NELSON EDUCATION LTD

McMaster University

Discover Psychology

NELSON EDUCATION

NELSON / EDUCATION

ISBN-13: 978-0-17-663125-3
ISBN-10: 0-17-663125-9

Layout and Design:
Science Media Lab
(McMaster University)

The following chapters are based on copyright work in collaboration with several authors and have been modified to accompany the web modules at McMaster University.

Table of Contents

Draft

Chapter 1: Foundations of Psychology

Introduction

It was the dead of winter, but here he was, sitting on a park bench, drenched in sweat, feeling agitated and nauseous, thinking about what had happened just a few days earlier. Steve's wife had caught him taking the painkillers to which he had become addicted. Years earlier, Steve had suffered an injury on the job, and had been given a prescription for OxyContin, a powerful narcotic pain reliever. Steve was amazed at the ability of these little pills to control his pain and this allowed him to return to work much earlier than he had expected. Soon he found himself using the drug to work through other minor injuries, colds, hangovers, and even days when he just didn't feel like going to work. When he started using the drug on a daily basis, the only days of work he ever missed were those days when he could not obtain the drug. On those days, he suffered from a variety of symptoms characteristic of influenza: Runny nose, watery eyes, diarrhea, muscle cramps and nausea. These symptoms, however, would disappear almost instantly once he managed to acquire some OxyContin or a similar drug. Before long, his wife became aware of what he was doing and confronted him, demanding that he stop using the drug. He agreed, and tried to quit several times, but each time some crisis would lead him to start using again. His wife finally issued an ultimatum, saying that if he did not get treatment for his addiction, she was leaving him. Steve begged his wife to give him one more chance. While she watched, Steve flushed the remainder of his stash of pills down the toilet. However, tonight the withdrawal was intense and the pain was real. All he could think was that he needed a fix to get him through. With his secret supply and credit line exhausted, he was a desperate man.

That's when he came up with a very foolish idea. Steve walked into the local pharmacy and asked the pharmacist if he had OxyContin in stock. As the pharmacist looked at him suspiciously, Steve motioned to the toy gun, taken from his son's room, hidden in his jacket. He demanded the pills and calmly walked out. He raced home to the safety of his garage. His hands shaking, Steve clumsily ripped open one of the bottles, spilling the contents all over the floor. He fell to his hands and knees frantically collecting the pills and popping them into his mouth one after another. He was still semiconscious when the police arrived.

Draft

If you were interested in understanding why some people are prone to substance abuse, where would you begin? This was my challenge as I began my graduate career as an experimental psychologist. A first step would be to define the problem. For me, this was clearly a *behavioural* phenomenon—an addict engages in persistent drug-seeking behaviour, which has a variety of consequences. In the opening case study, Steve's behaviour seems to have been influenced by some of the short-term consequences of his actions, such as the relief of his withdrawal symptoms. Other, longer-term, consequences, such as being in trouble with the law and harming his personal relationships seem to have been ignored, or at least viewed as less important. If we could understand how Steve's behaviour is related to the consequences of that behaviour, perhaps we could find a way to help him change that behaviour.

As a graduate student, I became involved in research that provided compelling evidence that environmental cues associated with drugs become important factors in relapse to drug use. (You will learn more about how cues become associated with drug actions through classical conditioning in Chapter 3). This may explain, for example, why a recovering alcoholic passing by a neighborhood bar may feel an almost irresistible urge to drink, even after years of sobriety. For the next several years I was focused on understanding these interesting behavioural aspects of drug addiction (e.g., Kim, Siegel, & Patenall, 1999). It should be noted, however, that there are numerous other ways of looking at the same issue. Many scientists approach the study of substance abuse primarily as a phenomenon to be studied at the cellular and molecular level. The approach taken by these researchers emphasizes the effect on various biological systems of the many chemical compounds contained in a wide range of drugs. We were studying the same problem but asking very different questions. When I presented my research at conferences that focused on this more biological approach, many researchers were surprised to learn that psychological factors could have such dramatic effects on drug action! In turn, I became increasingly interested in understanding the biological mechanisms underlying the behaviours I had been studying (Kim et al., 2008). Later, I would be exposed to the work of other scientists who were focused on understanding the socio-cultural factors that affected drug use. This broad experience helped me to appreciate that the study of a complex topic, such as drug addiction, benefits from a range of perspectives, methods and tools.

What is psychology?

Psychology is a very broad discipline and one of the goals of this book is to introduce you to the wide range of questions that might be of interest to a psychologist. This is likely the first psychology course you have been a part of and you may already have some ideas about the field. These ideas, which may have been informed by the popular media, may include a classic image of a leather couch and a man with a notepad thoughtfully stroking his beard and posing awkward questions about your mother. This is a popular cultural image depicting a simplified version of counseling therapy. While this is certainly an important application of psychology, referred to as **clinical psychology**, many psychologists do not treat clients in a private practice and are involved in research and teaching at universities. As you proceed through this book, you will be exposed to a variety of issues and perspectives that will expand your psychological horizons and introduce you to the breadth of the field.

I started this introductory chapter with a case study about drug addiction because it highlights an area of research that asks many questions that would be of interest to a psychologist. However, you will be exploring many diverse topics that are of interest to psychologists. Some psychologists want to know how we make decisions, perceive colour, or encode new memories. Others try to understand how we acquire phobias, choose our mates, or develop personality traits. Still other psychologists explore how networks of neurons give rise to consciousness, the regulation of hunger and eating, or the evolution of language. Given such diverse topics, it's not surprising that the modern study of psychology overlaps with a number of other disciplines, including biology, sociology, physics, genetics, medicine, economics, chemistry, political science and anthropology (among others).

Why are *you* studying psychology and reading this text? As part of an assigned course reading, you may have some initial reluctance to immerse yourself, and I can certainly sympathize with that. For my part, I have done my best to present to you a body of interesting ideas and processes to consider rather than a series of facts to memorize. In this text and the accompanying web lectures, I will provide you with a working foundation of information about some genuinely interesting concepts, along with theory and research for you to consider. However, this is just a starting point. After that, it's up to you! Actively engage: Don't just accept what's been presented to you. Ask questions: What is the evidence? Are there alternate explanations? Debate: Talk to your instructor, colleagues, and friends as you consider answers to important questions. Apply: Use your growing knowledge to understand everyday life situations as you join discussions and activities in the course tutorials and message boards. Once you complete your study of introductory psychology, these critical thinking skills will be applicable throughout your career.

Studying psychology should have great appeal because the applications for this knowledge are all around you. Every day you are exposed to loose psychological claims from friends, colleagues, and reports from news sources (credible or otherwise). Perhaps you have heard that opposites attract in romantic relationships, that humans only use 10% of their brain, or that a blind person's non-visual senses become more acute. While each of these widely held beliefs seem plausible, research in psychology has shown that they have no basis in fact (Beyerstein, 1999; Buss 1984, 1985; Morrongiello, Humphrey, Timney, Choi, Rocca, 1994; Rosenbluth, Grossman, & Kaitz, 2000). One goal of this text and accompanying web lectures is to train you to think critically as you consider problems as a psychologist would. This involves asking thoughtful questions, testing ideas and evaluating evidence. This systematic approach has allowed psychologists describe and understand human thought and behaviour, a process that is still very much in progress.

Let's begin with a definition of the field you are about to study. **Psychology** is the science of the mind and behaviour. By *mind*, I am referring to all the mental processes and subjective experiences that make up your sensations, perceptions, memories, thoughts, motives, and emotions. By *behaviour* I am referring to all your observable actions. Psychology uses the scientific method to answer questions through the systematic collection and analysis of data (see Chapter 2). Research in psychology is typically directed towards one or more of four main goals:

1. To accurately and objectively *describe* the processes of mind and behaviour
2. To *explain* the mechanisms of these processes and their causes
3. To *predict* how these processes will be affected by different conditions
4. To *control* and *influence* these processes in practical application

By describing, explaining, and predicting behaviour, psychologists can apply this knowledge towards designing programs and treatments to control and influence desired processes of mind and behaviour.

In the remainder of this chapter, I want to do three things that will get you started in exploring these different aspects of psychological research. First, I want to briefly review the history of psychology to give you a sense of how the field has evolved into the vibrant discipline it is today. Second, I want to explore how this history has led to the multiple perspectives applied to issues in psychology. Third, I will discuss the distinction between experimental psychology and applied psychology, the two main branches of the discipline.

Section 1: The History of Psychology

Philosophical Foundations

The term *psychology* is based on the Greek root words *psyche*, meaning soul, and *logos*, meaning word. In the 18th century the term began to be used to describe "the study of the mind." Although psychology as a formal discipline is relatively young, having emerged only a little more than 100 years ago, the central questions studied by psychologists are hardly new. People have always wondered about the mind and its connection to the outside world, about the reasons for various human behaviours and traits, about the accuracy of human perceptions and so on. One early researcher in the emerging field of psychology, Hermann Ebbinghaus, clearly recognized this when he said that:

"Psychology has a long past, but only a short history."

- Hermann Ebbinghaus, Abriss der Psychologie (Summary of Psychology), 1908

Psychology's long past stretches back to its intellectual roots in philosophy and physiology. Historians of psychology point to the classic works of Greek philosophers such as Socrates, Plato, Aristotle, and Hippocrates as a starting point for formally exploring issues of human thought and behaviour. The ancients explored important questions about humanity, such as the nature of free will, the source of knowledge, and the mind-body relationship that are relevant to this day. Several centuries later the French philosopher Rene Descartes (1596-1650) suggested that the mind and body are separate and distinct entities that are causally linked. He believed that the mind controlled the movements of the mechanical body, receiving information about the outside world through the sense organs. Although Descartes was wrong about some things, his description of the body in mechanical terms would become very influential on the work of physiologists.

By the 1800s, new experimental procedures emerged that allowed physiologists to begin filling in the knowledge gap and provide mechanisms for the abstract issues raised by philosophers. Johannes Müller (1801-1858) discovered that the messages transmitted by nerves were coded as electrical impulses traveling along different channels. He proposed that nerve connections to specific areas of the brain resulted in different sensory experiences. For example, activity of one brain region might lead to the experience of vision, while activity in another brain region might lead to the experience of hearing, and so on (Berrios, 2005). Müller's idea of localized function in the brain was supported by experimental work by Pierre Flourens (1794-1867). By damaging different regions of an animal's brain and recording the resulting deficits, Flourens learned which brain region controlled heart rate, breathing, and visual and auditory reflexes (Yildirim & Sarikcioglu, 2007). Hermann von Helmholtz (1821-1894) showed that the speed at which nerve impulses travelled was significantly slower that the speed of an electrical current flowing along a metal conductor. This suggested that neural communication involved processes that were much more complex than just an electrical signal traveling along a wire. All these developments suggested that physiologists could now ask serious scientific questions about the brain and nervous system.

The Science of Psychology Emerges: Wundt and Structuralism

Scholars working independently in separate fields were using different methods to ask converging questions about how the mind and body interact. The time was ripe for a new movement. A German professor named Wilhelm Wundt (1832-1920) advocated for a new independent discipline of psychology that would build on these foundations in philosophy and physiology. As it turned out, Wundt's timing could not have been more perfect. There was increasing intellectual curiosity concerning questions such as how sensations were turned into mental awareness and whether sensory perceptions of the outside world were accurate reflections of reality. In 1879, Wundt established the first formal psychology laboratory at the University of Leipzig. Having been trained in sensory physiology under Helmholtz, Wundt's approach to psychology would reflect the same rigorous experimental approach to understanding the mind and consciousness. By 1881, Wundt had launched the first academic journal devoted to psychology (**Bringmann, Balance, & Evans, 1975**). Many talented students were drawn to study under Wundt and the new discipline of psychology grew quickly across Europe and North America.

Psychology was brought to North America by one of Wundt's students, G. Stanley Hall (1844-1924), who started his own psychology laboratory at John Hopkins University in 1883. Shortly after in 1887, Hall established the first psychology journal in the United States, and in 1892, he founded the American Psychological Association (APA). Today, the APA is the world's largest psychological organization with over 150,000 members – and its success has led to the development of other important organizations, such as the Association for Psychological Science, the Canadian Psychological Association, and the Canadian Society for Brain, Behaviour and Cognitive Science. In an explosive decade from 1883-93, twenty-four new psychology research labs opened in the United States and Canada (Benjamin, 2000), many of which were established by researchers who were connected to Wundt's original lab.

Edward Titchener (1867-1927) studied under Wundt in Germany and came to teach in the United States at Cornell University. Titchener extended Wundt's ideas about psychology, and developed the approach to psychology known as **structuralism** (Thorne & Henley, 1997). The structuralist view was that psychology should focus on the elements of conscious thought and perception (i.e., the 'structure' of our mental experiences). Like their counterparts in physics who were studying the nature of matter by examining its basic atomic components, the goal of the structuralists was to reduce conscious experience to its core components such as sensations, feelings, and images. Given that it was not possible for these researchers to observe and analyze the conscious experience of another individual, their data were primarily collected through a method called **introspection** in which experimenters trained subjects to carefully observe and report their own experiences. These accounts were then analyzed in an effort to break down the experience into its basic component parts and determine the order in which they occurred and how they related to one another.

Most of the research inspired by the structuralist view focused on visual, auditory, and touch sensations and perceptions. A subject in a typical experiment would be exposed to sensory stimuli such as a tone or particular lighting condition in a carefully controlled laboratory setting. The subject would then report their experience in as much detail as possible. While you will still find many psychologists interested in these same questions about how our experience of the world around us is related to the physical reality of that world (in fact, this is the central question of a branch of psychology known as **psychophysics**), you are very unlikely to find any modern-day structuralists, at least in the strict sense of the word. Before we see why the structuralist school eventually disappeared from psychology, we need to examine two other schools of thought that arose soon after Wundt, Hall and others began to publish their ideas and findings.

SECTION REVIEW: History of Psychology

TABLE 1.1

Psychology began with philosophical questions about behaviour and the mind and developed into objective tests of these very questions		
Philosophical Foundations	**Transition to Experimental Psychology**	**Structuralism and Introspection**
• Western psychology can be traced back to the Ancient Greek Philosophers; the questions they posed and the observations they made have been apparent throughout history as humans have attempted to understand the nature of thought and behavior.	• In the 1800s came the start of **experimental psychology**; empirical tests were developed for the claims and assumptions held on human psychology leading to a modern understanding of the brain and nervous system through physiological tests of sensory mechanisms.	• In 1879, Wundt developed the **structuralist** school, focusing on the study of sensory perceptions to discover the nature of thought and perception. • Wundt advocated the method of **introspection**; since mental processes are not directly observable we must analyze and breakdown our experiences through self-reflection.

Section 2: Modern Developments

The Adaptive Nature of Consciousness: James and Functionalism

The functionalist school of psychology arose in the United States in the late 1800s. The central figure of this movement was William James (1842-1910), who published the highly influential *Principles of Psychology* in 1890. Where the Wundt and his colleagues viewed the subject matter of psychology as the structure of conscious thought, **functionalism** focused on *what conscious thoughts were for*, rather than of what they were made (Hunt, 1993). Note that his contrast between structural and functional analysis is one that is mirrored across a wide variety of disciplines, from biology to literary criticism. The functionalist view of psychology was greatly influenced by the work of Charles Darwin (Hillner, 1984), who had proposed his theory of Natural Selection in 1859. The central idea in Darwin's theory was that certain traits would be retained in a species, or not, based on the adaptive value of that trait. In other words, any evolved characteristic had to be something that helped the species to adapt to its environment in some way; if it was there, it had to have a purpose (Darwin, 1859). James and the functionalists therefore argued that what was important about conscious thought was what it allowed us to do (Galotti, 1999). The fact that this ability existed suggested that it must serve some adaptive purpose in the real world, so rather than examine consciousness in the laboratory, the functionalists were more interested in observing consciousness in the environments and situations for which it had presumably evolved to navigate.

Although James believed in careful observation, he was less interested in the rigorous methods promoted by Wundt. In James' psychology, there was room for emotions, values, and recognition of individual uniqueness, which could not necessarily be captured by test results. Indeed, explanation was emphasized more than experimental control (Arkin, 1990). One of the important contributions of the functionalist school of thought to modern psychology was the introduction of the use of tests and questionnaires to collect data on topics of interest. This emphasis on using objective data that could be observed and verified, rather than the introspective reports, highlights one of the main criticisms of the structuralist approach. James and his colleagues argued that the structuralists were using unscientific methods by relying on introspection, in that there was no way for anyone to verify the accuracy of this subjective data (Calkins, 1906). A second criticism was that the structuralists were missing the point entirely by trying to reduce consciousness to its individual elements. In other words, the structuralists were guilty of **reductionism**; by breaking a problem into successively smaller and smaller pieces, they were both losing sight of the big questions and losing the ability to answer them in a meaningful way. By way of example, imagine trying to describe the paragraph you are reading to a friend while talking only about the individual letters that appear in it, or even worse, all the lines, curves and angles that make up those letters. While it may be true that all those elements are there, and that they relate to each other in certain ways, your explanation will quickly become long and complicated, making it difficult or impossible to see the big picture.

Perception and Reality: Wertheimer and Gestalt

A third major criticism of structuralism came from another direction. The **Gestalt** school of psychology had also developed in Germany, centered on the work of Max Wertheimer (1880-1943), Kurt Koffka (1886-1941) and others. These researchers had yet another view of the appropriate subject matter for psychological research, suggesting that psychology should be the study of perception and problem solving. The Gestalt movement introduced two influential principles to the study of human thought and behaviour: The **principle of totality**, which stated that the study of any conscious experience must simultaneously take into account all of the mental and physical aspects of the individual, and the **principle of psychophysical isomorphism**, which stated that there was a systematic relation between any conscious experience and physical events occurring in the brain and central nervous system (Barlow, 1981). The primary criticism of the structuralist approach raised by researchers in the Gestalt school can be illustrated by examining Figure 1.1.

Figure 1.1 Subjective Contours in Visual Perception

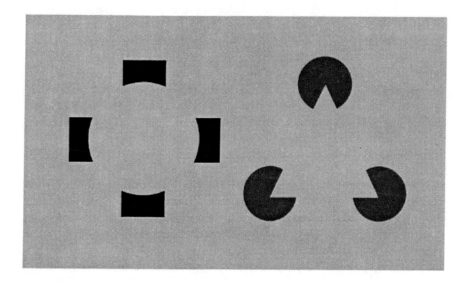

The above figures are examples of subjective contours in visual perception. While we can clearly see both the 'triangle' and the 'circle', there are no actual triangles or circles in the images. The red and blue shapes contained in the image suggest the partial outline, or contour, of a shape, and this suggestion is so powerful that we perceive the shape as being there even when it is not.

The subjective contour illusion illustrated in Figure 1.1 is just one of many examples raised by the Gestalt school that effectively put an end to any serious interest in structuralism as an approach to psychology. It was generally accepted that there was little point in introspectively examining the structure of our perceptions when it was so easily demonstrated that these perceptions were not necessarily an accurate reflection of the world, and that we had no control over our tendency to perceive things that were not really there. Related to this last point, it is important to realize that even the most highly educated and trained experts in visual perception will still see the non-existent shapes in Figure 1.1; knowing *why* these illusions happen does not make them any less powerful (although, as we will see later, it often makes them more interesting and informative).

The Black Box: Watson and Behaviourism

With the decline of structuralism and functionalism, a new school of thought emerged that would dramatically alter the course of psychology. At the turn of the 19th century, a Russian physiologist named Ivan Pavlov (1849-1936) reported experiments which demonstrated "involuntary" learning in dogs. Pavlov showed that dogs would learn to salivate to a previously neutral stimulus (such as a sound), if that stimulus had previously been paired with the presentation of food. This basic demonstration of learning provided a mechanism by which experience with the environment could alter behaviour. Pavlov's work, and its implications, will be discussed in more detail in Chapter 3.

Such studies influenced psychologists like John B. Watson (1878-1958) to focus exclusively on behaviour. In a classic 1913 paper entitled *Psychology as the Behaviorist Views It*, Watson argued that in the pursuit of understanding consciousness, psychology was diverging from objective science (Watson, 1913). Watson offered yet another definition of the appropriate subject matter, suggesting that psychology should be the study of behaviour. Note the absence in this view of any reference to thought or consciousness. It is important to realize that the behaviourists were not denying the existence of the mind, or suggesting that internal mental processes did not play an important role in producing the behaviour they studied. What they were saying was that these internal mental events *were not objectively observable*, and therefore such data were not suitable material for the scientific method. According to behaviourists, psychology should concern itself with *behaviour*, which is objectively observable.

For example, multiple observers can all record and verify the number of alcoholic drinks consumed by an individual on a particular occasion. While the occasional error in observation or recording might occur, in general any interested person should be able to reach the same conclusions about the amount of alcohol consumed.

This is an objective measure; there is no interpretation or guesswork involved, we simply count the drinks consumed. The evidence on which we base our conclusions is available to, and observable by, anyone. Any arguments that arise can be settled by carefully recounting. On the other hand, if we were interested in *why* the individual consumed the amount of alcohol they did, we are asking about mental events occurring inside that individual's head. How would we investigate such a question?

The obvious answer would be to simply ask the individual. The person might tell us they were drinking because a relationship had ended, or because they were celebrating a birthday, or because they were just trying to relax after a hard day, or any number of other reasons. Why would a behaviourist be unwilling to accept such answers as useful data for scientific analysis? The primary reason is that there is no way to verify such data. Despite the many technological advances that have allowed psychology to progress, we still do not have the ability to read minds.

Therefore, when the individual tells us why they are drinking, we have no way to look inside their minds to see if that is really the case. You might wonder why we should be unwilling to simply accept what the individual tells us as fact, but consider two important reasons to be skeptical: First, the individual may know perfectly well why they are drinking, but be reluctant to state the real reasons and provide some more socially acceptable explanation instead. Second, the individual may think they know why they are drinking, but may actually be unaware of the true motivating factors. In either case, their responses would provide an inaccurate picture of the situation. As we will see in later chapters, neither of the two possible problems suggested above is far-fetched; people are often unwilling or unable to report the real mechanisms behind their behaviour. It follows that, if we cannot trust an individual's description of his own internal mental state, there is certainly no reason to trust anyone else's description of that state.

For Watson and the behaviourists, anything happening inside someone's head was unobservable, and therefore off limits if psychology was to progress as a science. The mind was a 'black box' into which we could not see, and therefore any description of events taking place there was, by definition, not objectively verifiable or useful.

Box 1.1: The Behaviourists and Nature vs. Nurture

Are you the person you are because you were born that way, or are you the product of your experiences? This question reflects a long-standing debate that has concerned philosophers, biologists, psychologists and others for centuries. This debate is concerned with the extent to which a given trait is determined by biology and genetic inheritance ('nature') or by the environment and experience ('nurture'). The behaviourist position on this issue, as you might imagine, strongly emphasized the role of environmental factors. In an often quoted statement, John Watson, the founder of behaviourism, boldly claimed:

Give me a dozen healthy infants, well-formed, and my own specified world to bring them up in and I'll guarantee to take any one at random and train him to become any type of specialist I might select — doctor, lawyer, artist, merchant-chief, and yes, even beggar-man and thief, regardless of his talents, penchants, tendencies, abilities, vocations and race of his ancestors (Watson, 1924).

Note that what Watson is saying here is that Nature does not matter; everything of importance is determined by experience. This statement might strike you as rather extreme and, in fact, Watson himself recognized this too. While the quotation above has been reproduced countless times, what is often left out is the next part of the same statement in which he concedes "*I am going beyond my facts and I admit it, but so have the advocates of the contrary and they have been doing it for many thousands of years.*" In this last statement, Watson is suggesting that although his point of view may minimize the role of biology and genetics in human psychology, explanations of human thought and behaviour that relied only solely on upon in-born characteristics, and neglected the role of the environment, were inadequate and unlikely to be correct. Psychologists now accept that categorizing a particular behaviour as "innate" or "learned" is an artificial distinction and that we must consider both nature and nurture and how these influences interact. The modern field of psychology has largely stepped away from all-inclusive schools of thought that once defined the field.

In the 1950s, B.F. Skinner (1904-1990) emerged as the leading figure in behaviourism. Skinner acknowledged that internal mental events must exist, but, like Watson before him, concluded that it was impossible to make measurements in a scientific way – at least for the present. Moreover, Skinner argued

Draft

that we could learn everything that we needed to know about an organism by studying its behaviour without a need to appeal to internal mental events. Descriptions of these mental events were adding a layer of complication to our explanations that was neither scientific nor necessary. Any behaviour, or *response*, could be explained entirely as a result of some observable input, or *stimulus*, from the environment (Delprato & Midgley, 1992).

Behaviourism was highly influential, particularly in North America. Researchers taking this approach made numerous discoveries concerning the role of environmental stimuli in determining behaviour, and their work forms the basis for the material we will encounter in Chapter 3. You may be surprised to learn that the behaviourist influence even extended to the study of processes such as memory and language (Mahadevam, Malone, & Bailey, 2002). However, this program of research that emphasized stimulus-response associations had critical flaws as you will see in later chapters. It should be noted that behaviourism was primarily responsible for pushing psychology towards operating as a scientific discipline. There were, however, numerous critics who argued that to ignore the mind and mental processes was to ignore much of what was central to human experience. This helped to set the stage for the cognitive revolution in the 1960s, which will be discussed a little later in our history. First, we need to examine another very influential movement in psychology led by researchers with views quite different from those of the behaviourists.

Unconscious Motives: Freud and Psychoanalysis

In the late 19th and early 20th centuries, Sigmund Freud (1856-1939) became one of the most influential thinkers in recent Western intellectual history. Freud was trained as a neurologist, a physician specializing in disorders of the nervous system. Many of his early patients displayed symptoms that did not seem to have any obvious physical cause, such as paralysis of an arm or leg in the absence of any detectable damage to the nerves. Other patients presented a range of disorders, including depression, hysteria, and excessive anxiety. Over time, Freud began to develop theories concerning the nature of such disorders, and a set of techniques for treating them, that came to be known as **psychoanalysis**. At the core of psychoanalytic theory is the idea of **the unconscious**. Freud suggested that a large portion of our internal mental world was inaccessible to our conscious awareness. Certain thoughts, memories and desires, particularly traumatic or socially unacceptable ones, were often pushed down into this unconscious realm where the conscious mind did not have to confront them. This process of **repression** was a way for the conscious mind to defend itself against trauma and conflict. Also central to the psychoanalytic perspective is the idea that, even after traumatic material has been confined to the unconscious, it is still capable of influencing conscious thinking and behaviour in a number of ways. According to this view, the best treatment for a wide variety of mental or behavioural disorders was to seek out the underlying unconscious material at the root. We see here yet another perspective on the appropriate subject matter for psychology; for the psychoanalyst, psychology was the study of unconscious conflict and motivation.

Freud's ideas were adopted and adapted by his students and colleagues, many of whom went on to make significant contributions of their own. Carl Jung (1875-1961), Alfred Adler (1870-1937), and Karen Horney (1885-1952), all students of Freud, each took psychoanalysis in new directions and developed ideas that continue to influence psychology today. Modern psychodynamic theory, which emphasizes the role of relationships and self-image along with unconscious motivations in the assessment and treatment of psychological disorders, is one of several schools of thought that trace their roots directly back to Freud's work. Despite his influence, and despite the fact that both his ideas and his likeness are likely the first things to pop into the mind of the average person when the word 'psychology' is mentioned, Freud's ideas have also been the subject of much criticism, at least some of which is justified. Like anyone else, Freud was deeply influenced by the time and culture in which he lived and worked, and these influences certainly found their way into his thinking. Given that Freud's cultural setting was rather socially conservative, many of his ideas clash with our more liberal cultural values. For example, Freud clearly had a somewhat negative view of women in general, considering them to be psychologically weaker and more fragile than men. However, this is not to say that Freud's work should be, or has been, dismissed entirely. Much of the work that has been done by researchers and clinicians extending and applying Freud's original ideas has involved separating out the elements of cultural bias while retaining the useful core ideas. In fact, the views of Freud and his followers would dominate clinical thinking and practice for decades until the rise of cognitive-behavioural and drug-based therapies.

Box 1.2: What does a behaviourist have to do to get a coffee around here?

Despite the success of the behaviourist school, it became increasingly difficult to deny the importance of studying the cognitive processes that are so seamlessly tied in with the human experience. Consider just a few of the cognitive tasks that are part of my morning routine as I buy a cup of coffee. I first need to remember my current location and the location of my favourite coffee shop and navigate there from my present location. Along the way numerous tasks and decisions must be dealt with concerning traffic signals, the speeds and trajectories of various vehicles and pedestrians, recognition of familiar faces and landmarks, and detecting any relevant new changes in the environment. While all this is going on, I still have to remember where I am going and why. Once I arrive at the coffee shop, I need to distinguish between customers and staff, so I can direct my request to the right person. I also need to decipher the text on the menu while recalling my past experiences with various beverages in order to choose something that I will enjoy (a double-soy ½ caff vanilla latte). I will then use my language skills to communicate with a server. When the server asks me "will there be anything else?" I need to separate the sounds coming from the server's mouth from the sounds of other customer's mouths and the radio behind the counter. Finally, I use my knowledge of what each coin and bill in my wallet represents to pay for my purchase, while convincing myself that this beverage is so much better than the coffee I have at home that spending $4.95 on it was not a waste of my limited resources. When you begin (and the description above is just the beginning) to analyze this simple trip, you can start to appreciate the complex mental tasks that the mind engages in all the time. Is it really possible to capture everything important that is going on here by restricting ourselves to talking only about behaviour?

SECTION REVIEW: Modern Developments

TABLE 1.2

Work in psychology began to diversify and past methods were continuously questioned, challenged, and revolutionized		
James' Functionalism	**Progressions to Objectivity**	**Freud and Psychoanalysis**
• The field of psychology began to establish itself as an independent scientific discipline • James developed the functionalist school, an approach adapted from Darwin that looked at conscious experience in terms of its adaptive function and objections to structuralism began to develop	• The **Gestalt** school of psychology promoted the study of perception and problem solving and indicated that conscious perceptions are not necessarily accurate representations of reality, deeming introspection unreliable • The **Behaviourist** school of psychology attempted to refine scientific practices in psychology by proposing that internal mental events should not be studied, since they are not directly observable	• Freud's school of **Psychoanalysis** provided the foundations for modern clinical psychology through a focus on the treatment of disorders and the study of personality • Focus was placed on the role of the unconscious in affecting behaviour through various conflicts and motivations

Section 3: Recent Revolutions

Opening the Black Box: The Cognitive Revolution

Although behaviourism put psychological research on sound empirical footing, it also imposed limitations with its insistence that we give up any attempts to study the mind and consciousness (Mandler, 2002). Indeed, a generation of psychologists were discouraged from using terms such as 'mind', 'image', 'consciousness', and even 'memory' in their scientific writing (Murray, 1995). Given this reluctance to refer to internal mental events, you may be surprised to learn that the behaviourist influence even extended to the study of processes such as memory and language. However, this program of research that emphasized stimulus-response associations had critical flaws. For example, the behaviourist approach assumed that memory was a process of retrieving a static, unchanging and complete record of some event in response to an environmental cue. In other words, memories were like photographs in an album that presented exactly the same information each time they were viewed. The problem with this view is that much of what was being discovered in the realm of memory research suggested that this was not actually how memory worked; memory was a reconstructive process that resulted in the retrieved information being changed to better fit with our preconceived ideas and/or current circumstances. Rather than being a 'photograph' of some event, it was more like 'telling the story' of the event. Depending on who the story was being told to on that particular occasion, and why, various details might be omitted, emphasized, exaggerated, or otherwise altered to suit the occasion. While this idea, and the topic of memory in general, will be examined in more detail later, the point here is that it was becoming clear that researchers were going to have to start looking into the 'black box' of the mind if we wanted psychology to provide useful explanations of many important phenomena.

Mental tasks such as memory, attention, categorization and decision-making are the focus of **cognitive psychology**. Historians of psychology can pinpoint the exact date that the modern study of cognition began – the so-called "cognitive revolution" on September 11th, 1956. This was the day that the Massachusetts Institute of Technology hosted a conference on a new approach to studying mental processes. The work of psychologists such as George Miller (1920-), Donald Broadbent (1926-1993), and Noam Chomsky (1928-) showed that making reasonable inferences about internal mental states and events was necessary in order to fully explain much of human behaviour. The modern study of cognition was built on the methodology of behaviourism, but argued that we can use the information from overt behaviour to make inferences about the mind. More recently, exciting technological advances in **neuroimaging** have made it possible to more directly study the connection between the mind and brain. Today, it would be difficult to find an area of psychology that has not been altered by the increasing influence and power of the cognitive approach.

Human Exceptionalism: Rogers and Humanism

Another school of psychological thought also arose in the 1950s as a reaction against the dominant behaviourist and psychoanalytic perspectives of the day (Bühler & Allen, 1972). While behaviourism and psychoanalysis constituted radically different approaches, they did share one important implication for psychology that a growing number of researchers and clinicians found problematic: Whether the behaviour in question was the result of past experience with environmental stimuli or unconscious desires and conflicts, the important determinants of behaviour were things that were out of our conscious control. To Carl Rogers (1902-1987), the leading figure of the emerging school of **humanist psychology**, these perspectives were ignoring the central issues of human thought and behaviour. Rogers believed that the human **self-concept**, or internal self-representation, was central to understanding human behaviour. Further, he suggested that this mental self-portrait was a characteristic not shared by other species, and that much of the work done by behaviourists, which often used animal subjects as models, was irrelevant to the human condition (Thorne & Henley, 2005). Rogers and others, particularly Abraham Maslow (1908-1970), went on to identify the quest for personal growth as a primary motivating factor in human behaviour, which was also viewed as a uniquely human characteristic (Maslow, 1962). Rather than unresolved conflict in the unconscious mind, what motivated human beings (at least under ideal circumstances) was the conscious desire to maximize their potential.

The influence of the humanist movement in psychology was strongest in the area of clinical application. Rogers and the humanists had some very different ideas about how psychology should be used as a therapeutic tool. They argued that the goal of therapy should be providing a relaxed, accepting environment in which the client would direct the course of the interaction. Note the difference between this view and the position taken by Freud and the psychoanalysts, where the basic assumption is that the therapist knows more about what is really going on than the client does, and should therefore direct the course of therapy. Rather than have a client's interactions with a therapist be focussed on what was 'wrong' with the client, the focus should be on providing the client with the sense that they are valued, worthwhile human beings, regardless of their current problems or circumstances.

As you can see, relative to other scientific disciplines, the history of psychology is not all that long, but it has seen the rise (and sometimes the fall) of a number of different ways of defining and approaching the subject matter. In the next section we will examine some of the current perspectives directed towards psychological questions. You will see the influence of many of the major historical movements in the variety of methods used by researchers across the discipline, and should come to appreciate the value of having a range of different ways to think about human thought and behaviour.

SECTION REVIEW: Recent Revolutions

TABLE 1.3

Invaluable transformations were brought to both research work and therapy that contributed to the establishment of psychology as a scientific and beneficial field both experimentally and as an applied science		
The Cognitive Revolution • The **Cognitive Revolution** introduced the rejection of the behaviourist idea that unobservable mental events should not be considered; their importance was seen as undeniable • Much work was done to formulate empirical methods and technologies to be able to infer models and theories of mental processes from observable behaviours and processes	**Humanism and Its Role in Therapy** • The school of **Humanism** brought the focus of psychology solely onto humans through the valuing, growth and development of the human self	• It was proposed that therapy should consist of a relaxed environment where individuals are accepted for who they are, and their input is deemed important, despite struggles they may face • The hierarchical setting of therapy, with the therapist as the absolute knower, was eliminated

Section 4: Contemporary Perspectives in Psychology

Levels of Analysis

As should be clear from the preceding section, the current practice of psychology has been influenced by a wide range of different ideas. Many of these schools and ideas have risen and fallen in popularity over the years, but you can see their influence in the multiple perspectives that modern psychology brings to the study of human thought and behaviour. In several cases, advances in both technology and theory have allowed previously unanswerable questions to be addressed. Any psychologist seeking to investigate some particular human characteristic must first make some decisions concerning the **level of analysis** they wish to use to approach the problem. In reality, for any individual researcher this decision is largely already made by their training and area of specialization. For example, someone whose graduate training and research experience has emphasized the role of social relationships is likely to frame questions and look for answers in terms of social relationships, rather than molecular biology. One of the great benefits to psychology of having such a wide range of different perspectives is that many of them may be brought to bear on important questions. We will first look at three basic levels of analysis that might be used to address a psychological question, and then turn to a survey of the different perspectives that might be applied at each of these levels.

PSYCHOLOGICAL ANALYSIS

We are operating at the *psychological level of analysis* when we state our questions and look for our answers in terms of mental events taking place in our subjects. Whether we are interested in the workings of memory, the role of childhood trauma in personality, how children learn language, or any of an infinite range of psychological questions, the answers lie inside the heads of the people we study. In one sense, the problem raised by the behaviourists is still relevant; we still do not, and may never, have the ability to directly observe and record thoughts. The only way we can be truly objective is by examining public behaviour. However, one of the consequences of the cognitive revolution discussed earlier has been the development of models, along with the collection of large amounts of data to back them up, allowing us to make reasonable inferences about the mental events that produce the behaviour being measured. In many ways, explanations given at this level of analysis may be more intuitively sensible, in that they may be framed in terms of thoughts, emotions, memories, motivations, and so on, that we are all somewhat familiar with. Finally, it should be noted that using the term 'psychological level of analysis' here is not meant to imply that analyses on any other level are, therefore, not psychology. Both of the other levels of analysis we will discuss shortly are often employed to investigate phenomena of interest to psychology.

BIOLOGICAL ANALYSIS

At the *biological level of analysis*, psychologists try to understand human thinking and behaviour by examining the underlying physiological activity. The structure and function of the brain and nervous system, the genome and gene expression, the molecular mechanisms by which various drugs produce their effects, and the diagnosis and treatment of neuropsychological diseases are among the many issues relevant to psychologists that have been addressed at this level of analysis. One advantage of this approach to psychological issues is that from a biological point of view, other than size there is not much difference between a human brain and a rat brain or a monkey brain. They have almost all the same parts and work in pretty much the same way. Therefore, we can develop and use animal models for various phenomena and safely assume that the same biological principles allow us to make useful inferences about human biological functioning. In fact, this principle extends even to far less closely related species as well. For example, much of what we know about how brains learn, and the role of genetic factors in that process, comes from studying a species known as *Drosophila Melanogaster* (more commonly known as the fruit fly). Recent research has identified structures corresponding to parts of the human brain in the nervous system of the marine rag worm, a species hundreds of millions of years old (Benito-Gutierrez & Arendt, 2009).

None of the above is intended to suggest that the biological level of analysis restricts psychology to relying on animal models. Numerous technologies have been developed and adapted to allow us to examine the workings of the human brain as well. Developments such as magnetic resonance imaging (MRI), electroencephalography (EEG), electron microscopy and DNA sequencing have all enhanced our ability to understand the biological roots of thought and behaviour. We will encounter this level of analysis frequently as we survey the discipline in the following chapters.

ENVIRONMENTAL ANALYSIS

A third way to address a variety of questions in psychology involves the *environmental level of analysis*. This approach owes much to the behaviourist tradition, with its emphasis on the identification and control of environmental stimuli that can influence behaviour. As was the case with biologically oriented analyses, answering questions at the environmental level does not rely on our ability to infer anything about internal mental states. For the same reasons described above, psychologists working at this level of analysis have also developed numerous animal models of various phenomena. There is no reason, for example, to assume that the principles of reinforcement that keep a gambler sitting at a slot machine in a casino are any different from the principles that keep a rat pressing a lever to obtain the occasional food pellet. Much of the material we will encounter in Chapter 3 will be based on this level of analysis.

The social aspects of our environment have also been of great interest to many psychologists. Humans are a social species, in that we seem to be adapted to function best as part of a group. As a result, we are very sensitive to cues in our social environment, and they have been shown to exert a powerful influence over our behaviour.

Target Study

EEG EVIDENCE FOR MIRROR NEURON DYSFUNCTION IN AUTISM SPECTRUM DISORDERS

Researchers: Lindsay M. Oberman (University of California San Diego), Edward M. Hubbard (University of California San Diego), Joseph P. McCleery (University of California San Diego), Eric L. Altschuler (University of California San Diego, Mt. Sinai School of Medicine), Vilayanur S. Ramachandran (University of California San Diego), Jaime A. Pineda (University of California San Diego)

Source: Oberman, L. M., Hubbard, E. M., McCleery, J. P., Altschuler, E. L., Ramachandran, V. S. & Pineda, J. A. (2005). EEG evidence for mirror neuron dysfunction in autism spectrum disorders. *Cognitive Brain Research, 24,* 190-198.

Note: The material below is the author's summarized description of the original published article

Individuals with autism are known to exhibit certain deficits in social skills, communication, and other cognitive abilities such as language, imitation, empathy and theory of mind (the ability to understand the actions and intentions of others). While the deficits of individuals with autism are well documented, there is a large gap in understanding in terms of the neurological basis of behavioural and cognitive deficits. The current study draws on work in neuroscience on mirror neurons, a subset of motor neurons that fire in response to the biological motion of others. Mirror neurons are thought to play a large role in understanding the actions and intentions of others and are also believed to be responsible for aspects of language comprehension, imitation, empathy and theory of mind. What is particularly interesting about mirror neurons is that individuals with autism show impairments in basically everything that mirror neurons are responsible for! This has lead researchers to predict that perhaps damage to mirror neurons is the basis for certain autism deficits. In order to test this inference, researchers employed Electroencephalography measurements of mu wave rhythm, a representation of mirror neuron functioning, where mu wave suppression during the perception of biological motion represents mirror neuron firing. Thus it was theorized that individuals with autism would show a lack of mu wave suppression when observing biological motion. By comparing mu wave rhythms in both individuals with autism and control individuals in response to different forms of motion (self-initiated, observed biological motion, observed non-biological motion, and white noise), the researchers were able to uncover underlying neurological differences in mirror neuron firing that they believe are linked directly to the deficits noted previously.

METHOD

Participants   A total of 24 male individuals participated in the study, ranging in age from 6 to 47: Eleven ASD (autism spectrum disorder) participants and thirteen controls matched for age and gender. Of the ASD group, ten were high functioning autistic and one was diagnosed with Asperger's (a syndrome on the high functioning end of the ASD spectrum). During analysis, one individual with autism and two controls were excluded due to insufficient EEG data, and one more control was excluded due to technical difficulties, resulting in a total of ten ASD individuals and ten controls. All ASD participants were classified as high-functioning, that is, had an IQ of over 80 and age appropriate verbal comprehension and production.

Procedure   The experiment involved a total of four within subject conditions used for EEG data collection for both the ASD and control groups. The first condition, "Move own hand" instructed participants to open and close their right hand in order to provide a measure of self-initiated movement. The second condition, "Watching a video of a moving hand" instructed participants to view a black and white video of a hand opening and closing in the same manner as the instructions for the previous condition, in order to provide a measure of observed biological movement. The third condition, "Watching a video of two bouncing balls" instructed participants to watch two gray balls moving together and apart against a black background in order to provide a baseline measure for observed movement (non-biological). The last condition, "Watching visual noise" instructed participants to view television static in order to provide a baseline measure.

During the "Watching a video of a moving hand" and "Watching a video of two bouncing balls" participants were required to partake in a continuous performance task (counting the number of times the stimuli stopped moving throughout the video) to ensure engagement with the task.

The EEG analysis provided two measures of mu rhythm suppression. The first, the ratio of power during self-initiated hand movement and observed hand movement relative to the baseline. The second, the ratio of power during self-initiated hand movement and observed hand movement relative to the bouncing ball condition.

Results   Mu rhythms were measured over the sensorimotor cortex, the brain region believed to be the site of mirror neurons. For the control group there was significant mu wave suppression in comparison to baseline for the self-initiated hand movement and observed hand movement conditions. For the ASD group there was significant mu wave suppression in comparison to baseline for the self-initiated hand movement condition, but a lack of suppression during the observed hand movement condition. There were no significant differences in suppression during baseline between the control and ASD group, thus the differences in suppression for the observed hand movement condition was due to the particular manipulation and not differences in baseline suppression. As well, there was no significant suppression during the non-biological motion condition. The same measurements were conducted in comparison to using the non-biological motion condition as baseline, and similar results were obtained, further strengthening the results found. All participants performed with complete accuracy on the continuous performance task, thus differences in results are unlikely to be related to differences in performance. As well, there were no significant correlations between age and mu wave suppression. Another result of particular importance was the existence of suppression only in areas inferred to contain mirror neurons.

Discussion   Results indicate that individuals with autism exhibit selective deficits in the firing of neurons involved in the perception and understanding of observed biological motion, that is, a deficit in mirror neuron functioning. Other motor functioning in ASD individuals is normal, thus the deficit is not due to disorders of the entire motor system. The lack of a significant relationship between age and mu wave suppression indicates that it is unlikely to be a deficit that changes or is related to age. Such results have provided evidence for a potential neurological account of behavioural and cognitive deficits apparent in ASD. Since mirror neurons are responsible for cognitive abilities and behaviours that are dysfunctional in individuals with ASD, and such individuals exhibit dysfunctional mirror neurons, it is inferred that mirror neurons may be the key to understanding the neurological basis of certain ASD tendencies.

Limitations   Within the study the researchers address a number of potential issues and alternative possibilities in interpreting the data. For instance, the study used only male participants, and thus is not generalizable to females who may exhibit different tendencies. As well, the study includes a wide age range and thus does not account for within-sex variability that may result from differences in age, even though there is no significant correlation between age and suppression. As well, it is possible that ASD individuals may have focused more on the continuous performance task and perceived the moving hand as more mechanical, or may have been too distracted to process the moving hand as much as stimuli of the other conditions. However, previous studies with robot hands have still elicited mu wave suppression in 'normal' individuals, and mu wave suppression is similar in comparison to both the ball and the white noise, indicating that such stimuli were still processed despite also being focused on in the continuous performance task.

Despite such significant results, there are questions left unanswered. For one, although it is believed that the impairments resulting from mirror neuron dysfunction may be caused by early developmental deficits, it is not known whether mirror neuron dysfunction is the result of other specific impairments or is the primary dysfunction. As well, it is unknown as to whether mirror neuron dysfunction is the result of dysfunction in other brain areas or due to difficulty in visual processing of biological motion in general. In order to form a complete picture of mirror neuron functioning and the relation to deficits of ASD, further research must be conducted by exploring functioning in related brain areas as well as visual processing differences.

Comment   Although the study relies primarily on a biological level of analysis, by exploring the neurological basis of ASD, it also works to reveal how research projects in psychology can be approached with differing, converging levels of analysis, while continuing to promote empirical adequacy. As mentioned, one of the limitations of the study is the large age variance of the participants. Although no significant correlations were found, there were a low number of individuals in the study, and thus may not accurately represent the ASD population at large. From an environmental perspective, we can further consider this factor of age and ask questions about the developmental past of ASD individuals and whether particular similar experiences may have contributed to the autistic tendencies being studied. As well, we can explore potential clinical projects that may improve mirror neuron functioning. From a psychological perspective it is important to consider, here and in future research, established models about the behavior and mental processes of ASD individuals in order to inform biological research, especially when making inferences back and forth between hypotheses and data.

SECTION 4 REVIEW: Levels of Analysis

TABLE 1.4

The field of psychology is based on different levels of analysis and a variety approaches to understanding thought and behavior		
Psychological	**Biological**	**Environmental**
• The **Psychological** level of analysis studies the processes of internal mental events and makes inferences through the development of models	• The **Biological** level of analysis studies physiological mechanisms and activity through the structure and function of the brain and nervous system; diverse technologies and both animal and human models are used	• The **Environmental** level of analysis studies the role of the environment as the primary factor for influencing psychological processes; much emphasis is placed on the strength of the social environment

Section 5: Multiple Perspectives

Multiple Perspectives in Psychology

We will conclude this section by considering an example of how psychologists may operate on one or more levels of analysis when addressing a particular issue. We opened this chapter with the story of Steve and his struggles with drug use. Each of the following perspectives suggests different kinds of questions that might be asked in such a case. The first distinction we should make is between clinicians who would be interested in working with Steve to help him identify and solve his problems, and researchers who would be interested in Steve as a source of data to help them understand drug use in general, and identify solutions to widespread problems related to drug use. While it is certainly the case that many clinicians are also researchers, each role has a distinct focus. A clinician's primary focus is finding a way to help Steve. A researcher's primary focus is to understand the underlying mechanisms that produced his behaviour. Although there is certainly a great deal of overlap between these perspectives, consider some important differences. If, as clinicians, we find a way to help Steve solve his drug use issues, whether or not these

Draft

same techniques would help anyone else in a similar situation is not particularly relevant to Steve. Even if we do not completely understand why our client recovered, we are still going to consider it a 'win'. Our responsibility is to help each particular client, and we have helped Steve. As researchers, on the other hand, we would be interested in discovering principles that applied not only to Steve, but to everyone. Consider that, from a research perspective, we might learn as much from Steve's failure to deal with his problems as we would from his success.

Whether psychologists are working as clinicians, researchers or both, the types of questions they ask and the kinds of answers they look for depend further on the particular perspective they bring to the issue. As we have seen in some detail, psychology has been influenced by a range of different schools of thought, and you will see these in some of the approaches to issues illustrated in Steve's story.

- **Diagnostic Perspective:** Determining if Steve met the diagnostic criteria for psychological disorders such as substance dependence or substance abuse.

- **Behaviourist Perspective:** Identify and control the environmental stimuli that lead to Steve's drug use and examine the role of the drug as a reinforcer.

- **Psychodynamic Perspective:** Identify and examine unconscious conflict and tension at the root of Steve's drug use.

- **Cognitive Perspective:** Explore the thought patterns and processes involved in Steve's decision-making with regard to drug use.

- **Biological Perspective:** Examine the short- and long-term physiological effects of Steve's drug use, particularly within the brain, and the mechanisms by which the drugs produce their effects.

- **Developmental Perspective:** Investigate the role of genetic predisposition and environmental influences at critical periods of development, and their role in producing Steve's adult behaviour.

- **Evolutionary Perspective:** Consider why the biological systems and behavioural mechanisms affected by Steve's drug use exist in the first place, what their functions are in the normal, drug-free state, and how drug use interacts with these evolved characteristics.

- **Socio-cultural Perspective:** Look at Steve's social context and cultural background, and their role in determining customs, attitudes and expectations regarding drug use.

Each of these perspectives suggest questions that lead to very different kinds of answers, even though they are all directed at the same basic phenomenon. This is not to say that one particular approach is better than the other. In the modern practice of psychology, both clinicians and researchers are typically informed by multiple perspectives and levels of analysis. One of the principal advantages of having so many different approaches available is the opportunity for psychologists to integrate ideas and findings that these different approaches produce. This has led to the formation of exciting new fields at the intersection of multiple levels of analysis such as **behavioural neuroscience**, where behaviour is related to the underlying function of the nervous system, and **psychoneuroimmunology**, the study of the effects of psychological variables on the ability to resist disease. As for Steve, as you might imagine, his best chances for dealing with his drug problem lie in taking advantage of knowledge and practices developed by psychologists operating from a wide range of different perspectives.

SECTION 5 REVIEW: Multiple Perspectives

TABLE 1.5

Psychologists work generally as <u>researchers</u>, <u>clinicians</u>, or a combination of the two; by integrating different perspectives, psychology can provide well rounded, holistic answers to many questions		
Research versus Clinical Psychology	**Integration in Psychology**	
• Researchers work towards knowledge acquisition about various phenomena, and clinicians apply such knowledge to the treatment of individuals through therapeutic practices	• The different levels of analysis and perspectives may overlap or be combined when attempting to formulate robust answers to psychological questions	• Key differences in how questions and phenomena will be approached still remain and due to this, different factors and explanations may be employed when attempting to formulate answers

Section 6: Basic and Applied Research

Another distinction that we need to make is that between **basic research** and **applied research**. Much of the activity that takes place at research institutions and universities is carried out in order to acquire new knowledge for its own sake. This process is often referred to as *basic research*, in that there need not be an obvious immediate application for the knowledge gained. While such research is often the butt of jokes by politicians and talk-show hosts, it is important to realize that many of the most influential discoveries in science were not immediately recognized as such by the researchers that made them. For example, Ernest Rutherford, the founder of nuclear physics who discovered the structure of the atom (Thomas, 2008), thought that the notion that this atomic structure could be a source of power was absolute nonsense (subsequent developments suggest he was right about atomic structure, but somewhat off the mark on the nuclear energy question). In these basic research laboratories, theories of human thought and behaviour are developed, tested and refined.

Other researchers may be seeking to understand various psychological phenomena in order to apply that knowledge to the solution of an identified practical problem. Developing treatments for psychological

Draft

disorders, identifying effective methods in education, managing institutionalized populations and designing workplaces to maximize productivity are just a few examples of *applied research*. Where basic research is typically concerned with figuring out how things work, applied research is typically concerned with figuring out how we can make things work to our advantage. As noted above, this is not to suggest that basic and applied research operate independently of one another. The knowledge of human psychology gathered by basic research is the raw material for the development of useful applications, many of which may not be obvious at the time of the original discovery. Conversely, many of the applied breakthroughs in psychology over the last century might never have been made if we restricted ourselves to doing only research that was clearly 'good for something'.

Although we have considered multiple perspectives and levels of analysis, we have still only scratched the surface. There are many different sub-disciplines within the broad spectrum of psychology. Each of these is informed by a particular combination of the perspectives and historical antecedents that we have discussed in this chapter so far. Note that these various sub-disciplines are not separated by rigid boundaries, and many psychologists work at the intersections among various areas. In addition, many of these areas of interest also cross over into disciplines beyond psychology, such as biology, chemistry, sociology, medicine, anthropology and economics, to name just a few. We will encounter many of these as we proceed through the following chapters.

SECTION 6 REVIEW: Basic and Applied Research

TABLE 1.6

Psychological research uses a range of methods for asking and answering questions, notably in terms of the theoretical foundations of psychology as well as whether and how such theories apply in real world settings.		
Basic Research	**Applied Research**	**Interdependence in Psychology**
• **Basic Research:** acquisition of knowledge for the advancement of science; provides the necessary foundations for any claims or applications through the development and testing of theories	• **Applied Research:** application of knowledge of psychological phenomena for the solution of problems	• Basic and Applied research do not necessarily exist in isolation, and can be combined even in single research projects

Section 7: Sub-Disciplines in Psychology

Sub-Disciplines in Psychology

If you were to survey the faculty in the department offering the course you are currently taking, you would undoubtedly find an amazing range of research being undertaken. You will also find that many researchers focus their work within a relatively limited area. As a discipline, psychology encompasses such a broad spectrum of subject matter that it is inevitable that researchers cannot be experts in everything, or approach a question from all possible perspectives. Psychology has developed a number of sub-disciplines, and you will probably see these reflected in various sub-groups within faculty in your department, and also in the structure of most psychology degree programs. At the undergraduate level, there is almost always some emphasis placed on exposing students to a range of perspectives and subject material from different areas of the discipline. In particular, introductory courses such as the one you are taking need to provide a foundation for students to pursue multiple possible options within the discipline. Whenever possible, you should talk to your professors about their research. This will not only help you to identify your own interests within the field, it will also serve to acquaint you with many of the different sub-disciplines that exist within current psychological practice. Many, although not all, of the different research programs you encounter will fall into one (or more) of the sub-disciplines listed in Table 1.7.

Table 1.7 – Sub-disciplines in Psychology

Sub-discipline	Focus
Behavioural Neuroscience	Establishing links between the physical structure and function of the nervous system and behaviour.
Clinical Psychology	Assessment, diagnosis and treatment of psychological disorders.
Cognitive Psychology	Study of thought processes such as memory, attention, and perception.
Comparative Psychology	Comparison of psychological processes and behaviour across different species.
Community Psychology	Develop and evaluate programs and support structures within the context of community service and development.
Consumer Psychology	Application of psychological principles to the study of marketing and consumer behaviour.
Counseling Psychology	Diagnosis and treatment of psychological issues not severe enough to warrant a clinical diagnosis.
Developmental Psychology	The changes over the lifespan with regard to psychological issues such as attachment, cognitive ability, perception and language.
Educational Psychology	Develop and evaluate practices that encourage learning in a classroom environment.
Evolutionary Psychology	Understanding human psychology as the product of our evolutionary history, and examining the adaptive value of psychological processes

Health Psychology	Psychological factors affecting health-related issues, including disease processes, immune function, and the promotion of healthy behaviour.
Human Factors	Design and evaluation of interfaces between humans and technology such as operating control systems, visual displays and human-computer interaction.
Industrial/Organizational Psychology	Application of psychological principles to the function of a workplace or organization, typically to maximize efficiency and minimize stress.
Learning	Examining how behaviour is modified as the result of experience and the ability of environmental stimuli to control behaviour.
Personality	The stable psychological traits that identify us to ourselves and to others, and that influence and characterize our thinking and behaviour.
Psychometrics	Developing, evaluating, and conducting psychological and behavioural tests, scales and inventories.
Psychopharmacology	Investigating the mechanisms of drug action in the nervous system and elsewhere, and identifying psychological consequences of drug administration.
Sports Psychology	Working with athletes to maximize their performance through the application of psychological principles.
Social Psychology	The role of social forces and group dynamics in determining individual behaviour, thought and perception.

The list in Table 1.7 is not intended to be complete and exhaustive, and as previously mentioned, many exciting opportunities and discoveries arise when psychologists with different backgrounds and perspectives converge on a problem. Give the diverse range of questions, tools, and perspectives used by researchers and practitioners in psychology, it may be useful to conclude this chapter with some thoughts on what unites psychology: (1) the diversity of the discipline is a reflection of the complexity of the subject matter – YOU. In the chapters to follow, consider how the material being discussed is relevant to you as a thinking, behaving human and how it can enhance your understanding of the psychological world around you; (2) while each framework has made important practical and theoretical contributions, each captures only part of the puzzle. Together, multiple perspectives enrich a growing body of knowledge as psychology continues to evolve and incorporate new directions for research. Consider just one recent example. While your initial impression of psychology may be the treatment of mental illness, a recent movement called **positive psychology** puts a focus on exploring a largely neglected research area of positive human functioning to understand **effective interventions to build thriving in individuals, families, and communities (Seligman, 2003); (3) finally**, the most important theme uniting the various perspectives incorporated into psychology is a commitment to rigorous research methods. At a basic level, psychologists ask questions and seek answers. In the next chapter we will turn to a topic of fundamental importance to the rest of the content presented in this book, the methods used by psychologists to collect and analyze data and the logic behind these methods.

Box 1.3: Application: The Pervasive Role of Perspectives

In a field of study with such a variety of disciplines, we can see the strong role of numerous perspectives when taking on research projects. Psychology highlights, and in a way acts as a sort of microcosm of, the overarching importance of multiple perspectives. Adopting an outlook that acknowledges the legitimacy of different perspectives helps to tackle a variety of academic and social issues and questions. Psychology teaches us that there are multiple levels of analysis for viewing any problem. How we come in to knowledge projects, the background assumptions we bring in, the beliefs we have, the questions we ask and how we ask them frame the answers we seek and ultimately the answers we get. Different questions from different backgrounds and perspectives will get at different answers. By recognizing this we are able to take advantage of different perspectives; by exploring them and collaborating with others we can come together to formulate well rounded, inclusive answers that contribute more to our understandings of reality than single perspective answers. Not just any perspective is legitimate though. Perspectives still must be informed by empirical evidence and rationality.

In terms of academics we can see how this operates in the field of psychology. For any questions we have about the brain and behaviour we can use our knowledge of different perspectives to try and tackle issues. In this, however, we can also recognize that one single perspective is limited in terms of the scope of the answer it can provide. By definition, it is only one perspective, and any one perspective is incomplete. For example, a biological analysis may completely and accurately describe differences in brain structure between individuals with and without schizophrenia. However, an understanding of schizophrenia in this sense is incomplete for it lacks, for instance, an environmental analysis that would provide vital information about how certain experiences of individuals with schizophrenia may contribute to or alleviate certain symptoms. Such an approach, although often explicit and enforced in psychology, is important not only for psychology but for all areas of research and projects attempting to come to answers about the way the world works.

Each individual (or even groups joined by common interests and beliefs) is biased by the background knowledge they hold and the approaches they choose to take. This is why, for any

Draft

knowledge project, it is important to attempt to consider different perspectives, to incorporate the perspectives of different individuals, and approach academic problems or phenomena in different ways. Such knowledge and practices are not just the work of scientists and philosophers, though. It is a methodology that can be used by anyone – even, if not especially, undergraduate students! It is simply a way of tackling issues and an excellent way of going about any research project. How can this be done though? Simply by being open to alternative perspectives and making a conscious effort to consider data, experiences, or beliefs that may not necessarily fall in line with your own views, but still stand after being tested through the scientific method.

Taking this holistic approach to knowledge projects is not limited to the academic sphere though; it can actually extend into our social lives. Although it may not be obvious or done consciously, we tend to embrace such methods in our daily social interactions by being open to diversity in the lives and experiences of individuals and how this shapes the person they are, particularly during times of disagreement. Unfortunately, however, we often take the opposite approach by stereotyping and ostracizing individuals for their differences. We do not take the time to accept that perhaps their views and beliefs, opinions and philosophies may be equally valid, and the perspective we ourselves take is not the only or the best one. Being aware that all individuals come from different backgrounds and can make different contributions can facilitate social interactions and communication. No one individual has a complete and entirely informed view about the way the world works, but together we can bring a lot more to the table and potentially come up with more complete pictures of the way the world works.

We can see how multiple perspectives operate throughout various levels of experience, such as academics and social interactions. But we can also imagine other fields that it extends to, such as politics and economics. The most important thing to take and apply to our lives is the inevitable reality that multiple perspectives exist, and that one perspective is not the be-all end-all to knowledge.

SECTION 7 REVIEW: Sub-Disciplines in Psychology

TABLE 1.8

Psychology is a vast, diverse field, but a field that is rich with interdisciplinary understanding and interconnectedness		
Sub Disciplines	**Multidisciplinary Approaches**	
• A large variety of **sub-disciplines** exists in psychology; each sub-discipline has its general focus, but there is a high degree of overlap between them	• Convergence from different sub-disciplines emphasizes the strength of work being done and the robustness of theories under development	• The diversity and complexity of human beings is directly reflected in the field of psychology and the work done to understand humans at a deeper level

Key Terms

Applied research: Research conducted in order to apply the results to a known practical problem.

Basic research: Research conducted in order to acquire new knowledge, without necessarily having an immediate application for this knowledge.

Behavioural neuroscience: The study of the relationship between behaviour and the physical functioning of the brain and nervous system.

Behaviourism: A level of analysis concerned only with explaining psychological phenomena using learning methodologies, treating the mind as a black box.

Clinical psychology: The application of psychological knowledge and principles to the diagnosis and treatment of individuals with psychological disorders.

Cognitive psychology: The study of internal processes, such as memory, attention, and decision-making, involved in mental activity.

Comparative psychology: Concerns how behaviours have adapted over evolutionary time to deal with selective environmental pressures by comparing behaviour across multiple species.

Developmental psychology: A level of analysis concerned with explaining how behaviours develop over the lifespan

Draft

Evolutionary psychology: A level of analysis concerned with how behaviours develop over many generations.

Functionalism: The view that psychology should be the study of the adaptive functions of consciousness.

Gestalt: A school of psychology that emphasizes perception and problem solving.

Humanist psychology: A primarily therapeutic psychological movement focused on providing acceptance and encouraging person growth.

Introspection: The process of examining the contents of one's own consciousness.

Level of analysis: The basic type of approach taken to a particular question. Psychologists may investigate an issue at the psychological, biological or environmental level.

Neuroimaging: The process of capturing structural and functional information concerning the brain and nervous system.

Principle of psychophysical isomorphism: The Gestalt principle that the conscious experience of an event is directly related to the physical reality of the event.

Principle of totality: The Gestalt principle that analysis of any conscious experience must include all mental and physical aspects of a person's situation.

Psychoanalysis: The school of psychology, founded by Sigmund Freud that emphasized unconscious conflicts and desires as the motivators of behaviour.

Psychodynamic theory: A theory developed by Sigmund Freud that attempts to explain mental disorders, personality, and motivation by focusing on unconscious determinants of behaviour.

Psychology: The science of human thought and behaviour.

Psychoneuroimmunology: A field of study involving the relations among psychological events and the function of the immune system.

Psychophysics: The study of the relation between human perception and physical reality.

Reductionism: A philosophical problem based on the idea that if we continue to break a problem into smaller and smaller parts, we eventually become unable to answer larger questions in a meaningful manner.

Repression: The psycholanalytic concept that traumatic memories may be pushed into the unconscious in order to free the conscious mind from having to deal with them.

Self-concept: A person's internal image of themselves, which is central to humanist therapeutic techniques.

Social psychology: A level of analysis concerned with explaining the influence of an individual on a group, a group on an individual, or a group on another group.

Structuralism: The first school of thought developed in psychology, where the focus was on detailed introspective examination of the contents of consciousness.

The unconscious: The psychoanalytic concept of a portion of the mind not accessible to conscious thought.

References

Barlow, A.R. (1981). Gestalt-antecedent influence or historical accident. *The Gestalt Journal, 4*(2), 35-54.

Benito-Gutierrez, E. & Arendt, D. (2009). CNS evolution: new insight from the mud. *Current Biology, 19*(15), 640-642.

Benjamin, L.T., Jr. (2000). The psychology laboratory at the turn of the 20th century. *American Psychologist, 55*, 318-321.

Berrios, G.E. (2005). On the fantastic apparitions of vision by Johannes Müller. *History of   Psychiatry, 16*(2), 229-246.

B.L. Beyerstein (1999). Whence Cometh the Myth that We Only Use 10% of Our Brains? In Sala,   S.D. (Ed.). *Mind Myths. Exploring Popular Assumptions about the Mind and Brain.*   Chichester, UK: John Wiley and Sons.

Calkins, M. W. (1906) A reconciliation between structural and functional psychology.   *Psychological Review, 13*, 61-81.

Bringmann, W.G., Balance, W.D., & Evans, R.B. (1975). Wilhelm Wundt 1832-1920: a brief biographical sketch. *Journal of the history of the behavioral sciences 11*(3): 287–297.

Bühler, C., & Allen, M. (1972). *Introduction to humanistic psychology. Pacific Grove, CA: Brooks/Cole.*

Buss, D.M. (1984). Toward a psychology of person-environment (PE) correlation: The role of spouse selection. *Journal of Personality and Social Psychology, 47*, 361-377.

Buss, D.M. (1985). Human mate selection. *American Scientist, 73*, 47-51.

Darwin, C. R. 1859. On the origin of species by means of natural selection, or the preservation of favoured races in the struggle for life. London: John Murray.

Delprato, D.J. & Midglet, B.D. (1992). Some fundamentals of B.F. Skinner's behaviorism. *American Psychologist, 47*, 1507-1520.

Galotti, K. M. (1999). *Cognitive psychology in and out of the laboratory (2nd ed.).* Belmont, CA: Thomson Brooks/Cole Publishing Co; US.

Hillner, Kenneth P. (1984). *History and Systems of Modern Psychology.* New York: Gardner Press.

Hunt, M. (1993). *The story of psychology.* New York: Doubleday.

Kim, J.A., Bartlett, S., He, L., Nielsen, C.K., Chang, A.M., Kharazia, V., Waldhoer, M., Ou, C.J., Taylor, S., Ferwerda, M., Cado, D., Whistler, J.L. (2008). Morphine-induced receptor endocytosis in a novel knock-in mouse reduces tolerance and dependence. *Current Biology, 18*(2),129-135.

Draft

Kim, J.A., Siegel, S., Patenall, V.R. (1999). Drug-onset cues as signals: intra-administration associations and tolerance. *Journal of Experimental Psychology: Animal Behavioral Processes, 25*(4), 491-504.

Mahadevan, R., Malone, J. C., & Bailey, J. (2002). Radical behaviorism and exceptional memory phenomena. *Behavior and Philosophy, 30*, 1-13.

Mandler, G. (2002). Origins of the cognitive revolution. *Journal of the History of the Behavioral Sciences, 38*, 339-353.

Maslow, A. (1962). *Toward a psychology of being.* Princeton, NJ: D Van Nostrand; US.

Morrongiello, B. A., Humphrey, G. K., Timney, B., Choi, J., & Rocca, P. T. (1994). Tactual object exploration and recognition in blind and sighted children. *Perception, 23*(7), 833-48.

Murray, K. Narratology. In J.A. Smith, R. Harré, & L. Van Langenhove (Eds.) *Rethinking Psychology* (pp.179-195). London: Sage Publication Ltd.

Rosenbluth, R., Grossman, E. S., & Kaitz, M. (2000). Performance of early-blind and sighted children on olfactory tasks, *Perception, 29*(1), 101-110.

Seligman, M. E. (2003). Positive psychology: Fundamental assumptions. *The Psychologist, 16*(3), 126-127

Thomas, J. M. (2008). Lord Rutherford (1871–1937): The Newton of the Atom and the Winner of the Nobel Prize for Chemistry, 1908. *Angewandte Chemie International Edition, 47*(49), 9392-9401.

Thorne, B.M. & Henley, T.B. (1997). *Connections in the history and systems of psychology.* Boston: Houghton Mifflin.

Watson, J.B. (1913). Psychology as the behaviorist views it. *Psychological Review, 20*(2), 158-177.

Watson, J.B. (1924). *Behaviourism.* New York: Norton.

Yildirim, F.B. & Sarikcioglu, L. (2007). Marie Jean Pierre Flourens (1794-1867): an extraordinary scientist of his time. *Journal of Neurology, Neurosurgery & Psychiatry, 78* (8), 852.

Chapter 2: Research Methods in Psychology

Introduction

You are about to begin an extraordinary journey to explore some of the most interesting questions in science today: What drives a person to engage in socially positive behaviours such as volunteering or socially negative behaviours such as racism? How can we understand the seemingly odd and unpredictable behaviours of a person with schizophrenia? How could consciousness emerge from the coordinated activity of 100 billion neurons? While you might be tempted to view these kinds of questions in a general, abstract way, at a more personal level, there are questions about psychological processes that are directly relevant to the kinds of thoughts and behaviours you experience on a daily basis: What motivates you to follow social conventions? Why do you procrastinate? What makes the server at the coffee shop so attractive? To the extent that you have considered such questions at a personal level, you have most likely generated some *informal* answers to these psychological questions by relying on your personal experiences, common sense and reasoning. You follow social conventions in order to fit in with your friends. You procrastinate because you like playing video games more than you like doing math problems. The server in the coffee shop is attractive because red hair and a good sense of humour make for a great combination. These sorts of informal answers may satisfy you in many situations, but psychologists are interested in further exploring these questions using *formal* methods, primarily the set of techniques and concepts known as the **scientific method**.

Why is it necessary to formally study psychology as a science? Experience, common sense and reasoning are the tools we use every day to answer questions and solve problems. Why are the answers we get using these techniques inadequate for psychologists? As you will learn throughout this book, what appears to be 'obvious' or 'just common sense' may in some cases be entirely wrong. This is not to say that common sense and intuition are useless; these techniques are typically quite helpful in enabling you to successfully deal with your day-to-day life. They are, however, far from perfect. The psychological literature is full of examples of situations where the 'obvious' explanation turns out not to be the case. Consider the case of a particular kind of mouse that has been studied with great interest by psychologists interested in hunger and ingestive behaviours. The **ob-ob mouse** is the result of a genetic mutation. As you can see in the photo, ob-ob mice become massively obese. Without worrying too much about the details at this point, consider one of the most basic questions that arise here: Why are these mice so fat? It would seem that this question has an obvious answer…these mice are fat because they eat more food than normal mice. Indeed, ob-ob mice consume far more food than normal mice, but the use of formal scientific methodology has shown that the real answer is rather more surprising. The mutation in the genome of these animals results in their bodies converting almost all the food they eat into fat, leaving little food energy for the body to actually run on. Therefore the mouse needs to eat even more food, which also gets largely converted to fat, and so on. So, the real story is not that the mice are so fat because they eat so much, but that they eat so much because they are so fat.

Another major reason why it is important to use the formal research methods of science to study psychology has to do with the ability to perceive the world around you. As with the case of 'common sense', your perceptions are generally quite useful in allowing you to interpret and navigate the world around on a day-to-day basis. However when applying a more formal set of methods for investigating these abilities it turns out that what you see, hear, feel, smell, and taste may not be as accurate as you assume. One extremely important finding to emerge from the scientific study of perception is that you have a strong tendency to perceive what you *expect* to perceive, even when your expectations do not match up with reality. Stop now and quickly look at Box 2.1. You may assume that it reads: "Paris in the spring." If you look more carefully, you will see that it actually says "Paris in the the spring" (with an extra "the" added to the sentence). Part of the reason why you may have misread the sentence at first is that you read what you expected to read. In your extensive experience with reading sentences in the English language, barring the occasional typo, you have encountered thousands of examples of a single 'the' in a sentence but few, if any, sentences containing 'the the'. Interestingly, a child who is just learning to read would be much more likely than you to catch this error. As you may recall, when you were learning to read, you had to approach sentences like this by carefully examining the individual letters to determine what each word was, and then string the words together into a sentence. With practice, much of the work involved in reading has become less effortful and more automatic. While a more detailed discussion of effortful and automatic processing can wait for a later chapter, the point here is that while your reading has become far faster and more efficient with practice, in some ways it has also become more prone to making the kind of error illustrated in this example. Much of your hard-earned reading efficiency is the result of developing a set of expectations, based on experience, about how the written language works saving you from having to analyze everything you read letter by letter.

Box 2.1: An example of reading automaticity illustrating how prior knowledge influences your perceptions

In Chapter 1, you learned about the history of psychology and the variety of approaches that have been developed during its emergence as a science. In this chapter, you will be introduced to the varied research methods that psychologists use to answer the wide-ranging questions of psychology. This formal framework promotes the self-correcting nature of the scientific enterprise and prevents missteps in our understanding of behaviour. To illustrate the point, consider the case of Jaytee the psychic dog.

Why We Need the Scientific Method: Jaytee the Psychic Dog

Over the years, Pam has developed a special bond with her dog Jaytee. It was Pam's parents who first noticed that when Jaytee went out to the front porch to patiently wait for her, inevitably, Pam would arrive home shortly thereafter. Was this just coincidence? The timing seemed to be uncanny, even when Pam returned home at unusual times. Intriguingly, it seemed that Jaytee could *sense* when Pam was starting her journey home. This special ability did not escape the attention of the media and Jaytee was featured on several television shows that celebrated his paranormal powers. Things got even more interesting when a study supporting the claim was published by a researcher interested in 'psychic pet' phenomena (Sheldrake, 1998).

Although psychic ability is one possibility, there are several alternate explanations. Can Jaytee detect cues that his owners are not considering? Perhaps Jaytee can smell Pam's scent from a distance, hear the characteristic sounds of her car as it approaches, or pick up on her parents' anticipation as they look out the window and wait for Pam. It's also possible that correct responses by Jaytee just happen to coincide with Pam's normal routine. Finally, it's worth considering several factors with regard to the published studies conducted by Sheldrake and other researchers investigating this phenomenon.

To answer these questions in a systematic way, the psychic dog underwent a series of experiments by another group of researchers (Wiseman, Smith, and Milton, 1998). Wiseman was a paranormal skeptic who was highly critical of Sheldrake's original study. Importantly, Wiseman began by providing an **operational definition** of the key **variable**, psychic ability, which was "a trip to the porch preceding Pam's return home within 10 minutes." Without such an operational definition, it would be possible to consider a wide range of behaviours to be indicative of "psychic ability" under different circumstances. Next, several factors were controlled. The time of Pam's return home was randomly selected and unknown to her parents, and Pam drove home in a different car to eliminate any characteristic car sounds which could act as a cue, among other things. As with many sensational claims, when the data were carefully analyzed, it turned out that the simplest explanation was correct—under these controlled conditions Jaytee turned out to be a loyal, but entirely normal dog that showed no evidence of being able to predict Pam's arrival. It would seem that Pam's family, along with some researchers, had been rather selective in remembering and emphasizing those occasions when Jaytee's behaviour coincided with Pam's arrival, and had discounted or failed to remember the more frequent occasions where the dog's behaviour and Pam's arrival were unrelated. The scientific method, of which operational definitions are a key part, requires us to evaluate claims like the one above according to a set of rules that are designed to minimize the chances of being misled by stories that sound good, but are unsupported by the facts.

Box 2.2 Operational Definitions

Operational definitions are a key element in the design of any scientific study. In order to ask and answer questions, psychologists, need to agree on exactly how the variables involved are defined. For example, many psychologists are interested in various aspects of 'intelligence'. You may understand in a general way what is meant by the term 'intelligence', but can you say in a very precise and specific way exactly what is meant by the term intelligence? Think of all the behaviours that other people might produce that would lead you to think that they were intelligent (or not). This list might include things such as the size of vocabulary, ability to solve interpersonal problems, encyclopedic knowledge of baseball statistics, the number of languages spoken, university GPA, or the time it takes them to solve a Rubik's cube puzzle. Most psychologists would agree that all these things involve some form of intelligence, but do any of these qualify as a *definition* of intelligence? Could institutions save a lot of time and money by simply awarding university degrees on the basis of how long it takes the student to solve a Rubik's cube?

The challenge is that intelligence is a **construct**, or a theoretical idea that is quite useful for describing a concept in a general way, but difficult to measure in practice. There is no obvious way to measure intelligence itself (in fact, there are ongoing arguments concerning the very nature of intelligence). Is there something that <u>can</u> be measured that reflects this construct of intelligence as accurately and completely as possible? In practice, one of the most commonly used operational definitions of intelligence is the score obtained on a test such as the Wechsler Adult Intelligence Scale (Weschler, 1981), more commonly known as intelligence quotient or 'IQ'. These tests are designed to capture many different aspects of intelligence. They are objective tests, in that any researcher can look at your answers, add up the number of correct ones, and determine your IQ score. Any researcher who does this will come up with the same result. So, IQ seems to be a reasonable operational definition of intelligence; it can be measured, and when it is, any observer will agree that the results are what they are. Is IQ a <u>perfect</u> operational definition of intelligence? Almost certainly not; many researchers argue that important aspects of intelligence are not picked up by such tests, such as musical or social/emotional insight.

The two most important points to remember as you start to encounter psychological research in action are that a) operational definitions are essential, and b) they are always open to argument. Examining the operational definitions used by researchers is a key step in critically evaluating any research. To get an idea of what is involved in developing good operational definitions, try coming up with an operational definition (i.e., something that can be objectively measured) for each of the following constructs:

Fear

Happiness

Hunger

Sexual Attraction

Psychology as a Science

While it may seem obvious that you should be skeptical about sensational tales of psychic pets, consider that the story of Jaytee received a lot of media coverage (Matthews, 1994; 1995). The fact that a scientist initially published a report supporting the claim served to increase acceptance of the "psychic pet" idea with the general public. Before Wiseman's follow-up study, many people were adequately convinced of this apparently compelling example of psychic pet phenomena. Unfortunately, most of the general public does not read scientific journals where such reports are published, and "psychic dog" stories likely receive much more attention in the popular media than "non-psychic dog" stories. As a result, there are likely large segments of the general public who heard the original Jaytee story and still believe it to be true.

Now, think about the news reports, advertisements and stories you hear making extraordinary claims, often without any scientific research to back them up. It's often easier to passively accept these statements than to be a healthy skeptic. And so, half the college educated population believe the myth that you only use 10% of your brain ("Brain myths", 2003) and nurses working in maternity wards erroneously believe that more babies are born when the moon is full (Abell & Greenspan, 1979). More than likely, the mass e-mail message you received is misleading; the miracle pill is not so miraculous and a fortune is not waiting for you to claim. The greatest value of the scientific method is that it forces us to examine and test claims that we might otherwise be tempted to accept without much critical thought because they appeal to us for one reason or another. Who wouldn't want to have an amazing psychic dog or lose those unwanted pounds overnight?

Asking Questions and Multiple Methods of Analysis

Psychology, like many other disciplines, includes a wide variety of perspectives. Depending on their interests and training, two psychologists might take very different approaches to the same question. For example, different psychologists might look at the same situation and ask completely different questions. Some psychologists would be most interested in the nature of the relevant family and social relationships. Others might emphasize thinking and reasoning processes, or the physiological functioning of brain. Even before scientists begin collecting any data, they make certain choices that determine how the research will proceed. These choices are guided by the **level of analysis** that is applied to the problem. Some of the more common methods of analysis used in psychology include: learning, cognition, social, development, evolution, and neuroscience. The level of analysis that a given researcher uses influences the kind of questions that can be asked and answered. Because the problems and issues in psychology often thread across many contributing fields, researchers ideally will apply a multi-level approach, incorporating ideas and findings from across a variety of perspectives.

For example, researchers studying clinical depression may approach the issue using any of several different levels of analysis. How does a researcher determine at which of these levels she should start? One researcher may be interested in the cognitive aspects of depression: Chronically depressed people have somewhat different thinking patterns than the average 'healthy' person, and have a strong tendency to interpret events in a negative manner. Training people to break this cycle of negative expectations and outcomes (more or less, training in 'thinking positively') can produce great improvements. Another researcher may examine the levels of certain chemical substances in areas of the person's brain. Many aspects of chronic depression have been linked to the function of certain chemicals that carry signals in the brain. Numerous drugs have been developed to alter the action of these chemical systems, and these drugs are often effective in reducing the symptoms of depression. Other researchers may focus on the role of social relationships, environmental stressors, or significant emotional events in the person's life history.

Each of these researchers is operating in different **paradigms** asking very different questions, and probably getting very different kinds of answers. As you have seen in Chapter 1, a variety of paradigms have been developed over the history of psychology as a scientific discipline. Some of these paradigms have been discarded or lost influence as the discipline has evolved. The introspective techniques used by

Wundt and his colleagues to study perceptual processes have largely disappeared from modern psychology. The radical behaviourism of Skinner, while it continues to influence some areas of psychology, is far less influential than it was 50 years ago. While there is always some competition among different paradigms to provide the 'best' answers to important questions, this does not necessarily mean that there is one 'correct' paradigm and all the others are wrong and useless. Applying multiple methods of analysis to a question can be very useful because of the new insights that these additional viewpoints contribute to the answer of this question.

As discussed earlier, humans tend to see what they expect to see. This is no less a problem for researchers than the general population. If the only questions a researcher asks involve the levels of various chemicals in the brain, the only kind of answers they will ever get will involve chemicals in the brain. They will be extremely unlikely to pay attention to any of the other potential factors like relationships or thinking patterns, even if that information is sitting right in front of them. Therefore, it is important to attempt to integrate information from a range of different approaches in our attempt to understand human psychology. This often leads to the formation of exciting new fields at the intersection of multiple methods of analysis such as behavioural neuroscience and psychoneuroimmunology. Some therapies for depression such as cognitive-behavioural therapy specifically rely on a combination of techniques from research across multiple methods of analysis. The uniting theme in all the research we will explore into problems of psychology is the scientific method.

The goal of this chapter is to introduce you to how psychologists use the scientific method to answer fascinating questions about human thought and behaviour. In a very real sense, this makes it the most important chapter of the textbook. Because psychology covers such wide-ranging questions, you will come across a number of research methods used. You will also see how statistical reasoning allows psychologists to interpret data collected in their studies. You will finish by considering the ethical issues surrounding research in psychology. When you can understand these important steps, you have taken an important first step towards thinking like a psychologist.

SECTION REVIEW: Introduction to Research Methods

TABLE 2.1

The field of psychology is firmly based on the use of the scientific method and empirical accuracy in the formulation of theories		
The Scientific Method	**Levels of Analysis Approach**	**The Scientific Method Allows for Research**
• The **scientific method** is a formal way of asking and answering questions about human behaviour to get the most accurate, objective information possible and sidestep the inaccuracy of our common sense beliefs and assumptions	• Different questions based on different levels of analysis may be asked about the same subject matter and different answers may be formulated, but it is always important to consider **multiple levels of analysis** in order to get the most accurate, well rounded theories	• The scientific method allows for this approach to come into fruition and helps to avoid letting our presumptions of background knowledge preclude current research

Section 1: The Scientific Approach to Psychology

The Basic Rules of Scientific Inquiry

Science has a clearly defined set of rules about how valid knowledge should be obtained. By following a standard set of rules when designing their studies and collecting their data, scientists are able to trust each other's work and can build on the results obtained by others. An influential figure in the development of the modern scientific approach was Isaac Newton. Newton himself acknowledged the importance of using a common set of rules when, in a letter to fellow scientist Robert Hooke, he wrote "If I have seen further, it is by standing on the shoulders of giants". What Newton was referring to was that he could never have accomplished what he did without being able to use previous work by others as a starting point. In order to build on that work, he needed to believe it had been done using methods that would produce trustworthy data. If he had instead ignored all previous work and attempted to reinvent mathematics from scratch, for all we know he never would have made it as far as long division. Newton produced brilliant work in a variety of specific fields, and helped to establish four basic principles of the scientific method we employ today. Consider these principles as you progress through the textbook and encounter established and competing theories that attempt to explain psychological processes.

1. PARSIMONY

When presented with two *otherwise equally good* explanations for some phenomenon, scientists tend to prefer the simpler of the two. Generally, what makes an explanation 'simple' or 'complex' is the number of assumptions it makes. In some cases where there are competing explanations, one explanation can account for the known facts using fewer assumptions than the other. Both Ptolemaic (i.e., earth-centered) and Copernican (i.e., sun-centered) explanations of the solar system could explain various celestial phenomena such as the movement of planets or the phases of the moon. However, the earth-centered version required many more untested assumptions about the nature of the heavens to be accepted on faith. Partly as a result of this, and partly as the result of accumulating evidence to the contrary, earth-centered explanations faded while sun-centered explanations became more widely accepted. The principle of parsimony is specifically applied to the situation of competing explanations that do an *equally good job* of accounting for the known facts. Of course, in many cases two competing theories will not be equally good at accounting for the known facts, and in such cases we don't need to apply parsimony, we simply go with the better of the two. Parsimony is the equivalent of the 'penalty shootout' when a game ends in a tie. If one team clearly wins, it isn't required.

2. NATURAL ORDER

As far as is possible, we will attribute the same effects to the same causes. When we drop a dish and it hits the kitchen floor, we attribute that to the same gravity that keeps the moon orbiting the earth. Following this same principle in psychology, we assume that a behaviour (smiling for example) is a reflection of the same underlying mechanism in people all over the world. It is the same root mechanism (let's say happiness) that produces smiles on lottery winners and proud grandparents everywhere. Again, it is important to realize that this principle is only to be applied in situations when comparing the *same effects*. While smiling is likely always the result of the same cause (happiness) in humans, if we expand our investigation to include other species, we would likely find that in many cases the display of lots of teeth does not indicate any level of happiness.

3. GENERALIZABILITY

The principle of generalizability is closely related to the principle of natural order. Much like natural order dictates that we ascribe the same causes to the same effects when we observe phenomena occurring across different situations, we also need to operate on the principle of generalizability that the same causes that produce our effects in the lab also produce those effects in everyday life situations over which the scientist has no control. This assumption has important consequences in psychology, where experiments are typically conducted in contrived settings with mostly undergraduate students. In fact, many studies in psychology have been criticized for focusing heavily on a select demographic group in the studies; young, white, and middle to upper socioeconomic status, and then generalizing their conclusions to the entire human population. While such criticisms may be less relevant to certain research areas such as memory, such selective sampling may have important consequences on others such as social psychology. This concern over how well our laboratory studies reflect the 'real world' outside can sometimes be addressed by the use of some of the non-experimental methods described in Section 3 of this chapter.

4. CONSERVATISM

Scientists are conservative in the sense that they tend to support the current explanation until new facts accumulate that the current explanation can't deal with. This is not to say that scientists will stick to their ideas regardless of what the evidence says, just that they will not abandon their ideas until the evidence forces them to find a different explanation. The conservative scientist is like the person who drives the same car until it is no longer operable, and then gets the best new car available. The alternative would be like buying a new car every time a new model is introduced, regardless of the state of your current vehicle. As noted in Chapter 1, in the 1950s psychology was driven by behaviorism which was used to explain even internal mental processes such as memory. As technology developed and new ideas about these mental processes began to emerge, such behavioral theories were found to be increasingly lacking. Following the so-called Cognitive Revolution, starting in the 1960s, psychologists directed renewed emphasis to the internal mental events of cognition based on ideas very different from those of the earlier behaviourist researchers.

Empiricism and Objectivity

Following the four basic principles of scientific inquiry goes a long way towards shaping the conduct of scientific research. These principles, however, do not say anything explicit about accumulating the contributing 'facts' of knowledge. In his great work, *The History of Animals*, Aristotle presented a long, and apparently convincing, argument for why men and women *should* have different numbers of teeth. Note the use of the word 'should' in the previous sentence; this was an argument based on reason. Strange as it might seem to us, no actual verification was deemed necessary (nobody did any actual counting of male and female teeth). However, Aristotle's chain of reasoning was so convincing that this elegant argument was accepted as truth by the elite, educated class. In contrast, modern scientific methodology is based on **empiricism**, an approach that emphasizes that knowledge should be based on actual *observation* and not on reason alone (i.e., we are obligated to actually count some teeth before making our claims). This is not to say that logic and reason have no place in modern science; they play key roles. We certainly cannot carefully observe *everything* – we must pick and choose where to direct limited resources. However, the modern scientific method insists that logic and reason alone are of little use in the absence of observable, empirical data.

TABLE 2.2

In order to ensure that accurate claims are made, psychology research must follow several basic rules and be empirical and observable	
Basic Rules Central to Scientific Practice	**The Role of Empirical Adequacy**
• **Parsimony:** choosing the simplest theory with the most explanatory power • **Natural Order:** attributing the same effects to the same causes • **Generalizability:** ensuring the causes and effects observed in scientific practice are applicable in all situations involving the same causes • **Conservatism:** skepticism towards new theories until new evidence is undeniable • The basic rules of scientific inquiry are foundational for any scientific practice and must be used and enforced by all scientists in order to establish trustworthy and replicable theories	• Proper scientific research also requires that claims and theories are based on **observable, testable phenomena**, not merely reasonable claims, opinions or assumptions

Section 2: The Scientific Approach to Psychology II

Inductive and Deductive Reasoning in Science

While we might use empirical methods to accumulate a collection of facts about the world, we need a **theory** to explain and relate them. Facts and theories are related in two fundamentally different ways. We use *inductive reasoning* to move from a collection of specific observations (facts) to a theory that allows us to describe how these observations are related. For example, you may observe that cats, dogs, and cows are warm-blooded. Based on these specific observations, you formulate the Four Legs Theory, which states that all four-legged animals are warm-blooded. This theory manages to relate and explain the individual observations we have made; all the animals we tested had four legs and they were all warm-blooded as well. This is admittedly simplistic, but for now, it seems to account for the data. Note that there are plenty of four-legged animals that we have not *directly observed* to be warm-blooded. If our theory is a good one, it should also have something to say about temperature regulation in these species.

Draft

We can use *deductive reasoning* to test our theory by making specific predictions about situations or events that we have not yet observed directly. *If* all four-legged animals are warm-blooded, *then* elephants should be warm-blooded too, as they are also four-legged animals. No elephants were actually observed when we formulated the theory, but now all we need to do is catch a few elephants and gently coax them into accepting a thermometer in the name of the Four Legs Theory (just be glad we didn't choose grizzly bears). If it turns out that elephants are indeed warm-blooded, this will further support the theory. This hardly *proves* that the theory is perfectly correct, as there are still giraffes, tigers or any of a range of other four-legged animals yet to test. Each time we, or others, make another specific prediction based on our theory and obtain empirical evidence that the prediction is correct, the theory is further supported and more likely to be adopted by other researchers.

What if we make a testable prediction and the empirical evidence does not agree? What if the four-legged gecko lizard turns out to be cold-blooded? A good theory must be able to encompass *all* the known facts, not just *some* of them. If we modified the theory to state, "all four-legged animals, except the gecko lizard, are warm-blooded", this doesn't really do the job. We need a theory of 'warm-bloodedness' that explains *why* gecko lizards, while being four- legged animals, are not warm-blooded whereas all other four-legged animals are warm-blooded. You might wonder about our own two-legged, warm-blooded species, but note that our theory is that all four-legged animals are warm-blooded, not that all warm-blooded animals have four legs. Perhaps down the road, a brilliant researcher will develop a better explanation (a Unified Mammal Theory?).

This kind of thing happens routinely in the sciences; a theory is used to generate a prediction, new data do not conform, and the theory has to be modified or abandoned. This process of refinement is aided by the collaborative nature of science, where any given area is likely to be examined by many different researchers using a number of different methods of analysis. This reduces the chances that we will be fooled into making errors by our own preconceived ideas, as there will be other researchers, with different viewpoints and biases, to point out the flaws.

One final, but important, note with regard to scientific theories concerns the difference between a scientific theory and what we might call 'an idea'. The word 'theory' is often applied to explanations of various phenomena that are not proper theories in the scientific sense. What makes a scientific theory a scientific theory is that it generates *testable* predictions. For example, you might have some idea about what happens to people after they die. On the basis of this idea, you make a prediction about what will happen to you personally after you die. Many such ideas exist in the world, but it would be a mistake to call such an idea a theory because the predictions these ideas generate are not testable, and thus, unverifiable. In order to conduct a scientific test of your 'theory' we would need to have someone (or preferably lots of people – see the later section on replication) die, record some evidence of what they were experiencing, and then return with this objective empirical data in hand. If your 'theory' doesn't generate predictions that can actually be tested, it isn't really a theory. It should also be noted, however, that some predictions that are not testable today may become testable in the future as the technological means to do so are developed. The development of various brain-imaging technologies over the last 50 years has certainly allowed us to test many predictions in ways that would have been previously impossible. This ability to watch the brain in action has, in fact, been one of the driving forces behind the Cognitive Revolution in psychology referred to earlier. It is also important to remember that the scientific approach does not necessarily disagree with not testable ideas, such as those concerning the nature of post-mortem experiences. There are many questions that may be very important and central to many people that science is just not equipped to answer.

Target Study: Stereotypes

DO STEREOTYPES INFLUENCE WOMEN'S MATH PERFORMANCE?

Researchers: Steven J. Spencer (University of Waterloo), Claude M. Steele (Stanford University), and Dianne M. Quinn (University of Michigan)

Source: Spencer, S. J., Steele, C.M., & Quinn, D. M. (1999). Stereotype threat and women's math performance. *Journal of Experimental Psychology, 35,* 4-28.

Note: The material below is the author's summarized description of the original published article.

In a social situation in which others expect you to perform badly, the apprehension you may feel in response to these negative expectations may cause you to perform poorly and confirm their belief. This phenomenon is known as stereotype threat. In this study, comprised of three different experiments, Spencer, Steele and Quinn (1999) evaluated the effect of stereotype threat on performance of equally qualified men and women on a math test. We will examine one study in detail and briefly review the remaining studies afterward. The purpose of one of the studies was to determine if men and women would perform differently if they were told that the test had revealed gender differences in the past.

METHOD

Participants   The participants were 30 female and 24 male undergraduates attending Stanford University who were selected from an introductory psychology participant pool. All participants were pre-screened for high math abilities in that they all performed well in both university level calculus and scored above the 85th percentile on the math subsection of the Scholastic Aptitude Test (SAT) or the American College Test (ACT).

Procedure   Math questions originated from the advanced Graduate Record Examination (GRE) in mathematics. Most of the questions involved advanced calculus, although some also required knowledge of abstract algebra and real variable theory. The math tests were administered on a computer. For each question participants had the option of answering the question, leaving the question blank, or skipping the question, which allowed them to answer it later. The whole test consisted of eleven difficult questions divided into two parts. Part one was comprised of six questions and part two was comprised of 5 questions. Half of the participants were told that part one had shown gender differences in the past, and part two had no gender difference in performance. The remaining half was told the opposite concerning which test yielded gender differences. Thus, the order in which participants experienced the different conditions, as well as which part of the test was presented as biased, could not systematically influence the results. Participants had 15 minutes to complete part one and 15 minutes to complete part two.

Results   The researchers found that the two parts on the math tests were not the same difficulty level and only the results of part one were used to evaluate potential effects of stereotype threat. When participants were not made aware of gender stereotype vulnerability, women's performance was consistent with that of men writing the same test. However, when participants were told that the test had shown a gender difference in the past, women scored significantly lower than men (see Figure 2.1).

Figure 2.1

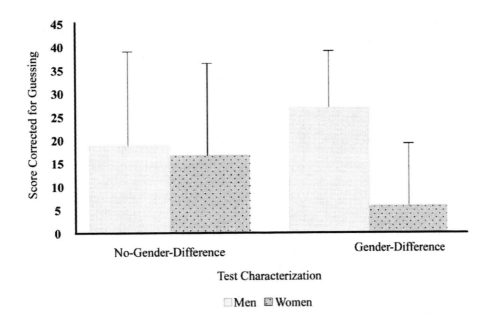

Performance on a difficult math test as a function of sex of participant and test characterization.

Source: Graph recreated based on the original graph presented in Spencer, S. J., Steele, C.M., & Quinn, D. M. (1999). Stereotype threat and women's math performance. *Journal of Experimental Psychology, 35,* 4-28.

Discussion   In one of the two remaining studies Spencer and colleagues found that women underperformed on a difficult test, but performed on par with men on an easy math test. These findings suggest that stereotype threat may be present even in the absence of an explicit suggestion of sex differences in mathematical capabilities. This suggests that stereotype threat may become an issue in any situation where difficulties are encountered, even when there is no explicit mention of the stereotype. In the second remaining study the gender difference in math test performance was replicated with students from a different university wherein math questions originated from the Graduate Management Test (GMAT). In addition, this second study also used a control group that received no information on potential gender differences. Based on the findings of these studies, it can be inferred that women perform less well than men on difficult math tests if they are informed that the expectation is that they will not perform as well as men, although they appear to perform as well as men in the absence of this expectation.

LIMITATIONS

The concept of stereotype threat may appear to be a relatively simple idea, but this study demonstrates that even when an idea may seem straightforward it can be challenging to design a well-controlled experiment. First, in this study, it was difficult to assess the true effect of stereotype threat due to the lack of a certain type of control group. Had there been a control group to which no explicit mention of gender differences was offered, the researchers would have been better able to interpret how stereotype threat influenced performance on the math tests. Furthermore, part one and part two of the test proved to have different levels of difficulty which forced the researchers to ignore data from half of their participants. Additionally, this study utilizes a lab environment as the setting to conduct the experiment; this makes the setting somewhat artificial and contrived. This is problematic because the results may not transfer to a real testing situation where the test is written in a naturalistic setting. While it may be difficult to orchestrate, it would be interesting to see how the results of these studies may have differed if the tests had been on paper in a classroom environment with other students seated around the participants.

COMMENT

While the results of these studies is certainly interesting and perhaps distressing to some extent, it is important to note that more research on stereotype threat is needed to fully understand its true effect and implications on performance. This study demonstrates that a relatively simple research design features both strengths and flaws. Both strengths and limitations are equally important to be aware of when reading journal articles to evaluate results and conclusions, and both should inform the design of your own experiments as a future psychologist.

The Process of Scientific Investigation

STEP 1: GENERATE OR ADOPT A THEORY

Scientists begin by studying the existing collection of information about the world, including previous work published by other scientists. This information helps them to construct a theory, a general set of ideas about the way that the world works. Alternately, they may adopt an existing theory, as was the case in the target study, and begin generating deductive predictions based on that.

STEP 2: GENERATE A TESTABLE HYPOTHESIS

This theory guides the creation of a set of testable statements called **hypotheses** (this is the term used to describe those testable predictions generated by a theory using deductive reasoning). A hypothesis makes specific predictions about the relationship between variables involved in the theory. Spencer et al (1999) used their knowledge of background research on stereotype threat to develop a hypothesis that they could induce gender differences in performance on a math test by telling participants that gender was a factor.

STEP 3: CHOOSE A RESEARCH METHOD

A scientist must carefully select a research method that is appropriate to test the hypothesis at hand. Some of these different methods are discussed in the following two sections of this chapter. What they have in common is that they allow scientists to collect data about how the events of the world unfold and whether they are in line with their hypothesis or not. In the target study the researchers opted to use an experiment. As you will see, other options are possible, with each option having benefits and liabilities.

STEP 4: COLLECT DATA

The next step involves actually collecting the data using one or more of several techniques. Each of these also has advantages and disadvantages as summarized in Table 2.5. Spencer et al (1999) used questions on a math test to collect data, which consisted of the participant's test scores.

STEP 5: ANALYZE DATA

Once the data have been carefully collected, a researcher uses statistical tools to analyze those data to reveal patterns and determine whether the hypothesis has been supported or not. Through the use of these techniques, Spencer et al., (1999) were able to determine that their results were **statistically significant,** meaning that their findings supported their hypothesis that gender specific stereotype threat could be induced in a math test setting by telling participants that gender would affect their scores.

STEP 6: REPORT FINDINGS

Finally, individual scientists and the scientific community as a whole review all findings on a topic to revise existing theories that define our current understanding about the world. Spencer et al (1999) documented their results in the form of a journal article and in doing so, shared their findings with the rest of the academic community. Many subsequent researchers built on the principles related to gender specific stereotype threat uncovered by Spencer et al. In the target study, however, only summarized data are reported; they do not report each individual score obtained by each subject under each condition. This level of detail is typically not reported in journal articles, although it is becoming increasingly common for researchers to make such data available either upon request or through some public forum such as a web site. This allows other researchers to perform their own, possibly different, analyses on the data.

STEP 7: REVISE THEORIES

Because science and research are constantly generating new data, some of which may not fit with current theories, these theories are continually being revised to account for this new information. Findings revealed in the Spencer et al., (1999) studies indicate that women perform badly on difficult math tests particularly if they are informed of the expectation is that they will not perform as well as men. These results strengthened the previous theory of stereotype threat as a factor that can influence performance in a variety of situations.

Testing our Hypotheses: Reliability and Validity

There are two important issues that arise when we perform a test of any kind. In order for a test to be considered useful for any sort of scientific inquiry, it must be both reliable and valid. **Reliability** is the ability of any test to give the same output when the same input is entered. Imagine stepping on a bathroom scale to test your weight. Every time you step on the scale, at least within a relatively short time period, the scale should produce the same reading. You are providing the same input each time (your actual weight), and a reliable scale should produce the same output each time (your weight as displayed on the scale). If instead the scale reads 25 kg one time, 78 kg the next, and so on, it clearly is not doing the job we expect it to do; the same input is resulting in very different output from one test to the next. As you can imagine, any test that is not reliable is pretty much useless. Establishing the reliability of any test is a primary concern for researchers. If a test cannot be shown to be reliable there is no need to concern ourselves with the next issue, we need a new test.

The second issue is somewhat more complex. There are several different forms of validity that may concern us, but we will confine our discussion to the most basic form of validity, **construct validity**. The term construct validity refers to the ability of a test to measure what we intend to measure. Imagine we are using a bathroom scale again, but this time we are using it as a test of intelligence, rather than body mass. You step on the scale and it reports that your IQ is 65. Naturally, you want to know if this intelligence test is reliable, so you step on the scale again, and receive the same IQ rating. You conduct a few more tests, just to make sure, and each time your IQ is measured to be 65. Clearly we have a reliable (and quick!) test of intelligence. It ought to be clear, however, that our intelligence test has no construct validity. While we may intend to measure intelligence, what our test is actually measuring is clearly body mass. The above example is quite extreme, but you imagine instead that we are developing a new test to diagnose a mood disorder such as major depressive disorder. We will want to be sure that our test is actually measuring depression, and not anxiety, anger, shame or any of a range of other conditions that might easily be confused with depression. While reliability will be our first concern, we also need to consider the validity of any test or instrument used to collect data.

TABLE 2.3

Through use of the steps of the scientific method we can both formulate theories and generalize theories to phenomena		
Inductive Reasoning	**Deductive Reasoning**	**Steps of the Scientific Method**
• **Inductive reasoning** allows us to build theories based on various incidents of observed phenomena converging on a hypothesis or set of hypotheses	• **Deductive reasoning** allows us to make predictions about certain phenomena based on the testable claims of a particular theory	• The **scientific method** involves 7 vital steps that must be followed rigorously in order to construct empirically accurate theories or deduce claims based on pre-existing theories

Section 3: Research Design: Case Studies, Correlations and Experiments

Now that we have established the relationship between individual observations of the world and the theories that explain them, we need to examine where those observations come from. There are a variety of approaches that we might take, and which we choose to investigate some question will depend on many factors. In this section we will look at some of the most commonly used, and useful, ways of collecting data about the world around us. Each has its own advantages and disadvantages, but by the end of this section it should be clear that relying on any one of these methods exclusively would greatly limit our ability to advance our knowledge. Psychology relies on using all of these methods to deal with different aspects of any given research question.

Case Studies

A case study is typically a detailed examination of one particular individual. Imagine that you are a neurologist, and one morning a patient walks into your office. This patient has recently experienced a traumatic head injury and seems to have lost the ability to speak. They can still understand what others say to them, but are unable to produce any speech of their own. While your first obligation is going to be treating this patient and doing whatever possible to remedy the damage, you may also be quite curious as to what exactly has happened to the patient's brain that resulted in this particular impairment. Using a variety of brain-imaging techniques, you determine that the patient's brain damage seems to be confined to a small area of the temporal lobe (just above and in front of the patient's left ear). You will encounter plenty of neuroanatomy later in this course, but for now let us just refer to this particular bit of brain as

'Area X'. The obvious conclusion would be that Area X is the part of the brain primarily responsible for the production of speech. Before getting too excited, however, remember what you have already read about 'obvious' answers; we still need to proceed with some degree of caution here.

With the patient's consent, you subject them to a series of tests designed to measure various aspects of brain function. The results of these tests consistently serve to reinforce your original conclusion; the patient's brain seems to be perfectly functional in any situation except those that require speech to be produced. To your surprise, one day you enter the testing room to find your patient singing along with the radio. You immediately run a number of tests again, and it still seems that the patient cannot produce normal speech (although they can sing). This makes things even more interesting. Not only have you identified a brain area that seems to be the 'speech center', but also that speaking and singing seem to be controlled by different brain regions. This is all very exciting, but there is one very important question remaining. How do you know that the injury sustained by your patient would produce the same results in *any* human brain? In other words, have you identified the speech center in the human brain, or just in your patient's brain? Could other brains be different?

Case studies are invaluable to psychology. In Chapter 6 you will encounter one of the most influential and interesting case studies in the history of psychology, that of HM (the subjects of case studies are typically identified in the literature only by their initials in order to protect their privacy). In areas where there may be no existing bodies of evidence to examine or theories to test and modify, case studies can provide us with some initial 'facts' to work with. They can also serve to support (or not) existing theoretical positions. Almost everything we know about the human brain and its function has roots in case studies such as the one described above. Brain injuries are unfortunately common, and the process of linking certain abilities to certain brain areas typically starts with the observation that an individual has lost both a particular bit of brain and a particular ability. We can learn how a healthy brain works by observing cases where damaged brains do not work. However, we can never be sure that what we observe in a single individual applies equally to all members of the human race. So how do we move from observations of an individual to conclusions that we can safely apply to everyone?

One possibility is to simply wait until more people show up in your office with injuries similar to those of your original patient. As you might well imagine, this could take a very long time, and might never happen at all. Another possibility is that you could go out into the world and actively search for such people. If you can locate a sufficient number of cases where similar brain injuries have occurred and/or similar disabilities are present, you may be able to use a different set of techniques to examine the relationship between certain types of brain damage and the ability to speak.

Correlational Studies

Another way we might choose to investigate the world around us is to look at existing relationships between pairs of variables. For example, we might be interested in examining the relationship between diet and life expectancy. Is it the case that there is a relationship between what you choose to eat and how long you will live? If so, what is the nature of that relationship? These are typically referred to as *correlational* studies. As with case studies, in correlational research we take the world as we find it; we don't manipulate anything, we just carefully observe and record. By definition, a simple correlation is a measure of the *direction* and *strength* of the relationship between two variables. Consider the following two variables: age and income. In any given person we examine, each of these variables could take on different values.

How might these two variables be related? To find out, we will survey a number of people and simply record, for each individual, their age and income. Once we have a sufficiently large sample of data we can use statistical techniques to analyze the relationship.

It might be the case that there is a *positive correlation* between age and income. If a correlation is positive, that means that as the value of one variable increases, the value of the other also increases. This would mean that the older someone was, the more money they made (the two variables increase together). Instead, there might be a *negative correlation* between age and income, where increasing values on one variable are associated with decreasing values on the other. In this case, our data would show that the older you are, the less money you made. The final possibility is the *zero correlation*, indicating no relationship. A zero correlation would indicate that age and income had no relationship whatsoever. What do we gain by knowing the nature of these relationships? The primary benefit is that, once the nature of the relationship is established we can measure one of the variables involved and use this to predict the level of the other variable. If the relationship between age and income is known, it allows us to predict a person's income based on knowing their age (or vice versa). Of course, if the relationship is a zero correlation, that tells us that knowing a person's age tells us nothing about how much money they make, and knowing their income tells us nothing about their age.

Correlations are typically described using a number called a **correlation coefficient**. This number ranges from -1.00 to +1.00. A correlation of +1.00 would mean there is a perfect positive correlation between two variables. If this was the case with the age-income relationship, that would mean that every single person on the planet who was older than you also made more money than you. Another way to view this is to imagine lining up the entire human population in order from youngest to oldest. By doing this you would also have, without exception, lined up the entire human population from poorest to richest. A correlation of -1.00, on the other hand, would tell us that there is a perfect negative correlation between two variables. In this case, every single person on the planet who is older than you also makes less money than you, and lining up the entire species from youngest to oldest would mean you had also lined them up from richest to poorest. In practice, at least in psychology, you are unlikely to observe many perfect correlations, either positive or negative. Relationships in the real world tend to be somewhat less neat and tidy. For example, if there was a positive, but not *perfectly* positive, correlation between age and income, statistical analysis might reveal a correlation coefficient of +0.70. This would indicate that while age and income generally tended to rise together, there would be plenty of exceptions (i.e., some rich young people and some poor old people). In other words, if we knew someone was older than you, we would predict that they made more money than you and be right most, but not all, of the time.

It is important to realize that the sign of a correlation coefficient (the '+' or '-' preceding the actual number) refers to the *direction* of the relationship, not the *strength*. The strength of the relationship is indicated by how far the number is from zero in *either* direction. Note that the stronger a correlation is, the more predictive power it has (i.e., the predictions we make on the basis of such data are more likely to be correct). While these predictions may not be perfect, they can still be valuable tools for understanding human psychology, as you will see in later chapters.

How might we use this approach to investigate the questions raised by our earlier case study, where we observed that damage to Area X in the brain seemed to result in an inability to speak? As was suggested at the time, it would be unwise to make assumptions about the entire human species based on observations made in a single individual. We could test our ideas in a more rigorous way by looking at a large sample of people who had a range of speech abilities and measuring them on the two variables of interest: How much damage is there in Area X and how capable are these people of producing normal speech? It might be the case that large numbers of people with no speech ability showed no damage at all in Area X. If this were so, it would strongly suggest that our original idea was not correct, and that the ability to speak was not entirely the function of that particular area of the brain. On the other hand, if we discovered that every person with an inability to speak had identical damage to Area X and that every person with normal speech ability showed no damage at all in this area, this would suggest that our original idea might, in fact, be correct. A more likely outcome might be that some of the people observed showed both damage to Area X and inability to produce speech, but others had either damage to Area X, or an inability to speak, but not both. This would result in a positive, but not perfectly positive, correlation, suggesting that while Area X clearly has something to do with speech production the real story of speech production must be somewhat more complicated and involve other areas of the brain as well.

A well-known study by evolutionary psychologists Margo Wilson and Martin Daly demonstrates how we can use correlational data to understand the nature of the relationships between variables. Wilson and Daly (2001) recorded homicide rates in Chicago in an attempt to determine the predictive value of income inequality (the difference between the incomes of the high earners and low earners) on homicide rates. They found a strong positive relationship ($r = +0.73$) between income inequality and homicide rates, meaning that as income inequality rose so did number of homicides. Interestingly, Wilson and Daly (1997) also found that the strongest variable relating to an increase in homicides was in fact male life span ($r = -0.88$). The variables in this study were not manipulated in any way by the authors; they did nothing to influence those that would or would not be murdered, nor did they do anything to influence the size of the income inequality. Wilson and Daly simply collected data from the world as it is and used their knowledge of psychology and statistical analysis to test hypotheses concerning these possible trends and relationships.

Figure 2.2 Positive and negative correlations

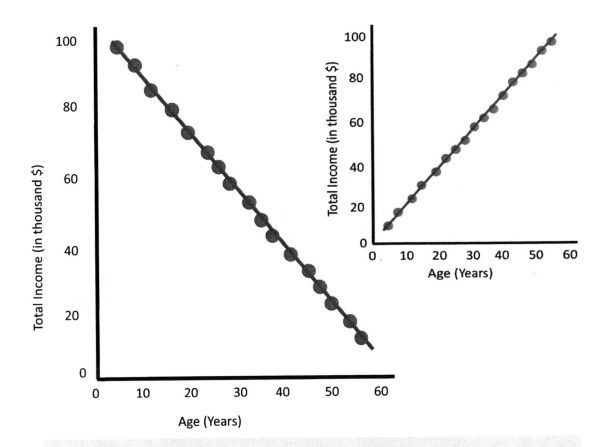

Correlational data are typically represented graphically using a scatter plot. In these figures one variable is represented on the horizontal (or X) axis and the other is represented on the vertical (or Y) axis. Each dot represents the value of each of the two variables recorded in a single case. The red line drawn through the dots is the *line of best fit*. This is a straight line which comes as close as possible to all the points on the graph and shows any positive or negative trends in the data (in the case of a zero correlation, this line would be perfectly horizontal). Scatter plots make it easy to see the general nature of the relationship between the two variables, although further statistical analysis is required before drawing any final conclusions.

While it is extremely useful to be able to identify relationships between pairs of variables, there is one important drawback to correlational studies: No matter how strong a relationship we observe, a correlation does not allow us to tell a 'cause and effect' story. If we observed a strong negative correlation between years of education and time spent in prison, we might be tempted to assume that spending more time in school *causes* you to spend less time in prison, and vice versa. Much as we might be tempted to draw such a conclusion from this data, it would be a huge mistake to do so. One well-established finding in psychology is that there is a positive correlation between height and intelligence. It is far from a perfect positive correlation, but neither is it a zero correlation indicating that the two variables have nothing to say about each other. If we try to extract a cause and effect story from this finding, we are left with two choices: Either being taller causes you to be more intelligent, or being more intelligent causes you to be taller. Neither of these explanations seems to make much sense, and yet the relationship clearly exists. This highlights another limitation of a correlational approach. By definition, a correlation is a relationship between *two* variables. You cannot have a correlation among 3 (or more) different variables. If you are dealing with variables A, B, and C, you can look at the correlation between A and B, between A and C, or between B and C, but this technique is not designed to look at all three together at the same time. The reality is that any given variable we choose to observe may be influenced by any number of other variables, but the correlational approach only allows you to examine one pair at a time. This brings to our attention what is called the 'Third Variable Problem' and the example concerning height and intelligence is a case in point. While there is clearly a relationship between height and intelligence, it is probable that neither of these is the causal factor. It is much more likely that increased height and increased intelligence are the result of some 'third variable' that we have not included in our analysis. One of the most obvious candidates would be early childhood nutrition, which could have a strong influence on both adult height and intelligence.

Consider another example in which you have found a positive correlation between amount of ice cream consumed and the number of violent crimes in a major city. Your first mistake would be to assume that eating ice cream *causes* people to commit violent crimes, or that an increase in incidence of violent crimes *causes* more people to eat ice cream. Remember: correlation does not mean causation. What 'third variable' might we be ignoring here, which might actually be the cause of both increasing violent crime and increasing ice cream consumption?

Finally, it should be said that although correlational research and case studies will never provide the kind of cause and effect explanations that we would ultimately like to have, sometimes it is the best we can do. In the next part of this section we will examine a research method that will allow us to derive cause and effect stories, but as you will see there are always going to be questions to which this method cannot be applied for either practical or ethical reasons (there is a section on research ethics at the end of this chapter). The limitations of research methods that involve simply examining the world as it exists, such as those already described will become clearer as we examine the research method preferred by most scientific researchers, the experiment. Refer to Table 2.5 for a review of advantages and disadvantages of descriptive and correlational research.

SECTION 3 REVIEW: Case Studies and Correlational Research

TABLE 2.4

<table>
<tr><td colspan="2">Certain methods of psychology research can allow us to explore particular phenomena and suggest relationships between variables</td></tr>
<tr>
<td>The Role of Case Studies</td>
<td>Correlational Research and What it Provides</td>
</tr>
<tr>
<td>

- **Case studies** involve the meticulous, long term study of an individual or small group of individuals, but are not necessarily generalizable to populations
- Such studies are still important starting points for much research and active replication and further research can help establish theories formulated

</td>
<td>

- **Correlational studies** seek to point out relationships between two or more variables by examining the **direction** (positive or negative) and **strength** (how far from zero in either direction) of observed relationships
- Correlational data can help us make accurate predictions but they do not indicate causes and effects; two variables may be strongly related but other unknown variables may actually be contributing to the observed relation

</td>
</tr>
</table>

Section 4: Experiments

Experiments

The procedure of choice used to systematically study a problem in psychology is the *experiment*. Unlike the methods previously described, where data are collected from the world as it exists, in an experiment a researcher *manipulates* one or more variables (i.e., they *make* something happen) and measures the changes that occur in a second variable. Careful observation and implementing measures to control other variables that could possibly affect results (more on this important concept shortly) allows us to detect cause and effect relationships. As has been implied already, it is these cause and effect relationships that will allow us to develop the most useful understanding of the world around us, at least from a scientific point of view. We are generally not content to simply know *that* things happen; we would also like to know *why* they happen.

INDEPENDENT AND DEPENDENT VARIABLES

A variable is anything that is free to take on different values. Some of the variables we might associate with humans would include height, IQ, age, or number of siblings, which, in any given person, might take on very different values. Some variables may have only two possible values (e.g., alive/dead, male/female, on/off, etc, such variables are often referred to as **binary variables**), while others may be free to take on an infinite range of values (e.g., weight, speed, temperature, etc). If there is only one possible value, such

---

65

as 'number of heads a human being has', that is considered a **constant**, rather than a variable. In an experiment, as with other research methods, it is critical that we work with operationally defined variables (see Box 2.2), and determining these operational definitions is required before you can proceed to investigate any question of interest.

There are two types of variables that are central to the experimental method. The first is referred to as the **independent variable** (IV). This is the variable that the researcher will explicitly manipulate. For example, if we set up an experiment to see the effect of room temperature on test performance, we might compare the test scores of students writing an exam in a cold room (10°C) to the test scores of students writing an exam in a standard temperature room (20°C). In this case, room temperature is the IV. We manipulated the situation such that one room was cold and the other was not. In the simplest case, an experiment will have one IV. It is certainly possible, and quite common to have experiments with more than one IV. It is also important to distinguish between an IV and the *levels* of the IV. In the above example, there was one IV (room temperature), and it was expressed at two levels (10°C and 20°C). It is also common, and in some cases highly desirable, to express an IV at more than two levels; we might have tested a much wider range of room temperatures rather than just the two we used.

The second important type of variable is referred to as the **dependent variable** (DV). This variable is measured by the researchers to see if their manipulation of the IV had any effect. In our example, the DV would be the test scores. If room temperature has any effect on test performance, we should see that by comparing the scores of the two groups of students. Again, some experiments have multiple DVs, but we will try to keep things simple.

There is a third class of variables that we also need to consider called **extraneous variables** (EVs), also known as **confounding variables**. These are variables that the researcher did not manipulate or measure, but that nonetheless could still affect the outcome of the experiment. In our Room Temperature experiment, we hope to demonstrate that a change in room temperature has an effect on test scores. But, think for a moment about all the other things that might affect those test scores. Are the students in the cold room smarter to begin with? Are all the students in one room male and all the students in the other room female? Imagine we only had a single room to work with, so we made it cold in the morning for one group and then warmed it up in the afternoon for the second group, resulting in the two groups being tested at different times of day. All of these variables (and many others) could *potentially* influence the results. What can be done to eliminate, or at least minimize, the potential influence of EVs on our data? The answer can be summed up in a single word: *Control*.

A good experiment seeks to control for the effects of all possible EVs. In a sense, we will seek to turn any potential EV we discover into a constant. If we thought gender might be an EV, we could eliminate gender as a potential EV by testing only female students. We have effectively eliminated an EV by making it a constant. One potential downside to taking this approach, however, is that we may now only be able to justifiably apply our conclusions to the female half of the species, rather than all humans as we might have hoped. This raises one of the difficulties of applying the experimental method; every EV we turn into a constant has the potential to limit the scope of our results. Another option is to *equate* our groups with respect to the EV, rather than eliminating it completely. In this case, we could ensure that each group had an equal number of males and females. While we haven't exactly turned the EV into a constant, to the extent that gender can affect our results it ought to have the same effect in both groups, which will still allow us to clearly see the effects of manipulating the IV.

EXPERIMENTAL AND CONTROL GROUPS

In the simplest case, an experiment typically involves two groups of participants, each of which is exposed to different levels of the IV. In many cases a **control group** will receive a 'zero level' of the IV. Whatever it is that we are manipulating, we do not manipulate it at all in these participants. We would therefore expect that these participants will reflect the 'normal' state of affairs. Data obtained from this group is compared to data from an **experimental group**, in which we have manipulated the IV in some way. Control groups are necessary in order for us to be able to see if our manipulation had any effect in our experimental group. Without data from a control group to compare to, we won't have any idea about the effect of our manipulation of the IV in the experimental group.

Let us return now to a research question we were discussing earlier, that of the relationship between damage to Area X in the brain and the inability to speak. On the basis of a case study, where one individual who could not speak displayed damage to this area of the brain, we used a correlational approach to examine the relationship between damage to Area X and speech ability in a large number of people. The data we obtained suggests that there is a positive, but not perfect, correlation between the two variables of interest. Remember also the limitations of the correlational approach. While we might be tempted to view our results as evidence supporting our theory that damage to Area X *causes* the inability to speak, we can't do that. Although it may seem unlikely, it is entirely possible that it is the inability to speak that causes the damage to Area X. After all, anyone who has spent time with an arm or leg in a cast (or in zero gravity) knows that muscles atrophy when they aren't used. Would it really be that surprising to see the same kind of atrophy in a part of the brain that was no longer being used? Of course, this would mean that the actual cause of the speech problems and the brain damage was some third variable that we have not yet discovered. Remember, we cannot infer cause and effect relationships from correlations. A correlation simply means that two variables are related to one another in some way.

If we want to test our theory that damage to Area X causes the inability to speak, we are going to need to perform an experiment. As ought to be clear by now, an experiment will require us to manipulate an IV, which in this case would be the amount of damage to Area X. In the simplest experiment we could design, there would presumably be a control group, in which we did no damage (the 'zero level' of the IV), and an experimental group in which we destroyed this area completely. You might want to skip ahead and read the final section of this chapter at this point if it is not already clear to you why we could never perform this experiment. No research institution, university, government, or any other sensible authority is going to allow us to permanently damage the brains of otherwise healthy people, regardless of how important or interesting our questions might be. Given that speech appears to be a uniquely human ability, we don't have the option of using non-human research subjects, as is sometimes done in similar situations. It would seem that we are unable to obtain the kind of cause and effect explanation that we would most like to have.

Fortunately for us, there have been some amazing advances in technology that might allow us to work around our problem. Using a technique called Transcranial Magnetic Stimulation (TMS) we are able to temporarily 'turn off' areas of the brain while causing no permanent damage. Using this technique, we can create an experimental group by taking healthy participants, people with no evidence of either brain damage or speech problems, and using TMS to temporarily stop brain activity only in Area X, and then give them a task that requires them to speak (answering a series of simple autobiographical questions, for example). Our DV in this case would be some measure of how much speech they could produce, which

---

67

we could operationally define as number of words spoken per minute. For our control group, we would take more healthy participants and treat them in exactly the same way with one critical exception; the TMS apparatus is never actually turned on. We can then compare performance on our DV between our control group, in whom normal speech ability would be expected, and our experimental group. If we then find that participants in whom Area X has been deactivated produce little or no speech, while our control participants are able to speak normally, we are now justified in claiming that damage to Area X *causes* speech deficits.

Box 2.3: Application / Twisting Science

The scientific method provides an important lesson in being critical about scientific claims and their legitimacy. We have come to understand that, although science is based on empirical adequacy and strives for objectivity, it is not perfect. Human error exists, theories are in constant need of replication and revision, and thus any claim made it not absolute. Popular media, however, will often have us think otherwise. Catchy news titles and emotionally driven phrases filled with astounding "hard facts" about the exciting world of science often seek to draw the public in. One of the biggest mistakes often made are the claims that scientists have "proven" that a certain phenomenon is caused by a particular factor, for example, that cancer is caused by the consumption of aspartame. Two major issues are apparent in claims such as this. For one, science does not ever "prove" anything; science is constantly being updated and is aware that humans are not capable of achieving absolute knowledge. Secondly, claims about causation are often inferred from correlational relationships. As we know, though, correlation does not mean causation; there are often extraneous variables involved in the relationship observed that are not being taken into account. For this particular example, although there may be a strong relationship between aspartame intake and cancer incidences, this relationship may be completely coincidental. There may be other specific variables such as exposure to radiation that just so happens to occur to people who like to drink diet soda or aspartame consumption simply is linked to another factor that contributes to developing cancer.

Popular media often uses these tactics to reel the public in; they may have an agenda they want to push and by appealing to the public in exciting ways, their messages are effectively sent out. Unfortunately the public may be lead down a path of falsehood and conceptions of scientific practice are skewed. Equipped with knowledge of the scientific method, though, we can hold ourselves back from being prey to the media and false information by being critical and constantly questioning the information presented to us.

ADVANTAGES AND DISADVANTAGES OF EXPERIMENTAL RESEARCH

The experimental method is so important to science because it allows researchers to develop cause and effect explanations. If we have done a sufficiently good job of controlling all the relevant EVs in an experiment, we can reasonably conclude that it was the manipulation of the IV that caused the changes in the DV. In our experiment investigating the role of Area X in speech production, we found evidence that damage to this area causes speech deficits. Remember that our earlier correlational study had suggested that there was a relationship between the two phenomena, but based on those data alone we were unable to conclude that either variable was the causal factor. This illustrates the primary advantage of the experimental method: The ability to say *why* something happened. There is, however, an equally important disadvantage to this approach that we need to keep in mind. One of the most common, and in many cases justified, criticisms of the experimental method is that there may be little resemblance between the carefully controlled conditions in the laboratory and the real world. After all, events in the real world are affected not only by those variables we might choose to manipulate or measure in an experiment, but also by all those EVs that we try so hard to eliminate in the laboratory. How justified are we in thinking that what we observe under laboratory conditions is an accurate reflection of how things work outside of the laboratory?

This is why we need a variety of experimental and non-experimental research tools if we intend to form a useful understanding of the psychological world around and within us. We need tools and techniques that allow us to investigate the world as it is, such as correlational and case studies, as well as tools that allow us to bring elements of that world into the laboratory where we can examine them under controlled conditions. While individual researchers may choose to concentrate on only one of these methods, psychology, like other sciences, is a collaborative effort where we rely on the fact that a variety of perspectives are directed at a question. Without data from the real world, our experiments would lack direction and relevance. Without experimental data, our understanding of the world would lack clear cause and effect explanations.

Table 2.5: Comparison of data collection techniques. This chart demonstrates information on the key research methods most frequently used in the field of psychological science. Each method has its own relative strengths and weaknesses.

Research technique	Advantages	Disadvantages
Case Study	Lots of in-depth information; can be helpful to provide direct evidence of a theory particularly when studying an unusual phenomena	Not generalizable to the population; can be subjective if researcher expects to find support for a specific theory
Direct Observation	If done in natural environment there is reduced artificiality compared to research lab setting; can allow for long periods of data collection rather than a snapshot observation or measure of behaviour; useful technique when little is known about subject or phenomenon of interest	Often observers cannot avoid being noticed or being intrusive which could bias response of phenomena under study; difficult to explain rationale of behaviours observed; observers may be biased or have subjective interpretations of what is observed
Experiment	Researcher has strict control over manipulation of variables and setting; allows for high accuracy in drawing conclusions of cause and effect relationships	Setting can be artificial and results may not translate to those found in natural settings; due to ethical and moral constraints many experiments cannot be conducted in this environment

Interviews	Often conducted one-on-one which allows interviewer to ask follow up questions for clarification and assess the honesty of the interviewee; can gather information on behaviours that may otherwise be difficult to observe	Interviewee may not be comfortable answering some questions or may be either unintentionally or intentionally dishonest due to social desirability bias, memory lapses
Questionnaire	Can gather information on behaviour that might otherwise be difficult to measure or observe; usually relatively simple to collect data from large samples; allows for collection of self-report or observations by someone other than the researcher	Difficult to assess truthfulness of self-report data due to social desirability bias, memory lapses, wishful thinking, response set; participant may not finish all questions rendering data inadmissible and difficult, if not impossible, to draw conclusions

Source: Table was created by the author

SECTION 4 REVIEW: Experiments

TABLE 2.6

Psychology experiments are used for the establishment of cause and effect relationships		
Fundamental Variables	**Component Groups of any Experiment**	**What Experimental Research Can Do**
• Experimentation involves the manipulation of a variable (**independent variable**) in order to test its effect on certain other variables (**dependent variable(s)**) • **Extraneous or confounding variables** are important to consider and control as much as possible as they may affect the data even if not manipulated or measured	• **Control groups** do not receive the manipulation of the independent variable and are used to increase certainty as to whether the independent variable has any significant effect of the dependent variable by examining any differences between the control group and **experimental group(s),** the group that does receive the manipulation	• Experiments allow us to establish cause and effect relationships but the amount of control in lab settings may deem the experiments as inaccurate representations of how things occur in the real world; this emphasizes the need for a variety of research techniques

Section 5: Coming to Conclusions

Samples and Populations

You may not yet have realized it, but you are now a part of the most intensively studied group of individuals in the field of psychology. There is an old joke that psychology is the study of first-year university students, and this reflects a real issue of some importance. It is highly probable that you will, as part of this course, have the opportunity to participate in psychological research. In many cases, this participation is encouraged by offering some incentive, such as money or bonus marks in a course, or may even be part of a course's grading scheme. Why are your professors so eager to have you act as a research subject? There are at least two important reasons. First, being a participant in a research study (or, as is often the case, several different research studies) will allow you to experience first-hand the kind of research that actually goes on at your institution. You will see many of the methods of collecting data described earlier being put into action in a concrete way. For those of you pursuing a degree in psychology, it will be very useful to know something about the research conducted by the faculty at your institution, as you may need to have one of these faculty supervise a research project that you undertake at some point in your undergraduate career. The second, somewhat related, reason is that your professor and his or her colleagues, along with their graduate students and others, all need to collect data in order to conduct research. As an introductory psychology student, you have the highly desirable quality of being part of a handy (some would suggest captive) group of potential research participants. Thus, there are large amounts of psychological data collected from students just like you. The potential problem in all this is that conclusions drawn from research on university students are frequently applied to much larger groups, in many cases the entire human race. Are such generalized conclusions justified? This is a complicated issue; if we find that a group of 20 students responds in a particular way to some manipulation we provide are we right in concluding that *every human* regardless of personal factors such as age, socioeconomic status, and cultural history would respond in the same way? The answer is a qualified 'maybe'.

Let us consider a basic question about human beings: What is the typical mass of a living adult human being? How would you go about answering such a question? First, we will need to define exactly what we mean by typical. This issue will be addressed in the next section on descriptive statistics, but for now the idea that we want to know the average mass of an adult human will probably be sufficient. With unlimited resources, we could answer the question with complete accuracy and confidence by weighing *every adult human on the planet* and computing the average mass. If we did so, there could be no arguing with our result. We collected all the available data and we can be 100% sure we know the answer exactly. Unfortunately, this is completely impractical – there is no way we have the time or resources to weigh everybody on the entire planet. Does this mean we have to abandon the question as unanswerable? While it may mean that we have to give up any hope of answering with 100% certainty, we may still be able to come up with some useful answers.

In the case of studying university students and subsequently applying our conclusions to the entire human race, the group of students tested would be our **sample**, and the entire human race would be the **population** from which that sample was taken. Before going any further, it is very important to realize that 'population' in this sense may be defined in an infinite number of ways. In many cases, including the one above, the population in question is the entire human race, which likely matches up well with our existing notion of the word 'population'. In many other cases, however, the population might be defined differently. Perhaps we are interested in some aspect of pregnancy, in which case the population of interest would be adult human females, rather than all humans of either sex. Maybe we are only interested in left-handed, red-haired, French-speaking auto mechanics. Populations can be defined any way you like, and in each case you are referring to all the individuals in the world that meet your criteria. The important consequence of this is that you can only generalize your conclusions to the population from which your sample came. In terms of our question about the mass of an adult human, we might have the time and resources to weigh sample of humans, perhaps a few hundred people, and calculate their average mass. Is this value likely to be a good indicator of the value we would have obtained if we actually had weighed every adult member of the species? The answer to this question involves one of the more important concepts in experimental design - randomness.

Whenever we take a sample and, based on what we observe in that sample, try to generalize to the entire population from which the sample came, we risk making an error. Remember that we can't be 100% certain of our conclusions without testing the entire population. How sure are we that our conclusions really apply to the whole population? The sample we tested was probably only an extremely small fraction of that population. If we want to generalize from our sample data to the larger population, we need to work with a sample that is truly *representative* of the population as a whole. With regard to our weight question, if 10% of the entire human population consumes less than 1000 calories per day, then 10% of our sample should also meet this condition. If 2% of the human race suffers from Anorexia Nervosa, which would have a profound effect on weight, then 2% of our sample should have anorexia. You can see the problem that arises here; if we need to make our sample perfectly representative of the population, we will need to know so much about the population already (the proportion of those with anorexia, vegetarians, redheads, left-handed people, etc) that we probably already know the answer to our original question about body mass. So it seems we are back where we started, with an unanswerable question. Given that we have already accepted that 100% certainty is impossible, however, there may be a way around this problem. Since we cannot guarantee that any sample we select is perfectly representative of the population we drew it from, we can maximize our chances of selecting a representative sample by selecting that sample *randomly* from the population.

Why does a randomly selected sample have the best chance of being representative? We are more likely to get a representative mix of all the relevant variables, known and unknown, if we pick our sample without using any preconceived criteria. This brings us to the one absolute requirement for obtaining a **random sample** from any population: If a sample is to be truly random, *every member of the population must have an equal chance of being selected for the sample.* Think for a minute about just what this means in terms of selecting a sample of the human race. To do so would mean that a cab driver in Bangkok, a priest in Copenhagen, you, and every other person on the planet would all be equally likely to be selected. The reality is that this is almost never the case. As mentioned earlier, you will likely find yourself included in a sample from some population as part of your exposure to research in this course. Depending on the nature of the research, you may or may not be aware of the identities of other people in the sample, but it is usually safe to assume that they are all university students like you (i.e., no Thai cab drivers or Danish priests). In some cases, the fact that the entire sample is composed of undergraduates presents no obvious reasons why the conclusions cannot be generalized to the entire human population. In other cases, there may be clear reasons why an all-student sample is not representative of the human race. It is probably safe to assume that regulating a heartbeat works the same way in students as in the rest of the species, given that this is a basic biological function that does not depend on income, geography, language, etc. It would not be safe to assume, however, that these (and other) socio-economic factors were irrelevant when the variables of interest were things such as intelligence, memory, and, for that matter, body mass. This is the very real problem at the root of the old joke referred to earlier. We need to be very careful about how we generalize our conclusions about populations when our samples may have been selected in a somewhat non-random manner, as is typically the case.

A final note on randomness: An equally important, and much less problematic, application of the same basic principle arises in experimental research. If we design an experiment with two or more groups of subjects that will receive different treatments to be compared to one another, we need to use **random assignment** when deciding to which group any particular participant is assigned. To see why this is important, consider a counter-example where we *systematically* assigned subjects to groups by placing all the female subjects in our control group and all the male subjects in our experimental group. If we later observe a difference between groups following some manipulation of an IV, is that difference due to our IV or to gender? In such a case we can never know. However, if gender can affect the results, and we randomly assign subjects to groups, we should end up with the same proportion of males and females in each group. If gender has an effect in this case, it should have the same effect in each group, and any difference *between* groups should be the result of our IV manipulation. The same logic applies to the entire range of EVs, known and unknown, that could possibly affect the outcome of our study. As with random selection, random assignment can help us avoid systematic errors with EVs. There are other ways to deal with this issue, such as explicitly assigning the same number of males and females to each of our groups. You will encounter such methods in more advanced courses, but for now you should at least be able to appreciate that this technique will only be applicable in cases of known EVs, and still leaves us vulnerable to the effects of EVs we have not thought of (and there will always be some of these).

Descriptive Statistics

After designing the study and collecting data comes the critical step of analyzing and interpreting the data. This will typically involve the application of statistical techniques that are largely beyond the scope of this course. At the introductory level, it is much more important for you to have a good understanding of the reasoning behind, and the differences between, the two basic types of statistics you will encounter: Descriptive statistics and inferential statistics.

It is likely that you already are familiar with **descriptive statistics**, which are used to organize and summarize data. Why do we do this? Imagine you conduct an experiment with two groups, each containing 50 subjects. After you manipulate your IV and collect data on your DV, someone asks you how it turned out. You could hand them a sheet of paper with 100 numbers on it (each subject's measured value on the DV). While this is surely an accurate representation of your data, it may be hard for your audience to appreciate in this form. If instead you calculate the average value of the DV in each group, and present your audience with just these two numbers, they will be able to see what happened in your study much more clearly. Note however that by summarizing the data in this way there is a loss of information, but this is generally considered an acceptable trade-off for making the data easily understandable. Three **measures of central tendency** that you have most likely run into before are **mean, median**, and **mode**, each of which provides a means of reducing a large set of data to a single representative value. What unites these techniques, and makes them *descriptive*, is that they are based entirely on the available data. If we take a sample of humans and want to know the mean age, we add up all the ages and divide by the number of people in the sample. What is more, any researcher can look at our raw data and calculate the exact same value for any measure of central tendency we might choose to use (i.e., it is objective – the mean of a set of numbers is what it is no matter who does the math). We will now look briefly at our three common measures of central tendency and examine why we might choose one over another in any particular situation.

If we need to use descriptive statistics to summarize a set of data, the mean is typically the most useful measure. This is largely due to the fact that many more advanced statistical techniques are based on knowing these means, and also partly because the mean is probably the most intuitively understandable way to summarize data. As mentioned above, calculating the mean is simply a matter of adding up all the values and dividing by the number of values to produce what you are likely familiar with as the 'average' (scientists prefer the term mean, and in fact what we are talking about here is the arithmetic mean…there are other kinds of means). While the mean is a simple and understandable summarization of the data, it is vulnerable to certain distortions in some cases. One factor that can render the mean less useful is the presence of what are called outliers in the data. An outlier is an extreme data point. By way of example, imagine that you measure the annual income of a randomly selected group of five people that just happens to include Bill Gates (who, for those who have lived a very sheltered life, is an extremely wealthy person). The mean income in your sample turns out to be 20 million dollars, which is in fact far more money than any sample member, except Mr. Gates, makes. In this case, the mean has been distorted by the presence of an extreme value, and may not be a useful way to summarize the data in a representative way. You certainly wouldn't want your income tax assessed on this basis (although Mr. Gates surely would).

The median is one alternative that reduces the influence of extreme outliers in a set of data. To calculate the median we simply arrange our data in numerical order, a process known as rank ordering, and select the value in the middle of the set. If there is an even number of values, we take the two middle values and calculate the mean of those two values. In this scenario, Bill Gates' income would simply be the highest in the list and how much higher it is than the next highest value no longer affects the outcome.

In other cases, we may be dealing with data where neither of the above approaches makes much sense. Imagine a study where the variable measured was country of birth. With this sort of non-numerical data, we cannot perform the kinds of arithmetic operations needed to calculate either the mean or median. What is the mean of France, South Korea and Argentina? How would we rank order such data to obtain a median? In such cases the preferred measure of central tendency is the mode, or the most commonly occurring value in the data set. You will encounter all three of these measures in psychology, although, as stated above, the mean is likely our first choice (data permitting), in that it will allow us more options in terms of later statistical analysis.

SECTION 5 REVIEW: Coming to Conclusions

TABLE 2.7

Proper selection of participants is necessary in order to accurately describe data collected		
Samples in Research	**Sample Selection**	**Descriptive Statistics and What They Do**
• **Samples** are groups of individuals selected for scientific study and are used as a representation of the larger population to which they belong	• In order to ensure samples are accurate representations and data collected is generalizable to the population, participants must be **selected randomly** (all must have equal opportunity to participate) and **assigned randomly** to control and experimental groups	• **Descriptive statistics** essentially organize and describe sample data • Common methods include **measures of central tendency (mean, median, and mode)** used to simplify and summarize immediately available data and deal with issues of distortion

Section 6: Inferential Statistics

Inferential Statistics and Variability

Things get a bit more complicated when it comes to the second general class of statistical techniques — **inferential statistics**. Where descriptive statistics are all based entirely on the data on hand, inferential statistics will require us to make some inferences (i.e., educated guesses) about the nature of those data. Typically, this comes up when we are engaged in trying to generalize what we have observed in a sample to the entire population from which that sample came. Our sample data are fairly objective; anyone performing descriptive analyses on these data will come up with the same answers. As we have already discussed, however, there are numerous questions that arise when we attempt to claim that the entire population would respond the same way our sample did. Inferential statistics are a set of techniques developed to assess how likely it is that our sample data are an accurate reflection of the population as a whole. In practice, these techniques are often used to determine whether a control group and experimental group in a sample actually reflect two different populations or just different parts of a single population. We will leave most discussion of this idea to more advanced statistics courses, but we will now turn to the idea that lies at the center of most of this advanced statistical reasoning, which is variability.

VARIABILITY

The single most important concept in statistics to understand is **variability**. A simple experiment was suggested earlier in which room temperature was manipulated and test scores were measured. Following our manipulation and measurements, we calculate the mean test score for each group. We discover that there is a 10 point difference between the means of the two groups. Can we generalize our result to the entire population? Let us be very clear about this— descriptive statistics reveal that we actually *did* find a difference between the two groups in our sample. Nobody is going to argue that our two groups do not, in fact, have different means. The question is: would any two randomly selected groups from this population show us the same difference between conditions? Are we really looking at two different *populations* here? Remember that populations can be defined in a number of ways, and in this case, if there are two distinct populations, they would consist of a) all humans writing such a test at 20° and b) all the same humans writing the same test at 10°.

As we have said, it is fairly straightforward to determine that two groups in an experiment are different on some measured DV; we just use some descriptive statistics. The more important question is *why* those group means are different, and there are two general possible explanations. The first (which we probably hope to be true) is that the group means are different because of *what we did* (i.e., our manipulation of the IV). The second, and this is the one that inferential statistics will actually evaluate, is that the only reason our two groups are different is that when we randomly selected and assigned groups, *by chance* we put all the people likely to score high on the DV in one group and all the people likely to score low on the DV in the other group. Remember that with truly random selection and assignment, this is still always a possibility. To evaluate the likelihood of that possibility, we need to ask another question. We have already asked and answered the question, "Are the two groups different from each other?", and it seems clear that they are. We now need to ask, "H*ow different are the scores within each group from each other?*" In other words, we need to look at variability.

Having run our Room Temperature experiment, we find that the resulting test scores range from 55% to 85%, but also that the test scores are not evenly distributed across this range. There are relatively few very high and very low scores and most are clustered in the middle or around the mean. That is to say, that in Room A, where the mean was 65%, the many of the scores are clustered between 62-68%. Conversely, in Room B where the average was 75% many of the scores are clustered between 72-78%. This kind of data is often represented graphically as a **frequency distribution**. You will see some examples of this kind of graph below. In these figures, the height of the curve at any point represents the number of occurrences of a particular value. The width of the curve shows the range of values obtained. The range, or difference between the lowest and highest values obtained, is one measure of variability. In some cases, typically those in which the mode is the preferred measure of central tendency, this may be the only useful measure of variability. In other cases, where the data permit us to calculate informative means, the preferred measure of variability is the **standard deviation**. For our purposes, we can think of the standard deviation as the 'average difference from the mean' of all the points in the data set. This value gives us a picture of the variability of a set of data summarized into a single number, just as the mean allows us to summarize the raw data into a single number.

Now, recall that in our room temperature study we were looking at two groups of subjects: The experimental group was exposed to the cold room and the control group was exposed to the normal temperature room. Let's first consider one possible outcome where the variability is low, which is to say, the scores *within each group* are all pretty close to each other. Another way to state this is to say that the group scores *cluster around the mean*. In Figure 2.3 below, the mean score for each group (Room A: 65% and Room B: 75%) is represented by the vertical dashed line and the *distribution* of all the scores in each group is represented by the solid curve. Each of these curves represents what is referred to as a **normal distribution,** a type of distribution commonly seen in psychological research, as well as the natural sciences. Normal distributions have a number of interesting mathematical properties which make them very useful for statistical analysis, but most of those are beyond the scope of this course. You should, however, note the characteristically smooth, symmetrical bell-shaped curve around a single peak (normal distributions are often referred to as 'bell curves'). As you can see in this diagram, the scores in each group tend to cluster around the group mean (all the scores tend to be within a fairly small *range*) and there is a 10 unit difference between the means of the experimental and control groups. Note that there is *zero overlap* between the two distributions of scores. One implication of this is that if you randomly selected one subject and looked at their score, you would know without a doubt which group they were in.

Figure 2.3 Low Variability

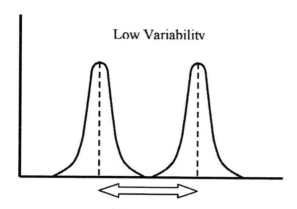

The next diagram below shows a different possible outcome of our study. Again, we find a 10 unit difference between group means (as the average from Room B-Room A is: 75-65=10), but now the scores within each group are much less tightly clustered around those means. In other words, the variability is much higher within each group. In this case, there is a considerable area of overlap between the two distributions (the area marked X). Now, if you randomly select a subject and look at their score, you might not be able to tell which group they were in, as there are a number of scores that occurred in both groups this time. Note that in both of these cases we have *the exact same difference between group means*, but after taking variability into account we might come to very different conclusions in each case. As a general rule, for a given difference between means, the lower the variability is, the more likely we are to attribute that difference to our IV manipulation. As within-group variability increases, we become less able to reject the explanation that our two groups are different only by chance, and that our manipulation had no real effect.

Draft

Figure 2.4 High Variability – increase overlap and label groups

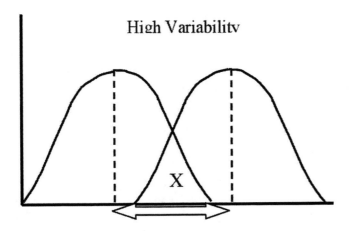

Ultimately, we need to decide how likely it is that the observed difference between groups is due to some failure of random selection and/or random assignment. Remember that these random processes are not perfect, they are just the best we can do in many cases. It is always possible that, even though selection and assignment were random, we accidentally and unknowingly ended up with more intelligent subjects in one group and less intelligent subjects in the other in our room temperature study. The primary purpose of most common inferential statistical analyses is to directly assess this possibility. In general, these analyses will tell us how likely it is that we could have randomly selected two groups with means this different if our manipulation had no effect at all. In other words, it is always possible that we randomly selected and assigned our subjects to groups in such a way that there was a difference between groups on our DV before we manipulated anything. Without getting bogged down in statistical details, the simple version of the story is that the less overlap there is between the data from two groups (i.e., the less variability there is in the data), the less likely it is that we could have obtained the difference between group means by accident. If a difference between groups is sufficiently unlikely to happen by accident, then we will conclude that the difference is actually the result of our IV manipulation. Coming to such a conclusion will require us to make some inferences (educated guesses) about the nature of the populations involved, hence the term inferential statistics.

If you go on to take a course or two in statistics, you will learn all the arithmetic required to actually perform these kinds of tests, and you may be surprised that most of it is pretty simple stuff that you have known since grade school. What makes statistics courses challenging for many people is not the math, but the underlying logic of why we do things in a certain way. A solid understanding of the concept of variability is essential for the proper application of statistical tests, and if most of the above makes sense, you are well on your way (if not, get the help you need to understand it now).

Draft

SECTION 6 REVIEW: Inferential Statistics and Variability

TABLE 2.8

By using and understanding methods of inferential statistics we can establish inferences about the data we collect		
Inferential Statistics and What They Do	**The Vital Role of Variability**	**The Measure of Standard Deviation**
• **Inferential statistics** employ a number of methods to answer questions about why the data is the way it is and to test whether differences between groups are due to significant, legitimate causes and effects	• **Variability**, how much the population strays from the mean, is vital to understand for it allows us to explore whether groups are significantly different or differences are due to chance	• **Standard deviation** allows us to answer questions about differences when combined with measures of the overlap and variability of the distributions of groups in an experiment • The less overlap, the smaller the variability, the stronger the differences between groups and the more likely differences are not due to chance

Section 7: Looking for Flaws: Evaluating Research

We have explored how psychological questions are formally examined using the scientific method, and discussed why we might prefer answers obtained in this way to answers obtained by relying on personal experience and common sense. It is important to realize that although the scientific method is preferred by psychologists, it is still subject to errors. One major advantage of the scientific method is that it has a built-in mechanism for correcting such errors, but before they can be corrected they first need to be identified. As you will learn throughout the remainder of this course, our perceptions of the world around us are full of inaccuracies, omissions and inventions. Your personal opinion of your professor aside, psychologists are human beings just like the rest of the species, and are no less subject to these kinds of biases and distortions in their perceptions than the typical human (the one difference being that psychologists may actually understand why their perceptions are flawed, although this will not prevent them from making the same kinds of errors we all make).

Fortunately, research in psychology is a large and collaborative enterprise with several checks that can minimize these errors. This begins with the peer review system used for publishing findings in journal articles. Before being published, a submitted study will be sent out for review by a number of experts in the field. If these reviewers find problems or errors, the article may be returned to the authors for revision, or rejected completely. Only after the concerns of these expert peers are satisfied will the article appear in a scientific journal. If a study passes peer review and is published, other researchers often become interested in following up on the study and testing related questions. Generally, any new finding or surprising result will be regarded with some degree of skepticism until such time as other independent researchers have conducted similar studies and obtained similar results, a process known as **replication**. Note that if we were to publish some finding of a difference between two differently treated groups, and this difference was actually the result of a failure of the random selection or random assignment processes discussed above, it is unlikely that another researcher conducting the same test on a different sample will obtain the same results. If a new finding does not stand up to the test of replication, it will come under question, and perhaps eventually be discarded. Over time, this process of review and replication helps to refine the accumulated knowledge in a field by identifying errors and unjustified claims. Even with such a system in place, there are still several potential sources of error that can affect the outcome of a study. In order to be critical consumers of research, we will need to make ourselves aware of the kinds of errors and biases that can sneak into the work of even the best, most respected researchers.

Type I and Type II Errors

As we have already seen, in cases where it is impossible or impractical to test an entire population, we typically select a sample from that population, perform the test on our sample, and generalize our conclusions to the entire population from which the sample came. In order to do this, we are required to make some inferences, and these inferences are not guaranteed to be correct. Those cases in which our inferences are not correct fall into one of two categories, which are referred to as Type I and Type II errors. In simple terms, we will make a Type I error when we claim that our IV manipulation had an effect when, in reality, any difference between groups is really the result of sampling error. Remember that it is always possible that we randomly selected and assigned subjects to groups in such a way as to make our groups different prior to any IV manipulation. Up to this point we have implicitly been assuming that any such sampling error will produce a difference between groups that is in the same direction as the difference we expect our IV manipulation to produce. In our room temperature study, we might hypothesize that subjects in the cold room will produce lower test scores. If, in reality, room temperature has no effect on test scores, but we accidentally assign lower performing subjects to this group, we may see a difference in our DV and conclude (incorrectly) that our manipulation had the predicted effect, thus making a Type I error. There is, however, another way things can go wrong. Imagine instead that we started with the same hypothesis (cold room = lower scores), but in this case accidentally assigned higher performing subjects to the cold room condition. Now, sampling error will produce an effect *opposite* in direction to our predicted effect of IV manipulation. In this case, if room temperature really does have an effect on test scores, we may end up with two groups with similar test scores. If this is the case, we will conclude that our IV manipulation had no effect when it actually did, thus committing a Type II error.

By way of an example, imagine that you are a radar operator whose job is to detect incoming enemy aircraft. Any approaching aircraft will show up as a blip on your radar screen, but so will flocks of migrating birds. If a blip appears on your screen, your first task is to determine if that blip is an aircraft, in which case you will sound an alarm, or a flock of birds, in which case you will do nothing. As long as you are correct in identifying aircraft and flocks of birds, there is no problem, but you may find yourself occasionally making the same two kinds of errors described above. If you incorrectly identify a flock of birds as an aircraft, you are making a Type I error (saying something is happening when it really isn't). On the other hand, if you incorrectly identify an aircraft as a flock of birds, you are making a Type II error (saying something isn't happening when it really is). Making either kind of error will have consequences, either sending your air force chasing after some geese, or allowing your enemy to bomb your cities.

The fact that these two types of error are always possible is one major reason why replication is so important. If some experimental result is actually due to manipulation of the IV, then it ought to turn out the same way when the experiment is repeated. In cases where a Type I or Type II error occurs, repeating the experiment with a different sample should not produce the same results, thus alerting us to the possibility that one of these errors occurred in the original study.

Box 2.4 Placebo Effects

Research in pharmacology has documented a remarkable phenomenon called the **placebo effect** when humans participate in drug trials. Control subjects are treated identically to experimental subjects as much as possible in order to control for the effects of possible EVs, and so, if the experimental group is given a pill to test the effect of a new drug on depression, control subjects are also given a pill. However, the pill given to control subjects has no physiological effects (it is a placebo). Intriguingly, for some control subjects, the mere act of taking a pill can lead to expectations that influence their feelings, reactions and behaviours. And so, many subjects assigned to the control condition of a depression drug trial, report improvement in response to the inert placebo (Walsh, Seidman, Sysko, & Gould, 2002)! Some researchers suggest that the placebo effect may shed some light on other related phenomenon of subject expectation such as faith healing (Humphrey, 2002, p. 226) and voodoo death sentences (Hahn & Kleinman, 1983).

Distortions in Self-Report Data

In Chapter 1, we discussed the divide that led Behaviourists to reject the use of introspective data in the study of psychology. The Behaviourists quite correctly argued that any data produced by asking people to report their personal experience, such as questionnaires, interviews, and personal inventories are subject to distortion and errors. As you will learn, our perceptions of the world and our memories of those perceptions are both subject to considerable error. Furthermore, there is no objective way to observe and verify these data. Although we can never be entirely sure that what someone *says* they experienced was actually what they *did* experience, such methods are still used because for some kinds of research questions and designs, there is no other way to collect such information.

One of the many complications that arise when working with human subjects is that they generally want to create a favourable image of themselves. We want to see ourselves in a positive way, and we want others to do so as well. This produces what psychologists refer to as the **social desirability bias**. This bias may lead people to answer questions in ways they think will make them look good, rather than answering with complete honesty. Imagine a person living in a socially conservative culture being asked questions about drug use or premarital sexual activity. Researchers have found, for example, that self-reports of racial biases may underestimate true biases (see Chapter 15).

In addition to systematic attempts to create a favourable impression, there are other problems that may emerge when collecting self-report data. A subject may misunderstand an ambiguously worded question, incorrectly recall personal information, or become bored with a repetitive task or series of questions. Some subjects may also demonstrate **response sets** – a tendency to respond to questions in a particular way regardless of the content (e.g., a person who answers 'C' to every question on a multiple choice test). Researchers often include control scales in surveys and questionnaires, which are designed to detect participants who are answering in some systematic, untruthful way. Even so, it is impossible to control for all such errors. For these, and other, reasons, researchers often measure other, more objectively observable DVs along with self-report measures. If we were showing subjects pictures of potentially frightening events, we might ask them how scared each picture made them feel, while at the same time measuring heart rate to detect any increases in response to the images. Obtaining similar patterns of results across multiple DVs will support the accuracy of the self-report data, while the self-report data may contain information that we would never learn by examining physiological variables alone.

Experimenter Bias

Although the scientific method aims to collect objective data and make sound interpretations, it's important to realize that research studies are conducted by researchers who are prone to the same personal biases, perceptions, and pressures as everyone else. Often, scientists develop theories, design experiments and collect data over a career that can span decades. Thus, scientists can have an emotional investment in the outcome of their research. Scientists must take precautions to avoid **experimenter bias** – personal expectations or preferences about the outcome of study, which can influence the results obtained, as well as how they are interpreted and communicated. Like everyone else, researchers can see what they expect to see. Experimenter bias can include 'honest' mistakes in recording a subject's response, although such mistakes tend to be heavily in favour of supporting the hypothesis (O'Leary, Kent, & Kanowitz, 1975). The researcher can also unintentionally reinforce a subject to behave in a particular way to support the hypothesis being tested. For example, the researcher may send subtle, nonverbal signals by nodding or smiling when the subject responds in a way that is favourable to the hypothesis in question.

These concerns for bias can be avoided by using the blind and double-blind procedures. In a blind study, the subject is unaware of the group condition to which they have been assigned. This avoids the bias that a subject may otherwise demonstrate by virtue of knowing their group assignment. In the **double-blind study**, both the subject *and* the experimenter are unaware of group assignment. This has the added benefit of ensuring that the experimenter is not inadvertently encouraging specific responses from the subjects.

TABLE 2.9

A number of errors arise in any psychology research and although they cannot be completely eliminated, there are a number of counter measures that bring us to the most objective information we can obtain		
Basic Errors and How They Affect Results	**Human Error in Experimentation**	**How to Deal**
• Errors are inevitable in research, but employing the scientific method properly through replication and error controlled, they can be strongly reduced • Type I errors involve claims that there are effects of the independent variable when differences are actually the result of sampling errors • Type II errors involve claims that manipulations do not have effects when they actually do	• **Self Report biases** involve errors of human perception such as responding in experiments in manner we feel is expected of us (**social desirability bias** and **placebo effect**) and responding a certain way no matter the content of the experiment (**response sets**) • **Experimenter biases** involve the influence of experimenters' presumptions on the experimental design and interpretation of data	• Many measures are put in place to counter this such as **blind** (participants are unaware of the condition they are in) and **double blind** (experimenters and participants are unaware of the conditions participants are in) procedures, but error is nearly impossible to completely eliminate

Section 8: Ethics in Research

Ethics in Human Research

All researchers are required to behave according to an ethical code in order for the scientific enterprise to work. Researchers must be able to trust that other researchers are reporting their data truthfully and objectively. Researchers also have to agree to allow others to access and evaluate both the collected data and conclusions. Researchers also agree to not appropriate the work of others, and give credit where credit is due. All of these principles apply across the range of scientific disciplines.

In psychology, where subjects are almost always living organisms and frequently living *human* organisms, researchers face an additional set of ethical challenges. In Canada, as in most countries, researchers are required by law to treat research subjects in an ethical manner. All research must be conducted according to certain ethical principles, and every university or research institution must have a committee set up specifically to review all research and make sure it conforms to ethical standards. These standards are set out by the three major agencies that fund research in Canada: the Natural Sciences and Engineering Research Council (NSERC), the Social Sciences and Humanities Research Council (SSHRC), and the Canadian Institute for Health Research (CIHR). These three agencies, operating jointly as the Tri-Council, have set out the standards for the treatment of human research participants, and all researchers, whether they receive funding from these agencies or not, are required to operate within these rules.

The Tri-Council Policy Statement Tutorial

The Tri-Council has an online tutorial available, which is designed to familiarize researchers with current policies concerning ethical conduct of human research. These policies are set out in the Tri-Council Policy Statement: Ethical Conduct for Research Involving Humans (TCPS) This tutorial can be found at:

http://www.pre.ethics.gc.ca/english/tutorial/

Registration is not required to view the tutorial, but it is recommended that you complete the registration page, as this will allow you to print out a certificate of completion once you have successfully finished the tutorial. Many institutions require that students complete this tutorial before becoming involved in the conduct of any research. Even when not required, completing the tutorial can help you to both evaluate and design research projects with regard to ethical issues.

The first principle of ethics in human research is respect for *human dignity*. Research participants have the right to expect that their physical, psychological or cultural integrity will not be threatened. You will see many examples, as you learn the history of psychology, that this was not always the case. However, our current standards dictate that we cannot attack the dignity of our subjects no matter how interesting or important the data we collect might be. One important consequence of this principle is that we must be particularly sensitive to respecting the dignity of vulnerable populations, such as the mentally ill. Studying these populations may be of great interest, but there may be questions about their ability to fully comprehend the research project and their role in it.

This leads to the next important principle, *informed consent*. You have the right as a subject to have the purpose and procedures of any experiment explained to you before you agree to take part. Note that we are talking about *informed* consent, not just consent. This means that researchers are not supposed to hide *anything* from their subjects; if they do, then the subjects are not fully informed when they give their consent to participate. This presents a particular problem for psychology. Human beings tend to be very *reactive*. That is to say, we tend to behave differently when we know we are being observed. This can be a big problem for psychologists studying human subjects. If our subjects know what we are looking for, that knowledge could alter their behavior. One aspect of the social desirability bias discussed earlier is that we tend to tell people what we think they want to hear (which will make them happy, which will make them like us). If this happens, we aren't getting an accurate picture of the behaviour we are interested in. This is not to say that subjects will necessarily lie deliberately; these effects can be very subtle and subjects may not even be aware that they are doing this.

Because humans can be so reactive, we often grant a small exception to the 'fully informed consent' principle in psychological studies, and allow some measure of deception. Researchers are frequently allowed to obscure the purpose of their research somewhat when describing it to potential participants and in some cases researchers may be allowed to explicitly mislead their subjects, although this is relatively rare and would not be considered ethical if there were any other way to obtain equivalent information. In cases where this is permitted, researchers are obligated to fully debrief (i.e., explain what was really going on, and why) at the earliest possible time once they have collected their data. They also need to provide a strong and compelling rationale for using deception or concealment.

We are also required to respect the *privacy* of our subjects, and to treat any data we collect from them in a confidential manner, as far as is possible, and also to make sure subjects are informed of who will have access to the data, where and how it will be stored and for how long. Ideally, our data would be anonymous, but this is not always possible or practical. If we do collect any kind of identifying information from our subjects (names, addresses, employer, etc), we are obligated to remove this information from the rest of our data at the earliest possible time and store it separately. We also usually publish only *aggregate* data, such as group means, rather than individual scores.

Finally, we are obligated to conduct our research in such a way as to balance the potential harms and benefits. If there is the potential that subjects could be affected negatively in any way by participating, there needs to be an equivalent potential payoff for the subjects, the scientific community, or society in general. Sometimes it will be seen as ethically acceptable to put subjects at some risk, but only if there is a correspondingly large upside. Note that when there is the possibility of some negative outcome, we must also have a plan in place for dealing with that possibility (e.g., referral to counseling or medical treatment). We are also obligated to try to maximize the benefits of our research and minimize the potential harms. If we are going to put our subjects at any risk, we are going to have to make the case that we will obtain important and beneficial information that we could not otherwise get. Even in such cases, there will still be strict limits on the kinds of risk to which our subjects can be exposed. An important concept here is that of *minimal risk*; if the risks a subject will be exposed to in the course of the research are no greater than the risks they would be expected to face in everyday life (after all, everyday life is not a zero-risk proposition), then the risks are generally considered minimal, and are usually acceptable.

Ethics in Animal Research

There are many reasons why non-human species may be used as research subjects in psychology. As you will learn in Chapter 11, evolutionary theory has provided psychology with a variety of insights into the

Draft

origins of many human characteristics and behaviours. Given the relatedness of different species, and their common evolutionary origins, we may be able to learn much about ourselves by observing other species in various situations. We might gain insight into human social behaviour, neurochemistry, or genetics by looking at the social behaviour of monkeys, the brains of rats, or the genomes of fruit flies. There are also ethical reasons why an animal model might be preferred. Many manipulations that would not be considered ethical in human subjects are seen as acceptable in non-human subjects (causing permanent damage to part of the brain, for example). While the issue of research on non-human subjects for human benefit is one that can provoke strong feelings and opinions, two points should be made clear. The first is that, regardless of your views on animal research, your life expectancy has certainly been significantly lengthened as a result of it. The second is that just because we are dealing with non-human subjects, does not mean that there are no rules. Like human research, all studies involving non-human subjects must pass a similar ethical review process, and need to pass a similar cost-benefit analysis. There are strict regulations concerning how various species of animals may be treated, and researchers are obligated to minimize the distress caused to any research subject, use the minimum number of subjects, and to clearly demonstrate that any negative impact on their subjects is offset by a greater gain in knowledge. Veterinary care and monitoring must be provided, and animal research facilities are regularly inspected to ensure they conform to standards for housing and care of non-human subjects.

Research Ethics in Psychology

It is also important to realize that research ethics evolve over time. Many procedures that would have been considered ethical 50 years ago would never get past an ethics review board today. As you proceed through this course, you will encounter several examples of studies that would be considered highly unethical by today's standards. Many of these studies are still influential and frequently discussed. In many cases, these landmark studies served to bring to light ethical issues that had not previously been taken into consideration. One such 'classic' study in the history of psychology you will encounter is the infamous Stanford Prison Experiment (Zimbardo, Haney, Banks, and Jaffe, 1973). This study is a prime example of what can happen when there is a lack of stringent ethical guidelines. In this experiment, Zimbardo set up a fake prison in the basement of the Psychology Department at Stanford University. He randomly assigned male participants to be prisoners and guards and then watched as his "fake" prison began to take on the characteristics of a real prison – his guards became abusive towards his prisoners, and the prisoners became rebellious and hostile. The behaviour rapidly became far more extreme than anyone had expected and the experiment had to be shut down early because of his participants' psychological distress. Such a study would never be considered ethically acceptable today, although it should be noted that one of the reasons for this is, in fact, what we learned from Zimbardo's original study. The ramifications of this experiment and its findings still echo today. For these and similar reasons, many of the classic experiments in some areas of psychology are now museum pieces and will never be replicated in modern research programs (barring substantial changes to make them ethically acceptable, which would mean that such studies are not replications in the strict sense of the term). This is not to say, however, that we cannot learn from these studies; they continue to inform both our knowledge of psychology and our ethical research practices.

SECTION 8 REVIEW: Ethics in Human and Animal Psychology Research

TABLE 2.10

Ethical concerns for both humans and animals are extremely important and allow for respect and dignity to be upheld in the quest for knowledge		
Human Ethics	**Animal Ethics**	**Fundamental Importance of Ethics**
• Basic rules of respect and honesty are established in scientific practice but additional rules are required for the use of living organisms in research • Extremely important standards for human research are the **respect for human dignity, informed consent, privacy** and **minimal risk**	• The use of animal subjects can be extremely helpful for human research and minimizes human risk but also requires respect for ethical protocols such as **minimizing distress, minimizing subject use** and **indication that benefits outweigh harms**	• Ethic protocols are continuously evolving but past work that is currently deemed as unethical can still be appreciated in terms of the knowledge such work has produced

Draft

Key Terms/Definitions

Anecdotal Evidence: Information evidence gathered from others or from one's own experiences.

Case Study: An in-depth investigation of an individual person or a small group of people, often over an extended period of time.

Confounding Variable: See Extraneous Variable.

Constant: A feature or quality that always takes the same value across all situations.

Construct Validity: The extent to which there is evidence that a test measures a particular hypothetical construct.

Control Group: A group of individuals designed to serve as an accurate comparison in an experiment.

Correlation: A measure of the strength of the relationship between two variables.

Correlation Coefficient: A numerical index of the degree of relationship between two variables.

Dependent Variable: Variable that is measured in an experiment.

Descriptive Statistics: Statistics designed to describe the data collected. Includes mean, median, and standard deviation.

Double-Blind Study: Experiment in which neither the experimenter nor the participants know which group each participant belongs to.

Empiricism: The philosophical perspective that states that knowledge should be gained by direct observation of the world as it is, as opposed to rational perspectives that used logic and reason to determine how the world ought to be.

Experiment: Scientific tool used to measure the effect of one variable on another.

Experimental Group: The participants in a study who receive the manipulation in regard to the independent variable.

Experimenter Bias: Actions made by the experimenter, unintentionally or deliberately, to promote the result they hope to achieve.

Extraneous Variable: A variable that the researcher did not manipulate or measure, but that nonetheless could still affect the outcome of the experiment

Frequency Distribution: A figure that plots values of a variable on the x (horizontal) axis and the frequency with which those values were observed on the y (vertical) axis.

Hypothesis: Testable statements guided by theories that make specific predictions about the relationship between variables.

Independent Variable: Variable that is controlled or manipulated in an experiment.

Inferential Statistics: Statistics that allow us to use results from samples to make inferences about overall, underlying populations.

Interview: A research tool during which the investigator asks the participant questions, often these may be structured or semi-structured in nature.

Levels of Analysis: Different perspectives that emphasize different aspects of a research question.

Mean: Average value of a set of data.

Measures of Central Tendency: Descriptive statistical techniques for summarizing a distribution of data into a single value that represents the entire distribution.

Median: The centre value in a data set when the set is arranged numerically.

Mode: The value that appears more frequently in the set.

Naturalistic Observation: A descriptive research method in which the researcher engages observation of behaviour in real-world settings.

Normal Distribution: A distribution with a characteristic smooth, bell and symmetrical-shaped curve around a single peak.

Paradigm: A set of assumptions and ideas about what kind of research questions can be asked and how they can be answered.

Ob-ob mouse: The particular term for a mouse that is the result of a genetic mutation associated with extreme obesity in the mouse.

Operational Definition: This describes the actions or operations that will be made to objectively measure or control a variable.

Participants: The persons whose behaviour is systematically studied or observed in a study or experiment.

Placebo Effect: When an individual exhibits an effect to a perceive treatment when no treatment is actually given.

Population: The full group of individuals you are seeking to understand.

Practice Effect: Improved performance over the course of an experiment due to becoming more experienced.

Psychological Test: A standardized measure of a sample of a person's behaviour e.g. IQ test.

Questionnaire: A research tool in which a participant responds to a written list of items or questions.

Random Assignment: Assigning participants to either the experimental or control group at random to avoid any biases that may cause differences between the groups of subjects.

Random Sample: Choosing a set of subjects at random from the population being studied.

Raw Data: Data collected from a study or experiment that has yet to be assessed using statistical analyses.

Reliability: The measurement consistency of a test (or of other kinds of measurement techniques).

Replication: The repetition of a study to see whether the earlier results can be duplicated, often times by independent researchers.

Response Set: A tendency of research participants to respond to questions in a particular way that is unrelated to the content of the questions.

Sample: The subset of the population you're interested in that you examine.

Sampling Bias: A problem that occurs when a sample is mot representative of the population from which it is drawn.

Scientific Method: The formal methods, primarily the set of techniques and concepts, used to examine and answer questions of a scientific nature.

Social Desirability Bias: A tendency to give socially approved answers to questions about oneself.

Standard Deviation: A measure of the variability of a set of data, specifically the expected difference between any randomly selected datum and the mean of the set.

Statistically Significant: The condition that exists when the probability that the observed findings are due to chance is very low.

Theory: A set of statements or principles that try to relate and explain a set of observations.

Variability: The extent to which the scores in a data set tend to vary from each other and from the mean.

Variable: A feature or characteristic that is free to take on (at least two) different values.

References

Abell, G., & Greenspan, B. (1979), "The Moon and the Maternity Ward", *Skeptical Inquirer* 3 (4): 17–25.

Anderson, C.A., Bushman, B.J., & Groom, R.W. (1997). Hot years and serious and deadly assault: Empirical tests of the heat hypothesis. *Journal of Personality and Social Psychology, 73*, 1213-1223.

Editorial: Brain Myths [Editorial]. (2003). *Nature Neuroscience, 6*(2), 99.

Gibbons, F.X., Eggleston, T.J., & Benthin, A.C. (1997). Cognitive reactions to smoking relapse: The reciprocal relation between dissonance and self-esteem. *Journal of Personality and Social Psychology, 72*, 184-195.

Greenwald, A.G., McGhee, D.E., Schwartz, J.L.K. (1998). Measuring individual differences in implicit cognition: The Implicit Association Test. *Journal of Personality and Social Psychology, 74*, 1464-1480.

Hahn, R. A., & Kleinman, A. (1983). Belief as pathogen; belief as medicine. *Medical Anthropology Quarterly, 14*(4), 3, 16-19.

Humphrey, N. (2002). Great expectations: the evolutionary psychology of faith healing and the placebo effect. In: C. von Hofsten & L. Bäckman (Eds.) *Psychology at the turn of the Millennium: Social, Developmental, and Clinical Perspectives* (pp. 255–285). New York, NY, USA: Taylor and Francis Inc.

Loftus, E.F., & Zanni, G. (1975). Eyewitness testimony: The influence of the wording in a question. *Bulletin of the Psychonomic Society, 5*, 86-88.

Matthews, R. (1994, April 24). Animal magic or mysterious sixth sense? *The Sunday Telegraph, 24 January,* 17.

Matthews, R. (1995). Psychic dog gives scientists a lead. *The Sunday Telegraph, 15 January,* 4.

Nisbett, R.E., & Schachter, S. (1966). Cognitive manipulation of pain. *Journal of Experimental Social Psychology,* 2, 227-236.

O'Leary, K.D., Kent, R.N., & Kanowitz, J. (1975). Shaping data collection congruent with experimental hypotheses. *Journal of Applied Behavior Analysis, 8*, 43-51.

Ratemyprofessors. "About Us" (June 18, 2009) http://www.ratemyprofessors.com/About.jsp

Sheldrake, R. (1998). A dog that seems to know when his owner is returning: preliminary Investigations. *Journal of the Society for Psychical Research. 62,* 220-232

Silva, K. M., Silva, F.J., Quinn, M.A., Draper, J.N., Cover, K.R., & Munoff, A.A. (2008). Rate my professor: Online evaluations of psychology instructors. *Teaching of Psychology, 35,* 71-80.

Spencer, S. J., Steele, C.M., & Quinn, D. M. (1999). Stereotype threat and women's math performance. *Journal of Experimental Psychology, 35,* 4-28.

Draft

Timmerman, T. (2008). On the validity of ratemyprofessors.com. *The Journal of Education for Business, 84*, 55-61.

Walsh, B., Seidman, S., Sysko, R., & Gould, M. (2002). *The Journal of the American Medical Association, 287*(14), 1840-1847.

Wechsler, D. (1981). *Manual for the Wechsler adult intelligence scale-revised (WAIS-R)*. The Psychological Corporation, San Antonio, TX.

Wilson, M., & Daly, M. (1997). Life expectancy, economic inequality, homicide, and reproductive timing in Chicago neighbourhoods. *British Medical Journal, 314*, 1271-1274.

Wiseman, R., Smith, M., & Milton, J. (1998). Can animals detect when their owners are returning home? An experimental test of the 'psychic pet' phenomenon. *British Journal of Psychology, 89,* 453-9.

Zimbardo, P.G., Haney, C., Banks, W.C., and Jaffe, D. (1973). The mind is a formidable jailer: A Pirandellian prison. *The New York Times Magazine,* April 8, Section 6, 38-60.

Draft

Chapter

3

Chapter 3: Learning

Introduction

> The brightly lit room was full of flowers, thoughtful gifts, and cards from friends. These cheerful surroundings belied the chronic pain John had been suffering. With advanced pancreatic cancer, he had not moved from his hospital bed in two months. At exactly 8:00AM, like clockwork, the nurse came in to administer the first of four daily morphine injections that helped to manage his pain. Over the preceding months, the prescribed dosage level had to be increased several times in order to control John's pain. As it became clear that there was little more that could be done for him, John decided to move to the privacy of his home under the care of his daughter Samantha. Samantha was trained to administer the morphine injections with the same procedures and dosage levels specified by the physician.
>
> John's own bedroom was very different from his hospital room. Here, John decided to keep things the way he liked: simple, uncluttered, and dimly lit. That evening, John awoke experiencing considerable pain. Samantha noticed that it was about the time for her father's scheduled morphine injection. She carefully prepared the syringe with the same dose of morphine he had been receiving in the hospital, and then injected the drug as she had been shown. Immediately, Samantha realized that something was terribly wrong. Her father's pupils became unusually small and his breathing was shallow. John was experiencing a morphine overdose. She double and triple checked the protocol and everything seemed right. Frantically, she called the hospital.

This scenario is based on a case study reported by Siegel and Ellsworth (1986). If Samantha had correctly followed the procedures for morphine preparation and injection, why did John experience an overdose in response to a drug dose that he had regularly, and safely, received over the preceding weeks while in hospital? One interpretation of these events is based on a *learning analysis* of drug tolerance. **Drug tolerance** is the decreased effectiveness of a drug such as morphine over the course of repeated administration. Research suggests that *learning* plays an important role in the development and maintenance of drug tolerance (see Target Study).

Draft

Target Study: Morphine Situation Specificity

Researchers: Shep Siegel (McMaster University)

Source: Siegel, S. (1976). Morphine analgesic tolerance: its situation specificity supports a Pavlovian conditioning model. *Science, 193*(4250): 323-5.

Note: The material below is the author's summarized description of the original published article.

The strength and applicability of Classical or Pavlovian conditioning is profound. Regarding the phenomena of drug tolerance, where theories of physiological systemic changes dominate, and this simple concept of learning seems to have greater explanatory power and has turned past literature on its head. Theories of drug tolerance have been based strictly on drug administration and physiological effects on the sensitivity of receptors; decreased sensitivity to drug effects occurs because of systemic changes either from increased frequency of use or blockage of receptor access. What is proposed in the current study, however, is a model of drug tolerance for analgesic (pain relieving) morphine that is founded on the principles of classical conditioning. The environmental context of drug administration is a vital factor in the development of drug tolerance and the mechanisms of drug overdose, and central to the conditioning theory of tolerance being purported.

What is the specific model behind this theory? Every episode of drug administration acts as a conditioning trial. In order to maintain homeostasis, physiological systems attempt to counteract drug effects. The stimulation provided by the drug acts as an unconditional stimulus, and the counteraction acts as the unconditional response. The environment of drug administration, however, becomes associated with the process of administration and counteraction. Over repeated trials of administration in a particular environment, the environment becomes associated with counteraction and the environment itself begins to elicit anticipatory responses – the body is prepared to compensate for drug effects simply by being in that particular environment, that is, tolerance is built towards the drug effects. The more this association occurs, the stronger it becomes, and the higher the drug tolerance in the particular environment.

One way of testing this theory is by building tolerance for a particular drug and then testing drug effects with a placebo. Previous work has explored this with rats that have been exposed to morphine use. When rats received a placebo in the environment of administration, hyper analgesic effects occurred – pain increased because the environment elicited compensatory responses but there was no drug to counteract. In order for tolerance to occur, though, the association between environment and morphine administration needs to be consistent.

Thus, based on the principles of conditioning as well as past literature, the current study predicts that morphine tolerance in rats will be selectively sensitive to the environment of administration. That is, rats in the environment that they were not tolerated in will respond to drug administration in a non-tolerant manner – the same amount of morphine ought to result in a stronger effect of the drug on pain (decreased pain sensitivity).

METHODS

As male rats have been used in previous studies of morphine tolerance, the current study utilizes experimentally naïve male rats in order to ensure previous drug administration experiences do not confound results. The experiment consisted of 10 sessions, the first 8 being the tolerance acquisition phase where the drug was administered in a particular environment, and the last 2 being the tolerance test phase. Half of all the experimental groups received tolerance acquisition in one environment: pain sensitivity was measured by an analgesiometer that applied paw pressure. The mean paw withdrawal threshold provided the measure of sensitivity. The other half of the groups were subjected to a hot plate procedure where paws were placed on a hot plate and pain sensitivity was measured by how long it takes rats to lick their paws.

For each environment, two groups were used, one group that had functional practice with the procedure during the tolerance acquisition phase and one that had non-functional experience with the procedure to ensure that any differences are due to environmental cues and not practice with responding to the stimulation of the procedures.

As well, 4 control groups, the same as all the other groups except that they were administered saline instead of morphine, were used to ensure that morphine was significantly more effective for pain relief before tolerance.

During the tolerance test phase, each group was tested in each environment, with order controlled for by counterbalancing.

RESULTS

Experimental groups displayed lower pain sensitivity on the first session than control groups due to the morphine use and as sessions continued –as tolerance occurred- morphine groups displayed greater pain sensitivity. As well, functional and non-functional groups of the same environment showed no differences in sensitivity ensuring differences are not due to procedure experience. When rats were tested in the environment that tolerance was not acquired in, pain sensitivity was significantly lower, that is, the tolerance built up in the original environment is not apparent and the morphine more effectively acts as an analgesic.

DISCUSSION

According to previous work on tolerance, the administration of morphine in the experiment should lead to tolerance no matter the environment, especially since all rats received the same amount of morphine on the same schedule. However, this is not what occurred- environmental cues played a crucial role in the mechanisms of tolerance.

LIMITATIONS

Although the experiment used experimentally naïve rats, no pre-tests were used to explore variance in pain tolerance amongst the rats prior to the experiment. Depending on how large this variance is, a sample size of only 12 rats per group may not be an adequate representation of the population. As well, the study uses male rats only; it may be useful to replicate the procedure with female rats in order to question whether effects are of the same strength.

The current study looks specifically at morphine use; it may be of value to explore whether these effects of conditioning on tolerance are generalizable to other painkillers as well as other types of drugs used for different purposes.

COMMENTS

The conditioning theory of tolerance is quite profound and extremely interesting. It is quite surprising that something as powerful as the effects of narcotics and the strong basis in physiology that it has can be so affected by the presentation and learning of associations. This goes to show just how powerful conditioning is and suggests that it may have a very important role in our daily functioning as well as situations of survival relevance, such as counteracting potentially harmful drug effects. However, it is not without its flaws. With conditioning and compensation also comes the issue of overdosing. Tolerance may be built in a certain environment, but when the same amount of drug is administered in a different environment, the cues that elicit compensation are not present, thus compensation is not elicited at the same level and the amount of administration may be too great to be compensated and extreme physical harm, even death, may occur. Being able to be so easily influenced by associations may be adaptive in a number of situations, it allows for efficiency and enhanced navigation through daily experiences, but it is also imprecise and just as easily may have negative consequences. By understanding the mechanisms of conditioning, we can build strategies to avoid such consequences.

The features of an environment (the **environmental stimuli)** that are present when a drug is administered become associated with the drug effect. These stimuli become cues for a dose of the drug, and trigger physiological responses that counteract the drug effect and contribute to tolerance. In this case study described at the start of the chapter, John was always administered morphine in the presence of particular environmental cues: a brightly lit, cluttered hospital room in which the same nurse administered morphine. John's bedroom, by contrast, is an environment in which morphine drug effects had never before been experienced, and the environmental stimuli were not cues for a dose of the drug. With the usual environmental cues absent, the usual physiological response that helped to counteract the drug effect was not triggered, exposing the patient to the full depressive effects of that amount of drug on the respiratory system: an overdose.

Although learned associations between stimuli can have life and death consequences, in a more general sense, you are exposed to associations (with less dramatic consequences) that are acquired effortlessly in your daily experience:

- You inhale the wonderful aroma of cinnamon as you walk past the bakery and feel your stomach growl
- You keep the dial at a radio station after hearing a familiar song that brings back a flood of nostalgic memories
- You grab a leash from the closet and ask "who wants to go for a walk?" and your dog jumps to attention
- You hear the enticing sounds of a nearby slot machine paying off and think to yourself, "Why not? Just a few coins won't hurt."

A Definition of Learning

In everyday use, the term *learning* may refer to a number of processes that lead to accumulating knowledge or skills. In psychology, the term learning has a more precise definition:

Learning is a relatively enduring change in the mechanisms of behaviour that occurs due to experience.

The definition of learning contains three key concepts:

1. THE MECHANISMS OF BEHAVIOUR

Why are we concerned ourselves with *mechanisms*? Why not simply consider 'changes in behaviour' to be an indication of learning? After all, when you learn to how to ride a bicycle, wear oven mitts before grabbing a hot pan, learning is apparent from observed improvements in performance. There are two compelling reasons to consider more than behaviour alone, both of which involve the distinction between *learning* and *performance*.

First, there are many reasons unrelated to learning why behaviour might change. Fatigue and motivational factors can alter behaviour. For example, imagine you have successfully trained your dog to roll over on command by rewarding her with treats. As she seems to have learned the behaviour well, one evening you attempt to have your dog perform this trick for some friends. Instead, your dog seems more interested in taking a nap. Rather than forgetting, there are more likely reasons for the failure in performance; perhaps your dog is just too tired or has already had so many treats that she is just not motivated to perform. On a later occasion, when your dog is hungry for more treats (or less tired), she may once again perform the trick indicating that the learning is intact.

Second, learning may occur yet not be immediately reflected in performance. In many cases, a learned behaviour may only be relevant in particular contexts. If you have learned to wear oven mitts before touching a pan on the stove, this does not mean that you should continue to wear oven mitts in any context in anticipation of a potential pan-handling situation. Rather, this learned behaviour is only optimal in contexts where there are hot items to be manipulated. Experimentally, we can observe the effects of learned behaviour that is not yet reflected in performance in the phenomenon of **latent learning**, see Box 3.1.

Box 3.1 Latent Learning

The type of experiment described below was first conducted by H.C. Blodgett in the 1920s, and more famously replicated by E.C. Tolman in his landmark paper *Cognitive Maps in Rats and Men* in 1949. These studies involved exposing rats to a relatively complex maze. Three groups of rats were given access to this maze under different conditions. Rats in the first group were exposed to the maze once a day with food in the goal box. These subjects quickly learned the correct route, and after several days they would *run* directly to the goal box, making almost no wrong turns. These rats had clearly learned the correct series of turns and this was obvious in their performance. A second group of rats was also exposed to the maze each day, but for these rats there was no food in the goal box. As you might expect, the second group of rats tended to wander around, and while one of the rats might occasionally wander into the goal box there was no increase in this behaviour across days.

A third group of rats was treated identically to the second group (no food in the goal box) for the first 10 days of the study. During this period, these rats behaved just like the rats in the second group; they wandered around and showed no evidence of learning the route to the goal box. However, on Day 11 food was introduced to the goal box for the first time. When these rats were placed back in the maze on Day 12, *they ran to the goal box just as quickly, and made no more errors than rats in the first group.* This strongly suggests that these rats had actually been learning the layout of the maze as they wandered around (forming what Tolman would call a cognitive map, or internal mental representation, of the maze). Notably, during the first 10 days, while this learning was taking place, there was no change in performance. Once food was available, and there was a reason to want to get to the goal box, performance began to reflect the learning that was already there. This study highlights the important distinction between learning and performance.

Given that behaviour might change for reasons other than learning, and that learning may not be instantly reflected as a change in behaviour, we need to define learning in terms of the *mechanisms of behaviour*, rather than the behaviour itself. When learning occurs, something changes in the processes and systems that produce behaviour, thereby altering the *mechanism* of that behaviour.

2. LEARNING INVOLVES CHANGE THAT IS RELATIVELY ENDURING

The definition specifies that the changes in the mechanisms of behaviour that occur as a result of learning must be *enduring*. This is not to say that these changes must be permanent (although they may be), but rather that learning should tend to be retained over time whether or not learning is being continually expressed in behaviour. Changes in behaviour that are the result of fatigue would presumably only last until the subject is rested. On the other hand, once you have *learned* to ride a bicycle, you can likely get back on after months or years of not riding and still perform at a similar level with just a little practice (it seems redundant in this case to say that it is 'like riding a bicycle').

3. LEARNING IS A PROCESS BASED ON EXPERIENCE

A third element in the definition of learning is that it occurs due to *experience*. To illustrate this concept, consider another possible reason why behaviour could change in relatively enduring ways. As you will see in Chapter X, there are dramatic changes in the physiology, skills, and behaviours of humans across the lifespan. While some of these changes reflect learning, others are largely a result of **maturation**. That is, there are behaviours that develop and change as an individual matures, often independent of experience. For example, as a tadpole develops into a frog, and shifts from swimming to hopping, this is not a learned behaviour- it has lost its tail and developed legs. In human development, maturation and learning are often closely coupled, and work together to alter the mechanisms of behaviour. Consider the process of language acquisition. A certain level of maturation is necessary before a child has developed motor control of the physical organs of speech production to produce language, but before this time, the child has already acquired considerable knowledge of words and their meanings. As the vocal apparatus comes 'on line', vocal ability and language ability develop in tandem.

In summary, the definition of learning makes a distinction between learning and factors that can influence performance. These factors may include transient states such as fatigue or hunger and long-term physiological maturation. The need to clearly distinguish such factors, and the primary reliance on observable behaviour as the measure of what has been learned, has led to an emphasis on the use of the experimental method in this research area. If the concepts of experimental and control groups are not sufficiently familiar, you may need to review the material in the previous chapter. Keep in mind that learning is not unique to the human species. Although there are some organisms that seem incapable of learning (as we have defined it), the range of organisms that do show this ability includes such distant relatives as *Caenorhabditis elegans* (c. elegans) a nematode (roundworm) about 1mm in length with a nervous system consisting of just over 300 neurons (compared to your 100 billion plus). The important point is that much of what you will read about in the rest of this chapter is based on the assumption that the learning process works the same way in human and non-human learners. Indeed, much of what we know about how humans learn comes from work with animal models in which a researcher has greater experimental control.

SECTION REVIEW: Introduction to Learning

TABLE 3.1

<table>
<tr>
<td colspan="2" align="center">Learning is based on the development of enduring associations, the mechanisms of their formation, and how such associations are adaptive</td>
</tr>
<tr>
<td align="center">Mechanisms of Behaviour</td>
<td align="center">Learning is Enduring & Based on Experience</td>
</tr>
<tr>
<td>
<ul>
<li>Learning is distinct from merely performance of or changes in behaviours; learning is often context specific and goes beyond natural responses to stimuli</li>
<li>Latent learning, acquiring associations that are not immediately expressed or expressed only in appropriate contexts, reflect this distinction and highlights the importance of the specific mechanisms of learning</li>
</ul>
</td>
<td>
<ul>
<li>Not all learning is permanent, but is often retained relatively strongly over time even if the behaviours involved are not continuously expressed</li>
<li>Experiences throughout the lifetime are key to learning and often distinct from developmental changes; adaptations to environmental cues through realizing associations form the foundations of learning</li>
</ul>
</td>
</tr>
</table>

Learning Theory

Almost four hundred years ago, John Locke (1632-1704) and the empiricist philosophers provided an elegant argument describing how we learn about the world by creating **associations** between ideas through experience. Relatively simple ideas such as 'hot pan' and 'burned hand' become associated as the result of experiencing those things together. More complicated forms of learning could be understood by involving more and more associations layered on top of each other. In this way, even the most complicated ideas could be broken down into associative links between individual ideas.

Looking Ahead

Psychologists have long been interested in understanding how associations are formed such that learned behaviours allow for adaptive interactions with the environment. As previously mentioned, in psychology the term *learning* usually refers to basic conditioning processes rather than the learning of abstract concepts. In this chapter, we will focus on questions such as: How do we associate stimuli and events? How do cues in the environment trigger behaviour? How are basic learning processes common across various species and circumstances? We will consider two basic perspectives on learning: Classical conditioning, which focuses on the ability to make associations between various stimuli that may appear in the environment, and instrumental conditioning, which focuses on the associations that form between our actions and the consequences of those actions. Before getting to those ideas, however, we first need to examine some basic phenomena that can produce changes in behaviour.

Section 1: Orienting Responses, Habituation, and Sensitization

You are programmed to notice novelty. When you become aware of a new stimulus or change in the environment it leads to a reflexive **orienting response** -- an automatic shift of attention toward that stimulus or event. Not every change in the environment will produce an orienting response; although it seems obvious, it is worth explicitly pointing out that the stimulus must be something that you are capable of perceiving. For example, flashing an infrared light would not be expected to produce an orienting response in a human subject, because we are not physiologically capable of perceiving it. However, if we consider a bird as a subject (which can detect this light) we may observe an orienting response.

Orienting responses are important for focusing attention on unfamiliar stimuli, which may signal sudden danger or unexpected opportunity. However, if your attention were attracted equally by every perceptible change in the environment, you would quickly become overwhelmed. It is important to be able to distinguish between stimuli to which we need to pay attention and stimuli we can safely ignore. Some environmental stimuli may change regularly without signaling anything very important to us. When Ted first moved into an apartment on a busy street corner in Calgary, he found the traffic and street noises to be very distracting as he tried to fall asleep. After a few weeks, he realized that he had stopped noticing the noises and was able to quickly fall asleep in spite of the traffic outside. It took him somewhat by surprise when, months later, his sister was visiting and asked, "How do you sleep with all that noise?" Stimuli that had originally produced orienting responses (and prevented Ted from sleeping soundly) were no longer causing the same effect. In fact, on subsequent visits to his parent's suburban home, Ted may find that the *absence* of traffic noise may interfere with his ability to fall asleep. The change in Ted's response to the novel sounds surrounding his urban apartment is an example of a simple form of learning called **habituation** – a decrease in response to a stimulus or event as it is repeatedly presented without any consequence. Habituation functions to limit an orienting response and to allow the organism to ignore inputs that have become familiar and have proved to be of no consequence. This keeps the focus on novel stimuli that have not yet been evaluated.

An everyday example of habituation involves your adaptation to constant **tactile stimulation**. When you first put on a hat, wristwatch, or ring, you are consciously aware of the sensation of pressure on that area of your body. As time passes, this sensory input does not change much and you stop being aware of it. However, this does not mean that have become incapable of perceiving the stimulus. Rather, you have learned that this constant stimulation is unimportant and can safely be ignored.

Box 3.2: Habituation to a scarecrow

Birds may initially be startled by the introduction of a scarecrow in a farmer's field. This makes adaptive sense since failing to attend to a potential predator can be fatal. However, as the birds become familiar with the presence of this new object, which proves to be harmless, habituation to the new stimulus will occur and it will no longer produce a response, allowing the birds to engage in more useful behaviours such as feeding on the farmer's crops.

Habituation is a useful response that allows you to ignore irrelevant stimuli that may otherwise be distracting and divert your limited attentional resources. However, imagine trying to follow the complicated plot of a movie while wearing an itchy wool sweater that is difficult to ignore. The process of habituation needs to be limited; otherwise there would be an ever-increasing range of stimuli being permanently ignored. At some point, the itchy sensation on your skin may not be related to wearing an item of clothing, but rather reflect an insect bite or rash. Although habituation can help us to concentrate our resources on relevant stimuli, in many cases it is just as important to be able to reverse the process.

Whereas habituation is a *decrease* in responsiveness, there are two alternate processes that can lead to an *increase* in responsiveness to a stimulus or event. **Dishabituation** is an increase in responding that follows a change in the stimulus to which habituation has occurred. Although you will habituate to the sensations resulting from wearing a hat, taking the hat off will not immediately return you to the former baseline state of not wearing a hat. Rather, you will first become aware of the sensation of 'not wearing a hat' until you habituate to the change in the constant pressure that was on your head while wearing the hat. Imagine you are in a forest and habituate to the sounds of birds chirping and small animals rustling. If these forest sounds in the background suddenly intensified *or* completely stopped, you would likely notice the change immediately. In both of these examples, dishabituation is important because a change in a familiar stimulus can indicate important new information. Perhaps the birds have stopped chirping because they have detected a nearby predator or you suddenly become conscious of your exposed head because the wind has blown your hat off.

While repeated exposure to many stimuli leads to habituation and a decrease in responding, in other cases repeated presentation leads to **sensitization**, or an increase in responding. Where habituation serves to keep us from being distracted by unimportant stimuli, sensitization focuses attention to stimuli that do have relevance. You can readily observe a sensitized response when watching a suspenseful movie with friends. As the music sets the mood and the tension builds, emotions and anxiety become heightened. A carefully placed poke or a well-timed loud noise can create a behavioral response with measurable success.

Sensitization can be adaptive because it prompts you to engage in behaviours appropriate to escaping a potentially harmful stimulus. The process of sensitization is also thought to play a role in many psychological processes, including drug dependence, asthma, the development of mood and anxiety disorders (Heim & Nemeroff, 2001), allergies and epilepsy.

Unlike the associative type of learning described by Locke and the empiricists, habituation and sensitization are considered simple forms of *non-associative* learning because they modify an existing stimulus-response relationship, rather than create a new one. The kind of process affected by habituation or sensitization is typically a **reflex**, which takes place independently of the conscious experience of the subject. When a physician taps the patellar tendon just below your kneecap, you reflexively extend your leg. You do not consciously *decide* to do it, it just happens. When a reflexive response habituates, as would happen if the physician repeatedly tapped your tendon, it is still a reflex, and you are not consciously deciding to extend your leg less and less. In fact, you would have great difficulty in consciously preventing your leg from moving if the reflex is activated; by definition, a reflex is independent of conscious control. It is for this reason that simple forms of learning such as habituation and sensitization are referred to as non-associative. In the next section, we will begin to look at associative learning. Although non-associative learning can be adaptive, there is more to learning than simply noticing and ignoring stimuli and events. Associative learning allows organisms to learn *relationships* between stimuli and events, and the widespread applications of this ability will become evident as we proceed.

SECTION 1 REVIEW: Orienting Responses, Habituation and Sensitization

TABLE 3.2

Mechanisms of non-associative learning are able to reflexively direct attentional resources and responses towards or away from stimuli in order to best adjust to and respond to the environment		
Orienting Our Attention	**Habituation**	**Increases in Responsiveness**
• In response to perceptible and salient stimuli, **orienting responses** allow us to selectively attend to potentially important stimuli in our environment, and to avoid being overwhelmed by unimportant stimuli or environmental changes	• Through repetitive experience with certain stimuli and a lack of negative consequences, responses are decreased but not eliminated, in order to selectively attend to stimuli of importance	• In response to changes in stimuli that are habituated to, **dishabituation**, or an increase again in sensitivity occurs to ensure appropriate environmental responses • With sensitization, an increase in the presentation of stimuli also leads to heightened responsiveness in order to respond suitably to stimuli that may be of direct threat

Section 2: Classical Conditioning

In an episode of the television show *The Office*, lead character Jim describes learning in school about "this guy who trained dogs to salivate by feeding them whenever he rang a bell." For the next few weeks, Jim secretly conducts his own study using his hapless co-worker Dwight as a subject. Each time he shuts down his computer (playing the familiar Windows sound effect) Jim presents Dwight with a mint. In time, simply playing the Windows sound effect quite literally leaves a bad taste in Dwight's mouth, leading him to reflexively reach for a mint.

This example demonstrates how learning relationships among events in the environment can be understood in terms of associations. Just as Dwight has learned to associate a computer sound with a minty treat, you have learned to associate thunder with lightning, and a farmer's cows have learned to associate a certain time of day with milking. These examples support the empiricists' argument regarding the importance of associations for an understanding of the world. However, it was not until the late 1800s, that the brilliant work of the Russian physiologist Ivan Petrovich Pavlov (1849-1936) finally moved the study of associations into the lab. His work would lead to the discovery of a form of learning called **classical conditioning**.

Pavlov's Psychic Secretions

Pavlov's groundbreaking work on the physiology of digestion laid the foundation for advances in theoretical and applied medicine. However, Pavlov is best known for his work on conditional reflexes, which he conducted late in his career. In his study of the reflex regulation of the digestive glands, Pavlov paid special attention to a phenomenon that he initially called "psychic secretion." Pavlov knew that salivation was triggered whenever food (especially dry food) was placed in the mouth. Interestingly, Pavlov observed that even food stimuli at a distance from the animal could elicit salivary secretions. How could this be possible? A series of experiments led Pavlov to conclude that psychic secretion was actually a physiological reflex. More specifically, it was a conditioned reflex shaped by learning. Later experiments refined our understanding of complex interactions between an organism and its external environment. In 1904 he was awarded a Nobel Prize for Medicine/Physiology for his early work on digestive physiology. In his Nobel Lecture address, Pavlov chose to focus much of his speech on his subsequent work on the conditioned reflex as the first sure steps down a new avenue of investigation. This new avenue would become the most important contribution of his career.

Pavlov was committed to the use of the scientific method and to experimental control while running a large lab with several assistants running simultaneous studies. As such, certain scheduled routines were followed: dogs would be tested at the same time for several days and often by the same assistant. In his work on reflexive salivation, a typical test would involve an assistant entering the housing room and placing a small amount of dried meat powder in the dog's mouth, and recording the amount of salivation that occurred. Salivation was measured by surgically diverting one of the dog's salivary glands so that it emptied into a small tube, where the contents could be measured, rather than into the dog's mouth (note that Pavlov was using the saliva production of one gland as an operational definition for the net total saliva production of all salivary glands). Using this preparation, Pavlov had reliably recorded reflexive salivation in response to food, and demonstrated the importance of this phenomenon to the digestive process.

There is an important lesson for all aspiring researchers in what happened next. The history of science includes important discoveries made by people who were looking for something else at the time. The list of prominent scientists who were observant and clever enough to recognize the significance of serendipitous findings includes Pavlov. Notably, Pavlov had already established himself as an eminent scientist recognized leader in his field. Nevertheless, when a novel and unexpected finding was observed, Pavlov seized the opportunity and essentially abandoned his previous line of productive research.

Pavlov observed that some of the dogs in his studies would begin salivating as soon as the research assistant entered the room, *before* any food had actually been placed in the mouth. Pavlov was quite familiar with salivation as a *reflexive* response to food, but a reflex requires some stimulus to set it in motion. What was this salivation a response to? How was this reflex being triggered when nothing had yet been placed in the dog's mouth? To Pavlov, it seemed clear that the dogs must have been responding to some cue in the environment that served as a signal that food was coming (perhaps the entry of the research assistant). This meant that the reflexive response of salivation was being triggered by some mental experience, rather than a physical stimulus, thus the term 'psychic' secretion.

Pavlov followed up on his ideas with a series of experiments known for their elegant design and use of careful objective measures. In a typical experiment, he used simple patterns of stimuli for the animal subject to detect and carefully recorded measures of activity. For example, a metronome would begin playing, and this would be followed by the presentation of food (a metronome is a mechanical device that produces a steady 'click-click-click' sound, allowing musicians to play along to a steady beat). After this pairing was repeated over several trials, Pavlov observed that the dog would salivate in response to the sound of the metronome alone. To understand this pattern of learning, Pavlov distinguished between two types of responses, and two types of stimuli that could produce them. An **unconditional response** (UR) is a biologically determined reflex that can be elicited in the absence of any prior learning. The stimulus that elicits the UR is called the **unconditional stimulus** (US). In Pavlov's procedure, the US was food being placed in the dog's mouth, and this elicited the UR of salivation. This salivation reflex is 'hard-wired' into the dog's physiology and happens automatically without requiring the dog to learn anything. You experience the same reflex when food is placed in your mouth. In both cases, the existing relationship between the US and UR is *not conditional* upon any prior learning, meaning that it happens independently of previous experience. Thus, the stimulus and response are said to be *unconditional*.

Box 3.3: Terminology.

A note on terminology: Some textbooks use the terms "conditioned" and "unconditioned" rather than the terms 'conditional' and 'unconditional' used here. Either form is acceptable though this textbook reflects a preference for the latter terms, which arguably reflects a more accurate translation of the Russian terms used by Pavlov.

A second type of response, called the **conditional response** (CR), only emerges after some learning has taken place (i.e., it is *conditional* upon experience). The CR is elicited by a **conditional stimulus** (CS), a stimulus that previously produced nothing other than a brief orienting response. The CS becomes *associated* with the US if they are repeatedly presented together. In Pavlov's procedure, the sound of the metronome is a CS that becomes associated with the US of food being placed in the dog's mouth. After a number of **conditioning trials** on which the CS and US were presented together, the initially neutral CS became capable of eliciting a CR of salivation.

As you may have noticed in the previous description of Pavlov's work, the UR and the CR are frequently very similar, if not identical. This raises an important question. How did Pavlov know, for example, that some responses were unlearned reflexes while other responses were the result of conditioning when all the responses in question were the same thing – salivation? The answer to this question is reflected in the typical design of a conditioning study. When the CS and US are paired together on a number of conditioning trials, there is a response on each of these trials. Each time Pavlov paired the sound of a metronome with food being placed in the mouth, the dogs reflexively salivated as we would expect. In fact, no matter how much a dog salivated on any conditioning trial, we would not yet have evidence of learning because the salivation could always be explained as the reflexive response to the US. To demonstrate that conditioning has taken place, and that the CS and US have become associated, we need to conduct **test trials** on which the CS is presented by itself. If salivation occurs when the *CS* is presented alone, and there is no US present to reflexively elicit a response, it is considered evidence that the CS and US have been associated and the subject has *learned* to respond to the CS.

By focusing on discrete stimuli and responses, and using animal subjects, Pavlov was able to tightly control his experiments and ultimately describe the general principles of classical conditioning.

Subsequent research has demonstrated that this simple form of learning can be observed across a wide range of species (snails, worms, rodents, humans) and under a variety of circumstances. Beyond the lab, classical conditioning is a part of your everyday life. As you will see, it is often rather straightforward to apply the results of conditioning studies in the laboratory to many common situations we face on a daily basis. Before proceeding, however, there is one further point about this type of learning that needs to be made clear.

Several references have been made already to learning in general, and classical conditioning in particular, as being adaptive. Saying this implies that the ability to learn benefits us in some important way. How is it benefitting the dogs in Pavlov's study to learn to salivate in response to a metronome? How are they any better off than a dog that could not learn to do this? First of all, remember that the metronome – food situation is just one example of the ability to learn associatively. As we have already seen, any stimulus that is going to function as a US must, by definition, be capable of producing some reflexive response (the UR). Those stimuli that we are 'hard-wired' to respond to in reflexive ways tend to be stimuli that have biologically important consequences. The US in Pavlov's study, food, is clearly a stimulus that has biological importance, and the fact that we reflexively salivate in response to food is an important element of our digestive process. As we will see across a number of different conditioning phenomena, the major adaptive value of classical conditioning is that it allows the organism to predict and anticipate these biologically important events, and prepare for them. By learning to associate the sound of the metronome with the food that followed it, and starting to salivate as soon as they heard the metronome, the dogs were prepared in advance for the arrival of food, making the digestive process faster and more efficient.

TABLE 3.3

Classical conditioning takes advantage of our tendency to learn associations between stimuli without being aware of this learning, even when stimuli do not have any natural relationship		
Pavlov's Experiments	**UR, US, CR, CS**	**US versus CS**
• Pavlov stumbled across the finding that the dogs' salivation was not only a reflexive response to receiving food, but a learned response based on the anticipation of food	• The **Unconditional Response (UR)** is a reflexive response to **Unconditional Stimuli (US)**, any stimuli in the environment • The **Conditional Response (CR)** is a learned response, the same as the UR, in reaction to the **Conditional Stimulus (CS)** after it has been paired with the US	• Evidence of learning occurs when the CS elicits the CR, the same as the UR, without presentation of the US • Classical Conditioning is highly integrated into many aspects of our lives and apparent in many species; it plays an adaptive role by tuning our cognitive resources towards important biological events

Section 3: Major Phenomena of Classical Conditioning I

In this next section we will examine a number of classical conditioning phenomena that will illustrate how this process works and how it is adaptive across a range of situations. We will begin by looking at the formation of an association that takes place over the course of conditioning trials, a process known as **acquisition**.

Acquisition of the CR

Before conditioning begins, the CS does not elicit a CR. The CS typically elicits an orienting response, and may result in some measurable behavioural changes, but such changes are considered neutral with respect to the response of interest. For example, if a light is used as a CS in an experiment where the US is food and the UR is salivation, the light could elicit changes in pupil dilation. However, this change would not be considered relevant to salivation, the measured response of interest, and the CS would therefore still be considered neutral. Following a number of conditioning trials where the CS and US are paired together, the CS (e.g., the light) comes to elicit a CR (e.g., salivation). After careful observation of this process, Pavlov came to two important conclusions about the acquisition of conditional responses. First, conditioning tends to be gradual, and the strength of the CR slowly grows over the course of conditioning trials. The strength of the CR is zero before any conditioning trials have taken place, and will increase somewhat after each pairing of the CS and US. Eventually, a point will be reached where further conditioning trials do not result in any further increases in CR strength. At this point the association between the CS and US would seem to be as strong as it is ever going to get, and we would say that learning has reached an **asymptote**. In Pavlov's studies, for example, the metronome CS initially produced no salivation. However, as the metronome was paired with food over a series of conditioning trials, the metronome began to produce a salivation CR. Eventually, the amount of salivation elicited by the metronome reached a peak. At this point, there are two possible reasons why a CR might 'level out' and not continue to increase despite the addition of more conditioning trials. First, we may have reached the subject's maximum physical ability to respond to the stimuli. After all, a dog is only capable of producing so much saliva. Second, it's possible that we have reached the maximum conditioning possible with the given specific stimulus pair. Some of the factors that determine how effective any particular stimulus will be as a CS or US will be discussed later in the chapter.

Pavlov's second major conclusion was that acquisition of the CR was dependent on stimulus **contiguity**, or the extent to which the two stimuli occur together in time and space. All that was required for the sound of a metronome to become associated with the presentation of food was that the two events occur at more or less the same place and time. This implies that there does not need to be any pre-existing connection between the stimuli used as the CS and US, and that any stimulus that produces an orienting response can be used as a CS and paired with any stimulus that produces a reflexive US. In other words, you will learn to associate any two stimuli that meet the above requirements if you experience them together some number of times. While this view dominated the early study of classical conditioning, it eventually became clear that there were a number of problems with the idea that contiguity was all that was needed in order for two stimuli to become associated. Before getting to those problems, however, we will need to explore a range of conditioning phenomena beyond the acquisition of a conditional response.

TABLE 3.4

Learning through classical conditioning is based on acquisition, but there are certain limitations on the intensity of associations formed and the responses to them		
Acquisition & the Learning Curve	Contiguity	
• **Acquisition** is a gradual process that occurs through continuous presentation of the US and CS together • Conditioning increases in strength, but levels off at a certain point either when physical responsiveness is maximized or no further condition can be acquired with the stimuli involved	• Important to acquisition is the presentation of the US and CS together in time and space continuously in order for learning of the association between the two to occur	• Acquisition can occur for any two stimuli, even if completely unrelated, so long as there is **contiguity**, according to early work in classical conditioning, but more modern research has since shown classical conditioning to be more complex

Section 4: Major Phenomena of Classical Conditioning II

Extinction of the CR

Although the ability to acquire associations can be adaptive in terms of allowing you to anticipate important events, a truly adaptive mechanism for learning also needs to be able to work in the opposite direction. Imagine that you were the subject of a conditioning study where, on each conditioning trial, a red light started flashing a few seconds before you received a mild (yet unpleasant) electric shock. Prior to any conditioning, experiencing the shock would cause a general increase in muscle tension, while the flashing light merely produced a brief orienting response. After a number of trials where the shock was paired with the flashing red light, you show an increase in muscle tension in response to the flashing red light alone, thus demonstrating that you had learned to associate the flashing light with the shock. At this point, the study is over and you are free to go on about your regular life, during which you are certain to encounter many flashing red lights. In almost all cases, these flashing red lights will not be followed by an electric shock, and may in fact be meant to indicate other events such as 'your parking meter is about to expire' or 'your battery is running low' or 'you have a voicemail message'. It would not be adaptive to, based on your experience in one conditioning session, then spend the rest of your life tensing up

---

whenever you encounter a similar flashing red light stimulus. Although you might experience muscle tension in response to flashing red lights for a while, eventually this response would fade away with each subsequent encounter with a flashing red light that does not coincide with an electric shock. This process is referred to as **extinction**, and is observed experimentally when a CS is repeatedly presented alone following acquisition of the CR.

In the case of Pavlov's dogs, each conditioning trial during acquisition involved presenting the CS followed by the US. At the end of the conditioning phase, the dogs showed a strong CR; they would salivate in response to the metronome CS. During an extinction phase, on each **extinction trial,** the CS is presented alone. The dogs would now hear the metronome on each trial, although food was no longer delivered. At first, the dogs continued to show some salivation in response to the metronome, but eventually this behaviour diminished until the dogs no longer showed any CR. The reduction of the CR suggests that the association between the CS and US that had developed during acquisition had now been *extinguished.*

Box 3.4 Extinction Trials and Test Trials

If you have been paying careful attention, you may have noticed that we have used two different names for what is essentially the same procedure. During acquisition, if we want to know the strength of an association, we cannot measure this on a trial where both the CS and US have been presented. On any trial where the US is present, any responding may be considered to be a UR. We therefore need to present trials where only the CS is present in order to see if our subjects have learned to associate this stimulus with the US. During acquisition, we would consider such a trial, where the CS is presented alone, to be a *test trial*, and these are occasionally required in order to see if any association is developing.

This type of trial, where only the CS is presented, is also conducted *repeatedly* during extinction training. In this case, we would refer to the trial as an *extinction trial.* The procedure is exactly the same, but depending on the context it may be referred to by different names. These trials also have the same effect in both situations: every time the CS is presented without the accompanying US the ability of that CS to produce a CR is reduced. While this is generally the goal of extinction training, it is the opposite of the goal of acquisition training, where we typically want to see the development of a CR. It is for this reason that test trials are conducted relatively infrequently during acquisition (for example, a test trial may be conducted only following many conditioning trials). What would you expect to happen if, during acquisition training, we alternated conditioning trials and test trials (i.e., one conditioning trial, then one test trial, then one conditioning trial, and so on)?

The fact that acquired associations can be extinguished allows animals to adapt to changing circumstances in their environment. Remember that the ultimate benefit of being able to learn this way is to be able to predict the occurrence of biologically important events. If the situation changes, and a CS is no longer a good predictor of the US, then it will not be beneficial to keep responding to the CS as if it *was* a good predictor. This brings us to the question of what is actually happening during the extinction process. This is still the subject of some debate, but for our purposes it is more important to consider what *is not* happening during extinction.

Extinction is not the same thing as *forgetting*. As we will see in Chapter 4 on Attention and Memory, it is possible to lose access to information over a period of time. However, classically conditioned responses tend to be maintained robustly. In other words, it typically takes more than the passage of time to extinguish a learned association. Notably, a CS can continue to elicit a CR following a period of weeks and months during which there was no exposure to the CS (Schwartz, Wasserman, & Robbins, 2005). In contrast, the process of extinction can be very rapid, with measurable decreases in the CR after only a few trials of presenting the CS alone.

Despite the 'mirror image' nature of the acquisition and extinction curves, these two processes are not necessarily the same process operating in opposite directions. Importantly, extinction *is not* is the complete erasure of the acquired association. Note that many early learning researchers assumed that extinction actually was the 'opposite' of acquisition. Let us consider this idea for a moment. If extinction involved completely undoing whatever had been done during acquisition, this would imply that when the CR was no longer seen at the end of extinction training, the subject was now *in exactly the same condition they were in prior to the start of acquisition*. Before any conditioning trials took place, the CS produced no CR, presumably because there was no association between the CS and US. Now, following extinction, the CS again produces no CR, suggesting that any association between the CS and US has been erased. This view of extinction was popular for a time, but several experimental phenomena strongly suggested that this view of extinction could not be correct.

One phenomenon suggesting that extinction is not 'unlearning' is **reacquisition**. As the name suggests, this is observed when experimental subjects are first exposed to conditioning trials during an acquisition phase. Once a strong CR has developed, extinction trials begin, and these continue until there is no longer any evidence of the CR. At this point we will add an additional phase to our procedure, and reintroduce conditioning trials where the CS is now paired with the US again. If extinction has actually erased the learning that occurred during the initial acquisition phase, then reacquisition should proceed at the same rate as the original acquisition, with the same number of conditioning trials required for the CR to reach an asymptote. As it turns out, this is not the case. A number of studies have shown that reacquisition is faster than acquisition. This could only be the case if at least some of the original learning was retained following the extinction process. Otherwise, there is no reasonable explanation for the fact that fewer conditioning trials are required to reach an asymptote the second time around.

A second phenomenon indicating that extinction does not involve the complete erasure of previous learning is **spontaneous recovery**. Consider a group of subjects that are exposed to a series of conditioning trials. Over the course of these trials, as the CS and US become associated, a CR develops and eventually reaches an asymptote. Extinction trials are now initiated and continue until no CR is observed. At this point, the subjects are finished for the day. The next day, the subjects return and are presented with more extinction trials. Given that the CR had been extinguished at the end of the previous day, we would not expect to see any response to the CS. However, when our subjects now experience the CS on the day following extinction, they display some of the previously extinguished CR. With further extinction trials this response will again diminish to zero, but the important observation here is that the CR, which had disappeared following extinction on the previous day, had reappeared to some extent despite the fact that the subjects had not had any further exposure to either the CS or the US during the intervening time. In other words, the extinguished CR was 'spontaneously recovered'.

It seems clear that some elements of the learned association are retained even when the CR appears to have been extinguished. What is going on during extinction trials that cause the CR to diminish and disappear? This is a question that continues to be debated among researchers, but it appears that extinction, like acquisition, is actually a form of learning. Where acquisition involves learning an association between two stimuli, extinction involves learning that that association 'no longer applies', at least on a temporary basis.

One possible explanation for the observation of incomplete extinction of the CR is the phenomenon of **renewal.** If a response is extinguished in a different environment than where it was acquired, the fully expressed CR is observed if the animal is returned to the environment in which acquisition originally took place. This has application to the treatment of phobias. Therapy typically takes place in a setting that is different from the actual context in which the patient may be exposed to the CSs that elicit the CR (e.g., the therapist's treatment room). This suggests that patients undergoing treatment for aviophobia (fear of flying in an airplane) have the best chance of success if they directly confront the very cues that elicit fear and anxiety in the actual context (e.g., directly in an airplane). Although this may complicate matters, this strategy seems to be successful in at least one treatment plan. In the DePlour Training Center program, individuals follow a typical therapy plan that is augmented by riding in a realistic flight simulator, and they graduate with a short "liberty flight" from Montreal to Toronto to test their new approach to flying: this acts as the ultimate extinction trial.

Inhibitory Conditioning

Taken together, the spontaneous recovery and reacquisition phenomena described above suggest that extinction is more complex than it might appear. An explanation preferred by Pavlov was that extinction training leads to **inhibitory conditioning**. To this point we have been discussing conditioning as a situation where a CS and US become associated. In fact, what we have been describing is **excitatory conditioning**, where what is learned is that the CS signals the *presence* of the US. For Pavlov's dogs, the metronome signaled the presence of food, and acquiring this association allowed the dogs to anticipate the occurrence of a biologically important event. In many cases, it can be just as useful to be able to anticipate the *absence* of a biologically important event. Learning that certain cues indicate the absence of food, potential mates, or predators can be just as important as learning to anticipate the presence of such things.

Using Pavlov's basic conditioning procedure, consider how some fairly simple changes could produce different results. In this case, the dogs are presented with the food US regularly (i.e., every 10 minutes). When the metronome CS is presented, the food presentations stop for a period of one hour, before resuming their previous schedule. In such a situation, the dogs will learn that the CS signals that no US will be presented for some time. In the case of excitatory conditioning, Pavlov concluded that the association between the metronome and food had been learned when the CS alone began to produce an increase in salivation. How would we measure learning in a case where the CS instead predicts the *absence* of the US? Consider that the baseline level of salivation, when nothing related to food or digestion is taking place, is not zero; there is typically some level of salivation occurring even when food is not being consumed (or anticipated). Therefore, when dogs learn that a CS predicts the absence of a food US, we could expect to see salivation decrease from its baseline level, which is in fact what is observed in such a situation.

SECTION 4 REVIEW: Major Phenomena of Classical Conditioning II

TABLE 3.5

For adaptive purposes, we must be able to counter conditioning when optimal, but it is important to realize that extinction if quite complex and not absolute		
Extinction		**Inhibitory Conditioning**
• Through continuous presentation of the CS without the US (**extinction trials**) it is adaptive for acquired responses to be extinguished in order to prevent physical and/or mental resources to be used unnecessarily • Extinction trials differ from **test trials**, in that test trials are presented only once after acquisition to test conditioning strength	• Extinction does not lead to forgetting though, as is seen through **reacquisition**, where reintroducing the CS and US after extinction can reform the acquisition faster than originally, though forgetting would suggest a slower rate of acquisition • Study of **spontaneous recovery**, responding to the CS even after extinction, has indicated the importance of context: extinction is stronger if in the same environment as acquisition	• The complexity of extinction suggests it may also be a form of learning, though inhibitory – learning based on the anticipation of the absence of a biological event • Essentially, individuals learn a new acquisition on top of the old **excitatory conditioning**, but the original learning is not forgotten

Section 5: Higher-Order Conditioning

Higher-Order Conditioning

In a typical conditioning experiment, an initially neutral stimulus (CS) comes to elicit a CR after some pairings with a US. In **higher-order conditioning**, the established CS is now paired with a new stimulus, allowing the new stimulus to become another CS capable of eliciting a CR. Imagine an experiment in which a tone (CS1) is paired with food (US), leading to a response of salivation (CR). After robust conditioning has been established, the tone (CS1) is now paired with a light (CS2), but without any food. After some CS1-CS2 pairings, the light and the tone will separately elicit salivation (CR).

As you might have anticipated, the CR elicited in higher-order conditioning is typically weaker and more vulnerable to extinction compared to the original CR (e.g., the original tone CS elicits more robust salivation than the second-order light CS). Despite these limitations, higher order conditioning greatly expands the power and influence of associative learning. For example, as a child Joe had a fear of being injected with a needle at the doctor's office. Just the sight of the needle (CS) caused Joe to experience fear as he had never known it. In time, many associated stimuli -- the sight of the doctor's office, the familiar route there and even the word "doctor" -- came to elicit a fear response. Now, Joe gets to relive the whole experience in his annual visit to the veterinarian. His cat knows exactly what is going on as soon as Joe places him in the enclosed laundry basket that marks the start of the ritual of the trip to the veterinarian's office. Consider how these principles are applied outside the lab to trigger positive emotional responses to affect what you *like* and *dislike*. Commercials pair beautiful people and popular songs with a specific brand, and savvy politicians plan photo-ops to associate with celebrities, well-received public projects, and patriotic symbols.

Generalization and Discrimination

Pavlov used precise control in his experiments to train animals with particular stimuli and collect objective measures of responding. In the course of testing, Pavlov observed that although his subjects would show a CR in response to the CS they had been trained with, they would also show some degree of responding to stimuli that were similar, but not identical, to the original CS. For example, if the original CS was a 1000 Hz tone, the subject might also respond to a tone of 950 or 1050 Hz. While it might seem like a failure of learning when an organism responds to stimuli other than those used during conditioning, consider that the hot pot on the stove that can burn your hands comes in many different shapes and colours. To achieve the maximum benefit from an earlier learning experience, it may be very useful for an organism to be able to apply that learning to stimuli that may not be identical to the original CS. If you have to burn yourself on every piece of cookware you own before learning to handle it with oven mitts you are at a distinct disadvantage when compared to someone who, after burning themselves on one particular pot, learns to handle anything that looks like a hot pot with care.

The process of applying what has been learned with a particular set of stimuli to a wider range of similar stimuli is referred to as **stimulus generalization**. This does not imply that what has been learned will be applied equally in all cases; generally the more similar a stimulus is to one that has been conditioned, the greater the response. Consider an experiment in which a rat experiences a mild electric shock (US) that is paired with a tone (CS) of a particular pitch. When tested, the rat will typically show the strongest fear CR to a test tone of the same pitch. However, the rat will also show a fear CR to tones of similar pitch. As the test tone becomes more and more different from the pitch of the original CS, the elicited CR will be correspondingly weaker and weaker. This pattern of responding is often represented in graph showing what is called a **generalization gradient**. Consider the important adaptive function served by stimulus generalization. A mellow mouse may initially ignore rustling sounds coming from behind a bush only to be confronted by a waiting cat. If he survives this learning trial, stimulus generalization will allow the mouse to develop an alarm response to a range of similar rustling sounds and avoid possible future attacks from predators.

Stimulus generalization can be an adaptive response because it allows the learning organism to apply previous learning to new, but similar, situations. However, a tendency to uniformly generalize what has been learned does not always work to the learning organism's benefit. For example, if you were to

---

115

generalize your experience with hot pots on a stove to the extent that you were unwilling to handle any round objects without oven mitts, this would likely interfere with your ability to play basketball successfully. In some cases the ability to generalize what has been learned may be less useful than the ability to learn to respond *only* to particular stimuli. This is referred to as **stimulus discrimination**, and reflects an organism's ability to fine-tune its responding such that a CR occurs to one stimulus but not to other, similar, stimuli. Like generalization, discrimination has important adaptive value. Consider a rabbit that has experienced several informal conditioning trials on which footprints in the snow (CS) were paired with the presence of a dangerous predator such as a fox (US). It makes sense for the rabbit to be fearful and avoid stimuli paired with the presence of predators, but to what particular CS should these behaviours be optimally directed? If the rabbit generalizes what it has learned over a very wide range of stimuli it may avoid all footprints, thus greatly limiting its ability to forage for food. If, on the other hand, the rabbit can learn to avoid fox footprints specifically, and to ignore the tracks left by other rabbits, squirrels, mice and other non-threatening species, this will allow the rabbit to maximize its foraging while still avoiding danger.

The phenomenon of discrimination can be demonstrated more precisely in a controlled experiment using **discrimination training**. Imagine an experiment in which you are exposed to a puff of air directed at your eyes (US) that reliably produces a reflexive blink response (UR). In the acquisition phase, a red light (CS) is paired with the air puff (US). After several pairings, the red light elicits a blink response (CR). This describes a typical acquisition procedure, and if you were subsequently presented with a pink light, it would not be surprising if this stimulus also produced a blink response as a result of stimulus generalization. Now consider another conditioning procedure involving two different types of trials. On some trials, you experience the red light and air puff pairing, and other trials you will experience a pink light in the absence of the air puff. At first, generalization will likely cause you to give a blink response to both the red and pink lights. However, as training proceeds, discrimination will allow you to fine-tune your responding such that a blink response is directed specifically toward to red light only.

In this discrimination training design, the red light is termed the CS+ and the pink light is termed the CS-. It is clear that the CS+ signals the onset of the US, but what is learned about the CS-? As we have already seen, a CS can also predict the absence of a US. The CS- therefore acquires an inhibitory association with the US while the CS+ acquires an excitatory association with the US. This ability to learn to respond to particular stimuli, while suppressing responding to similar stimuli can be very valuable. In Chapter 2 we discussed the situation faced by a radar operator who needs to make the distinction between those signals on his screen that are produced by aircraft and those that are produced by flocks of birds. If the signals produced by the two sources are different in some perceptible way, and the operator can learn to distinguish the airplane CS+ from the bird CS-, then the operator will be able to perform her job in a much more efficient manner.

The Temporal Arrangement of the CS and US

We have so far described excitatory conditioning trials as involving the 'pairing' of a CS and US. Before proceeding further, we should explore the *temporal arrangement* of the stimuli (how the stimuli are related in terms of time) in more detail, as this can influence how much, if any, learning will take place in any given conditioning procedure. For most excitatory conditioning procedures, the optimal arrangement is **short-delay conditioning**, where the onset of the CS occurs first, followed by the onset of the US. Both stimuli typically terminate at the same time in this procedure. The interval between CS onset and US onset is generally in the range of half a second to a few seconds. Short-delay conditioning is considered to be the most effective arrangement and acquisition of the CR will reach an asymptote following fewer conditioning trials than would be the case with any other temporal arrangement of CS and US. When the interval between CS and US presentation is too great, conditioning tends to become less effective. Similarly, conditioning drops off sharply if the CS-US interval is made too brief, or when there is no interval at all and the CS and US are presented simultaneously. It is possible, however, to see excitatory associations form even when the US is presented before the CS, a procedure known as backward conditioning, although this procedure more often results in inhibitory learning (Rescorla, 1988).

We can make intuitive sense of the relative effectiveness of conditioning resulting from these various CS-US delay intervals by considering how the signaling role of the CS can be optimized. Consider the following: one summer you are in Sicily driving on a beautiful mountain road winding up to Taormina. Your beautiful view of the Mediterranean is interrupted by two factors: some very confident locals who fearlessly raced up the mountain and some rather dangerous hairpin turns in the road. If you were in charge of putting up signs warning tourists of these turns, where should they be optimally placed? Placing the sign right in the middle of the turn is obviously a poor option. The information comes too late and is of no use to the driver. This is analogous to simultaneous conditioning. An even poorer option would be to place the warning sign after the dangerous turn. This is analogous to backward conditioning. (In fact, placing the sign after the turn would signal a driving period free of dangerous turns!). Your best option is to place a sign just before the turn to alert the driver to pay close attention to the upcoming turn. This is analogous to conditioning with the effective short-delay CS-US interval. If you think it would be wise to give the driver more time to prepare, you might consider placing the caution sign farther ahead of the turn. However, if you place the sign too far ahead, the driver may ignore or forget about it as the turn approaches. This is analogous to the less effective long-delay CS-US interval. The only question remaining is *chi contatto circa mettere su alcuni segni di avvertenza* (whom do I contact about putting up some caution signs)?

Contiguity vs. Contingency

As noted in our discussion of acquisition, Pavlov's view of classical conditioning emphasized contiguity – the CS and US must occur together close in time. Indeed, Pavlov considered contiguity to be a *necessary and sufficient condition* for the acquisition of a learned association, a view that dominated learning research for decades. To say that contiguity is a *necessary* condition is to say that you must have contiguity in order for learning to happen. To say that contiguity is a *sufficient* condition is to say that all you need is contiguity in order for learning to happen. In other words, if two stimuli occur together in time, they will become inevitably associated. While learning theorists would likely still agree that contiguity is a necessary condition, much research has emerged in the last 40 years that suggests that contiguity itself is not a sufficient condition for learning. You have learned that optimal conditioning occurs when the CS can act as an effective signal to prepare the organism for the US (or non-occurrence of the US). This property of the CS to provide information about the presentation of the US is called **contingency**. As we will see, having stimuli occur at the same time does not necessarily mean that one stimulus provides useful information about the occurrence of the other.

The importance of contingency over contiguity was neatly demonstrated in a classic experiment by Robert Rescorla (1966). Dogs were initially trained to jump across a barrier in a "shuttle box" to avoid an electric shock. If they successfully jumped to the other side, the shock could be postponed. The frequency of jumping was used as a measure of fear conditioning. Once the dogs were well trained, they entered the second phase of training. In the Random Group, a shock (US) was presented at random times independently from a tone (CS). On some trials, the CS and US were temporally contiguous, but critically, the US was *just as likely to occur* in the absence of the CS. This meant that overall, the CS had no predictive value of whether or not the US would follow. In the Contingency Group, the CS was always paired with the US. Thus, the CS had good predictive value.

Now the dogs were returned to the shuttle box. The question was, what would happen when the tone (CS) was played to signal the coming shock? Would this CS affect their jumping escape behaviour? Playing the CS helped the dogs in the Contingency Group but not the Random Group. Importantly, both groups were exposed to the same number of contiguous pairings of the CS and US, but the CS only became an effective signal that guided behaviour when it had a contingent relationship with the US. Therefore, it is the information value contained in contingency, and not the contiguity, that is important for conditioning. It is important to note that the dogs in the Random Group have learned something different, but just as important – in this case, that the CS is irrelevant. This will impact their ability to later learn a contingent relationship between the CS and the shock, making it more difficult to make this association.

Classical Conditioning and Physiological Regulation

The French physiologist Claude Bernard (1813-1878) observed that every organism has an internal environment that interacts with a larger external environment. The internal environment consists of all the body's physiological functions including blood oxygen and glucose levels, ion concentrations and core temperature. To remain healthy, these physiological markers must be kept fairly constant, fluctuating only within narrow limits. For example, human body temperature can fluctuate within a typical range of 35-39°C. A core temperature that falls below (hypothermia) or rises above (hyperthermia) this range can put an individual at serious risk. The external environment consists of all the elements of the physical world that an organism is exposed to including climate conditions, access to nutrients, contact with toxins, and interactions with predators, prey, kin and potential mates. These elements of the external environment can fluctuate widely with the time of day, season, and random variations. To meet the challenge of maintaining an internal equilibrium in this shifting world, the process of **homeostasis** initiates changes in behaviour and internal adjustments. For example, in response to a drop in environmental temperature, a fox may shiver and seek shelter (behaviour) and restrict blood flow to its extremities (internal adjustment).

Classical conditioning is an important homeostatic mechanism that helps to maintain physiological regulation. Consider the ingestion of a food that contains high levels of glucose. The sudden influx of the sugar raises blood glucose levels above the normal internal equilibrium. To compensate, there can be changes in behaviour (e.g., stop eating the sweet food) and internal adjustments (release of insulin to uptake and store the excess glucose). Remarkably, such homeostatic mechanisms can become more efficient with conditioning. The presence of excess glucose (US) elicits a physiological response of insulin release (UR). There are a number of reliable cues that precede the US, notably, a sweet taste (CS) that is paired with the introduction of glucose into the bloodstream. With a lifetime of associative pairings, the sweet taste (CS) alone can elicit anticipatory insulin release (CR) in preparation for the expected rise in blood glucose.

Box 3.5: Application | Conditioning and Drug Effects

Let's take a closer look at the case study that opened this chapter in which the clinical use of morphine demonstrated that drug effects are influenced by conditioning. Drug effects can introduce a challenge to the individual's homeostatic internal environment. For example, among its many drug effects, morphine can disrupt pain sensitivity, respiration (breathing rate), and mood levels. Many drug effects decrease with repeated administration – drug tolerance. The full expression of drug tolerance can be understood as a combination of URs and CRs that act to neutralize the drug effects. Let's consider morphine's effect to *decrease* pain sensitivity and respiration. In response to these drug effects (USs), the body responds (URs) with mechanisms that act to restore homeostasis. These URs may include an *increase* in pain sensitivity and respiration. With each drug administration, there are cues associated with the drug effect which include all the stimuli that signal the drug is about to arrive – the sight of the needle, physical environment, and so on. These cues form a complex CS that elicits a CR to prepare for the arrival of morphine. Together, URs and CRs act to neutralize the drug effects and contribute to tolerance. So now, can you understand the events that may have led to the drug overdose suffered by the patient in the opening case study? Many reports have confirmed the predictions of a conditioning analysis of drug tolerance (Kim, Patenall, & Siegel, 1999; Siegel & Kim, 2002). Research in conditioning of drug effects further demonstrates the important role of classical conditioning in preparing an organism to adaptively respond to stimuli that challenge homeostasis.

Final Thoughts on Classical Conditioning

The study of learning has an important place in the history of psychology and continues to influence contemporary research. From the 1920s until the mid-1960s it was the dominant general paradigm in experimental psychology. Most aspects of human behaviour were assumed to be heavily determined by experience or learning, and the entire field of psychology was dominated by learning-based theories. For example, as noted in Chapter 1, even the work of psychologists studying human memory was dominated by the behaviourist approach. Early memory researchers theorized that memories were formed in much the same way that they assumed conditional responses developed: by the association of ideas or items that occurred close together in time (contiguity). According to this view, forming memories and conditional responses relied on an essentially mechanical process in which the learner played little or no active role.

However, we can now see that a view of classical conditioning as an inevitable mechanical process is oversimplified and ignores the richness of its flexible mechanisms. The complexity of classical conditioning is summarized by Robert Rescorla (1988), a leading researcher in the field of associative learning: "Conditioning is not a stupid process by which the organism willy-nilly forms associations between any two stimuli that happen to co-occur. Rather, the organism is best seen as an information seeker using logical and perceptual relations among events, along with its own preconceptions, to form a sophisticated representation of its world." In studying the principles of learning, behaviourists taught us much about adaptive processes which have important applications across all fields of psychology ranging from treatment of phobias to understanding drug tolerance. Shep Siegel, a leading researcher in the conditioning of drug effects has succinctly summarized the adaptive nature of classical conditioning as follows: "The study of homeostatic regulation *is* classical conditioning."

SECTION 5 REVIEW: Higher Order Conditioning

TABLE 3.6

The complexity of conditioning is further realized with higher order conditioning and the extent to which environmental context is incorporated to provide adaptive advantages		
Generalization & Discrimination	**Temporal Arrangement**	**Contiguity versus Contingency**
• Acquisition of the CR often occurs in response to stimuli similar to the original CS, with response intensity decreasing with decreases in similarity, advantageous for novel, similar situations • **Stimulus discrimination** though can occur when needed; organisms are able to modify the level of generalization, or it may be achieved through **generalization training**	• **Short delay conditioning**, where the CS is presented approximately several seconds after the US, is often the most effective method of forming associations • **Simultaneous presentation** or delays over several seconds often prevent conditioning	• Despite Pavlov`s stress on the role of **continuity** as necessary and sufficient, **contingency** has been shown to be of higher importance • **Contingency**, the information in the presentation of the US in response to the CS, has greater relevance for the acquisition of associations • Not only is classical conditioning relevant for responding adaptively to the environment, it is important for maintaining homeostasis for physiological regulation

Draft

Section 6: Instrumental Conditioning

For a number of years, there was an unusual display in the lobby of the psychology building at Harvard University. Remarkably, two pigeons would hit a ping-pong ball back and forth to each other in a spirited match. Visitors were amazed at how such a complex skill could be taught to birds. Although impressive, training was actually straightforward and less complicated than people realized. The trainer was psychologist B.F. Skinner. Skinner began by training each pigeon individually. The desired behaviour of hitting a moving ping-pong ball was broken down into particular bits of behaviour and reinforced with food. The bird might first be **reinforced** for just approaching the ball, then for touching the ball, later for pushing it, and finally only for hitting a moving ball. All that was left was to place the two trained pigeons at opposite ends of a specially designed table and start keeping score.

By a similar process, Skinner taught pigeons to walk in figure eights, dance with each other, and even operate a prototype missile guidance system (Skinner lamented that no one would take this research application seriously). The reality that actions can be **shaped** by the environment, and maintained by their consequences, are principles that are widely used in many applied settings including cognitive behaviour therapy, game design, and educational psychology. However, Skinner went a step further and believed that these principles could be used to positively change society as a whole. As summarized by one interviewer, "In the Skinnerian world, man will refrain from polluting, from overpopulating, from rioting, and from making war, not because he knows that the results will be dangerous, but because he has been conditioned to want what serves group interests."

In the first part of this chapter you were introduced to non-associative forms of learning that allow you to orient towards stimuli and either respond more (sensitization) and focus attention or respond less (habituation) and ignore. You were also introduced to an associative form of learning called classical conditioning, which allows you to anticipate biologically important events. These types of learning involve behaviours that are automatically triggered – there is no conscious decision-making that takes place. However, you also behave in ways that produce environmental changes and have consequences. A cat meows by the door and Jen lets him out. Mary inserts a coin into a vending machine and receives a snack. You fill in the correct words and scribble on a test sheet and are reinforced with an excellent grade. In each of these examples, the behaviours are initiated by, and are under the control of, the organism. We will next consider the mechanisms of learning that govern these types of behaviour in another form of associative learning called **instrumental conditioning.** If classical conditioning involves forming new reflexive responses, instrumental conditioning involves forming new voluntary behaviours that direct goal-directed actions.

Thorndike's Law of Effect

In the wake of Darwin's theory of evolution by natural selection, a debate was sparked concerning the extent to which mental abilities, such as problem solving, were conserved across species. Darwinian naturalists reported seemingly amazing accounts of intellectual achievements in animals, including stories

Draft

of cats baiting a lawn with scattered breadcrumbs to lure unsuspecting birds. How could this apparently sophisticated problem-solving behaviour in animals be objectively evaluated? Recall that the data emerging from Pavlov's laboratory concerned only reflexive learning, which was different from this type of skill. A new line of research originating from the lab of Edward L. Thorndike (1874-1949) provided an answer. While Pavlov was investigating conditional reflexes with dogs in Russia, Thorndike was investigating a different type of learning with cats in America.

CATS IN A BOX

Thorndike's general procedure was to provide a problem for an animal to solve. His most famous experiments involved placing a hungry cat inside a 'puzzle box' with a latched door, with food available just outside the door. The door could be opened to reach the food if the cat performed a simple action such as pulling a string or pressing a lever. The cat would then be placed back into the box for another learning trial and observed to see how long it took to master this escape response.

Put yourself in the place of a hungry cat placed in a strange box. What's a cat to do? At first, you have no idea, so you meow loudly and claw aimlessly, getting you no closer to your goal of escaping the box. This may go on for a while until you accidently claw at a dangling string, which opens the trapdoor. On subsequent trials, the experimenter may observe gradual improvement, as you take less and less time to produce this correct response. Later in training, there is an almost immediate approach to the string and the correct response is produced leading to freedom and reward. A casual observer witnessing the later trials may conclude that you are a reasonable cat with good understanding; however, Thorndike would argue otherwise.

It turns out that cats and humans solve this puzzle very differently. If you examined a record of the total time to escape, cats show a *gradual decline* across repeated trials. This is not the pattern that would be expected if you (as a human, now) were placed repeatedly in the same situation. Once you identified the correct response (an insightful "Aha!" moment) we would expect to see your response time permanently drop as a step function in subsequent trials, rather than gradually decline from trial to trial. In contrast, the observed learning curve for a cat suggests that the escape response was gained in small increments with no evidence of insight into problem-solving. It would be the equivalent of observing James Bond placed repeatedly in a diabolical trap with the same solution ("Aha! Use the device that Q gave me!"), yet show only marginal improvements in escape time with each successive experience.

THORNDIKE'S LAW OF EFFECT

Thorndike observed that cats in the puzzle box initially engaged in a variety of responses like biting, jumping, clawing, and meowing that were unrelated to the final target response. Across trials, the frequency of these irrelevant behaviours gradually decreased, while the cat's tendency to perform the correct response increased. Thorndike described this process as consisting of target responses becoming "stamped in" and irrelevant responses becoming "stamped out". The mechanism for stamping was summarized in Thorndike's **Law of Effect**: A response followed by a *satisfying effect* is strengthened and likely to occur again in that situation, while a response followed by an *unsatisfying effect* is weakened and less likely to occur again in that situation. Just how strongly these responses are stamped in or out are proportional to the consequences (satisfying or unsatisfying) of the response. Consider how Thorndike's experimental situation is very different from the paradigm used by Pavlov. The puzzle box presented a set of sights, sounds, smells, and other cues, but none of these stimuli directly elicited string-pulling as an *involuntary* response or reflex. Instead, the stimuli associated with the puzzle box acted as an occasion setter for many possible *voluntary* responses, only one of which was set as the correct response. The satisfying effect of access to food increased the probability of the response that produced it when the cat was placed in the same situation. In this view, there was no need to attribute any special intellectual sophistication to the cat. Rather, the apparent problem-solving behaviour was more accurately described as a change in the probabilities of the various possible responses.

SKINNER AND OPERANT BEHAVIOUR

If Thorndike was the father of instrumental conditioning, B.F. Skinner was its doting uncle. It was Skinner who popularized the Law of Effect and pushed instrumental conditioning to the forefront of learning theory. While both classical conditioning and instrumental conditioning are forms of associative learning, they differ in terms of what becomes associated. In classical conditioning, the association forms between two stimuli (the CS and US), whereas in instrumental conditioning the association forms between a stimulus and a behavioural response. Where Pavlov's dogs had no control over when the CS or US appeared (i.e., neither of these things were affected in any way by the dog's behaviour and were entirely under the control of the experimenter), in instrumental conditioning the subject's behaviour directly causes the satisfying or unsatisfying consequences. Skinner used the term **operant** to describe these behaviours, as these voluntary actions *operate* on the environment to produce change leading to a specific consequence (instrumental conditioning is also frequently referred to as **operant conditioning**). Instead of referring to a 'satisfying effect' or 'reward' that followed a response, Skinner preferred the term **reinforcer**, which implied no assumptions about judgments being made in the mind of the individual responding. In keeping with the tenets of behaviourism, the term *reinforcer* was chosen as an objective descriptor of behaviour. Following a response, a reinforcer (e.g., food) is defined as anything that increases the probability of response being emitted again in future. While some stimuli are **primary reinforcers** that have intrinsic value – like access to food, water or a mate – **secondary reinforcers** only come to be reinforcing through previous learning. A good example in the realm of human behaviour is money. Paper rectangles, round pieces of metal, and small plastic cards have little intrinsic value (i.e., by themselves, they do not produce any particularly satisfying effects), but can be used to obtain items that are natural reinforcers. Consequently, these secondary reinforcers can be powerful motivators of behaviour. Similarly, grades, air miles, gold stars, coupons, and status symbols act as powerful reinforcers and influence your behaviour, but only to the extent that they have been associated with other primary reinforcers. The principle here is the same as was discussed in the earlier section on classical conditioning with respect to higher-order conditioning.

Among Skinner's many contributions to the field of learning is the design of an apparatus called an **operant chamber**, which he used for the experimental study of operant (instrumental) conditioning. The operant chamber (also commonly referred to as a 'Skinner box') consisted of a special chamber with a lever or other mechanism by which an animal could respond to produce a reinforcer such as a food pellet. The Skinner box had many advantages over Thorndike's puzzle box. Trials could be shorter, there were no constraints on responding, and after completing a response and experiencing its effect, the animal remains in the box, and is free to respond again (and again and again!). The response rate (e.g., lever presses over time) was automatically recorded with a device called a **cumulative recorder**. In a typical experiment, an animal stayed in the chamber for a set interval of time and analyzing the output of the cumulative recorder would allow learning to be assessed.

Draft

Major Phenomena of Instrumental Conditioning

Although learning researchers like Skinner emphasized the distinctions between classical and instrumental conditioning, modern learning theorists point out that there is also a lot in common between these conditioning processes, both of which ultimately involve learning about relationships. It may not surprise you then that there are many parallels between the major phenomena of classical and instrumental conditioning. For example, in instrumental conditioning, the more pairings there are between an operant response (e.g., lever press) and its consequence (e.g., food pellet), the stronger the acquired learning. If conditions change and the operant response is no longer paired with its consequence, the result is a decline in responding leading to extinction. As in the case of classical conditioning, extinction in instrumental conditioning does not involve "unlearning" of the response. Rather, new learning is layered on top of the previously learned response. This is supported by the observation that following extinction, an instrumental response can show spontaneous recovery and faster reacquisition.

GENERALIZATION AND DISCRIMINATION

As with classical conditioning, there is an important role for environmental cues present in the context of instrumental conditioning. These cues are called **discriminative stimuli** and signal to the organism when a given response-reinforcer relationship is valid. Imagine an experiment involving a Skinner box modified for use by a pigeon. Instead of a lever, there is a *key light* (an illuminated plastic circle on the wall of the chamber), which the pigeon can peck. When the key light is green, pecking it results in the delivery of a small quantity of food. However, when the key light is red, pecking it has no effect. In this design, the green light is functioning as positive discriminative stimulus (S+) and the red light as a negative discriminative stimulus (S-). As conditioning proceeds, the pigeon will learn to perform the response (pecking the key) in the presence of the S+ (green light) but not the S- (red light). Presumably, you follow a similar pattern of discriminative control of responding with your gas pedal at traffic signals. You can probably think of many more examples. A student may learn to complain (response) about his heavy workload in the presence of friends (S+) who offer sympathy and attention (reinforcer), but withhold these complaints in the presence of his parents (S-) who are not so sympathetic but offer a review of their financial support along with anecdotes concerning walking miles to school and back in blinding snowstorms (uphill both ways). Similarly, a child may learn that eating her spinach (response) leads to access to ice cream (reinforcer) when her father is present (S+) but not on her mother's watch (S-).

How do the S+ and S- of instrumental conditioning compare with the CS+ and CS- of classical conditioning? The CS+ informs you about what *will* happen; "look alive, the US train is about to arrive." In contrast, the S+ informs you about what *could* happen *if* you produce the appropriate behaviour; "if you act now, reinforcers are standing by." The CS- informs you of what *will not* happen; "the US train will definitely not arrive in the next 20 minutes." In contrast, the S- informs you that a response-reinforcer is not currently valid; "there's no point in acting now, wait for a better opportunity." Despite these qualitative differences in information, the mechanics of both instrumental and classical conditioning function similarly with respect to stimulus generalization and discrimination. For example, in the experiment described earlier in which a pigeon is trained to peck a key when the S+ (green light) is presented, an experimenter can test responding in the presence of a variety of coloured lights. In a stimulus generalization gradient curve, she would observe that the key pecking response was strongest in the presence of a green light and lights of similar wavelength. However, the key pecking response would become weaker as the colour of the light became increasingly different from the original S+.

Draft

TABLE 3.7

Instrumental Conditioning is a form of associative learning that requires overt behaviours to be performed for learning to occur and emerged out of the work of Skinner and Thorndike		
Thorndike & Stamping In	**Skinner & Operant Behaviour**	**Major Phenomena**
• In any random environment, voluntary behaviour leading to satisfying consequences becomes more frequent, is **"stamped in"**, and behaviour leading to displeasing consequences diminishes	• Essential to instrumental condition is the association between stimuli and voluntary behaviours that operate to produce certain consequences, a **reinforce**; anything that increases the probability of the behaviour occurring again	• Many parallels in the mechanisms of learning exist between classical and instrumental conditioning, such as the role of environmental cues • **Positive discriminative stimuli (S+)** indicate the presence of a reinforcer based on the response, whereas **negative discriminative stimuli (S-)** indicate the absence of a reinforce in order to fine tune behaviour in response to generalization

Section 7: Reinforcers, Reinforcement, and Punishment

Reinforcement and Punishment

When you consider the adaptive nature of operant conditioning, you likely think about examples where obtaining a satisfying consequence selectively increases the behaviour that produced it. A child's completed piano lesson earns her a gold star, thus increasing piano practicing; a purchase at a particular shop allows you to obtain a loyalty reward, thus increasing shopping at that location; pushing a lever results in the delivery of a food pellet, thus increasing the frequency of lever pressing. Gold stars, card stamps, food pellets, and words of praise are examples of reinforcers. Up to this point, our discussion has focused on how obtaining these desirable reinforcers can increase responding. There are, however, other ways that the consequences of behaviour can alter the probability of that behaviour being repeated.

Skinner used the term reinforcement to refer to an outcome that *increases* the probability that the response will occur. We can consider two distinct ways that this can happen – *positive and negative reinforcement.*

Positive reinforcement occurs when the *arrival* of a stimulus following a response increases the probability that the response will occur again. This is the kind of scenario we have been discussing so far and in everyday language, we call this *reward training*. A rat presses a lever to receive a food pellet, and placing coins in a vending machine leads to a candy bar. There is, however, another method we might use to increase the probability of a particular behaviour. Consider that there are two ways that a parent might increase the probability of having their child finish his homework each involving a different type of stimulus. Using positive reinforcement, the child is given access to homemade chocolate chip cookies when the homework assignment is complete. In this case, the cookies serve as an **appetitive stimulus**, or something that produces satisfaction when received. Alternately, the parent could allow the child to be excused from his normal dishwashing chores as an incentive for finishing his homework assignment. **Negative reinforcement** occurs when the *removal* of an **aversive stimulus** (i.e., something unpleasant) follows a response and leads to an increase in the probability that the response will occur again. This type of learning is also called *escape* or *avoidance training*. A rat presses a lever in order to avoid being shocked and you open an umbrella to avoid getting wet while outside. In both these examples, the failure to proceed with an instrumental response leads to continued exposure to an aversive stimulus. Importantly, both positive and negative reinforcement increase responding, but do so by different means.

Skinner used the term **punishment** to serve as the opposite of reinforcement. Punishment is an outcome that *decreases* the probability that the response will occur again. Again, there are two distinct ways in which this can happen. **Positive punishment** occurs when the *arrival* of an aversive stimulus follows a response, thus decreasing the likelihood that the response will occur again. This is like the everyday use of the word punishment with which you are familiar. A rat presses a lever and this results in an electric shock, thus decreasing the probability that the rat will press the lever again. You make fun of your boss and this results in you being assigned a particularly unpleasant task, thus decreasing the probability that you will make fun of your boss in the future (as least within earshot). **Negative punishment** occurs when a response leads to the *removal* of an appetitive stimulus, which decreases the probability of that response occurring again. This type of learning is also called *omission training*. A rat's free access to food pellets is terminated if he enters a running wheel and so the rat is less likely to enter it; a parent takes away access to a favorite toy from a child who has pinched his sister and so he is less likely to pinch his sister again; being caught street racing results in the confiscation of your car (and a substantial amount of your money). Again, both positive and negative punishment lead to the same result – the target behaviour is less likely to be produced in future – but do so by different means.

IMMEDIATE AND DELAYED CONSEQUENCES

Reinforcement and punishment are administered most effectively when the consequence immediately follows the target behaviour rather than being delayed. This allows an organism to accurately associate the correct behaviour with the reinforcer. This is especially evident when training animals. When you first get a new cat (let's call him Gilbert) there is probably an adjustment period. There are things he will do that you do not like and there probably are things that you could change, too. One of these "pet" peeves might be climbing up on the kitchen table (his habit, not yours). Reasoning with Gilbert will likely just leave you both walking away frustrated, so you do what any inspired psychology student might do: try a positive punishment procedure. When he jumps onto the table, you give him a quick spray with a water bottle. This method is very effective *if* the arrival of the spray of water immediately follows the undesired behaviour. You can imagine the problem if there is a long delay. If Gilbert has been lounging on the table for several hours before you discover his transgression and spray him, he is far less likely to associate the aversive stimulus with the behaviour of jumping on the table. In fact, he would be more likely to associate getting sprayed with your entering a room, inadvertently teaching him to avoid you rather than the kitchen table.

While having the consequences of behaviour follow quickly generally facilitates instrumental learning, in some circumstances both human and non-human subjects show the ability to respond to reinforcers that may not be immediately delivered. In most employment situations, you are required to wait until your scheduled payday to receive your financial reinforcement (assuming that love of the job is not your primary motivator). Although payday may not always occur at the most convenient times, we accept this practical arrangement rather than demanding to be paid following each bolt we tighten, or each cup of coffee we serve. Similarly, a rat in an operant chamber does not need to be reinforced following every lever press in order to keep pressing. The ability to tolerate **delay of gratification** begins to develop in childhood, and young children who show difficulty tolerating such delays tend to have more difficulty in coping with stress and frustration later as adolescents. In adults, the inability to delay gratification may play an influential role in substance abuse and addiction. In part, the immediately rewarding consequences of drug taking behaviour may overshadow the delayed, and possibly greater, benefits of abstinence.

Box 3.6: Application / Roediger and the Testing Effect

The testing effect refers to the phenomena that learning is better facilitated by testing –forced memory recall- than repeated episodes of studying and reviewing material. Therefore, it seems the best way to learn new concepts i.e. at school, is through lots of testing…even pop quizzes perhaps! However, there is a catch. In order for this effect to really work, test material must have a level of difficulty that allows for relatively high success rates. So if professors make the tests so hard that recall is, on average, nearly impossible, successful learning will not occur. Another important factor to consider is the role of feedback. Receiving full feedback after the completion of tests is extremely important for it allows individuals to realize where they have made mistakes and why, and to learn the correct answers and why they are correct. If students do not know what they have done wrong, how is it expected that any proper learning will occur as a result of taking the class? Roediger and Karpicke suggested that the testing effect results from processes of encoding during studying and testing. When material is studied, the processes used to retrieve the items when attempting to recall is also encoded. This process of retrieval is what is activated during testing, and by testing, individuals have practice accessing the material, something that simply reviewing material cannot offer. The testing effect has obvious benefits for testing in educational systems. As long as tests are fair and the appropriate feedback is given, frequent testing is actually a beneficial, effective way of learning. However, the testing effect is also quite relevant for test preparation. Instead of reading information repeatedly, it is best to continuously test yourself! Either come up with different methods of testing yourself, or get friends and family to help out. Either way, the more practice retrieving the material, the stronger and more long-lasting the learning.

SHAPING AND CHAINING

The simple target behaviours of a typical instrumental conditioning experiment are readily learned – a rat presses a lever for a food pellet and a pigeon pecks a key for a morsel of grain. What about complex or less obvious responses? If you were a trainer at a marine park, how would you train a dolphin named Flipper to gracefully leap out of the water and through a flaming hoop? You could simply hold the hoop above the pool and patiently wait for an opportunity to arrive to reinforce the target behaviour with a fishy treat. However, this strategy may leave you waiting for a very long time.

Skinner developed a method called **shaping by successive approximations** which can be used to train such a complex response. The target behaviour of jumping through a hoop can be broken down into gradual stages of behaviour and reinforced. You can begin by reinforcing Flipper with a fish simply for swimming near the hoop. This is the first approximation toward the final goal. Once this response is established, you now reinforce him only if he pushes his head out of the water. This is the second approximation. Next, you reinforce Flipper only when he extends his torso out of the water. At each stage, there may be natural variations in behaviour, but as the trainer, you can selectively reinforce successive approximations of your choosing. Following these steps will gradually lead to the target behaviour (an amazing jump through a flaming hoop) and a theatre full of dazzled visitors. Even when the target behaviour could otherwise be learned through trial and error, shaping can dramatically reduce acquisition time. Consider how much more quickly a cat in Thorndike's puzzle box could learn to perform the correct response with a little "coaching" using a shaping procedure. A parent teaching a child to properly eat with utensils uses essentially the same technique, as does a tennis coach imparting the secrets of a slice backhand.

Chaining is another procedure used to develop a sequence (chain) of responses to build even more complex behaviours. In chaining, a response is reinforced with the opportunity to perform the next response. For example, a rat is initially trained to press a lever for a food pellet as the last step in a chain of responses. The next challenge for the rat is an overhanging string placed nearby. The rat must pull the string to gain access to the lever. The response of pulling the string is reinforced by the *opportunity* to make the original lever press response that leads to food. Again, note the similarity to the higher-order conditioning procedure described earlier. Step by step, a chain of responses can be built leading to a final sequence of behaviours that can appear to be quite complex.

There are numerous applications of shaping and chaining in clinical and educational settings. For example, in a hospital, a patient suffering from mental illness and limiting his behaviour to mainly sleeping can be encouraged to gradually get of bed, leave his room, and eventually socialize with other patients to gain a more functional living standard.

TABLE 3.8

The use of instrumental conditioning is brought on by a variety of intentions and different methods of reinforcement and punishment can modify behaviour in different ways		
Reinforcers and Punishment	**Consequence Timing**	**Shaping and Chaining**
• **Positive Reinforcement** or **Reward Training** involves the presentation of an appetitive stimulus after the desired behavior is performed that will increase the likelihood of the behavior • **Negative Reinforcement** or **Escape Training** involves the removal of an aversive stimulus to increase desired behavior • **Positive Punishment** involves the presentation of an aversive stimulus in order to decrease undesired behavior • **Negative Punishment** or **Omission Training** involves the removal of an appetitive stimulus in order to decrease undesired behaviour	• The most effective way to ensure associations are formed between behaviours and consequences is to present consequences immediately after • This may not be ideal in real-world settings, but we are often raised to be able to deal with delayed gratification and still learn in response	• **Shaping** by successive approximations is the method used to train organisms to perform complex behaviour by breaking the behaviour into is component parts and reinforcing their acquisition through successive levels of difficulty • **Chaining** involves adding on increasingly complex behavioural requirements to the original requirements in order to receive the original reinforcer

Section 8: Complexities in Reinforcement

The Complex Nature of Reinforcement

There are other important factors to consider when behaviour comes under the control of reinforcement and an individual comes to *expect* a reward for the target behaviour. This is illustrated in experiments that test **contrast effects**, in which changes in the value of a reward lead to shifts in response rate (Flaherty, 1996). Imagine an experiment in which one group of rats is trained to press a lever to receive a sip of a 10% glucose solution (high reward) and another group is trained to press a lever to receive a sip of a 2% glucose solution (low reward). Over the course of acquisition, it is not surprising to observe that the 10% glucose group responds at a higher rate than the 2% glucose group. What would you predict would happen if we suddenly switch the rewards presented to both groups? You might expect that rats moving from a high to low reward would respond even more to make up the difference. However, just the opposite happens. Rats that were used to responding for a high reward then switched to a low reward will now respond at a *slower* rate than the rats receiving exclusively low reward from the beginning – this is a **negative contrast**. However, the rats switched from low to high reward, experience a **positive contrast**, and respond at a *faster* rate than the rats receiving exclusively high rewards from the beginning. How powerful a given reinforcer is, therefore, depends not only on the absolute value of the reinforcer itself, but also on the relative value of that reinforcer compared to other reinforcers that have been experienced.

These reward contrast effects make intuitive sense when you think of its application to humans. Imagine you have a part-time business in which a restaurant paid you $5 for every homemade pie you baked. If the owner of the restaurant suddenly decides to pay you $10 per pie, you may become motivated to bake even more pies and benefit from the extra income. Note that in this case you could actually earn the same amount of money (in absolute terms) every week by baking fewer pies. However, now that the same pie-baking behaviour leads to an even larger reward, the behaviour will likely increase, rather than decrease. If, instead, the restaurant owner changed the rate of pay from $5 to $1 per pie, you may lose motivation and bake very few pies, even though you would actually need to bake five times as many pies to earn the same amount of money. On the other hand, a competing baker, who has been paid $1 per pie all along, will continue to work for this level of reinforcement. As you can see, it is not always the level of reinforcement, but how that reinforcement compares to previous reinforcement, that will determine its motivational value. If a particular response leads to less reinforcement than before, it may be optimal to seek out alternate sources of reinforcement. Interestingly, animals placed in a negative contrast effect condition also show an increase in exploratory behaviours, akin to "shopping around" for a better reinforcement opportunity (Pecorraro et al., 1999).

Another phenomenon called the **overjustification effect** further illustrates the complex nature of reinforcement. In a classic experiment by Lepper and Greene (1978), nursery school children were given the opportunity to draw pictures, an activity that the children found to be enjoyable. Some of the children were then rewarded for making drawings with a "Good Player" certificate. Not surprisingly, the rewarded children spent more time on drawing than another group of children who were not rewarded. However, when the certificates ran out, the previously rewarded children drastically dropped their drawing time to a level below the unrewarded children and chose to pursue other activities instead. The cautionary tale of the overjustification effect is that a newly introduced reward for a previously unrewarded task can alter an individual's perception of that task. A task that was previously regarded as having intrinsic value (an activity pursued because it is, in and of itself, rewarding) now becomes viewed as work with extrinsic value (an activity undertaken only because it leads to reward coming from other sources). Does a student volunteer at a youth center for the pleasure of helping others (intrinsic value) or to build a competitive resume (extrinsic value)? If you were interviewing job candidates, accurately judging how relevant behaviours are being reinforced may help you to make a wise selection. In a broader sense, reward contrast and overjustification effects demonstrate that a reinforcement relationship is more complex than you may initially think. Reward systems that are not planned properly can have unintended negative effects which can be especially important for considerations in educational and applied settings.

SCHEDULES OF REINFORCEMENT

We have discussed several examples of reinforced behaviour in which a reinforcer regularly follows a specific response. In a **continuous reinforcement** (CRF) schedule, the reinforcer follows *every* correct response made by the individual. For example, on a CRF schedule, a pellet of food follows *every* time a rat presses a lever. However, instrumental responses in the real world, and in many lab experiments, are often rewarded on a **partial reinforcement** (PRF) schedule, where the reinforcer follows only some of the responses. Interestingly, partially reinforced behaviours are much more resistant to extinction than continuously reinforced behaviours; that is, partially reinforced subjects, for whom it is not uncommon to have a response go unrewarded on a particular trial, may take far longer to conclude that reinforcement is *never* coming again and modify their behaviour appropriately.

In cases where reinforcement is not continuous, there are two basic methods for determining when reinforcement will be delivered. *Ratio* schedules are based on the number of responses made. Although not every response is reinforced, the more responses that are made, the more reinforcements will be obtained. *Interval* schedules, on the other hand, are based not on the number of responses made, but on time elapsed since the last reinforcer was delivered. The critical factor here is not *how often* a response is made, but rather *when* a response is made.

Both ratio and interval schedules may be implemented in either a *fixed* or *variable* manner. In a fixed schedule, the number of responses required, or the time that must pass before reinforcement is available, is always the same. In a variable schedule, the number of responses (for a ratio schedule), or the interval of time (for an interval schedule) before a reinforcer is delivered varies randomly within some range around a set mean. As well, variable schedules are more resistant to extinction than fixed schedules since, like with partial reinforcement, individuals are less likely to have expectations about when reinforcement is coming thus it takes longer to realize reinforcement is never coming again. If we consider both factors, (ratio vs. interval and fixed vs. variable) we can define four different schedules of partial reinforcement, and these different schedules affect the resulting pattern of behaviour in dramatic ways.

In a **Fixed Ratio (FR) schedule**, reinforcement follows after a fixed number of responses. For example, on a FR-5 schedule, a rat is reinforced after completing 5 lever presses. Note that a continuous reinforcement would be considered an FR-1 schedule, where every response is reinforced. Because reinforcement is based on the number of responses, producing those responses quickly will cause the reinforcer to be delivered sooner. Following reinforcement, there is often a period, called a **post-reinforcement pause**, during which the organism momentarily stops responding before starting up again. This leads to an overall pattern of responding where periods of high response rates alternate with periods of no responding. As you might imagine, there are practical limits on the number of responses required to obtain a single reinforcer. A rat might press a lever 5, 10 or even 50 times to obtain a single food pellet, but as the number of responses required increases the post-reinforcement pause tends to get longer. This phenomenon is known as **ratio strain**, and if the required responses continue to increase the organism will eventually reach **break point** and stop responding completely.

In a **Variable Ratio (VR) schedule**, reinforcement follows after a variable number of responses have been completed. The average number of responses required characterizes a particular VR schedule. For example, on a VR-5 schedule, a rat is reinforced, on average, after 5 responses have been completed. However, unlike a FR-5 schedule, the actual number of responses that are required from trial to trial can be different. And so, over the first 20 responses completed, reinforcement may follow after response 4, 7, 11, and 19. In total, 4 reinforcements have been delivered over 20 trials, for an average of 5 completed responses required per reinforcement. VR schedules produce high, steady rates of responding without the post-reinforcement pauses seen in FR schedules. This makes sense when you consider the difference in reinforcer predictability between FR and VR schedules. If an FR schedule is in effect, the subject can learn the precise number of responses required and produce those responses whenever reinforcement is desired. If a VR schedule is in effect, and the response requirement changes from trial to trial, pausing after reinforcement would make less sense, as the requirement for the next reinforcer could be relatively high (so it would not be in the subject's best interest to waste any time).

In a **Fixed Interval (FI) schedule**, the first correct response that occurs after a fixed interval of time is reinforced. For example, on a FI-1 min schedule, a rat is reinforced for the first lever press that occurs at least 1 minute after the last reinforcement was delivered. Note that the subject is free to respond at any time, but these responses will have no effect until the interval has passed. Like FR schedules, FI schedules create a characteristic pattern of responding, called an **FI Scallop**. Responses are typically produced at a low rate early in the interval, with the response rate gradually increasing over the interval. Following reinforcement, the same gradually increasing rate of responding is repeated. This pattern of responding is often observed in the study habits of students following a FI schedule of assessments. In a course with scheduled tests every 3 weeks, a typical observation is that very little studying occurs immediately following a test, but gradually increases leading to a peak of cramming just before the next regularly scheduled test approaches.

In a **Variable Interval (VI) schedule**, reinforcement follows the first correct response to occur after a variable interval of time has passed. For example, on a VI-5 min schedule, a rat is reinforced for the first lever press that occurs after an average interval of 5 minutes. However, the actual amount of time that must elapse before reinforcement is available will vary from trial to trial. And so, over a 30 minute session, a rat can earn up to 6 reinforcers, but may receive them following responses that occur after 3, 4, 9, 15 22, and 30 minutes. Again, the unpredictable availability of reinforcement results in a steadier rate of responding in VI schedules, as compared to FI schedules. This suggests that quizzes delivered randomly over a semester will lead to steadier rates of studying than will quizzes at regularly scheduled intervals. The same principle makes random drug testing of athletes more effective than regularly scheduled testing in promoting drug-free training behaviour.

Box 3.7: Application | Phone Checking Behaviour

In our modern technological age, cell phone use has become an integrated, normal part of everyday behaviour and communication. However, becoming heavily reliant on cell phones has also left us somewhat obsessed with the next message, update or call we're going to get and what often results is compulsive checking behaviours. As I am sure many of us know we feel the constant need to check our cell phones for any sort of update or bit of communication that keeps us in tune with the greater social network we are a part of. Why does this happen though? It is not simply an obsession with technology and keeping in touch with the world; mechanisms of learning, operant conditioning in particular, play a large role. Receiving messages is based on a variable interval schedule of reinforcement. The first thing to note is that this is a partial schedule of reinforcement, meaning there is a high resistance towards extinction: we don't necessarily get constant messages so when there is a period of time without messages, we don't think that we're never going to get a message again. As well, because the reinforcement is unpredictable it encourages a steady rate of responding. We don't always know when messages are going to come, so we constantly check our phones in hopes that one will be there. Thus what results is a form of operant conditioning where the behaviour elicited is the constant checking of the phone in hopes of the reward of receiving the message. Whether cell phone companies realize this or not, the abundance of cell phone use has led to this conditioning that works to their benefit through obsession and dependency of cell phone use.

Observational Learning

In both classical and instrumental conditioning, learning occurs as a result of direct experience; subjects must actually experience the US or the reinforcer/punisher in order for behaviour to be modified. Keeping in mind the distinction discussed earlier between learning and performance, we have already seen that learning may remain latent until the subject is put in a context where this learning is relevant. This latent learning is still based on the subject's own direct experience, it is just the case that this experience will not be reflected in performance until the subject is in the appropriate context. In many cases, however, we can see instances where an individual learns by observing the experience of others. Depending on what we observe, we may imitate or avoid behaviours based on the consequences we have observed when others performed those behaviours. We all find ourselves in unfamiliar situations from time to time, where we are not sure what behaviours are expected or appropriate. In such situations, it is often the case that we will look to the behaviour of others, and its consequences, to determine our course of action. Having spent some time in airports, I have observed that when there is a vacancy in first class, and one lucky passenger will be selected for a free upgrade, this lucky person is always someone who is nicely dressed, and never the guy in sweatpants and a baseball cap. Luckily, this has happened to me once and now I always dress nicely when travelling by air, just in case.

The first experimental demonstrations of observational learning were conducted in the 1960s by Albert Bandura and colleagues (e.g., Bandura & Walters, 1963). Bandura was investigating the extent to which children learned to behave aggressively as a result of observing aggressive behaviour in others, a phenomenon that continues to inspire much research and debate today. These studies used an inflatable figure called a Bobo Doll – a one meter tall figure with a small weight in the bottom which caused it to stand itself up again when knocked over. In these classic experiments, children were placed in a room containing several toys, including a 'Bobo Doll'. Prior to being placed in this room, some children viewed a short movie clip showing an adult kicking or punching the doll. When these children entered the room with the toys, they showed a strong tendency to immediately begin attacking the doll, often displaying behaviour that was even more aggressive than what they had observed in the movie clip. Other children, who had not observed the example of adult aggressive behaviour, were much less likely to display this type of behaviour when given the same opportunity to play with the toys. Clearly the children were modeling their aggressive behaviour on what they had observed others doing; they had learned by observation to direct aggressive behaviour at a particular target.

Bandura's work on the observational learning of aggressive behaviour directly addressed an issue that continues to be of concern today, which is the relationship between viewing violence in media (particularly on television and in video games) and aggressive behaviour in children. It is undoubtedly true that many children who watch television or play popular video games are exposed to numerous depictions of violent aggressive behaviour, and in the context of these shows and games such behaviour often leads to desirable results (e.g., you will not get very far in many popular video games, such as the Grand Theft Auto series, by taking a non-violent approach). Given the results of Bandura's pioneering work, it is understandable that many parents and authorities are concerned that exposure to such media will teach their children to behave aggressively in real-life situations. Other research suggests that the average North American child spends as much time viewing or engaging with entertainment media each week as the typical working adult spends at their job - about 40 hours (Bushman & Anderson, 2001). Furthermore, children (and adults, for that matter) who are exposed to more aggressive behaviour in the media appear to display more aggressive behaviour and have more aggressive thoughts (Anderson et al, 2003; Anderson, 2004).

A more recent discovery, with major implications for the importance of observational learning, was the identification of cells in the brain known as **mirror neurons**. The structure and function of neurons will be discussed in much detail in Chapter X, but for now, just note that neurons are the 'brain cells' that appear to do most of the information processing in the nervous system. A mirror neuron is a cell that responds in the same way when performing an action as it does when the animal possessing that cell observes someone else perform the action or even imagines performing the action. In other words, if these cells are activated when you reach for an object sitting in front of you, they will also be activated by watching someone else reach for an object or even by just visualizing the act of reaching for an object. These findings have led many researchers to conclude that these mirror neurons are involved in the *internal representation* of actions. As such, they would play a central role in the process of observational learning by allowing us to form mental representations of actions we have observed, and to subsequently reproduce those actions. Incidentally, mirror neurons are thought to play essential roles in speech communication – both for children learning how to talk, but also for ensuring that what is said by the talker, and what is heard by the listener, share a common representation. You say 'cup' and I hear 'cup' and they are, in terms of what the sound represents, the same word.

SECTION 8 REVIEW: Complexities in Reinforcement

TABLE 3.9

The reinforcement of behaviour through Instrumental Conditioning is marked by a number of complexities and factors that when manipulated slightly, can change the behaviour of individuals in different ways		
Indications of Complexity	**Schedules of Reinforcement**	**Observational Learning**
• **Contrast effects** are changes in response rates as a result of changes in reward values • **Negative Contrast** – lowering of reward value • **Positive Contrast** – increasing reward value • The **Overjustification Effect** displays how changes in reinforcement i.e. presentation of rewards for behaviours already naturally performed, alter the perception of the behaviour by increasing it	• **Continuous Reinforcement:** reinforcers for all correct responses • **Partial Reinforcement:** reinforcers for a portion of correct responses • **Fixed Ratio Schedule:** reinforcement after a set number of responses • **Variable Ratio Schedule:** reinforcement after random number of responses • **Fixed Interval Schedule:** reinforcement after a fixed period of time • **Variable Interval Schedule:** reinforcement after a random period of time	• Associative learning involves direct experience and often leads to imitation or avoidance behaviours when appropriate, especially in unfamiliar situations • Understanding learning in such ways has applications for behavioural issues as well as understanding the neurological basis of imitation

Draft

Final Thoughts on Learning

Beginning with the initial studies of Pavlov, Thorndike and Bandura, learning theorists have pointed out important ways in which classical conditioning, instrumental conditioning, and observational learning are different. Whereas classical conditioning involves elicited behaviour triggered by a stimulus, instrumental conditioning involves voluntary behaviours emitted by the organism, and observational learning need not involve any immediate change in behaviour. Furthermore, classical conditioning involves learning the relation between stimuli (the CS and US), whereas instrumental conditioning and observational learning involve learning the relation between a behaviour and its consequence. In some ways these assigned categories may be artificial distinctions and some learning theorists have suggested that the same underlying mechanisms may be responsible for all forms of learning. At the very least, we can observe that classical and instrumental conditioning work together in learning situations in the real world. For example, as a graduate student (in a learning lab), one of the chapter authors had a colleague who introduced him to the world of pungent French cheeses. One day, the author had the unfortunate experience of food poisoning following the consumption of a special type of cheese called Petite Muenster, which has a characteristically strong odor. This single trial has had long-lasting effects. To this day, the pungent odor is a CS that automatically triggers a CR of queasiness. The odor also plays another role, acting as a discriminative stimulus for the author to plug his nose (an instrumental response), which is reinforced by the desirable consequence of reducing the inflow of the offending odor (negative reinforcement). This incident impressed upon him the complexity and adaptive benefits of learning. More importantly, it taught him to beware of smiling French researchers bearing gifts of cheese.

4

Chapter 4: Attention and Memory

Introduction

> How did President George W. Bush first hear the news of airplanes flying into the World Trade Center towers on Sept 11, 2001? Bush's public recollections were documented by news agencies. On one occasion, Bush recalls being informed by senior adviser Karl Rove before later conferring with Chief of Staff Andy Card. One two other occasions, Bush recalls seeing the first plane hit the tower on live television as he entered a Florida classroom. However, at the hour of his Florida event, there was no video footage available of the first plane crashing into the building. How could Bush be so wrong about the details of such a significant event?

Think about the sights, sounds, smells and details of events that compete for your attention as you experience the world. Now, try to recall a vivid memory that can place you at a significant moment in history. I can clearly recall exactly where I was and what I was doing when I first heard the news that Princess Diana had died in a tragic car accident. I was watching late-night TV with two friends when a news report appeared making the announcement. For the next several weeks, the news media extensively covered the story. My recollection includes attention to many fine details: there were three of us there; we complained about the humid weather; we each wore the same uniformed shirts from work (I was working as an instructor at a summer camp at the time) and we ordered pizza with anchovies. These vivid experiences are described as **flashbulb memories,** which have a 'live' quality feeling almost as if a person is looking at a photograph of a moment locked in time (Brown and Kulik, 1977). Years later, I saw an actual photo taken from that evening and I was very surprised to learn that I was completely wrong about at least one detail. Although the three of us worked together over the summer and often met after work, in the photo, we were wearing our regular clothes. This makes sense, because the summer program had ended the week before. Without seeing the photo, I would have found it difficult to believe that I could be so wrong about a detail that seemed so vivid in my memory.

The arousal and emotional experience of flashbulb memories illustrate the strong interplay between attention and memory – we remember what we pay attention to and our attention is shaped by what we remember. In this chapter, as you consider the mechanisms of attention and memory, keep in mind the intimate connection between these cognitive processes which determine how we experience and remember the world around us.

Section 1: Introduction to Attention

Just before making an announcement, your instructor asks the class "May I have everybody's attention?" and you know exactly what she is asking of you. If your friend later remarks, "I wasn't paying attention in class, what did she say?" you would have a good idea of whether his mental resources were directed toward the announcement or the competing demands of his cell phone. More than a century ago, in his classic textbook *Principles of Psychology*, William James commented on the obviousness of attention: "Everyone knows what attention is. It is the taking possession by the mind, in clear and vivid form, of one out of what seem several simultaneously possible objects or trains of thought."

Try putting this description to the test by reading the following message written in **bold** while ignoring the other words in the passage:

Among *hidden on a* **the** *empty beach* **most** *near the* **important** *ocean,* *a* **cognitive** *pirate* **abilities** *from old* **is** *has* **the** *concealed* **ability** *a box* **to** *of treasure* **select** *won in a* **signal** *fierce* **from** *battle* **noise.** **You** *Incidentally* **do** *Jen and Molly should* **this** *stop reading* **by** *the* **focusing** *bold type face* **attention** *found* **on** *in* **certain** *this* **cues** *passage* **such** *and* **as** *then* **type** *continue.* **style.** *Rumor* **When** *has we it* **focus** *that 300 our paces* **attention** *due* **on** *west* **certain** *from* **stimuli** *tribal* **the** *council* **message** *and in* **then** **other** *200* **stimuli** *paces* **is** *due* **not** *north* *X marks* **clearly** *the spot.* **identified.** *Apparently* **However** *enough* **some** *gold* **information** *can* **from** *be* **the** *had* **unattended** *to* **source** *purchase* **may** *the* **be** *very* **detected** *island!*

It would be impossible (and a completely overwhelming experience) to process all of the sensory stimulation in the environment competing for the limited capacity of your attention. In the exercise above, you probably had little difficulty in following the message written in bold face, which demonstrates your ability to selectively process incoming information. This ability comes in handy living in a digital world of information overload with many stimuli competing for your attention. On my drive to work, I often change the radio station to avoid advertisements I dislike while trying to maintain focus on the cars in my lane and the traffic signals ahead. Part of the challenge of my daily commute is to sift through the noise to select important messages for preferential processing. The same need for selective processing was also present for humans living in the context of a hunter-gatherer society. Hunters needed to focus on relevant visual, olfactory, and auditory stimuli that directed them to the their prize. Gatherers need to carefully analyze the details of a potential patch that would yield fruits, nuts and roots. At the same time, both groups also had to be wary of distant sounds and cues that could indicate predators and enemies lurking in the background. To achieve all of these ancient and modern goals, we rely on the cognitive process of attention.

Psychologists are interested in understanding how attention shapes our perception and memory and how attentional processes are guided by two competing needs of:

1. Focusing limited mental resources on the immediate task.

2. Monitoring ongoing stimuli to evaluate their potential significance and shifting the allocation of mental resources when necessary.

In the example, your task was to focus on reading the words in bold type to reveal a message. At the same time, you still processed some of the words and context of the rest of the passage as part of your normal monitoring process. If your name happens to be "Jen" or "Molly", you may *also* have been especially drawn to the fourth line of the passage, which contains information of personal significance:

Jen and Molly should **this** *stop reading* **by** *the* **focusing** *bold type face* **attention**

Psychologists have developed many tools to bring the study of attention into the controlled setting of the lab. We will consider these tools next.

Section 2: Tools to Measure Attention

The Cocktail Party Effect

It's a bustling Saturday morning at your local coffee shop. While waiting for your free-trade organic coffee, you and a friend are engaged in a deep philosophical conversation about the meaning of William James' description of attention. You suddenly realize that you are a living example in action: despite the many other conversations taking place at the same time and in close proximity, you can effortlessly follow your friend's voice while "turning down the noise" of the background din. When your name is called, you can instantly pick out this important bit of information and pick up your order. This scenario is commonly referred to as the **cocktail party effect** – despite competing background noises, a listener can focus on a single channel and still pick out relevant salient information from the background.

The first way that the cocktail party effect was simulated in a laboratory was using what is now called the **dichotic listening paradigm** (Broadbent). In this paradigm, headphones are worn so that one message can be presented to one ear and a different message can be presented to the other ear. The participant is instructed to "shadow" or immediately repeat the messages in the attended ear. As in coffee shop scenario, the attended message is shadowed effortlessly without interference from the message sent to the unattended ear. The words of the attended message are easily and accurately repeated even if they are about a difficult topic. Furthermore, attention can be switched between ears at random or periodic intervals demonstrating flexible control over attention. As you might have guessed, the semantic content of the message sent to the attended ear is well remembered. Although semantic content is vague, some information *is* still processed in the unattended ear. For example, subjects can report the physical features such as pitch and tone of the voice in the message presented to the unattended ear.

The results of the dichotic listening task illustrate that attention and memory are inextricably linked. Items that are selected for attention are better perceived and later remembered than are items that are not attended. However, consider that the dichotic listening paradigm simplifies the problem of the cocktail party effect so that it can be effectively studied in the controlled setting of the lab. Only two messages are typically presented (the attended and unattended message) whereas in the real world, there could be many simultaneously messages competing for attention. Furthermore, in the dichotic listening paradigm the experimenter specifies the to-be-attended item whereas in the real world, selection is not so prescribed.

Bottom-up and Top-down processing

How do we select items to attend to from so many to choices in the environment and construct meaning from the noise? Attention researchers have described a two-way flow of information: raw data is gathered through the senses (bottom-up processing), which dynamically interacts with information already stored in memory (top-down processing).

Bottom-up processing refers to a stimulus-driven mechanism in which attention is captured by salient change in the environment. For example, while enjoying a quiet dinner at a restaurant, you gently rock back and forth on your chair but tragically go a bit too far – you and your chair fall backwards and hit the floor with a dramatic thump. Even though there are many interesting sights, sounds and smells happening all over the restaurant, for the moment, it's safe to say that the crash instantly captures the attention of your date (along with everyone else in the restaurant)[1]. Similarly, bottom-up processing automatically captures your attention to alert you to a police siren, telephone ring, fire alarm, or (perhaps less dramatically) your name being called.

Attention can also be purposely directed through **top-down processing**. That is, instead of a reflexive reaction, you can strategically direct your attention to match your current goals and expectations from past experience through memory. For example, out of habit, I usually put my keys on the front desk when I return home. This helps me in the morning when I am usually in a rush to get out the door. As I think about my keys, I do not have to begin a systematic scan of the entire entrance hall. Rather, I can purposely direct my search to the front desk because that is where my keys can usually be found.

In the lab, we can directly observe how goals shape attending strategies by monitoring where a subject looks by using eye-tracking technology. For example, Yarbus (1967, and more recently DeAngelus & Pelz in 2009) monitored the eye movements of a participant as he answered questions about a painting. When asked to give the ages of the people in the painting, the participant looked mostly at the faces. When asked to estimate the financial circumstances of the family, the participant looked more at the clothing and furniture. When asked to remember the positions of people and objects in the room, the participant scanned all items in the painting equally. In other words, the participant changed their scanning behavior depending on the current task. Prior knowledge about the environment helps us to efficiently find information pertinent to our goal. Note that the *controlled* nature of top-down processing in directing attention contrasts with the *automatic* nature of bottom-up processing in the capture of attention.

Orienting and the Spatial Cueing Paradigm

The act by which attention moves across a scene is known as **orienting**. Posner's spatial cueing paradigm (Posner, 1980) is a classic psychological task for measuring orienting. This task allows the experimenter to measure shifts in attention in the absence of eye movements. It may seem strange that attention can move in the absence of eye or head movements because most of the time you look directly where you are attending. For example, in the previous case of the embarrassing chair incident at the restaurant, attention was automatically directed to the location of the accident, and this was accompanied by the

---

[1] This has actually happened to me on at least two documented occasions.

movement of every set of eyes in the restaurant to see the source of the commotion. **Overt attending** is obvious because where you are attending is also where you are looking.

However, you can also attend to things without looking. This is called **covert orienting**, which reflects "invisible" shifts of attention. For example, as you wait for your friend Waldo who is running late, your gaze may be politely focused on Wayne who is in conversation with you, but your attention covertly shifts toward the door in anticipation of Waldo's arrival. This improves the speed with which you will notice Waldo when he finally arrives. We can formally measure covert orienting in the lab using Posner's spatial cueing paradigm. Covert shifts in attention are reflected in the efficiency with which targets are detected at cued locations. In a typical experiment, you stare at a centrally presented fixation cross that is flanked by two boxes. The brightening of one of the two side boxes acts to cue your attention. After a brief period (less than 300 milliseconds) following this cue, the target is presented. The general finding is that you will be faster to detect the target if it was presented in the cued box than if it was presented in the uncued box. Interestingly, the time between the cue and target presentation (less than 300 milliseconds) is too brief for eye movement to occur! This indicates a shift in attention that is independent of eye movement.

Another interesting wrinkle is that if the time between the onset of the cue and the target is *more* than about 300 milliseconds (which allows you sufficient time to direct an eye gaze), you are actually *slower* to detect to the target at cued locations than at uncued locations! This is known as **inhibition of return** (IOR; initially demonstrated by Posner & Cohen, 1984; later reviewed by Klein, 2000). IOR occurs when you attempt to redirect to a previously attended location at which the target was not found. For example, imagine you are now searching for your friend Waldo who is lost in a large crowd. You know that Waldo will be wearing his lucky red hat and so you scan the crowd for red items. As a red blur catches the bottom right of your visual field, you turn to look but quickly realize it is not Waldo, but rather a red fire hydrant. As you continue searching, IOR tends to prevent your gaze (and attention) from revisiting the location of the fire hydrant. In turn, this promotes orienting towards new and previously unsearched locations, which should result in a more efficient search. Of course, that is so long as your friend Waldo is not now standing by that very same red fire hydrant.

Exogenous versus Endogenous cueing

So far I have described Posner's spatial cueing paradigm with peripheral cues – i.e., the sudden brightening (or dimming) of one of the boxes flanking the center of a computer screen. This is an example of an **exogenous cue** that physically orients you to a specific peripheral location. However, attention can also be oriented in response to centrally presented **endogenous or symbolic cues**. Imagine that, instead of having a peripheral box to the left or right light up (as would be the case for a typical *exogenous* cue), in the *center* of the screen is an arrow pointing to the left or right (or, alternately, the eyes of a face looking to the left or right, or even the word LEFT or RIGHT). Unlike exogenous cues, endogenous cues require interpretation. From experience you have learned that an arrow pointing to the left means attend to the left of the arrow (not the arrow itself). A major difference between these two cue types is that endogenous cues can be ignored if they conflict with task demands, suggesting they are under volitional control; in contrast, exogenous cues seem to automatically capture attention (Jonides, 1981; see also Friesen, Ristic, & Kingstone, 2004). In this way, top-down processing may be better suited to the handling endogenous cues, whereas bottom-up processing may be better suited to handling exogenous cues.

SECTION 1 REVIEW: Introduction to Attention

TABLE 4.1

Attention is defined by the ability to selectively focus, consciously or unconsciously, on relevant stimuli in our environment in order to navigate successfully and economically through daily experiences		
Cocktail Party Effect	**Bottom Up & Top Down**	**Cuing**
• When engaged in a certain task our attention is still able to attend to relevant stimuli, such as our name being called, from the background of our focus • This effect is demonstrated with the **dichotic listening task,** where semantic information from unattended channels are remembered in addition to information from attended channels	• A two-way flow of information guides our attentional selection • **Bottom Up**: attention is guided by salient stimuli or environmental changes; automatic • **Top Down**: attention is guided by conscious directed in order to fulfill a goal or meet memory expectations; controlled	• **Spatial Cuing Paradigm**: measures the movement of attention across a scene and factors involved • **Overt Attending**: the direction of attention is made clear through eye movements • **Covert Attending**: direction of attention not guided by eye movements but can be measured by spatial cuing where cues lead to faster target detection in periods too short for eye movement • **Exogenous cues**: allow attention to be physically and automatically oriented • **Endogenous cues**: allow attention to be consciously directed by interpretation of cue information

Section 3: Further Measures of Attention

VISUAL SEARCH PARADIGM

Although research questions can be studied in the controlled conditions of a lab, cognitive psychologists are ultimately interested in understanding how attention works in the real world. The challenge in real environments is to sift through an abundance of information to find what you are specifically looking for. Imagine that you are searching for your friend Waldo in a crowd again. This time, you know that he is not wearing his lucky red hat (which was lost in a freak laundry accident). In fact, you don't know what he will be wearing. How do you find him?

The visual search paradigm has been used to model how we search for items in our environment. In a typical experiment, the task is to locate a target item among a set of distracter items on a computer monitor display. For example, you may be asked to find a red circle (target) among a set of blue circles (distracters). The total number of items on the display, or **set size**, can vary from trial to trial. Your task it respond as quickly as possible as to whether you think the target is present or not. Performance is measured by response time as a function of set size.

POP-OUT EFFECT

In the example of searching for a red circle among blue circles, the color red uniquely marks the target in its present context (among an array of blue). Consequently, the target seems to "**pop out**" of the display. The pop-out effect reflects bottom-up capture of attention driven by the salience of the physical properties of the target (in this case, a unique colour). When a target "pops out", the time it takes to respond to it is *independent* of set size such that processing of the whole set of items seems to happen simultaneously (or in parallel).

CONJUNCTIVE SEARCH

Sometimes the target is not the most salient item in the scene, as might be the case when you are searching for your average-looking friend in a crowd of average-looking people. We can recreate this condition in the laboratory using the same visual search paradigm but adjusting the similarity between the target and distracters. Instead of searching for a red circle among blue circles, imagine that you are asked to search for a red circle among a set of blue circles and red squares. This becomes a much more difficult task; you cannot simply rely on a single unique feature of the target to distinguish it from the distracters. Instead, you need to search for two distinct features that characterize the target (the red circle). This type of search is called **conjunctive search** because you are searching for a target defined by a combination of features. Not surprisingly, for conjunctive searches, response time increases with set size such that there is a cost to processing each additional distracter. When the target is absent, you effectively have to inspect every item, one after another, only stopping when the target is found or when you have checked every item.

CONTEXTUAL CUEING

Fortunately, in most real world situations, objects rarely occur in isolation – they are typically found in rich structural environments. For example, we can reasonably expect to find the toaster in the kitchen and not in the bathroom. When you are in the kitchen, your search for the toaster can be focused on the counter and not the floor. Through experience and accumulation of knowledge, a **schema** can guide your search – a representation depicting the range of plausible objects and likely configuration of those objects within particular scenes. We can use these invariant structural properties of the visual environment to guide our attention, allowing for very efficient searches of highly familiar environments.

This important role of context can be observed experimentally using the contextual cueing paradigm (Chun & Jiag, 1998). This paradigm is similar to the typical visual search paradigm.

In this task, you would search for a "T" amid a background display of randomly oriented "Ls" of different colours (that's a sample stimulus, at right). The distracter display repeats over trials, although the location and orientation of the "T" target changes every time. Interestingly, you would find the target "T" more and more quickly, over successive trials with the same distracter display, compared to your search time for a new display that you've not seen before. This is because your memory for the global spatial configuration of the old display provides a helpful context to guide your search for the target.

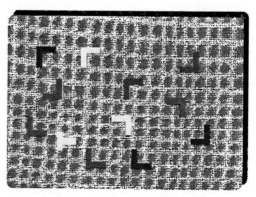

Interestingly, although participants are faster at identifying the target in the unaltered old displays, they are unaware that these displays have been repeated! This suggests an **implicit** memory mechanism.

WHAT IS THE FATE OF UNATTENDED ITEMS?

So far we have been discussing the benefits of selective attention. Overall, attended items are better remembered than unattended items. Moreover, our memory for unattended items can be vague, containing only some details about the physical characteristics but nothing of the meaning. Does this imply that the meaning of the unattended message was unprocessed? Not necessarily. In fact, MacKay (1973) demonstrated that we process the meaning of unattended words, although we may not have an explicit memory of doing so. MacKay used the typical dichotic listening paradigm but presented an ambiguous message to the attended ear. For example: "They threw stones at the bank yesterday", where "bank" could mean the side of a river or a savings and loan association. Participants were asked to shadow this message by writing it word for word without delay or mistakes. Meanwhile, the message presented to the unattended ear contained either the word "River" or "Money". Subsequently, participants were asked which sentence was closest in meaning to the sentences they shadowed: "They threw stones at the side of the river yesterday" or "They threw stones at the savings and loan association yesterday". If participants had heard the word "River" in the unattended ear they were more likely to pick the sentence about the river, whereas participants that heard the word "Money" in the unattended ear were more likely to pick the sentence about the financial association. Interestingly, participants reported no **explicit memory** for unattended message content. This illustrates that word meaning may be processed **pre-attentively** or before attention is selectively committed.

Another example in which meaning seems to be processed pre-attentively is when the unattended message contains your own name. In the cocktail party effect, I noted that you can selectively follow a single conversation against a backdrop of competing voices and sounds, yet still pick out salient information from the noise, as in the case when you suddenly hear your name in a conversation from another group. This might prompt you to direct your attention to this suddenly very interesting new conversation to hear what is being said about you! When assessed scientifically using the dichotic listening paradigm, participants often detect their name presented in the unattended messages (Moray, 1985; Wood & Cohen, 1995). Some researchers have proposed that certain stimuli such as your own name are special in their ability to automatically capture your attention irrespective of the current goal.

INATTENTIONAL BLINDNESS

The phenomenon of **inattentional blindness** demonstrates that our limited attentional processes can be susceptible to missing out on some very important and salient things. A car driver may be forced to swerve to miss a cyclist that suddenly appears from. In a striking experimental demonstration, Simons and Chabris (1999) used a selective looking paradigm where participants are asked to focus on one aspect of a video portraying multiple things. This is essentially the visual analog to the investigation of the cocktail party effect using the dichotic listening paradigm. In Simons and Chabris' experiment, the particular video consisted of six basketball players, three dressed in white shirts and three dressed in black shirts. Each team had a basketball that they passed back and forth. The players were arranged in a circle, alternating by team, so their passes overlapped in space. The task of the participant was to count the number of times the team dressed in white passed the basketball. As expected, participants were quite good at counting the number of passes the made in the target team without being distracted by the number of passes made by the distracter team. However, about half of the participants failed to see the black gorilla that walked through the center of the circle in the middle of the game. When shown the video later, participants were often shocked and some exclaimed, "I missed *that*!"

CHANGE BLINDNESS

Even when you are looking for a change you might not see it. When looking for your keys, you may fail to notice them on the desk even though they're right in front of you. In the laboratory, we can test factors that prevent people from detecting change using the **change blindness paradigm** (Rensink, O'Regan & Clark, 1997). In a typical experiment, two visual scenes are repeatedly presented in quick succession with an intervening blank screen. The task of the participant is to correctly identify the change between the original scene and its modified form – this may be a single addition, deletion, color change or location change of an object in the image. The intervening blank screen causes "flickering" as the display changes from one image to the other. It takes a surprisingly long time to identify the changing part of the image especially if it is in a peripheral part of the scene (like the presence or absence of a cloud).

We are faster at detecting the change if we know which part of the image is changing. This demonstrates the benefit of top-down directed attention. We are also faster at detecting the change if the intervening blank scene is removed. In this case, we can benefit from bottom-up capture of attention. With the blank scene intervening, everything seems to change between flickers since the scenes are completely different from the blank screen. However, when the blank screen is removed, the single change in the modified scene becomes more obvious and captures attention. The change blindness paradigm illustrates the important role of attention in perceiving change.

Box 4.1: Attention / Keeping the Focus

A phenomena that I'm sure we are all very familiar with is mind wandering – whether in class, while doing our homework, or listening to our parents lecture us. If you have not noticed, we tend to drift off without even being aware of it, and though it might be kind of relaxing, it can also have somewhat negative consequences. If, for example, when trying to study, our minds wander, it is almost impossible to get anything done and perform well, especially if the material is quite…boring. How can we prevent this? How can we transform studying into a process that captures our attention, maximizes processing of material and increases the likelihood of success when tested? In order to ensure that material catches the focus of attention, we need to rework it, make it novel and exciting, draw pictures or write bizarre stories that incorporate the material and make it more interesting and engaging. In addition, it is also a good idea to rework material in a way that is more self-relevant. Mechanisms of mind wandering explore how personally relevant information is more likely to capture attention, even automatically, than other types of information. So the next time you're studying, for example, a bunch of terms and concepts, try to use them to tell a funny story that somehow relates to an experience you've had, and it's likely that your mind won't wander so much anymore!

STROOP TASK: WHICH ACTIONS REQUIRE ATTENTION AND WHICH DO NOT?

So far, you have learned that attention is needed to search for specific things in a complicated scene, to listen to one speaker while ignoring others, and to follow the actions of one group while ignoring similar actions of another group. These are all fairly complex actions and at this point you may be wondering whether attention is required for all complex processes. Interestingly, not all complex things we do require our attention. Remember back to when you were first learning to drive a car. Remember how difficult it was to apply the right amount of pressure to the brake and gas pedals. Perhaps you awkwardly inched the car by moving from stop to fast while your driver instructor held on (for dear life) to the dashboard. Now after years of driving experience, you accelerate and stop smoothly, effortlessly and without much thought. Practice has made you (near) perfect. Practice has also helped to automate complex actions so they can be executed with little attention.

Another classic example of an automation in a complex process is word reading. Because you have a lifetime of practice reading words, it is easy to forget that this was once a challenge for you. In fact, word reading is so automatic that you can't help but do it, even if it makes the task you're supposed to be doing more difficult (i.e., it can override your explicit goal-directed processes). In the **Stroop paradigm** (Stroop (1935), the text of color words are presented in colored ink. The color word may or may not match the ink color it is printed with. Trials in which the word matches the ink are called *congruent,* for example the word "red" printed in red ink. Trials in which the word does not match the ink are called *incongruent,* for example the word "red" printed in green ink. If the participant is asked to read the color word, she does so swiftly regardless of the colored ink. In contrast, if the participant is asked to name the colored ink, she is significantly slower and more error-prone if the colored ink does not match the color word (incongruent) than if it does match (congruent). This type of error tends to result from automatically reading the word rather than naming the ink color like they were instructed to do. The automatic process of word reading is said to have *interfered* with the ability to name the colored ink when the word and ink color are incongruent. Since its first use, the Stroop paradigm has become one of the primary tools in attention research (MacLeod, 1991).

We can learn to exert some control over automatic processes like word reading. Consider naming ink color in the Stroop paradigm but with an uneven proportion of congruent and incongruent trials (Logan & Zbrodoff, 1979; Lowe & Mitterer, 1982). In a situation of mostly congruent trials (~ 75%), your best strategy is to go with automatic word reading since this will usually give you the correct response. In turn, your performance really suffers for the few incongruent trials, resulting in a big difference between congruent (fast) and incongruent (slower).

In contrast, in a situation of mostly incongruent trials (~ 75%), your best strategy is to not go with automatic word reading since this will usually give you the incorrect response. Indeed, you seem to suppress your automatic tendency to read the word; your performance does not suffer as much for incongruent trials and this reduces the difference between congruent and incongruent trials. In other words, there is overall less interference from word reading on incongruent trials, suggesting that you've demonstrated some control over this automatic process.

SECTION 3 REVIEW: Further Measures of Attention

TABLE 4.2

<table>
<tr>
<td colspan="3">Stimulus features and contextual information play a large role in how attention is directed and the limitations of attention are highlighted by instances of failure to attend to salient environmental information</td>
</tr>
<tr>
<td>Visual Search & Contextual Cuing</td>
<td>Inattentional & Change Blindness</td>
<td>The Stroop Task</td>
</tr>
<tr>
<td>
<ul>
<li>The visual search paradigm allows attention to be measured as a function of environmental complexity i.e. set size</li>
<li>The pop out effect indicates that visually salient information automatically captures attention regardless of set size whereas conjunctive searches slow down processing</li>
<li>Familiar environmental settings and our general knowledge about their contexts (schema) guide our attention in a more efficient manner</li>
</ul>
</td>
<td>
<ul>
<li>Inattentional Blindness demonstrates that when the focus of attention is placed strongly on a particular stimulus, even highly salient stimuli may go unnoticed</li>
<li>Change blindness demonstrates that salient changes in the environment often go unnoticed, even when we are looking for them</li>
</ul>
</td>
<td>
<ul>
<li>Not all complex processes require attention, numerous experiences or practice with tasks allow us to perform them almost automatically</li>
<li>An example of how this automatic processing can be a hindrance is the Stroop paradigm – the automatic processing of words interferes with colour naming</li>
</ul>
</td>
</tr>
</table>

Section 4: Models of Attention

Despite your new knowledge of attention, you may be wondering what attention is. One way of asking "What is attention?" is to ask "What is attention *like*?" The use of metaphors is a common strategy among scientists when they are trying to understand something. Indeed, many theorists before you have wondered what attention is (or 'is like') and we will consider key models of attention that have been developed.

ATTENTION AS A SPOTLIGHT

Draft

One idea is that attention acts like a spotlight, enhancing things than fall within its focus. Think back to the last time you went to a play. Consider how the spotlight worked to move your attention across the stage. People or objects in the spotlight were more easily seen than those outside the spotlight. You were more aware of what was going on in the spotlight than outside the spotlight. The spotlight moved around the stage, following the action. These are the essential features of the spotlight model of spatial attention proposed by Posner and colleagues (1980). Although the model does a good job of explaining the result for Posner's spatial cueing task, it has been less successful in explaining many of the other scenarios described earlier. Thus, although there does seem to be some relevance for location-based selection, the spotlight metaphor is limited.

ATTENTION AS A FILTER

Another idea is that attention acts like a **filter** with a bottleneck that only allows certain information to pass on to conscious awareness. According to Broadbent's filter model of attention (1958), the physical characteristics (color, shape) of sensory information are briefly stored and initially analyzed. Incoming information then encounters a *bottleneck*, which selects (based on physical characteristics) only a limited amount of the information to pass on for further processing.

Broadbent's model has often been described as an **early-selection theory** because it filters information out relatively *early* before it can be analyzed semantically. This early-selection model was well received by Broadbent's peers as it successfully accounted for a range of empirical evidence. Recall our discussion of the dichotic listening task, where participants noticed the physical properties of the unattended messages but not necessarily the meaning. These results clearly support an early-selection theory of attention processing with the unattended information being filtered out prior to semantic processing.

Broadbent's theory was a great achievement in the field of cognitive psychology, not only because it was the first to describe humans as information processors but also because it stimulated a lot of research on attention. That said, his early-selection model does not tell the whole story. Consider the cocktail party effect discussed earlier. Some key bits of information (like your name) can still be recognized from an unattended channel. According to early-selection views, it would not be possible for semantic aspects of any unattended information to capture your attention. Also, in MacKay's 1973 study described earlier, the meaning of information from the unattended ear does influence interpretation of the material in the attended ear.

To help explain why some data from the unattended channel can still be meaningfully processed, Treisman (1960) proposed the **attenuation theory** of attention. According to this model, unattended information is not completely filtered out but rather "turned down" or attenuated. The attenuator replaces the filter in Broadbent's model, allowing all information to pass but with differently assigned weightings depending on whether the information is physically similar to the target or not. Information that fits the description of the target is more heavily weighted and passes through the attenuator at full strength whereas irrelevant information passes as a weaker signal. This model is sometimes described as a "leaky filter" model as the unattended message also gets through albeit in much attenuated form. Treisman further proposed that some of this "weak" information might trigger recognition especially if that information is semantically relevant to us or semantically similar to the target information. This may be why the word "money" presented to the unattended ear biases a listener into interpreting an ambiguous sentence about "banks" presented to the attended ear to mean a financial institution rather than a river.

Another way to explain the recognition of unattended information is to place the filter at a later stage, that is, after all the incoming information has been analyzed for both its physical properties and semantic content. This is the **late-selection model** (Deutsch & Deutsch, 1963; Norman, 1968). However, due to our limited processing capacity (discussed in more detail later in reference to short-term working memory), only selected information can be maintained and so the unselected information fades. Like the attenuation theory, a late-stage filter model could also account for why our memory can be influenced by the meaning of unattended information.

The diagram below depicts the main differences between the three types of filter models. Each theory has strengths and weaknesses, but the attenuation filter model seems to be most consistent with neurological evidence (Driver, 2001).

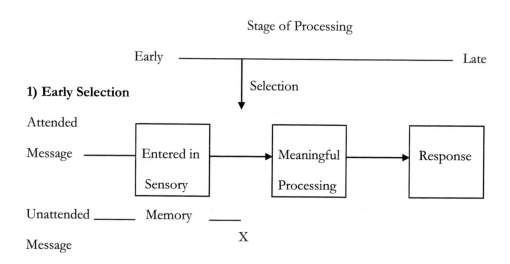

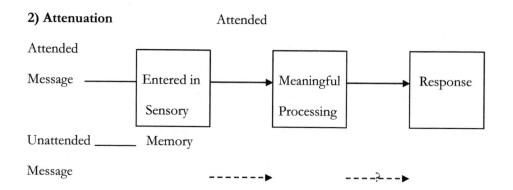

3) Late Selection

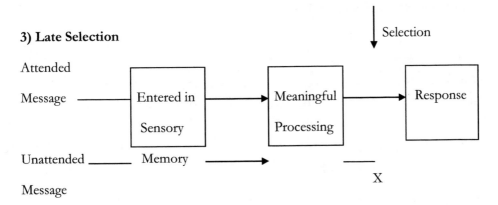

CONCLUSION TO ATTENTION

In the first half of this chapter, we have explored the characteristics, mechanisms, and tools used to study the cognitive processes of attention. Attention helps us make choices, search for information, and compare among competing bits of data. In the second half of this chapter, we investigate how attention interacts with another important cognitive process – memory – to provide a rich experience of the world around us.

TABLE 4.3

Original ideas on attention suggested that focusing is central attention, however, further work has indicated that mechanisms of filtering and analysis play a strong role		
Spotlight Model	**Early Filter Models**	**Late Filter Models**
• Early attempts to describe attentional mechanisms suggest they operate in the likeness of a **spotlight** • Focus moves towards different stimuli and when in the focus of the spotlight are more easily perceived and processed, however, this model is limited with more complex spatial paradigms	• Further work came to suggest attention acts more like a filter, where selected information goes on towards conscious awareness • **Broadbent's Early Selection Theory** suggests physical information is filtered before semantic processing, accounting for the Dichotic Listening Task but not the Cocktail Party Effect • **Treisman's Attenuation Theory** attempted to compensate by suggesting physical information is just attenuated and if relevant may be brought to the focus of attention	• **Late Filter Models** suggest filtering occurs after physical and semantic analysis and only selected information goes on for further processing due to limitations in processing capacity • Both this model and the attenuation model may be able to account for the Cocktail Party Effect

Section 5: Introduction to Memory

Imagine what it would be like to live in a world where new memories could not be formed. The film <u>Memento</u> tells the story of Leonard Shelby, a man who has recently lost his ability to form new memories. He describes his condition: "Everything fades. If we talk too long, I'll forget how we started. The next time I see you I won't remember this conversation. I don't even know if I've met you before. I've told you this before, haven't I?" Shelby's world is confusing and disorienting. It's not always clear where he is, what he's doing, or how he got there. He wakes up each morning completely lost; like a forensic detective who has just arrived at the scene of the crime, he searches for clues to help explain his current situation and his whole life.

Memento provides an interesting perspective on memory, presenting thoughtful ideas about what memory is and what it means to remember the past. Without the ability to form new memories, Shelby often seems hopeless: "I have to believe in a world outside my own mind. I have to believe that my actions still have meaning, even if I can't remember them. I have to believe that when my eyes are closed, the world is still there. We all need mirrors to remind ourselves who we are." Despite his impairment, some of Shelby's remaining memory processes remain intact; he maintains a temporary storage of his experiences, (i.e., at least of the past few seconds), he can still remember things that happed before his accident, and he can still use these memories to predict and plan his future. This scenario illustrates the critical interplay between attention and memory, which work together to create our current experience, the world as we remember it, and plans for the future. Because these processes operate invisibly and seemingly effortlessly, their function can be easily overlooked. Only when memory fails do we fully appreciate the extent of its importance, as in case of the fading memory in an elderly relative and the more devastating conditions of memory failure observed in special populations of patients suffering from Alzheimer's and memory disorders like amnesia as experienced by Leonard Shelby in the opening case study.

What is memory?

Psychologists organize memory into the three successive processes of encoding, storage and retrieval:

1. **Encoding** reflects data entry or how information initially enters into memory, a selective process that is highly dependent on attention.

2. **Storage** concerns how the record of memory is maintained over time. Notably, this record is not fixed and can be modified.

3. **Retrieval** is the act of recovering stored information. Memory retrieval is dependent on **retrieval cues** — a key piece of information that has the potential to activate a memory in full. For example, the mere smell of lilacs (the cue) makes me think of the time my grandmother and I picked flowers at her farm.

Cues become integrated with the memory at the time of encoding, and so processes of encoding and retrieval are considered highly interconnected. Although memory can be broken down into these three seemingly basic stages, the operations are highly malleable, which in turn, have the potential to create fallible memories.

Target Study: False Memories

"YOU AND YOUR BEST FRIEND SUZY PUT SLIME IN MS. SMOLLETT'S DESK": PRODUCING FALSE MEMORIES WITH SELF-RELEVANT DETAILS

Researchers: Tracy Desjardins (University of Windsor) and Alan Scoboria (University of Windsor)

Source: Desjardons, T. & Scoboria, A. (2007). "You and your best friend Suzy put Slime in Ms. Smollett's desk": Producing false memories with self-relevant details. *Psychonomic Bulletin & Review, 14*(6), 1090 – 1095.

Note: The material below is the author's summarized description of the original published article.

Due to the reconstructive nature of memories, we know that we can be quite susceptible to false memory implantation. This particular study focuses on the mechanisms of false memories, specifically how different types of details in a false narrative affect the likelihood of recalling false events. Past work in the field has explored false memories through autobiographical memory, memory for personally experienced episodes. A popular method used is what is known as the familial informant false narrative paradigm, where details about true events are collected from parents and individuals are guided to remember past events (two true and one false). The ability to implant false memories in individuals is quite strong, but little is known about the underlying mechanisms and critical factors involved. Certain facts, such as the believability of events and the effects of imagination, are known to play a strong role, however much is left to explore in terms of factors such as social pressures. Work in false memory has also looked at how event information is presented, whether through photographs or narratives, and if there are any differences. Narratives are more likely to elicit the formation of false memories likely because individuals have to use imagination and reconstruction to picture the event, making it easier for false details to be used to fill in the gaps, and less restriction is provided than with pictures. Thus it is sensible to use narratives when attempting to induce false memories.

Another interesting finding is the increased likelihood of self-relevant details in producing false memories in comparison to non-self-relevant details. Two general mechanisms are proposed as underlying this phenomenon. First it is suggested that self-relevant information is better constructed and formed because we are so familiar with it and we use it quite frequently. Second, according to what is known as the fluency hypothesis explores, self-relevant details are highly familiar and thus fluently processed; this fluency may lead individuals to judge details as coming from true past events. As to why non-self-relevant details do not have the same effect, essentially they lack fluency and may even have the complete opposite effect. The more unfamiliar or bizarre the details are, the less fluent they are and the less likely they are able to produce false memories. For the current experiment, self-relevant details used were unique to the individuals, ensuring they were directly self-relevant, and specific details included vivid information that was not the main focus of the narratives. The events individuals were told about involved getting in trouble in elementary school, with three true and one false narrative. Researchers hypothesized that events using self-relevant details in a narrative would significantly increase susceptibility to false memories in comparison to just specific details.

METHODS

Forty-four undergraduate students, five males and thirty-nine females, participated in the study. In order to ensure self-relevancy, parents were used to help customize narratives for each participant. The self-relevant details included: the name of their first grade teacher, a friend and their favourite toy at the time. Specific details included the general story of putting a slime toy on the teacher's desk and blaming the friend for convincing them to do it. The length and amount of detail was matched across false and true events to ensure the false event did not stand out for such reasons. Three main measures were used: the AMBQ, an assessment of event plausibility completed by participants; judges' ratings of the strength of participants' memories; and memory questions or participants' ratings of memory qualities. Participants attended a series of three interviews where they were told about events and encouraged to recall them; when unable to remember, interviewers used guidance to help. Following the interview, the three measures were used, and participants were told one event was false and asked to choose which one before being told.

RESULTS AND DISCUSSION

As predicted, participants that received narratives with self-relevant details had a greater amount of images and full memories of false events. In terms of self-ratings of memory strength, the subjective sense of recall was enhanced for self-relevant details. As well, AMBQ ratings and judges' scores matched up, ensuring credibility of responses. A trend, though not significant, was also seen: higher ratings of belief and memory were given for narratives with self-relevant details. Lastly, participants were more likely to be unable to tell which memory was false if they received self-relevant narratives. What this study highlights is the critical, robust role of self-relevant details in the likelihood of false memory formation, and thus further reveals the mechanisms of false memory formation, and memory processes in general, with support from the fluency hypothesis.

LIMITATIONS

Although findings were quite robust, further work is definitely in store for this field. For example, it is worth asking what would happen if the specific details, instead of being neutral and non-self-relevant were bizarre, and whether this would affect false memory formation any differently. Certain limitations exist within the experimental design as well. Although narratives have shown to produce higher likelihoods of false memory formation, it would be worth comparing self-relevant details and specific details between both pictures and narratives in order to examine all possible effects. As well, it is feasible that the memories provided by parents may indeed be false, or remembered incorrectly, thus confounding the assumption that only one of the memories is false. Lastly, it is also possible that the false narratives may in fact be very similar or the same as an actual event that had occurred but that the parents may not have remembered or been aware of. Although the study provides great insight into the mechanisms of false memory, it is important to keep in mind just how tricky a concept it is to study and how important meticulous experimental design is.

COMMENTS

The study of false memory is a key area of research invaluable for understanding processes of memory in general. As will be emphasized throughout this chapter, memory and remembering is based strongly on processes of reconstruction. This study certainly re-emphasizes this by pointing out how easy it is for false memories to be implanted and believed to be true, and generalizes to the entire study of memory by providing support for memory as a process rather than just information storage in different parts of the brain. Through this, the role of familiarity and fluency in reconstruction is also highlighted. Understanding false memory is important for understanding memory, but also in realizing the implications of such findings. Eyewitness testimonies, for example, we now know to be unreliable. Seeing how easily individuals can be manipulated into beliefs by those guiding recall, especially for situations that individuals are personally involved in, and the conviction that false memories are true, leads to the conclusion that additional evidence must be provided in the court of law. False memory research does not seek to discount the abilities of human memory, but instead reveals factors that must be taken into careful consideration when processes of memory are relied on for everyday use.

Section 6: Sensory and Short Term Memory

For decades, psychologists have thought of memory as the accumulated operations of three separate stores: sensory memory, short-term memory, and long-term memory (Atkinson & Shiffrin, 1971). This so-called multistore model of memory provides a relatively simple way to conceptualize types of memory.

Sensory memory

Take a moment and look around. Pay attention to how you scan the environment. Your eyes move across the scene, stopping for brief intervals to gather information. Although this is akin to taking snapshots at different locations, you perceive the world as a continuous representation. This is because each snapshot is briefly maintained and then replaced by the next. This is **sensory memory**, the transient maintenance of perceptual and physical information from the very recent past. Think back to when you played with a sparkler on a Canada Day as a child. The movement of the sparkler against the dark night sky brilliantly displays sensory memory in action. As you move the sparkler through the air to write your name, the trace of light briefly persists even after you have finished. When discussing attention, and in particular when discussing the dichotic listening paradigm, you learned that participants could recall the physical (sensory) characteristics of the unattended things. This suggests that sensory memory is not limited by attention and therefore may have a fairly large capacity.

All of your senses maintain a similar transient memory representation. For example, **iconic memory** for visual information is represented by the visual system whereas **echoic memory** for auditory information is represented by the auditory system. Sensory representations are displaced or overwritten by new incoming information from the same modality. How long is sensory memory? This is the question that puzzled Sperling who used a very simple method to find out. Sperling (1960) tested the longevity of sensory memories by briefly (50 milliseconds) and simultaneously presenting arrays of three rows of three numbers. Participants viewed the arrays and then listened for a tone of high, medium or low pitch to indicate which row to report. Despite the brief presentation time, if the tone sounded immediately after the array was presented participants were surprisingly accurate at reporting the numbers. However, if the tone sounded just one second later they recalled nothing, illustrating the extremely fast rate at which sensory memory decays.

Short-term (working) memory

Only some of the information in sensory memory is selected for further processing. This selection requires attention. Information that is selected from sensory memory enters consciousness and is maintained in the short-term or working memory buffer. **Short-term memory** is thought to operate like RAM on a computer, whereby the selected information is held online for a short period of time but not necessarily stored permanently. For example, short-term memory allows you to keep in mind all the words of this sentence. This temporary record of what you have just read allows you to understand the meaning of the entire sentence and decide what to do with that information. In the film *Memento*, despite losing his ability to form new lasting memories, Leonard Shelby maintains his short-term memory capabilities, illustrating that maintaining information online and storing it permanently are uniquely independent processes.

If unrehearsed, selected information can be maintained in the short-term (working) memory buffer for about 20 seconds. Peterson and Peterson (1959) tested participants' memory for three consonants (for example the letter *CHK*) over varying lengths of time (3-18 seconds). To prevent participants from rehearsing during the delay, they were asked to count backwards from a three-digit number by threes or fours. Although participants were quite good at recalling the consonants after a three-second delay, by 18 seconds their memory had almost completely faded.

However, when information is **rehearsed** (repeated over and over), it can be maintained for longer periods of time. I am sure that you have had the experience of trying to remember a phone number and you repeated the number over and over to yourself to maintain the number in short-term memory for a longer period of time. Now imagine that as you are looking for your phone and repeating the number to dial, your friend interrupts you by asking you a deep philosophical question on the role of memory and the concept of reality. As you ponder the question, you realize that this brief distraction has caused you to forget the number! This scenario illustrates the temporary and fragile nature of short-term memory with its limited capacity. It seems that you can reply to your friend's philosophical query or rehearse the phone number, but not both.

There has been much research on short-term memory capacity. According to Miller (1956), the "magic number" of items that can be held in (or processed by) short-term memory is seven plus or minus two. Obviously this is not a large amount of data and you can probably remember a time when you held more than nine pieces of information in mind at once. Indeed, one way to increase the amount of information maintained in short-term memory is by chunking (Simon, 1974). **Chunking** refers to the process by which information is organized into sets of familiar groups or categories of items. For example, trying to remember the following sequence of letters may be difficult: fbicbcbmocia because the 12 items exceeds your short-term memory capacity. However, grouping the letters into familiar acronyms: fbi, cbc, bmo, cia makes the task much easier because you only have to remember four chunks of information. Thus, you can use prior knowledge to impose structure on to-be-remembered items to help chunk the information into more manageable bits. In turn, this strategically increases the capacity of your short-term memory.

WORKING MEMORY: SHORT-TERM MEMORY GETS AN 'UPGRADE'

I mentioned *working* memory when I first introduced the topic of a short-term memory store. With respect to psychological history, the working-memory model was introduced many years after the idea of a short-term store had been proposed. In a sense, working memory can be thought of as Short-Term Memory 2.0, or an upgrade to the original conceptualization of short-term memory.

Working memory consists of three short-term buffers (or stores): 1) the phonological or articulatory loop, 2) the visuospatial sketchpad, and 3) the episodic buffer.

The **phonological loop** encapsulates the original notion of short-term memory, i.e., a temporary online store that can maintain seven plus or minus two bits of phonological information for a short period of time. The phonological loop maintains information that can be rehearsed verbally. It is, for example, engaged when rehearsing the number of your favorite pizza place.

The **visuospatial sketchpad** is a new addition to the working memory model; it is thought to temporarily represent and manipulate visual information. For example, the visuospatial sketchpad is engaged when trying to remember a mental map of how to get to your favorite pizza place.

The **episodic buffer** is also a new addition of the working memory model; it is thought to draw on the other buffers (phonological loop and visuospatial sketchpad) as well as on other stored long-term memories. This aspect of working memory is engaged when remembering specific past episodes. For example, in thinking about the last time you ordered pizza from this place, you recall that they mixed up your order of pineapple for anchovies.

In addition to the multiple buffers, the working memory model includes a **central executive**, which coordinates and manipulates information that is temporarily maintained in the buffers. The central executive allows working memory to be much more flexible and controllable than short-term memory was originally conceived to be.

SECTION 6 REVIEW: Sensory and Short Term Memory

TABLE 4.4

The role of memory is invaluable to all daily functioning and processes such as encoding, storage and retrieval are essential to successful memory operation		
Sensory Memory	**Short Term Memory**	**Working Memory**
• **Sensory Memory** represents brief, transient perceptual and physical information about immediate experiences and is not limited by attention • Representations exist for each of the senses, such as **iconic memory** for visual information and **echoic memory** for auditory information, and decay after approximately 50 ms	• Information selected for further processing in sensory memory is held in conscious awareness for short periods of time, but not permanently • Rehearsal of information increases the amount of time it can be held online for • Short term store can be increased by **chunking**	• **Working Memory** represents a refined version of short term memory and consists of 3 buffers • **Phonological Loop**: storage of information through verbal rehearsal • **Visuospatial sketchpad**: represents and manipulates visual information • **Episodic Buffer**: uses other buffers and long term memory to remember and hold online past episodes • The **central executive** is responsible for managing and manipulating the buffers

Section 7: Long-Term Memory

Long-term memory

When you think of "memory", perhaps what comes to mind are things that happened a long time ago: the toy you played with as a child, the story your mom read to you at bedtime, your first kiss, your last day of high school. Indeed, these are all examples of long-term memories. Long-term memories are thought to be stored permanently. Of course, this does not mean we remember *everything* that happened in the past. This is partly because only some memories make it to the long-term store. According to the multistore model, information can be copied from short-term memory to long-term memory but this transfer is largely dependent on the rehearsal of that information. Another way to get information into long-term memory is through elaborate encoding, an important topic that will be discussed in greater detail later.

Once in long-term memory, new information seems to be organized according to prior knowledge. We have a tendency to recall related information in clusters or groups even if that information was learned in random order (Bousfield, 1953). For example, imagine that you first studied the following word list extensively, and then were asked to recall it some time later: apple, screwdriver, hammer, lemon, pear, level, wrench, peach. You would very likely list all the fruits (apple, lemon, pear, peach) and all the tools (screwdriver, hammer, level, wrench) separately. Semantic networks depict such organization. Semantic networks represent concepts by nodes, and connections between concepts by lines connecting the nodes (Collins & Loftus, 1975). Concepts that are more closely related are more directly connected. The activation of one concept may be akin to throwing a pebble into a pond such that the activation may spread (or ripple) throughout the network, activating neighboring concepts to a lesser extent according to their distance from the source. For example, pizza makes me think about pineapple and that horrible time they mistakenly put anchovies on my pizza. Thinking of pizza may also remind me that I have not yet had dinner, so that I suddenly realize I'm very hungry. When I think of how hungry, hungry I am feeling, I naturally think of hippos. In this semantic network, "Pizza", "toppings", "dinner", "hungry" and "hippos" are all closely related concepts that activate each other.

It is also important to note that the flow of information between short-term and long-term stores is not unidirectional. Information is also transferred from a stored state into a conscious state (i.e., from long-term to short-term). This is effectively what happens when we are remembering the past. As mentioned earlier, the success of retrieving a memory from long-term storage is largely dependent on the effectiveness of its retrieval cue. Since retrieval cues are established at encoding, they play a major role in elaborate encoding, discussed in more detail later.

We retrieve stored information to help interpret the world around us. Based on past experiences, we have expectations about what will occur in a particular environment and in turn, we are more likely to remember things that fit within our expectations. Obviously, this is largely linked to attention and we know that attention can be under the influence of top-down control. Think back to the change blindness experiments in which an image and its modified version are presented and your task is to detect the change. This task should be easy but it turns out to be difficult because the change is in an unexpected location. For example, in one example, the engine of an airplane has been deleted from the original picture, an unexpected change when you may have instead expected a change in the faces of the passengers. However, once you detect the change in the engine, you can't help but see it. This is because your newly acquired knowledge of the engine change now guides your search of the scene.

It is also the case that we expect certain things to be part of an environment and we remember them as being there, when in fact, they were not. Such expectations reflect **schemas**—mental frameworks for interpreting the world around us based on prior experiences. Brewer and Treyens (1981) demonstrated this concept in a clever experiment. They had participants wait in an office that was set up like a typical graduate student's office. It contained the usually things you'd expect to find (at least in 1980s): some tables, a typewriter, a coffeemaker, and a Skinner box. It also contained some unusual things, such as a screwdriver, and it purposely did not contain some things, like books, that you would normally expect to find in an office. After 35 seconds of waiting in the "office", participants were taken into another room and told that sitting in the office *was* the experiment. When asked to describe all the items they remembered seeing in the room, almost 33% of participants reported seeing books that were *not* really there and only 10% reported seeing the screwdriver that *was* actually there. This experiment highlights the reconstructive nature of our memories: it demonstrates that human memory is fallible. (We will discuss more about this topic later, under the section *Memory Errors)*.

Long-term memory systems

The long-term memory system can be subdivided into separate systems based on the type of information stored. The diagram below depicts a common way in which LTM is subdivided.

Declarative memories (memory for factual information, explicit memories) are an example of the prototypical conception of memory. I ask you what you remember and you can tell me. This information could include general knowledge or **semantic memories** that are not tied to a particular place or time (e.g., roses are red) as well as specific memories of your past personal experience: these are **episodic memories** that are tied to a particular place and time (e.g., I remember how red the roses were that day at the park). On the other hand, **nondeclarative memories** (learned actions, skills, conditioned responses, implicit memories) are memories that are difficult to articulate. For example, you know *how* to ride a bike but you probably would have difficulty describing all the actions required to do so.

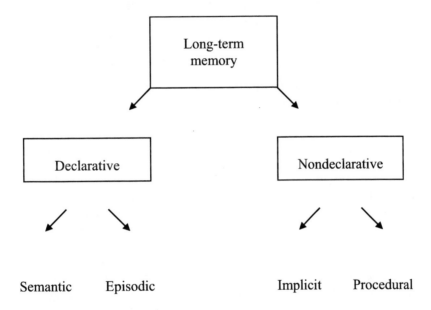

WHERE IS LONG-TERM MEMORY STORED IN THE BRAIN?

We have learned a great deal about the neural properties of long-term memory from patients with acquired amnesia. Patient H.M. is one of the most famous cases. In his late twenties, H.M. had his medial temporal lobes removed in an attempt to mitigate his severe epilepsy. The removal included the hippocampus and other neighboring structures. The surgery was successful in that it reduced the severity and frequency of seizures, however, it left H.M. with a debilitating memory deficit; H.M. could not remember events that took place shortly before his surgery (retrograde amnesia) and more critically, was unable to form new lasting memories (anterograde amnesia). However, the surgery did not disrupt H.M.'s memory entirely. His remote memories (childhood birthday parties, high school prom) were fully intact. He was able to follow short conversations, as long as they stayed within the range of working memory storage (about 20 seconds). He could also learn a new skill by performing it over and over again (procedural memory). H.M.'s condition is more or less portrayed by the character Leonard Shelby in the film *Memento*.

Although H.M.'s memory complaints were more severe than most amnesic patients, medial-temporal lobe related memory issues are fairly consistent across the board. Of the medial temporal lobe structures, the integrity of the hippocampus seems to be most critical for memory formation. A short-term memory trace is established in the hippocampus upon initial exposure to a particular item. This experience modifies the connections among neurons to create an active link that can be temporarily maintained. This is referred to as long-term potentiation (LTP), a subject you will encounter in more detail in your study of Neuroscience. Subsequent processing of the item via the same link among the same neurons changes the neural response, and these changes are thought to be a mechanism for temporary memory.

However, the hippocampal system does not seem to be a storehouse for long-term memories. Long-term memories appear to be represented in a more distributed fashion throughout the cortex, which is why HM could remember so much from before his operation. That said, the hippocampus may assist in coordinating the activation of distributed cortical regions that are involved in representing parts of the whole memory. When all the parts are simultaneously active, the memory is reinstated into consciousness. Repeated co-activation by the hippocampus strengthens the connections among the distributed regions so that eventually the distributed parts of the same memory co-activate without assistance from the hippocampus.

THE EFFECT OF REHEARSAL AS EVIDENCE FOR A MULTISTORE MEMORY MODEL

Let's now consider evidence that supports the view of memory as consisting of three separate stores (sensory, short-term, long-term), where information flows into and out of the short-term store. The most compelling and intuitive evidence for a multistore model of memory comes from the free-recall paradigm. In the **free-recall paradigm**, participants study a list of random words presented one at a time. Each word is associated with a specific position in the list. Following the study phase, participants are asked to freely recall the words in any order. The general finding is that there is greater recall for first few words presented in the list (**the primacy effect**) as well as the last few words presented in the list (**the recency effect**) with words in the middle of the list most poorly recalled. The primacy effect is thought to reflect retrieval of words from long-term memory whereas the recency effect is thought to reflect the readout of short-term memory. Designing an experiment that selectively affects short-term memory but not long-term memory (and vice versa) can test these ideas.

Short-term memory maintenance relies on rehearsal whereas long-term memory storage does not. Therefore, introducing a distracting task between study phase and test should selectively disrupt short-term memory. In this situation, the typical primacy effect (which is dependent on long-term memory) remains, but the recency effect is selectively diminished. Thus, the recency effect seems to be dependent on information maintained in short-term memory.

Enhanced rehearsal has the potential to make information more permanent (i.e., "transfer" information from short-term into long-term memory). Therefore, slowing the rate at which words are presented during study, in order to provide participants more time to rehearse each word, should enhance long-term memory. In this situation, the typically observed primacy effect is enhanced as is recall for mid-list words, whereas the recency effect remains unchanged. Thus, the primacy effect seems to reflect retrieving information from long-term memory. Critically, the recency effect is not affected because the words at the end of the list are still maintained within the short-term store.

SECTION 7 REVIEW: Long Term Memory

TABLE 4.5

Long term memory (LTM) is a complex network marked by semantic organization; retrieval is aided by cues and general knowledge based on years of experience guides much of what we do and how we function		
LTM & Its Systems	**LTM Storage**	**Rehearsal**
• **Schemas** are knowledge structures and expectations built through experiences and memories and aid in navigation – memory is reconstructive though and we often let schemas take control even if they lead to false judgments • **Declarative Memory**: memory for specific facts or episodes; general knowledge or semantic memories • **Nondeclarative Memory**: implicit and procedural memories, not overtly recalled but apparent in functioning	• Patients with amnesia have revealed much of what is known about LTM • The **hippocampus** has been shown to be vital for STM memory formation and trace formation but LTM processes are apparent throughout the cortex • The hippocampus us still thought to be important though for the coordination of memories for activation in consciousness	• The **multi-store model** suggests we have 3 stores for memory: sensory memory perceives sensory information which is selectively held online by STM and with rehearsal through STM components may be transferred and stores in LTM • Evidence for this comes from the free recall paradigm through **primacy and recency effects**

Section 8: Levels of Processing

Although the nature of the primacy and recency effects provide some support for the multistore memory model, this does not necessarily mean that human memory is really organized in this way. In fact, there are several issues with dividing memory into separate stores. It is unclear how information is transferred between stores or whether information must pass through short-term memory to get to long-term memory. It is also unclear whether short-term memory is really capacity limited (one of the features distinguishing it from long-term storage). Short-term memory can exceed it seven-plus-or-minus-two capacity by chunking. However, a "chunk" can only be identified as a result of its memorial consequences, and so is a completely circular explanation.

One of the most influential alternative frameworks for understanding human memory is the '**levels of processing**' framework proposed by Craik & Lockhart (1972). According to their framework, memory is not subdivided into separate stores. Instead, memory is conceived of as a continuum; items encoded at a deeper level (more attention, more elaboration) result in a longer lasting memory trace than items encoded at a more shallow level (less attention, less elaboration). This framework emphasizes the importance of the encoding processes that underlie the formation of a memory trace. Moreover, since memory traces are not maintained in separate stores, there is no need to understand how information is transferred between stores. The main criticism of this model is its vagueness, particularly concerning the definition of a "deeper" level.

To examine the levels-of-processing framework, Craik & Tulving (1975) tested participants' memory for words that were encoded in different ways. To manipulate the depth of processing, each word was preceded by a question about either: a) the case of the text (e.g., "Is this word in capital letters?"), b) a rhyming word (e.g., "Does this word rhyme with train") or c) the meaning of the word (e.g., "The girl placed the _____ on the table". Can the word replace the 'blank' to make a semantically congruent sentence?). A surprise memory test followed. As predicted by the levels-of-processing framework, words that were processed to a "deeper level" were more likely to be remembered, with semantic processing deeper than phonological processing, and phonological processing deeper than processing based on the physical characteristics of the word (i.e., meaning > rhyme > case). These results highlight the importance of encoding processes on remembering.

Enriched encoding

Since the inception of the 'levels of processing' framework, enriched encoding as a memory tool or **mnemonic strategy** has been strongly emphasized. One such mnemonic strategy is to think about the to-be-remembered information as it pertains to you. Generally, information encoded with 'me-in-mind' is better remembered than information encoded with something or someone else in mind. This effect is referred to as the **self-referent effect** (Rogers, Kuiper, & Kirker, 1977; Symons & Johnson, 1997). Interestingly, it seems to be the most effective way to encode information. Words processed according to 'self' are better remembered than words processed by case, rhyme or meaning (i.e., self > meaning > rhyme > case). In other words, self-referent encoding may reflect the deepest level of processing. This makes sense if we consider all the personal information we have in mind that can be used to elaborate and organize new material.

Encoding specificity

When we encode a particular item, the item is not processed in isolation but together with the surrounding context. As such, we may be able to access our memory for an item by thinking about its original context. The effectiveness of the context as a cue is largely dependent on the specificity of its relations to the item. This is known as the principle of **encoding specificity** (Tulving & Thompson, 1973).

Context can be defined as the physical environment in which the to-be-remembered item is presented (Godden & Baddeley, 1975). For example, scuba divers who studied word lists underwater subsequently remembered more words underwater than on dry land. Likewise, scuba divers who studied word lists on dry land subsequently remembered more words on dry land than underwater. In general, memory is better for items that were encoded and retrieved in the same environment, suggesting that the extraneous environmental cues that were encoded with the target item can be used to help retrieve memories for the target items themselves. ·

Context can also be defined as your internal or "mental state" at encoding. For example, in the 1970s Eich and colleagues (1975) demonstrated that information encoded under the influence of marijuana was best recalled while in the same drug state. Their experiment consisted of four study-test phase conditions: placebo-placebo, marijuana-marijuana, placebo-marijuana, and marijuana-placebo. As with the external environmental cues, recall was better when participants' internal state was the same at study and test. Notably, worse performance was observed for participants who studied under the influence of marijuana and then were tested under the placebo.

Transfer-appropriate processing

Similar to encoding specificity, **transfer-appropriate processing** proposes that memory is aided when similar processes are engaged at encoding and retrieval. Morris and colleagues (1977) first demonstrated transfer-appropriate processing using a similar procedure as Craik and Tulving (1975). A sentence with a blank space preceded each word and the participant determined whether the target word could replace the blank to create a meaningful statement. There were two sentence types: semantic ("The _____ had a silver engine") and rhyme ("_____ rhymes with legal"). A recognition task immediately followed. One group performed a standard recognition task in which they discriminated old words (previously seen in the experiment) from new words. This group performed according to the levels-of-processing account; words previously processed in semantic sentences were better remembered than words previously processed in rhyme sentences. Another group performed a special rhyme recognition task in which they determined whether the new words either rhymed or did not rhyme with a previously presented word. In contrast to the levels of processing framework, this group showed better recognition for target words previously presented in rhyme sentences than in semantic sentences. Thus, invoking a process (i.e., rhyming) was sufficient to boost recognition for words that underwent that the same process during encoding.

Draft

Principles of attention can help us focus, and mechanisms of memory can give us strategies about how best to remember information once we're paying attention to it. One of the most critical things we can take advantage of when studying is context. Studying in both a physical and mental context as similar to that of the testing environment as possible can be quite helpful. So when studying and testing yourself, try and set up your desk like an exam table, and get mentally prepared by putting away all your notes, turning off your phone, and timing yourself. Some more tips that we can use from knowledge of context specificity: try studying in a variety of different contexts with breaks in between before testing yourself, and use mnemonic strategies that are self-relevant. The more contexts that information is encoded in, the more links there are to memories that can be used for retrieving information more successfully. As well, by using self-relevant mnemonics, information is much easier to remember given that the knowledge structures we have for ourselves are so strong. Another thing we can take advantage of is transfer-appropriate processing. When studying, try to test yourself in the same way that you will actually be tested: this enhances memory by utilizing the same processes that the memories were linked to when encoded. So now tricks to manipulate memory can help you *remember* the tricks to manipulate memory to help you out on your next psychology exam!

Forgetting

As you have learned, getting information into memory is highly dependent on how the information was initially encoded. This stored information can be retrieved with the aid of an effective retrieval cue. Forgetting occurs when we lose the ability to retrieve previously stored information. Although forgetfulness is not considered a virtue, our ability to forget previously stored information may actually have an adaptive function. Consider for a moment what would happen if you forget nothing. Part of your problem would be an excess of information stored in your long-term memory, some of which was undoubtedly useless or outdated. Forgetting reduces the potential *interference* from such out-of-date or irrelevant memories and in turn, allows us to remember current information more effectively (Bjork, 1989; Kraemer & Golding, 1997). Interference is an important topic in memory that will be discussed in detail later in this section.

THE RATE OF FORGETTING

Ebbinghaus (1885) was one of the first to document the characteristics of forgetting by assessing the rate at which stored memories were forgotten. In one year, Ebbinghaus conducted 163 memory tests on himself. In order to reduce interference from prior knowledge, Ebbinghaus' studied nonsense syllables, like PIW, ZIB, MEH.

For each test, he memorized a series of nonsense syllables. Then, after a specified time, he re-memorized the same series of nonsense syllables. Ebbinghaus assessed his **memory savings** as a difference (the savings) in the time it took him to memorize the list at test versus retest. He calculated his memory savings across delays of 19 minutes, one hour, nine hours, one day, two days, six days, and 31 days. Immediately after memorizing the list, his memory savings was 100 percent. After one hour had elapsed, his memory savings was down to about 40 per cent and from then on it continued to decline more gradually. Memory savings plotted over time is referred to as the forgetting curve. Although it was later revealed that Ebbinghaus had a particularly steep forgetting curve, his experiments were the first to illustrate the basic characteristics of the rate of forgetting.

WHY DO WE FORGET?

According to **decay theory**, forgetting occurs because memories fade with time. Although decay may account for short-term memory loss, it cannot explain long-term memory forgetting. For example, forgotten memories can be later remembered. Furthermore, the passage of time is not always a good predictor of forgetting previously stored information. Instead, as discussed earlier, many memory theorists believe stored memories are more or less permanent and that forgetting is merely the consequence of not having the right cue to retrieve the specific memory. For example, a cue that was once useful for retrieving a memory may have since become associated with different information and consequently, may be no longer be able to retrieve the original memory. Such explanation of forgetting is referred to as **interference**.

Proactive Interference
Interference is said to be proactive if the interfering information was learned prior to the specific memory. Imagine that you have studied French in high school and now at University you want to learn Spanish. Although your previous knowledge is helpful, sometimes when trying to remember a specific Spanish term you remember the corresponding French term instead. In other words, your old memory for high school French is interfering with the retrieval of your newer memory for Spanish words. This is an example of proactive memory interference.

We can measure proactive interference in the laboratory using a very simple paradigm. The experimental group studies word list A and then immediately studies word list B. A control group only studies word list B. After a brief interval, both groups recall words from list B. Proactive interference has occurred if the experimental group remembers fewer words than the control group.

Retroactive Interference
Interference is said to be retroactive if new information interferes with the retrieval of old information. Consider your dinner two weeks ago. Unless you eat the same thing every day you are probably can't remember. This is partially because you have eaten several times since then and these new dining experiences are interfering with your retrieval of meals past. In the laboratory, we can measure retroactive interference using a similar paradigm to that used to measure proactive interference. In this case, the experimental group studies word list A and then immediately studies word list B. A control group only studies word list A, and then plays Tetris (or does some other distracter task) while the first group studies list B. After a brief interval, both groups recall words from list A. Retroactive interference has occurred if the experimental group remembers fewer words than the control group.

Temporary forgetting
Forgetting the name of someone you know is a common complaint. You know their name is in memory but (at the moment) it cannot be properly retrieved. This experience is referred to as a tip-of-tongue state, which often occurs for people's names and common words.

In the laboratory, we can induce tip-of-tongue states using a paradigm similar to Jeopardy. The participant is presented with a definition ("The liquid portion of blood") and is asked to generate the corresponding word (What is plasma?). Low frequency words are used to ensure that enough tip-of-the-tongue states are generated. In a tip-of-tongue state you may remember part of the word, like its first letter, the number of syllables, or related words (Brown & McNeill, 1966). Interestingly, words that have induced the tip-of-tongue state in the past are more likely to do so in the future (Warriner & Humphreys, 2008). The word is said to become more associated with this error-prone retrieval process each time it's on the tip of your tongue.

Repression   Can we purposefully forget specific memories about horrific events like childhood abuse? According to Freud, horrific memories can be repressed as a defense mechanism. Indeed, there is evidence to suggest that people can actually forget child sexual abuse. For example, Williams (1994) interviewed 129 patients who were medically treated for sexual abuse that had occurred about 20 years before. Surprisingly, a large proportion of those interviewed (38 percent) failed to recall the abuse. Of those that had forgotten, many were under the age of six when the abuse was originally documented.

Is this really evidence for memory repression? It is possible that forgetting a horrific event is simply an example of ordinary forgetting. We seem to have a general bias for remembering positive events. When remembering events, we tend think of pleasant memories over unpleasant memories (Lindsay et al., 2004; Linton, 1975; Wagenaar, 1986). Also, physically painful experiences like childbirth are not well remembered (Robbinson, Rosen, Revill, David, & Rus, 1980). Moreover, we are capable of intentionally forgetting things. In the directed forgetting paradigm, participants are instructed to intentionally forget a subset of studied items and subsequently recall fewer intentionally forgotten words compared to the other studied material (Allen & Vokey, 1998; McLeod, 1999).

Repression and repressed memories were hot topics of popular media in the 1990s. Many publicized cases of repressed childhood memories surfaced, usually while the person was in therapy for something else (Lindsay & Read, 1994; Loftus, 1993; Pope, 1996). It was not true in all cases, but in a subset it appeared that the particular therapy technique used (like hypnosis) seemed to be capable of planting false memories about abuse that never happened.

Draft

TABLE 4.6

Recent work has questioned the explanatory power of the multi store model and alternatives such as the Levels of Processing framework have been presented suggesting memory is based on how information is processed, emphasizing deeper, semantic processing as most effective

Encoding	Forgetting	Interference & Repression
• **Mnemonic Strategies** are tricks used to make to-be-remembered information more relevant and easier to remember i.e. **self-referent effect**, especially if it takes advantage of deep processing • **Encoding Specificity** points out how memories are not encoded in isolation but along with the context they are a part of and thus context can act as a **retrieval cue** • **Transfer Appropriate Processing** suggests memory is enhanced when encoding and retrieval utilize the same or similar processes	• **Forgetting** can be helpful in reducing interference from irrelevant memories • **Decay theory** suggests forgetting is based on the passage of time, but can only account for STM loss • Forgetting is often attributed to **interference** – cues are no longer associated with a certain memory but with other memories	• **Proactive Interference** occurs when knowledge learned prior to a memory prevents its retrieval • **Retroactive Interference** occurs when new knowledge prevents the retrieval of old memories • **Tip of the Tongue** experiences display how memories can be temporarily forgotten • **Repression** of negative memories is a controversial topic due to the fact that it is difficult to determine whether repressed memories remembered are true or not

Section 9: Memory Errors

In 2002, police were investigating the case of the Washington Sniper, a serial killer targeting random victims in Washington, DC. Several eyewitnesses came forward claiming that a suspicious white van was spotted near the scene of several of the murders. However, no evidence of the white van was ever discovered and the murderer's vehicle was actually a dark green car. How did this memory of a white van come to be? Intriguing work from Elizabeth Loftus suggests that our memories are far from perfect and that we are even susceptible to having false memories. Loftus noted that an early eyewitness had participated in a media interview mentioning a white van. This idea stuck and subsequent eyewitnesses also (inadvertently) made the same false claim.

Loftus provided experimental evidence that false memories could easily be implanted. In one study, Loftus and Pickrell (1995) assessed participants' memory for childhood events. Participants read four stories about their childhood (4-6 years old) as recounted by a relative. Unbeknownst to the participant, one of the stories was false. The fake memory depicted a crying child lost in a mall; with assistance from an elderly woman, the child was eventually reunited with her family. Although this event was not actually part of any of the participants' pasts, about 30 percent claimed to have "remembered" the event. This result illustrates the fallibility of memory. Our memories are not replicas of the past but rather reconstructions that can be shaped by related but misleading information. The fallibility of memory has important implications for the reliability of an eyewitness's testimony. In particular, the malleability of memory calls into question the practice of convicting alleged perpetrators on eyewitness testimony evidence alone.

Misinformation effects

The misinformation effect refers to the creation of false memories by incorporating new erroneous information with an old memory. Braun, Ellis & Loftus, 2002 demonstrated this by asking participants, all whom had visited Disneyland as a child, to evaluate a new (fake) advertisement for Disneyland featuring Bugs Bunny. Although Bugs Bunny is a Warner Brothers cartoon character and would never be associated with Disneyland, 16 percent remembered shaking hands with Bugs Bunny when they visited Disneyland as a child.

The language used during questioning can also introduce new and not necessarily correct information. In turn, this information may alter one's memory representation of a past event. For example, Loftus & Palmer (1973) presented participants with a film depicting a car accident and then asked "About how fast were the cars going when they _____ into each other?" Participants' estimations of speed varied according to speed implied by the verb of the leading question (smashed > collided > bumped). Furthermore, the word "smashed" led more people to remember broken glass, even though there was no broken glass actually present in the film of the accident.

Source confusion

Extraneous information that may be incorrect influences our memory, in part, because we fail to discriminate it from the facts. Consider where you first learned about the benefits of drinking two liters of water a day. Did you read about it in a magazine? Was this something your doctor told you about? The process by which we make attributions about the origins of memories is referred to as **source monitoring**. By failing to recall exactly where you learned this information, you have committed a **source monitoring error**.

One way in which we can commit a source monitoring error is by misattributing fluency (i.e., ease of processing) gained from prior processing. Read the following list of names: Brad Pitt, Joe Kim, Steve Brown, Angelina Joli, Jennifer Heisz, Molly Pottruff, Cal Broadbent. Now cover up the list with your hand. Is Steve Brown famous? If you answered 'no' then you are correct. You probably found this exercise to be trivial because it was quite simple to recall that Steve Smith was one of the names on the list. However, if I was to ask you the same question tomorrow, you would be more likely to mistakenly judge Steve Smith as famous (Jacoby, Kelley, Brown & Jasechko, 1989). In other words, Steve Smith would have become 'famous' overnight. This false fame effect is the result of a source monitoring error; the previously read name is incorrectly judged as being famous because it seems familiar (is fluently processed). This is considered to be an implicit influence of the past, as you do not realize that your prior experience has influenced your current behavior.

Another way in which we can commit a source monitoring error is by remembering imagined events as something that really happened. Our ability to discriminate real memories from those that are thought or imagined is referred to as **reality monitoring**. Previous research has shown that participants can misremember performing an action that they had merely imagined performing at an earlier time (Seamon, Philbin & Harrison, 2006). In this study, participants walked around campus either performing or imagining that they were performing familiar actions ("check the pop machine for change") or bizarre actions ("propose marriage to the pop machine"). Two weeks later, participants' memories for these actions were assessed. Interestingly, imagining the actions once caused participants to falsely remember performing the actions. This was true both for familiar actions and for bizarre actions.

SECTION 9 REVIEW: Memory Errors

TABLE 4.7

Our memory system is actually quite prone to error and false memories can be easily implemented and believed to be true with conviction	
Misinformation Effects	**Source Confusion**
• The **Misinformation Effect** occurs when new information is thought to be part of an old memory and false memories are in turn formed • This can occur simply by introducing associations between new information and old memories	• **Source monitoring errors** occur when we fail to recall the true origins of memories • This occurs often when we attribute familiarity and ease of processing to the source of memories • **Reality monitoring** is our ability to discriminate false memories from true memories

Conclusion to Attention and Memory

In this chapter you have learned the important role of attention and memory. We remember what we attend to and in turn, our attention is guided by our past experiences. Together attention and memory shape our experience of the world around us.

Attention works to selectively process information that is salient or relevant to our current goals. Without attention we would be unable to listen to a friend in a noisy bar, find a friend in a crowd, or notice important events in the environment like the siren of an oncoming ambulance. Although attention makes us generally more efficient, attention is also fallible and sometime our expectations lead us to miss highly salient items.

Memory is our record of the past. The very recent past is held temporarily before it is lost or stored more permanently. The strength of our memories depends on the conditions at encoding: how much attention was paid and to what depth the material was processed. The brain doesn't appear to have a storehouse for memories. Instead, memory is represented in distributed parts of cortex; when remembering the past, our representation of a particular event is reconstructed by co-activating the distributed parts. The reconstructive nature of this process may be why our memories are so malleable and have the potential to be influenced by erroneous information. For adaptive purposes we forget but memories are not "deleted"; we have only lost the way to retrieve them.

Let's end by remembering your flashbulb memory on 9/11. That day, your attention was heighted by the emotional significance and surprise of the event. Consequently, you paid more attention to and established a stronger memory for the event as well as other the typical things that took place around the

Draft

event. This flashbulb memory illustrates the strong interplay between attention and memory. If we consider that both of these cognitive processes are fallible, how much do you really trust this flashbulb memory, or any of your other memories for that matter?

Chapter

Chapter 5: Language

Introduction

> Ellie and Janet are sitting in an art class working on their self-portrait painting project. Ellie, who is just beginning to explore her artistic side, turns to Janet looking for approval. Janet takes a look at Ellie's painting and casually says, "Actually, that's good." Ellie goes back to her work unsure what to make of the comment. Was this a compliment or an underhanded dig? The problem is the word 'actually'. Remove it from the sentence and it's clearly a compliment. But add that single word and an innocent comment can take on a negative connotation. The word 'actually' implies a sense of surprise that what follows is not expected. Ellie can translate the comment to mean, "Wow, usually what you do is not very good, but this time, it's good." You can probably think about a similar incident in which a misinterpreted conversation or email originated from a single word. It's something that speechwriters, editors and advertisers think about very carefully. A single word or turn of a phrase can profoundly alter the meaning, impact, or legality of a sentence. Consider the sensational case of the Clinton-Lewinsky affair in which the question of whether Bill Clinton perjured himself before the grand jury depended on the definition of the word "is". Clinton rationalized that he wasn't lying when he said to his top aides that with respect to Monica Lewinsky, "there is nothing going on between us." According to Clinton: "It depends on what the meaning of the word 'is' is. If 'is' means is and never has been, that is not—that is one thing. If it means there is none, that was a completely true statement....Now, if someone had asked me on that day, are you having any kind of sexual relations with Ms. Lewinsky, that is, asked me a question in the present tense, I would have said no. And it would have been completely true."

Every day, you communicate by sending and receiving information. When you think of how you do this, you probably think in terms of using language: you place an order with the attendant at a coffee shop, you speak with fellow students on the way to class, and you email a friend to make weekend plans. You use spoken and written words to communicate with the people around you to convey your thoughts, feelings, and needs.

But communication is by no means limited to words and language. Communication occurs across the animal kingdom in a wide variety of ways. If you see a horse laying his ears back against his head, you would be correct to interpret that behaviour as a sign of aggression. When a male peacock displays his large, colourful tail, he is communicating his worthiness as a mate to peahens. When a stranger smiles at you, he can be indicating friendliness or nervousness in a novel situation. Perhaps the form of communication we most commonly think of is auditory communication. When you hear a dog growl, you interpret the auditory information to guide your decision to not to pet the dog. Despite the richness of information that can be transferred in these examples, humans are unique in their use of the most complex form of communication – language. According operational definitions of language accepted by most psychologists, no other species of animal except humans use language.

Think for a moment about what sets language apart from other forms of communication. Is it the words? It may seem so, but how are the sounds that we call "words" different from the purr of a cat? Is it the way that language allows us to combine words into sentences? How is that different from a bird combining sounds into a song? Perhaps it's the fact that language is symbolic? How could that be any different from a bee using carefully directed movements to tell her siblings the location of a food source? In the next section, we will discuss the characteristics of language which make it is such a unique form of communication.

Section 1: What Sets Language Apart from other Forms of Communication?

The Four Criteria

Language is a uniquely human form of communication that is symbolic, involves arbitrary associations, is productive, and is rule-governed.

1. **Language is symbolic.** To communicate using language, a user must understand that various language stimuli represent different meanings and concepts. In an oral language, the relevant stimuli are the sounds that you emit in the form of words. Of course, different oral languages have different types of stimuli for the same meaning: the sounds that make up the word "friend" in English are different in French (*amie*) or Korean (*cheengu*). However, in all languages, the relevant stimuli (words) are not necessarily concrete examples of the concept, but rather, *represent* the concept as a whole[2].

To understand this distinction, think about the difference in requesting a cookie from a tray of various baked goods by *pointing* to it or using the *word* 'cookie' by name. In the first case, you can only physically indicate the item you want if it happens to be present in the environment. In this way, your communication involves a concrete item. This is a type of communication we might see in pre-linguistic toddlers, other primates, or me when I am visiting Iceland, a country which uses a language for which I have an extremely limited grasp of the native vocabulary. In the second case, you ask for the item by using the word instead. Now, there is no need for the item itself to be present at that time. You can use

---

[2] In sign language, the language stimuli are signs, each of which represents a different word or letter of the alphabet.

the word to ask for the cookie even in its absence, since the word is a symbol that *represents* the cookie. The benefits of the symbolic nature of language cannot be understated. The ability to refer to objects in their absence opens the possibility to communicate about complex ideas and hypothetical concepts. It allows you to communicate memories of past events and hopes for the future. If I stop by my local Icelandic bakery and do not immediately see any of my favourite dried fig cake, I can ask the baker when I can next expect a fresh batch of *gráfíkjuterta*. It even allows us to discuss objects that we might never directly see and only exist in theory such as a black hole[3]. Language provides an organized system to represent concepts symbolically and communicate simple and complex ideas about them.

2. **Language involves arbitrary associations.** One consequence of the symbolic nature of language is that the words we use for concepts are arbitrarily assigned. Look at the shape below. Is it properly called a bliggo, cripton, or a dingo-bingo? There really is no correct answer as I just made this shape up, and any of the words (or others) could arguably be used to name this novel shape (though my personal preference is 'dingo-bingo'). The word used to represent the shape is not constrained by any characteristics of the shape itself, allowing the word chosen to be completely arbitrary.

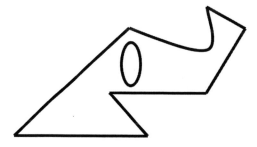

Figure 5.1.

Because language involves arbitrary associations of sounds to meaning, this shape could be called a bliggo, cripton, dingo-bingo, or any other assigned name.

Other forms of communication do not involve arbitrary associations. For example, all dogs instantly recognize that when another dog snarls and shows his teeth, he is indicating aggression and serving a serious warning. However, arbitrary associations allow various languages to use different sounds to label the same item. If the sounds used to identify items and concepts were associated with their inherent meaning, all languages would use the same sound to identify a given item. It is worth noting that there are some examples of words whose sounds *are* associated with their meanings; we term this rather unusual situation **onomatopoeia**. Some examples of these in English are the words 'meow', 'splash' and 'hiccup'.

---

[3] Another notable example is the proposed existence of a "Control" key on the keyboard of Chuck Norris' computer. In theory, this would not be possible (since Chuck Norris is always in control), but the fact remains that we can talk about its existence in theory.

In these exceptional cases, the sounds of the words are not set arbitrarily but attempt to imitate natural sounds to reflect their meaning[4].

3. **Language is productive.** Language is designed to use a small number of components to produce and understand a wide range of symbols (Kuczaj & Kirkpatrick, 1993). For example, language has a limited set of rules that can be used to combine a limited set of symbols in infinite ways. In this way, new combinations are constantly being created. An oral language is made up of phonemes, which are the smallest sound units of language (we will talk more about these later in the chapter). At first thought, it might seem like there are many phonemes, but in fact English only uses about 40 phonemes. From this relatively small set of phonemes and limited rules about how they can be combined emerges a vast vocabulary of over 500,000 words listed in the compendious Oxford English Dictionary. In turn, these words can then be combined into a functionally infinite number of sentences.

The productive nature of language allows its users to combine a series of representative symbols to express novel meaning in groupings of words that may never have been presented together before. If I said to you "I furiously dyed my bold hair purple on the flipside", you are likely hearing a novel sentence that you have not heard before. Nevertheless, you can still understand my general message, because you understand the individual components of the novel sentence.

4. **Language is rule-governed.** Despite the fact that the productive nature of language allows an infinite number of combinations to be created, each combination must follow a defined set of rules in order to make sense. Although someone could utter the following sequence of words: *"helmet count pick the red"*, the sequence does not follow the phrase structure rules of English, and so the sentence is nonsensical. Thus, while the productivity concept holds, the infinite combinations of symbols are constrained by the rules of each language.

It is important to note that different languages have different rules about how symbols can be combined. For example, each oral language has its own set of rules about which phonemes can occur in succession. In English, the phoneme /l/ is allowed to follow the phoneme /b/, as in the words 'blue' and 'blubber', while the phoneme /d/ is not. In Czech, the phoneme /k/ is allowed to follow the phoneme /d/, as is in the words 'kdo' (who) and 'kdy' (when), while in English we would never see these two phonemes in succession. As a native English speaker, you might be quite amazed by the Czech word for 'fourth' (ctvrty), which includes several phoneme combinations that are not permissible in English!

---

[4] It is interesting to note that given the same source of natural sounds, various languages apply slightly different onomatopoeia words to familiar animal calls. At a family reunion, an English duck would say "quak, quack"; Swedish: kvack; Dutch: kwak, kwak; Hebrew: ga ga ga; Japanese: gaagaa; Russian: krya-krya; Polish: kwa kwa.

HOW DEEP ARE THE EFFECTS OF LANGUAGE ON THOUGHT? TIME ESTIMATION IN SPEAKERS OF ENGLISH, INDONESIAN, GREEK, AND SPANISH

Researchers: Daniel Casasanto, Lera Boroditsky, Webb Phillips, Jesse Greene, Shima Goswami, Simon Bocanegra-Thiel, Ilia Santiago-Diaz (MIT Department of Brain and Cognitive Sciences), Olga Fotokopoulu, Ria Pita (Aristotle University of Thessaloniki), and David Gil (Max Planck DCenter for Evolutionary Anthropology)

Source: Casasanto, D., Boroditsky, L., Phillips, W., Greene, J., Goswami, S., Bocanegra-Thiel, S, Santiago-Diaz, I., Fotokopoulu, R.P., & Gil, D. (2004). How deep are the effects of language on thought? Time estimation in speakers of English, Indonesian, Greek, and Spanish. *Proceedings*, 186-191.

Note: The material below is the author's summarized description of the original published article.

Here researchers take a modern approach to the Whorfian hypothesis by systematically testing whether language metaphors about the concept of time can affect how time is represented non-linguistically, or the mental conceptions of time. The Whorfian hypothesis suggests that the particular language individuals' use can shape thought, a theory that breaks from traditional views of language and non-linguistic concepts as universal. Problems exist within the Whorfian hypothesis that has prevented it from mainstream acceptance. First, the linguistic data used to indicate that different languages differ in terms of, for example, metaphors, is subjective and anecdotal; an empirical database of such language differences had not been established. Secondly, there is a lack of non-linguistic data to make any inferences about how differences in language affect mental concepts. The Whorfian hypothesis seems to be based on a circular argument: claims about differences in mental activity are only supported by differences in language use. Current research has sought to take a more substantial and empirical look at the Whorfian hypothesis and as a result, the 'thinking for speaking theory' has been developed. Essentially this view purports the idea that we think about things and pay attention to stimuli in our environment in ways that are shaped by and match how we conceptualize them through language; in essence, our thought, abstract mental concepts in particular, is shaped by how we speak. In this experiment, though, researchers seek to discover whether there are influences beyond the thinking for speaking theory, for concepts that cannot necessarily be uttered e.g. explaining colour to a congenitally blind individual. This possibility has been explored, specifically by looking at high-level linguistic and symbolic representations of the concept of time, and has shown evidence for the shaping role of language. The current question, however, is whether low-level non-linguistic non-symbolic representations of time can also be shaped by language by exploring the effects of spatiotemporal metaphors on time estimation tasks. In order to do this, experimenters decided to first establish empirically verified differences in temporal metaphors across different languages, and to then compare whether any differences in turn affect mental representations of time.

EXPERIMENT 1

In order to conceptualize abstract non-spatial phenomena, spatial metaphors are often used; this allows for phenomena to be better understood in more concrete terms e.g. she is of *high* social status. For the concept of time in particular, languages such as English and Indonesian tend to conceptualize time in a spatiotemporal sense, or in measures of distance e.g. he ran for a *long* time, she was only gone for a *short* while. However, other languages such as Spanish and Greek tend to conceptualize time as quantity e.g. he was gone for *much* time; she had a *big* day at work (we can see how this does not quite seem right in English).

METHODS & RESULTS

Experimenters sought to empirically verify such cross-linguistic differences. This was done by gathering a variety of distance and quantity time phrases for each language, entering them into the Google search engine, and recording the number of hits for each phrase. With controls set in place, such as search restrictions to ensure hits found used the appropriate language, the researchers found significant differences between English and Indonesian metaphors in comparison to Spanish and Greek metaphors that matched predictions, and continuous work is being performed to ensure the empirical validity of such results.

EXPERIMENTS 2 & 3

Following, experiments sought to look at the effects of language on temporal thinking on a non-linguistic level, not just a 'thinking for speaking' level. Past work by Cassanto and Boroditsky (2001) has found that non-linguistic, non-symbolic conceptions of time are influenced by spatial factors. More concretely, individuals were asked to estimate how far and for how long lines growing across a screen were in growing; answers were indicated by clicking the mouse. For English speakers, lines that grew a longer distance were estimated to take a longer time to grow than lines that grew a shorter distance, even though the time taken was actually the same; that is, conceptions of time were influenced by spatial factors. However, when judging the distance of line growth, individuals did not show any influences of time, thus suggesting that because English speaks of time in terms of distance, distance had a substantially larger influence on conceptions of duration. Here we see the extension of language's influence into the non-linguistic realm. This study, though, looked only at English speakers; in order to ask whether language can influence non-linguistic concepts, researchers must explore potential cross-linguistic differences in influence.

METHODS

Two tasks were used in order to shed light onto the puzzle of whether metaphors of time influence mental conceptions of time. Experiment 2 utilized a growing line task, similar to the task of the former research discussed. In order to indicate distance estimations, participants used the mouse to click on the screen for the start of the distance, drag the mouse across the screen and click to indicate the end of the distance. In order to indicate duration estimations, participants used the mouse to click on the screen, wait as long as they felt the interval to be, and to then click again. Experiment 3 utilized a water container filling task, where individuals were required to watch a container of water fill and to estimate the length of time taken for it to fill, or for how long the filling occurred. The procedure was identical to that of Experiment 2, however, for the estimation of the fullness of the container, participants were required to use mouse clicks to indicate the estimated water levels. The experimental groups consisted of 65 individuals: native speakers of English, Indonesian, Spanish and Greek. Again, English and Indonesian were considered distance languages, and Spanish and Greek were considered quantity languages. It was

Draft

hypothesized that for Experiment 2, time measurements were expected to be significantly influenced by distance for English and Indonesian speakers, as the results of Cassanto and Boroditsky's work suggest, but only mildly for Spanish and Greek speakers. For Experiment 3 it was hypothesized that the fullness or quantity of water in the container would have a significant influence on time estimation for Spanish and Greek speakers, but only mildly for English and Indonesian speakers. That is, even if it actually took the same amount of time for 2 containers to fill, the one with more water in it would be predicted to have taken more time to fill.

RESULTS

The first result of interest is that individuals were fairly accurate in their time estimates, and equally so for both tasks across all groups. There were, however, key subtly, but significant differences that fell in line with the theoretical predictions. That is, English and Indonesian speakers were significantly influenced by distance in Experiment 2 in comparison to Spanish and Greek speakers, who were significantly influenced by quantity in Experiment 3 in comparison to the English and Indonesian speakers. Analyses indicate a strong correspondence between metaphors and non-linguistic behaviour, at least for time related non-linguistic behaviour.

DISCUSSION

Results seem to suggest that thought, is, in certain ways, affected by the language that we use. However, it is possible that we have inherent universal concepts of space and time, but through the learning of particular languages and their corresponding metaphors, our conceptual mapping may be shaped in certain ways. Or it is possible that language is fundamentally responsible for the conceptual mappings that we have and use, that is, language creates how we perceive the world and related non-linguistic concepts. What experimenters hope to establish with this body of evidence is support not only for the role of language in shaping linguistic representations, but even non-linguistic representations that form the foundation of our perceptions and cognitive processes.

LIMITATIONS

Although a well-controlled study, it is still early to make the strong claims purported. Being that only four languages are used, and the concept of time is the only non-linguistic concept explored, it is unsure as to whether it is legitimate to generalize these findings to all non-linguistic, low-level, non-symbolic concepts. It is worth exploring a greater number of languages, larger populations, and different non-linguistic concepts. As well, the database built in Experiment 1 is preliminary; indeed it is empirically founded, but remains a work in progress that needs replication in order to ensure that the work they have done is verifiable and that the researchers have been exhaustive enough in their searches and phrase use.

COMMENTS

This modern approach to the Whorfian hypothesis allows us to question the long held assumptions about the universality of non-linguistic concepts and the ignorance of the influence of language on thought. Although results so far are not convincing enough to suggest an entire lack of any universal non-linguistic concepts, or that our concepts are entirely the result of linguistic influences, they definitely make it hard to deny at least a partial role of language influence. This study highlights the importance of considering the role of nature and nurture, not necessarily just one or the other, not only for language development in itself but in how language development interacts with the development of non-linguistic mental concepts. Mental concepts, like language, may have some sort of universal, species-wide foundation, but it is through development, interaction with the world, and particular experiences that mould and shape those concepts, with language being one of the most important and foundational factors that helps in that shaping.

SECTION 1 REVIEW: What is Language?

TABLE 5.1

Language is a sophisticated form of communication unique to our species, characterized by the use of symbolism, arbitrary associations, productivity and rule use.		
Symbolic	**Arbitrary Associations**	**Productive and Rule Governed**
• Words and gestures are used as representations of specific concepts • This allows for communication of abstract and hypothetical concepts as well as ideas, things, etc that are not present	• Words used to represent concepts in language are made up and arbitrary • This is why various languages exist – the same concept is represented by different words in different languages as a result of this arbitrary nature of language	• With the limited set of sound combinations and words in a language, a potentially infinite number of expressions can be made, including completely novel expressions • With each language, though, rules about what makes sense still exist despite the productive nature of language

Section 2: The Structure of Language

There are at least 3000 oral languages active in the world today. While these languages are based on combining different sounds in various ways, all languages contain some similar features in their underlying structure. These structural characteristics allow scientists who study language (**linguists**) to define components of language and make cross-linguistic comparisons of structure.

Morphemes: the symbols of language

The symbols of language used to transmit information are called *morphemes*. In oral languages, **morphemes** are the smallest units of sound that contain information[5]. Morphemes are often words, but a single word can be made up of more than one morpheme. For example, the word *lady* is a single word that contains a single morpheme, but the word *ladybug* is a single word that contains two morphemes: *lady* and *bug*, each of which provides a discrete piece of information. Each of these morphemes can also stand alone as individual words: you would know what I was talking about if I mentioned either a lady or a bug. However, not all morphemes can be used as individual words; some must be added to another morpheme to make sense. For example, the word '*bugs*' is made up of two morphemes: the morpheme *bug* identifies the object, and the morpheme *s* indicates that there is more than one.

Analysing the morphemic structure of language in this way can reveal much about its origins and development. How many morphemes do you think make up the term *laptop computer*? You might be surprised that the word *computer* actually has two morphemes: *compute* and *r*. Together these label a machine that does computing. Thus, the term *laptop computer* has four morphemes: *lap, top, compute*, and *r,* which together label a machine that does computing and can sit on your lap.

Phonemes: the building blocks of symbols

Although in oral language morphemes are the smallest units of sound that contain information, they are not the absolute smallest units of sound. A morpheme can be broken apart into its constituent sounds, which are called **phonemes**. For example, the word (morpheme) *drag* has four phonemes: /d/, /r/, /a/ and /g/. Various languages typically use a set of between 30-50 phonemes. However, some African languages use over 100 phonemes (Konig, 2008) which linguists estimate is at about the limit of the human capacity to distinguish and recognize basic phonemic sounds. (Many of the phonemes used in languages with extensive phonemic libraries are similar to those used in English, but may also include unique phonemes such as *clicks*). Each language also has rules about how phonemes can be combined. To produce English sounds, we can combine certain phonemes, such as /m/, /a/, /p/, but not others, such as /c/, /v/, /t/. However, a different language may allow phonemic combinations that are not allowed in English.

It may be tempting to think that each letter of a written language represents a single phoneme, but it is often more complicated. In English, some letters can represent more than one phoneme. For example,

---

[5] In a sign language, morphemes are units of signs rather than units of sound.

the letter *c* can make a /s/ sound or a /k/ sound. The letter *g* can also make two sounds, as in the words green and gentle. Furthermore, combinations of letters can make new phonemes, as in the case of *th* or *sh*. Some languages (such as Italian) have a more consistent letter-to-sound correspondence, so that a given letter will always make the same sound. We call these **transparent orthographies** and they have important consequences for reading development. Children learning to read languages with transparent orthographies have a much easier time than children learning to read English and master reading relatively quickly (Spencer & Hanley, 2003).

Syntax: the rules for constructing sentences

Syntax (or grammar) refers to the rules that govern how we put words together to form a sentence. Differences in syntactic rules between languages are common. Some languages (such as French) assign gender to different objects. When using articles (words like *a* or *the*) in French, speakers must take into account the gender of the noun the article is introducing. Other languages (such as English) only assign grammatical gender where it corresponds to biological gender. For example, we specifically say 'he' or 'she' when referring to the sex of an individual but the object 'table' does not have a gender assigned in English, although it does in French.

Table 5.2.

English article	English noun	French article	French noun
The	Paper	le	papier
The	Car	la	voiture
A	Book	un	livre
A	Cup	une	tasse

French uses articles to assign gender to inanimate nouns, but English does not.

Languages also differ syntactically in terms of the order in which words occur in a sentence. English uses a *subject-verb-object* order of presentation, while Hindi and Japanese use a *subject-object-verb* order. Thus, while in English a child might say "I bought cookies", a direct translation of the same sentence to Hindi or Japanese would be the equivalent of "I cookies bought." These syntactic differences can be very challenging for a person learning a second language that uses a different word order from their native language. Languages also have rules about the parts of speech that must comprise a grammatical sentence. On account of these rules, although the following sentences may make some sense, they do not quite meet the rules of syntax:

This sentence no verb.

Drum vapour worker cigarette flick boom.

This is not a complete. This either.

(all sentences taken from Pinker, 1994)

But what about the following sentence? Can you identify what's wrong with it?

You have to really be careful[6].

In spite of the fact that you use syntax with language, you probably find it difficult to directly describe the syntactic rules of your native language – you just seemed to intuitively know it. Children learn these rules quite automatically through simple exposure to the language. This is an impressive task that adults learning a new language often find very difficult. Nonetheless, even for children, learning syntax does not proceed without mistakes. Children often make *overregularizations* in their syntax, as in the sentence "The boy runned home" and "My foots is growing fast". These types of errors indicate that children are in the process of learning the rules of the language, but have yet to master the exceptions to the rules.

Semantics: the meaning of it all

The **semantics** of a language refer to the meaning contained within. Remember, language consists of a set of symbols (words) that each represents a specific meaning. As a child's vocabulary increases, linguists would note that *semantic knowledge* increases. Semantics can also refer to the fact that we are able to understand different meanings for a word depending on the context in which it is presented. For example, you would interpret the word 'present' very differently in the following three sentences:

1. Were all of your group members *present* in class?

2. What was your favourite birthday *present*?

3. You can't always worry about the future – focus on the *present*!

---

[6] This is an example of a split infinitive, where an adverb occurs between *to* and the *verb*. To meet formal rules of grammar, this sentence should read 'You really have to be careful'.

Table 5.3

Although each language is composed of four important parts, how they are defined differs across languages		
Morphemes & Phonemes	**Syntax**	**Semantics**
• **Morphemes** are the smallest unit of sound or signing that contains meaning; these can be full words or parts of words • **Phonemes** are the smallest units of sound; the number, type, and how they may be combined varies across languages	• Unique to each language, syntax represents the rules that govern how morphemes and words may be combined in order to make sense • This includes gender assignment, the order of types of words and so on • Syntax is commonly automatically understood although difficult to describe	• The meaning that is produced through the use and combination of certain words and morphemes; language can have meaning and be understood without syntax

Section 3: Language Development

Humans are born with the ability to communicate their very basic needs through crying and basic reflexive behaviours during infancy to have their basic needs met. However, it is not until children develop language that they can move beyond this basic communication. As presented in Table 5.4, children develop language skills in a very consistent order and reach milestones at predictable ages, meaning that we can use a child's language skills to assess whether she is developing at a normal pace.

Table 5.4: Language milestones seen over the first 5 years of life.

Age	Language-related skills
0-5 months	Turns head towards sound source; makes noise when spoken to
6-11 months	Babbles, understands 'no'; tries to imitate sounds
12-17 months	Answers simple questions non-verbally; points to objects and people; follows simple directions paired with gestures; uses 1-3 words in combination
18-23 months	Follows simple verbal directions; asks for familiar items by name; starts combining words ('more juice'); imitates animal sounds
24 months	Understands approximately 50 words; uses approximately 40 words
2-3 years	Speaks in 2-3 word phrases; answers simple questions; begins to use plurals and past tense
4-5 years	Uses approximately 200-300 words; answers 'why' questions
5 years	Understands more than 2000 words; uses longer sentences (at least 8 words in length), can engage in conversation

Source: http://www.nidcd.nih.gov/health/voice/speechandlanguage.html#mychild

Universal phonemic sensitivity

A fascinating branch of research has demonstrated that infants have **universal phonemic sensitivity** – the ability to discriminate between virtually all phonemes even before they learn language. This is an ability that is lost into adulthood. Much of this research has been done with very young infants who are far too young to speak. How we can tell what infants can perceive? Infant researchers have had to develop some very creative techniques to address these issues. One commonly used approach is the *conditioned head-turn procedure*. This approach uses a number of the concepts you read about in Chapter 3 on learning. It begins by playing two different phonemes that are very easy to discriminate (e.g., /ba/, /da/) over a set of speakers. By pairing these sounds with a reinforcer, such as a puppet or a stuffed animal, the researcher conditions the infant to turn her head toward the speaker whenever she hears a new sound. Once established, they can then habituate the infant to a particular sound (e.g., /ba/) by playing it over and over again. If they then play a novel sound (e.g., /pa/) and the infant turns her head towards the speaker playing that sound, the researchers infer that the infant can discriminate between the two sounds. In this way, researchers can determine exactly which sounds infants are able to discriminate which can be compared with adult discrimination abilities. Because the infant is sitting on her mother's lap during the procedure, it is important that the mother is wearing headphones. Why? The mother's headphones ensure that she can't hear the sounds being played over the speakers which may lead her to inadvertently respond to the sound and cue the infant to respond as well.

Interesting implications come from comparisons of phonemic perception in infants and adults from different language cultures. Remember that not all languages use the same phonemes. In one experiment, researchers in Janet Werker's lab at the University of British Columbia compared 6-8-month-olds from English-speaking families, English-speaking adults, and Hindi-speaking adults on their ability to discriminate two different /t/ sounds which are present in Hindi but not in English (Werker, Gilbert, Humphrey, & Tees, 1981). An adult English speaker typically has a difficult time perceiving the difference between these two Hindi phonemes[7]. Using the conditioned head-turn procedure, Werker and her colleagues (1981) found that *infants* from English-speaking families were almost as good at the Hindi phoneme discrimination as the Hindi speakers. Interestingly, the English adults were significantly worse than the Hindi adults *and* the infants. Researchers have found a similar pattern across a wide variety of languages (e.g. Werker & Tees, 1984).

Well before infants develop sophisticated language skills, they can discriminate more phonemes than adults can. Why do adults lose the phonemic sensitivity that they enjoyed as infants? The answer appears to deal with experience with relevant phoneme contrasts. For example, the Korean and Japanese oral languages do not differentiate between the phonemes /r/ and /l/. Because adult speakers of Korean and Japanese do not have practice using this phonemic contrast in their language use as adults, they have difficulty perceiving the difference between these sounds. As a result, adults who only speak Korean or Japanese would have trouble discriminating the words *rash* and *lash*. However, Korean or Japanese infants (and infants from all cultures) are able to easily discriminate these sounds.

---

[7] If you focus carefully on the /t/ phoneme in the words *top* and *stop*, you should be able to hear a slight difference that is similar to the Hindi contrast.

The process of losing the ability to distinguish between contrasts in sounds not used in native language is called **perceptual narrowing**. A key question to this issue is when does the ability to discriminate non-native sounds disappear? Werker and her colleagues (Werker & Tees, 1983; Werker & Tees, 1984) tested teenagers, children, and infants, and found, to their surprise, that universal phonemic sensitivity was lost during the first year of life! When they compared 6-8-month-olds, 8-10-month-olds, and 10-12-month-olds on their ability to discriminate between the two Hindi phonemes, they found that over 96% of the youngest infants could discriminate the difference, approximately 70% of the middle age group could, and only 20% of the eldest infants could. They also demonstrated a similar pattern of decreasing perceptual ability using phonemes that are used in Nthlakapmx, a language used by aboriginals in British Colombia.

The pattern of perceptual narrowing in language development indicates that there may be a biological basis for phoneme discrimination that is influenced by experience in the first year of life (Werker, 2000). Specifically, our perceptual abilities are influenced by the stimuli to which we are exposed. Infants who are immersed in an English-language setting will benefit from being able to discriminate between /r/ and /l/, since both sounds are used in English. In contrast, infants immersed in a Japanese-language setting will not benefit from maintaining that ability, since the distinction between these sounds is irrelevant. Thus, infants are born prepared to deal with any language and as their perceptual system is exposed to a particular language setting, it develops accordingly.

Research from Laurel Trainor at McMaster University has provided insight into an important factor that may help infants learn about the patterns in their own language. When people talk to infants, they tend to speak in a higher pitch and exaggerate changes in pitch and use of rhythm. This type of speech is called **infant-directed speech,** informally known as *motherese*. Dr. Trainor found that the exaggerated changes in pitch used in infant-directed speech help 6-7-month-olds discriminate between different vowel sounds, possibly helping them learn the categories of vowel sounds that are present in their native language (Trainor & Desjardins, 2002).

Box 5.1: Application | Foreign Accent Syndrome

Neurological and cognitive research has provided strong evidence for the specialization of certain brain areas for the production and comprehension of language. For example, damage to Broca's area, a small area in the left frontal lobe, leads to difficulty in the production of fluent speech. Individuals are likely to understand what is being said to them, but they seem to have trouble finding the words to respond. Damage to Wernicke's area, located in the left temporal lobe, allows individuals to speak fluently, but their speech makes no sense. Such individuals also have difficulty understanding written and spoken language. However, these are not the only syndromes that exist within the domain of language.

A remarkable yet rare language syndrome that resulting from brain damage is Foreign Accent Syndrome (FAS). Patients with FAS have typically suffered from a stroke or head injury that has damaged areas in the left hemisphere involved in motor control of speech (Mariën & Verhoeven, 2007). When individuals regain speech after the incident, they are able to speak their native language, but they seem to have a foreign accent. Their language skills otherwise typically seem unimpaired to the casual listener (Katz, Garst, & Levitt, 2008). The first example of FAS came in the early 1900's and since that time only about 60 cases have been reported. Despite its rarity, this syndrome can teach us a lot about the brain areas and processes involved in speech production.

FAS has been reported in speakers of a variety of languages. For example, Mariën and Verhoeven (2007) worked with a 57-year-old Dutch speaker who suffered a stroke and subsequently developed an accent that sounded "French or German", according to listeners. Another patient they worked with spoke Dutch with a North African accent after his stroke, although with 6 months of speech therapy, his accent diminished substantially. Luzzi et al. (2008) worked with a patient who began speaking Italian with a Spanish accent. Atypically, she had not suffered a stroke or traumatic brain injury, but subsequent medical appointments over the course of year showed that her language began to deteriorate in other ways and she was having trouble producing fluent speech. Her FAS was in fact the first sign of a degenerative neurological disease.

An especially relevant case of FAS comes from a woman in Windsor, Ontario who suffered a stroke and subsequently spoke with what sounded like a Newfoundland accent. She had lived in Southern Ontario her whole life and had only traveled to Florida. Her case was unusual since patients diagnosed with FAS are typically perceived as having an accent of a different language instead of a different dialect of their native language (Naidoo, Warriner, Oczkowski, Sévigny, & Humphreys, 2008). Indeed, the fact that her accent sounded Canadian delayed diagnosis of FAS, as healthcare professionals working with her assumed she was from Atlantic Canada.

FAS seems remarkable to its observers because there is often no logical explanation for its appearance. Monolingual patients often start using an accent of a language they have never used or heard (e.g. Luzzi et al., 2008). How then can we explain how this phenomenon occurs?

The answer continues to be a working progress, but careful analysis of FAS patients' speech indicates that while it *sounds* like they are speaking with a foreign accent, in fact this perception is caused by fairly simple but consistent changes in the way they speak. For example, in Luzzi et al.'s (2008) case study of the Italian woman's FAS, her pronunciation of the Italian sound 'il' changed slightly so that it sounded more like a Spanish 'el'. Similar changes occurred with her pronunciation of several Italian consonants, making Italian words containing those consonants sound as though they were being spoken by someone with a Spanish accent. Similar basic changes were observed in a Texan woman who only spoke English developed FAS following an allergic reaction and spoke with what people described as a Swedish or Eastern European accent (Katz, Garst, & Levitt, 2008). Careful analysis of the speech of FAS patients often reveals that their speech is modified in its basic timing and rhythmic properties, or prosody (Blumstein & Kurowski, 2006), leading to the perception of a foreign accent. In fact, analysis by linguists indicates that these accents do not actually meet all of the patterns neither of the foreign language (Naidoo et al., 2008) nor of any particular language (Blumstein & Kurowski, 2006).

Our tendency to organize sensory input into a meaningful whole perhaps contributes to our perception of a consistent foreign accent in these patients (Naidoo et al., 2008). Fitting with this explanation is work indicating that the foreign language that is perceived often depends on the listener. The same patient can be perceived to speak English with an Asian, German, or Swedish accent (Ingram, McCormack, & Kennedy, 1992) or Italian, Polish, or Czech (Moen, 2000). In order to make sense of the changes in prosody that are heard, it is possible that the perceivers conclude that such individuals are all of a sudden talking in a different accent!

Early language skills

The first year of life is a busy period in which an infant experiments and refines her use of sounds tailored to her native language. Although infants do not start producing language until late in their first year of life, they show language-related skills very early in life. For example, even very young infants will respond to the presence of another person. In the **still-face procedure,** an adult looks at an infant while maintaining a non-responsive, neutral facial expression. Infants who are only 2 or 3 months old will become distressed during this procedure (Weinberg & Tronick, 2008), indicating that even at this young age, they have some expectations about how a face-to-face social interaction should proceed. Sometime during the first two months of life, we also typically see an infant's first social smile – a smile in direct response to a social interaction.

These social behaviours are followed by the pre-linguistic behaviour of cooing. Infants begin **cooing** between the ages of 2-4 months, making sounds that combine consonants with 'oo' and 'ah' sounds. During this stage of development, parents can practice "conversational skills" with their infants by taking turns cooing or vocalizing with them (Kuczaj & Hill, 2003). This turn-taking is an important component of later conversational skills: trying to have a conversation with someone who does not take turns well is quite a frustrating experience! The skills that allow children to communicate appropriately and effectively in a social situation (as is done in a conversation) are called **pragmatics**. Although early experience with turn-taking and other conversation-related skills does exist, pragmatic abilities continue to develop throughout childhood (Kuczaj & Hill, 2003) and are fine-tuned into adolescence (Obler, 1993).

Between 4-6 months of age, infants start babbling. This often sounds like they are playing with sounds, as they make a wide range of repetitive combinations of consonants and vowels such as 'bababa' and 'nananana'. Cooing and babbling may constitute a form of practice for later language production, as the infant gains some control over his vocal system and uses sounds present in his native language (Boysson-Bardies, De Sagart, & Durand, 1984).

As infants progress in her language development, she begins to repeat certain combinations of sounds which eventually form her first words; these typically emerge somewhere around 1 year of age. Typically, her first word refers to something that is important in her infant environment; people such as 'Mama', actions such as 'up', familiar labels such as 'hot,' or moving objects such as 'cat'. At this stage, there is a tendency to use more nouns than verbs (Bornstein et al., 2004). Infants next enter the **holophrastic phase**, where a single word is used to indicate the meaning of an entire sentence. For example, a child may say 'ball!' to indicate that he wants you to give him his ball, or may cry 'mommy' to indicate that he misses his mother.

Draft

At first, the infant is learning only 2-3 new words per week, but at a point between the ages of 18-24 months, vocabulary expansion hits a rapid increase called the **naming explosion** or **word spurt**. Although there have recently been questions as to whether this is actually a typical and qualitatively unique stage in language development (e.g., Bloom, Hall, & Waxman, 2004; Ganger & Brent, 2001), children typically acquire a vocabulary of about 250 words by the time they are 2 years old. By the time they are 2½ years old, this vocabulary grow to over 850 words and continues to increase very rapidly until they are about 6 years old, by which point she has mastered a whopping 10 000 word vocabulary. A characteristic process observe during this time of rapid vocabulary growth is **fast mapping**, whereby children learn the meaning following only 1 or 2 encounters with a new word. At around 6 years of age, the increase in vocabulary starts to slow down and most children have mastered a large majority of the vocabulary of their language, although the complexity of their syntax may continue to improve with throughout childhood.

It is important to note that there are large individual differences in vocabulary size. For example, Bates et al. (2004) found that vocabularies of 1½-year-olds ranged in size from 6 to 357 words. One important factor involved in individual differences is gender; girls typically have larger vocabularies and overall better language skills than boys between the ages of approximately 2 and 6 years (Bornstein, Hahn & Haynes, 2004). There are many potential reasons proposed for these observed sex differences including both biological factors (differences in brain maturation rates between boys and girls, especially in language areas of the brain) and environmental factors (perhaps girls play in ways that encourage more language interactions). Interestingly, birth order may also play a role in individual differences observed in vocabulary size. First-born children tend to develop larger vocabularies earlier than their second-born siblings, at least based on mothers' reports of vocabulary (Bornstein, Leach, & Haynes, 2004). There are also differences in the age at which girls and boys start using particular types of words. For example, Wehberg et al. (2008) found that girls start using words about social relations and for objects that need to be cared for (e.g., doll, baby) earlier than boys. In contrast, boys start using words for loud moving objects earlier than girls.

Receptive and expressive vocabulary

The words that children use to speak are referred to as the **expressive vocabulary**. However, if you have ever interacted with infants and toddlers, you may have noticed that they can understand a lot more complex words and sentences than they are able to produce. Words that children can understand but may not yet use are referred to as **receptive vocabulary.** Receptive vocabulary develops well before expressive vocabulary (Golinkoff & Hirsh-Pasek, 1995).

Along with task of learning how to produce language, infants must learn how to understand language – they must develop language comprehension. To appreciate just how difficult this task can be, imagine listening to your lectures for this class in a foreign language. Your challenge would include understanding the meaning of foreign words and even segmenting the stream of sounds to determine where one word ended and the next began. Unlike written language, there are no simple discernable "spaces" between spoken words. In print form, imagine if we removed the spaces between words, and you are faced with a segmentation challenge similar to that faced with oral language. You might have no trouble segmenting the following sequence into words since you are familiar with English: *Themealwasverygood.* Unless you know German, you would likely have a very difficult time doing the same task for the following sequence which says the same thing: *eshatsehrgutgeschmeckt.*[8]

SECTION 3 REVIEW: Language Development

Table 5.5

Early shaping of language skills set the stage for how inherent biological factors will be formed, including appropriate social communication		
Universal Phoneme Sensitivity	**Early Language Skills**	**Receptive & Expressive Vocabulary**
• Within the first year of life, infants are able to discriminate between the phonemes of all languages, as measured by the **conditioned head turn procedure** • **Perceptual narrowing**, the loss of universal phoneme sensitivity, occurs when individuals begin to specialize in a particular language and suggests that this phenomenon is somewhat inherent but shaped by early experiences such as **infant directed speech**	• Language related skills are present quite early in development • The **still face procedure** demonstrates understanding of expectations of face-to-face social interaction • **Pragmatics**, the understanding and use of appropriate communication, develops through conversational cooing and vocalizing with parents • **Cooing and babbling** represent precursors for the **holophrastic** and **word spurt phases**, as well as rapid vocabulary growth	• **Expressive vocab** refers to spoken words used to express languages • **Receptive vocab** refers to the understanding of more complex words and expressions by children that they are not yet able to use; language comprehension is just as important as production for language development

---

[8] The correct segmentation is *es hat sehr gut geschmeckt.*

Draft

Section 4: Further Characteristics of Language Development

Characteristics of early language

I mentioned earlier that children start their language use with holophrastic speech, where a single word is used to indicate meaning of a more complex idea. This phase of language development typically starts sometime between 10-18 months of age. During this stage, children make some very characteristic errors in their language. **Overextensions** are errors that involve using a fairly specific word for a broader set of related items. For example, a child may use the word *car* to label a bus, a truck, a wagon, and a bicycle. Overextensions can occur with verbs as well; an infant may use the word 'open' to describe opening a door, turning on a light, and peeling an orange. A less frequent error is **underextension** where a general term is used for only a very particular instance of an item. For example, a child may use the word *dog* only for his particular dog, but not for the dogs he sees at the park. Both types of errors decrease as children learn more words to help them discriminate within and between categories of items and verbs. Interestingly, overextensions in *production* persist longer than overextensions in *comprehension* (Naigles & Gelman, 1995). This means that the same little boy who uses the word *car* for a bus, a truck, and a wagon can point to the correct items if asked. This pattern is consistent with the pattern of expressive vocabulary developing later than receptive vocabulary.

Once children have established a more substantial vocabulary, they enter a phase of **telegraphic speech**. In this phase (which starts sometime between 18-24 months), they use short phrases that contain only the most crucial information they are trying to communicate, much like those that would be used if you were sending someone a telegram. For example, a child might request more to drink by saying *'more juice'* or ask for his teddy bear by saying *'where teddy'*. As they enter the naming explosion, children are able to use more and more telegraphic expressions to communicate their questions and demands.

As children come to use more complex language, they start to use **overregularizations** -- syntactic errors which involve using a grammatical rule too broadly. Overregularization errors can occur with a variety of syntactic rules; several common examples are given in Table 5.6. As children gain more exposure to language and gain feedback from adults about their use of syntax, their tendency to use overregularizations decreases.

Table 5.6: Common classes and examples of overregularization errors. The correction to the error is given in parentheses.

Pluralization	Past tense
foots (feet)	goed (went)
mans (men)	runned (ran)
mouses (mice)	dooed (did)
sheeps (sheep)	breaked (broke)
teeths/tooths (teeth)	feeled (felt)

Higher language skills

Language development does not end as children enter their school years; it continues throughout childhood and even into adolescence. Most children are 10 years old before they achieve **metalinguistic awareness**: the ability to reflect on language as a symbolic, rule-based communication system. Once they have developed this understanding, they are able to discuss the properties and uses of language, in much the same way that we did at the opening of this chapter. Children make use of metalinguistic awareness when making judgements of grammaticality and understanding figurative language. Before developing metalinguistic awareness, children use language and apply its rules, but they have difficulty talking about language abstractly.

As a child's vocabulary increases, he also gains an understanding that a given word can have multiple meanings (homonyms). Although a basic understanding of homonymy develops sometime between 3 and 4 years of age (Doherty, 2000), children tend to have difficulty applying different meanings appropriately until they are approximately 10 years old (Doherty, 2004, Mazzacco, 1997). Nonetheless, jokes and riddles that play on this developing understanding abound during the early school years[9]. Children also begin to understand sarcasm and irony, where the underlying meaning contrasts with the literal words being spoken. Evidence from Glenwright and Pexman (2010) indicates that this skill

---

[9] How do you make a sausage roll? Push it down a hill.
Why is it easy for elephants to go on holiday? They always have trunks with them.
Why did the teacher have her eyes tested? Because she had bad pupils.
(Taken from Yuill, 2009)

Draft

develops during middle childhood. They tested 5-6-year-olds and 9-10-year-olds on a task that asked them to identify when a statement made by a puppet was sincere or sarcastic. For example, the children would observe two puppets taking turns jumping on a trampoline. When puppet Dave falls and lands on his face, puppet Mike says either "Great trampoline tricks" (sarcastic) or "Awful trampoline tricks" (literal). The researchers found that the older children were very good at attributing Mike's underlying meaning, correctly identifying it as sarcastic or literal over 95% of the time. In contrast, the younger children were good at correctly identifying the literal meaning (93% accuracy) but showed deficits in understanding the sarcastic criticism, correctly identifying Mike's meaning only 52% of the time.

Another higher language skill involves using different language in different settings. You probably speak very differently with your friends than when you are speaking with your professor or making a presentation in class. The ability to modify speech in different settings begins in childhood and continues to develop into adolescence. An early example of language depending on social context at a young age comes from observations of children with their siblings. When interacting with an infant sibling, 2-3-year-olds are more likely to make repeated attempts to maintain the sibling's attention and more likely to speak in shortened sentences (Dunn & Kendrick, 1982).

Box 5.2: Application | Are bilingual children smarter?

A multitude of research over the 20th century has seemed to suggest that bilingual children are less intelligent than monolingual children, citing such factors as lower IQ scores for bilinguals. Such research, however, was restricted by limited measures of intelligence and confounds in research, including the failure to incorporate important variables like socio-economic status and whether tests were in the language bilingual children were more familiar with (Barac & Bialystok, 2011). Through an examination of past literature, Barac & Bialystok (2011) explored a variety of factors such as intelligence, metalinguistic awareness, school achievement and cognition across bilingual and monolingual children, and have come to find that bilingualism tends to have no effects at all (for intelligence) or positive effects (for all other factors). Further work has shown a number of specific enhanced non-verbal cognitive abilities in bilingual children such as selective attention, inhibition of distracters, task switching (Bialystok, 2010), working memory and abstract and symbolic representations (Adesope, Lavin, Thompson & Ungerleider, 2010), abilities honed by the use of two separate linguistic systems. However, findings also suggest that bilingual children do in fact perform worse for factors such as language processing and proficiency. Bialystok (2010) suggests that this is due to underdeveloped vocabulary; bilinguals have a smaller vocabulary for each language than native, monolingual speakers of each language.

What about factors such as long term memory? It may be reasoned that because of increased overall vocabulary from knowing two languages may allow for an increased number of memory traces; both languages may be used as associations for memory retrieval. Kormi-Nouri, Moniri & Nilsso (2003) found significant advantages in both episodic and semantic memory in bilingual children in comparison to monolingual children. Why? By handling two languages and the different sets of rules that go with each, individuals are better able to organize information, keeping them separate when necessary and ensuring that cross-over does not occur across the languages. As well there is increased flexibility: individuals are able to automatically select or access both languages depending on which one is currently in demand. Although bilingual children do not outperform monolingual children in all respects, there definitely are notable advantages across a number of cognitive abilities and makes decisions such as whether to place children in French immersion, or teach them the language of their cultural background, worth considering.

The Whorfian hypothesis

Although there are many similarities in common to the structure of all languages, let us consider the implications of the variability that exists between languages. Of course, we use language to communicate with others, but some theorists have proposed that our very *thoughts* are shaped by language. From this idea came a proposal by Professor Edward Sapir and his student Benjamin Whorf: *language may influence how we perceive and experience the world.* This idea is known as the **Whorfian hypothesis** or the **Sapir-Whorf hypothesis**.

Recent research testing this hypothesis involved a tribe of hunter-gatherers in Brazil called the Piraha. The Piraha language contains only three counting words which correspond to: one, two, and many. If the Whorfian hypothesis is correct, the Piraha should have trouble understanding numerical concepts since their language doesn't contain them. To test this hypothesis, researchers asked members of the tribe to match groups of objects according to how many items were in each group. The Piraha performed well on this task when the groups contained one or two items, but performance dramatically worsened as groups of items increased in size (Gordon, 2004). These findings thus supported the Whorfian hypothesis.

However, consider evidence that counters the Whorfian hypothesis. The Arapaho Indians in Wyoming have only one word in their language to describe a senior male relative. Thus, unlike English speakers, Arapaho speakers use the same word to refer to an older brother, a father, an uncle, and a grandfather. Despite this, the Arapaho clearly understand the differences between these individuals and are able to understand precisely how they are related to each one. Further evidence against the hypothesis comes from cultures that differ in the number of words they have for colours. Davies and Corbett (1998) selected people from several cultures, each of which used a language that had a different number of words for colours, and asked them to sort a set of colour chips, much like the paint chips you might see in a paint store. Despite the fact that some of their participants used languages that had twice as many colour words as others, the participants generally sorted the colours into very similar categories.

Draft

SECTION 4 REVIEW: Further Characteristics of Language Development

TABLE 5.7

With the learning of language's complexities come a number of characteristic errors and corresponding stages of language mastery, and researchers have come to explore just how important language development is in shaping our perceptions of the world		
Early Language	**Higher Language Skills**	**Whorfian Hypothesis**
• Early language development, 10-18 months of age, is characterized by certain errors such as **overextensions**, where specific words are used to refer to a more general group of related items, and **underextensions**, where terms that are too general are used to refer to more specific items • This phase is also characterized by **telegraphic speech** • **Overregulization** errors, where grammatical rules are used too broadly, begin to occur with increased complexity in language development	• Around 10 years of age, children develop **metalinguistic awareness**, or the understanding of language as symbolic and rule based • From here on comes understanding of homonyms, sarcasm and irony, including the ability to adjust language use in different social settings	• The **Whorfian hypothesis** suggests our perceptions and experiences are shaped by language, specifically the particular language(s) we use • Evidence in support comes from the Piraha of Brazil • The study of the Arapaho has brought counterevidence though: although they had one word for a number of family members, they could still discriminate their relations to each member

Section 5: Theories of Language Development

In theories of language development, questions about the relative influence of nature (genetics and biology) and nurture (experience and environment) inevitably surface. If we consider that only humans use language, it suggests that a genetic predisposition allows for this complex skill to develop. But language must also have learned components. After all, the native language you learn to speak depends on where you live and the environmental interactions provided by your parents. Language theorists have developed several theories to understand the important role of both these influences in language development.

Social learning theory of language development

Social learning theory grew out of the principles underlying operant conditioning that you encountered in Chapter 3. According to social learning theory, children learn language through a combination of imitation and operant conditioning. Proponents of this theory (like Skinner) noted the important role of positive reinforcement that comes with language and language-related behaviours. Think about what happens when an infant babbles, randomly and repetitively combining sounds. On one occasion, he may end up babbling *'mamamama'* as his mother hands him his bottle. What will be the mother's reaction? His mother likely responds excitedly with praise and excitement! Mother's social responses provide positive reinforcement for the infant's behaviour and increase the chance that he will repeat that sequence of sounds in the future[10]. The use of positive reinforcers can also encourage more advanced language attempts. Consider Sylvie, a two year old girl who has recently learned that ice cream is incredibly delicious. Sylvie is developing rudimentary language skills. Now that she can ask for *'ice'* (her term for ice cream), she is much more likely to continue with this behaviour. Sylvie's younger brother Gerald, who does not yet speak, can only point when he sees ice cream to indicate his request, whereas Sylvie is be able to ask for ice cream by name at any time. These consequences will encourage her to continue using language to develop more advanced skills.

Support for social learning theory comes from case studies of children who have not been exposed to language throughout their childhood. One of the most famous examples is Genie, a young girl who was removed from an abusive home situation at age 13. Throughout her childhood, she had been locked in a small room and had had virtually no interactions with other people. When she was rescued from this situation, she had virtually no language skills. Such cases seem to indicate that without exposure to adequate models of language, children will fail to develop language skills (although some researchers have questioned whether Genie had developmental delays from birth that would have prevented her from developing normal language even in a normal setting).

Critics of social learning theory point out that language development in children is far too rapid and complex to be driven by imitation and reinforcement alone. Once children have learned to produce words, they combine them in novel ways that have never been modeled or reinforced. Furthermore, as discussed earlier, a young child's language contains errors that would never be heard in adult speech. Adults speaking their native language do not use overextensions or overregularizations, yet children consistently pass through a phase of language development that includes these errors. In a strict behaviorist view, an undesirable behaviour (such as a syntax error of overextension) will persist unless it is paired with negative consequences. Considering this argument in the context of language, we might expect that parents actively correct a child's use of overextensions and overregularizations as well as reinforce correct language use. Although there may be some direct reinforcement that occurs due to

---

[10] Instead of waiting for a spontaneous utterance to reinforce, parents may provide explicit models of language use for their children to imitate. For example, a father may repeatedly say *'dada'* hoping to influence his infant's first word through imitation.

correct use of language (as in the case of encouraging an infant's request for a *bottle* instead of a *'baba'*), analyses of conversation transcripts between parents and children indicate that reinforcement is not uniformly consistent and overt corrections of grammatical errors are actually quite rare.

It seems unlikely that this pattern of reinforcement is sufficient to explain the rapid progress and breadth of language development. In other words, social learning may play a role in language development, but it is insufficient as the sole explanation.

Innate mechanism theory of language development

On the opposite camp are theorists who believe that humans are born with an innate mechanism that allows them to learn language. Perhaps the most famous proponent of this view is Noam Chomsky, who has argued that language develops rapidly due to an innate mechanism that he termed a **Language Acquisition Device** (**LAD**). Chomsky noted that although different languages have variations in grammatical rules, all languages follow certain universal rules. The innate mechanism allows humans to understand and use these universal rules. Without these mechanisms, Chomsky suggested that language skills could not develop as rapidly or extensively as they do.

Evidence to support the idea of innate language learning mechanisms comes from work with children born deaf whose parents have chosen to teach them to learn to lip-read instead of use sign language. In spite of this parental choice, when these children come together, they have been observed to spontaneously develop a sign language, even without being taught the formal rules of how to sign. Even more striking is the observation that the sign language did not necessarily follow the exact grammar structure of the parent's oral language. This suggests that the spontaneous sign language was not learned and may be based on an innate understanding of grammar.

Two additional observations further support a genetic component to language development. First, data indicates that very young infants and even newborns prefer listening to speech over non-speech sounds (Vouloumanos & Werker, 2007). This preference indicates an innate predisposition for exposure to language that cannot easily be explained by social factors, since the infant is so young. Indeed, infants show specific neurophysiological responses to the first language to which they are exposed (Cheour et al., 1998). This indicates that infants' brains are pre-wired to adapt to the sounds and their associated meanings that are present in their environment. Second, universal language milestones occur in a consistent pattern at certain ages.

Like social learning theory, the innate mechanism theory of language development is not without its problems. For example, there is evidence that infant monkeys and chinchillas also show very specific neurolophysiological responses to some aspects of language. This finding does not necessarily refute the possibility that humans are hard-wired for language development, but it does call into question whether language is indeed a uniquely human quality and whether other animals have similar responses to language, and if so, why such skills are underdeveloped.

Draft

The world over there are groups of individuals who are deaf that use sign language to communicate because of limitations in communicating orally Although there are now several different official sign languages formally taught in schools for the deaf, there is also evidence for the spontaneous development of sign language in deaf populations. Pinker (1994) reviewed the development of Lenguaje de Signos Nicaraguense (LSN). Until the late 1970's, deaf children in Nicaragua had been isolated in their home communities; this changed when the government brought them to centralized school systems and tried to teach them to lip read and use speech. Despite the failure of the government's program, the children developed a basic sign language on their own, while playing and interacting with one another outside of the classroom. Over the years, this language evolved into a complex and fully symbolic language.

Similar to oral languages, people from different cultures use different sign languages. For example, there are several different Asian sign languages, and within Canada two different sign languages are taught: American Sign Language (ASL) and Langue des Signes Québécoise (LSQ). Sign languages are independent languages in their own right. Their structure and syntax do not necessarily mimic the oral languages spoken in their culture of use. For instance, American Sign Language (ASL) is more similar in some ways to Navajo and Bantu languages than to the oral English that is used in North America (Pinker, 1994). A given sign language can also have different dialects that are used in different regions, similar to the way that people in different regions of the United Kingdom speak different dialects of English.

Sign languages meet the defining characteristics of language: they are productive and rule-governed (see Petitto, 1994), and they consist of symbolic, arbitrary associations. As in oral languages, the symbolic and arbitrary associations between meaning and symbol allow different sign languages to use different signs for the same meaning. While there are instances of onomatopoeia (symbols reflecting their meaning) in sign languages, the vast majority of signs are more a representation than a simple 'copy' of the physical item. For example, in ASL, the sign for tree is a motion of the hand that looks like it is blowing in the wind, but the sign for pig involves waving the hand under the chin.

The symbolic nature of these languages is also clear from work done by Laura Ann Petitto, at the University of Toronto. If you have ever talked with a toddler, you may have noticed that they have trouble using the referents 'you' and 'me' correctly. This is not surprising, since the referent changes depending on who is speaking: when the child is speaking, the words have the opposite referent to when the adult is speaking. In ASL, however, the signs for 'you' and 'me' are simple pointing gestures: 'me' is a point to one's own chest, while 'you' is a point to one's conversational partner. Even 1-year-olds can use pointing to indicate what they want, so it may seem surprising that Petitto found that 2-year-old children learning sign language mixed up these pronouns in much the same way that 2-year-olds using oral pronouns do! Even more intriguing is the fact that the signing children were able to point accurately at a younger age, but as they developed an understanding of language, their pointing diminished and then re-emerged in this error-prone fashion. This developmental trajectory indicates that the children were using the signs as much more than a direct point; they were using them as symbols representing meaning and assigning that meaning correctly was a learning process (Petitto, 1987).

Oral babbling emerges sometime around 7 months of age, even in deaf children, but after that they seem to need oral input to continue oral language development. Nonetheless, there is evidence of babbling in sign language (manual babbling) (Petitto, Holowka, Sergio, Levy, & Ostry, 2004; Petitto & Marentette, 1991). At the same time hearing infants exhibit oral babbling, deaf infants (or hearing infants who are being taught only sign language) make systematic and rhythmic motions that seem to be precursors for more advanced or complex signing.

Although the symbols used to represent meaning are different in kind to those used in oral languages, sign languages and oral languages follow similar developmental trajectories, activate similar areas of the brain, and have similar underlying structures. This suggests that although the physical methods of communicating languages may differ due to developmental limitations, the fundamental bases of human language are the same, suggesting at least a partially inherent foundation for human language.

Interactionist theories of language development

As is often the case when scientists try to make an exclusive argument, explanations that rely solely on nature or nurture on language development have bee found to be insufficient. This outcome has led to the proposal of **interactionist theories** of language development that argue for a combined role of nature and nurture. They recognize that children are biologically prepared for language, but also require extensive experience with language in the environment for adequate development. According to the interactionist view, children play an active role in acquiring language by formulating, testing, and evaluating hypotheses about the rules of language. It is this active role, paired with brain maturation that eventually leads to language mastery. Interactionist theories thus integrate three influences on language development: biological maturation of the brain, social interaction, and cognitive preparedness.

SECTION 5 REVIEW: Theories of Language Development

TABLE 5.8

Much debate has long existed over whether language is a product of nature or nurture, but modern views hold that it is a combination of both factors that results in human language		
Social Learning Theory	**Innate Mechanism Theory**	**Interactionist Theories**
• **Social learning theory** suggests that language abilities are acquired through imitation and operant conditioning, with support from case studies of language deprivation during development e.g. Genie • Criticism includes the suggestion that language is too complex and acquired too rapidly to be learned, errors early in development are not performed by adults so they cannot be imitated, and patterns of reinforcement used are insufficient	• Chomsky has suggested the existence of a **Language Acquisition Device** and basic universal rules for all languages; support comes from the spontaneous development of sign language in deaf children, preference for speech sounds and neurophysiological responses to native languages • Criticism includes evidence that infant monkeys and chinchillas show the same neurophysiological responses to language	• Nature or nurture is insufficient, both are needed to explain language • Children's experiences and experimentation with language and individuals that already use language, combined with brain maturation, produces language abilities

Section 6: Concluding Thoughts

What makes language unique?

Let's close by revisiting the original problem posed at the beginning of this chapter: why do psychologists consider language to be a uniquely human form of communication? There are certainly many examples of communication in non-human animals, but tonne of these fulfill the defining characteristics of language (it is productive, symbolic, rule-governed, and involves arbitrary associations). Although scientists would not classify any naturally-occurring form of non-human animal communication as language, some have tried to determine whether primates (specifically chimpanzees) can learn to use language. Although some chimps have learned to use what appear to be remarkably advanced forms of communication, scientists still lack conclusive evidence that they are using language per se. Let's consider example of a famous chimp to understand why.

Washoe was a chimpanzee who was captured in Africa in the 1960s and raised by scientists Allen and Beatrix Gardner. Previous work trying to teach chimpanzees to use language had centered on attempts to vocalize and had predictably failed miserably. The Gardners reasoned that a language that did not require a human vocal system, such as American Sign Language, would be a better tool to allow a chimpanzee to communicate through language. Using operant conditioning and social modeling, Washoe was eventually taught to use approximately 250 signs. Remarkably, she used them spontaneously and even combined them in new ways, indicating that her signed communication was productive. Washoe's communication also involved using symbolic signs that had arbitrary associations with meaning (e.g. pulling her hand away from her mouth to sign 'good'), although many of her signs were somewhat less arbitrary (e.g., her sign for 'eat' involved bringing her hand to her mouth). Nonetheless, the critical characteristic lacking from Washoe's communication system was that of a rule-base: her communication was not governed by any reliable grammar. You can see this from the following two examples of communicative episodes between Washoe and a scientist (Jensvold & Gardner, 2000). These interactions were designed to test whether Washoe could respond to questions on-topic, essentially testing her conversation skills. Signs are written in upper-case letters.

Episode 1:
Washoe: FRUIT GIMME
Scientist: WHO FUNNY?
Washoe: ROGER
Scientist: WHERE CAT?
Washoe: ROGER GIMME
Scientist: WHERE CAT?
Washoe: GIMME.

Episode 2:
Washoe: ME OIMMEX (unfamiliar sign)
Scientist: questioning expression
Washoe: GIMME
Scientist: WHAT?
Washoe: ME OIMMEX
Scientist: NOT UNDERSTAND?
Washoe: FOOD GIMME

Despite numerous subsequent attempts to teach chimpanzees language, to date there is no conclusive data indicating success at this task. This means that to date, humans remain the only species to use language.

Chapter

6

Chapter 6: Psychological Disorders

Introduction

DEFINING ABNORMALITY

How can we determine what is abnormal? And perhaps more importantly, how can we be certain that what one person thinks is abnormal is agreed upon by everyone else? Clinicians generally rely upon a set of important criteria when they assess and diagnose psychological disorders. The most prominent themes in these criteria are: deviance, distress, dysfunction, and danger; also known as *the four D's*.

Deviance. This criterion refers to the idea that thoughts, emotions, and behaviours that we define as abnormal deviate from those deemed acceptable by society. An important aspect of the deviance criterion is the understanding that the practices of minority groups are labeled as deviant not necessarily because they are wrong, but simply that they are different. Therefore, we define abnormality by whether or not the individual's behaviour is accepted by the culture to which that individual belongs. Many of us may talk or mutter to ourselves as we recite a list of chores or when we stub our toes – these behaviours are likely to be considered within the bounds of normality. However, if we encountered a stranger on the street having an argument with someone that was not there, we would conclude that this behaviour is abnormal and deviates from how we expect people to act in everyday life. Another important consideration is that both those who fall below and above the norm are labeled deviant. Consider the example of mood: in major depressive disorder individuals experience an excessive decrease in normative mood regulation, whereas in bipolar disorder, individuals experience episodes of mania in which they feel excessively elated. Both of these experiences are deviant, although two different extremes, and thus both are considered to be a part of a psychological disorder.

Distress. The distress criterion accounts for negative feelings of individuals with psychological disorders. Many people, though not all, who have forms of mental illness report feelings of being deeply troubled by their illness. A classic example is individuals with anxiety disorders. Can you imagine feeling anxious about making everyday decisions, from what to wear and what to eat, to where to go for university and your future career? Individuals with generalized anxiety disorder experience a pervasive and seemingly never ending sense of dread and anxiety. The feelings of distress associated with anxiety disorders are part of the requirements for the clinical diagnosis. However, it is important to note that not all disorders are accompanied by feelings of distress. For example, sociopaths feel little if any guilt or remorse about any of their wrongful behaviours.

Dysfunction. The dysfunction or maladaptive behaviour criterion entails a marked impairment in the ability to perform everyday functions. These behaviours render the individual unable to engage in normal social or occupational functioning, and may contribute to failed marriages and friendships, or job loss. The behaviours in some psychological disorders are described as maladaptive because they prevent the individual from living a functional, full life. It is possible that someone may engage in maladaptive behaviour intentionally, such as a hunger strike for some purpose or demonstration, but these protestors should not immediately be regarded as having a mental illness simply because they are not eating food to make a point. We must be careful when evaluating the rationale behind maladaptive behaviours.

Danger. This criterion involves dangerous or violent behaviour directed at oneself or at others. For instance, someone engaging in suicidal behaviour would be regarded as being a danger to their self. As with the previous criteria, this pattern of behaviour alone does not qualify for the diagnosis of a psychological disorder. An example of risky and dangerous behaviour may be skydiving, or simply not taking the proper medication for physical diseases (e.g., heart problems). Both of these are dangerous to a degree, but performing either one of them does not necessarily conclude that an individual is suffering from a mental illness.

No matter how we define abnormality, the fact remains that the boundaries between normal and abnormal are fuzzy. The four D's criteria do not stand-alone, and clinicians use these criteria in combination with a number of other factors to determine whether someone can be diagnosed with a psychological disorder.

Stigma of Psychological Disorders

Despite the leaps and bounds taken toward furthering our knowledge of psychological disorders, individuals afflicted by mental illness are still subject to stigmatization and commonly held stereotypes perpetuated by cultural myths. The *labeling theory* of mental illness, originally proposed by Scheff (1970), posits that the application of a deviant label to an individual can result in changes of self-perception and perception by others, and a decrease in social opportunities. Scheff purports that mental illness stereotypes are learned during socialization and are then reinforced as to create rigid stereotypes. One of the most dramatic illustrations of labeling is a classic study entitled "On Being Sane in Insane Places" by David Rosenhan (1973), in which he demonstrates that even health professionals are subject to the effects of labeling and stereotyping. Rosenhan had himself and seven other "pseudo patients" committed to different psychiatric hospitals around the United States. All eight individuals were deemed sane prior to becoming involved in the study. The pseudo patients included a psychiatrist, a psychology graduate student, a housewife, a pediatrician, a painter, and three psychologists. Upon intake at their respective psychiatric hospitals, all eight faked symptoms of schizophrenia, by issuing complaints of hearing voices saying "empty", "hollow", or "thud." All but one were admitted and subsequently diagnosed with schizophrenia. Once admitted, they reported being dehumanized and essentially ignored by hospital staff despite returning to their normal behaviour and asserting that they no longer heard voices. Psychiatric staff continued to interpret their behaviour as abnormal and as further evidence of mental illness. For example, when the pseudo patients took copious notes while in the ward, hospital staff commented in their records about their "peculiar note-taking behaviour." After an average stay of 19 days, all pseudo patients were discharged and given the label of 'schizophrenia-in remission' (when we say 'in remission' we mean that an individual no longer appears to have the symptoms of that disorder). The results of this study are unnerving because they demonstrate the serious influence that labeling may have on the interpretation of future behaviours.

The important 'take-home' message is that everyone has quirks and eccentricities that make us deviant in some way, and while sometimes these peculiarities may warrant clinical diagnoses and labels, we should not be defined by these actions.

In an attempt to assuage the problems associated with labeling, the American Psychiatric Association (APA; 2000) recommends that clinicians apply diagnostic labels only to people's disorders, not to the people themselves. Thus, a client with schizophrenia should be referred to as *a person with schizophrenia* or *a person afflicted by schizophrenia* rather than as a schizophrenic. This forces the primary focus to be on the individual rather than on the diagnosis.

Medical Students' Disease

As you progress through this chapter, you may begin to feel that you have at least one or possibly many of the psychological disorders we will discuss. This is the phenomenon of *Medical Students' Disease* (or more appropriately entitled, *Introductory Psychology Students' Disease*), a condition reported in medical students when they perceive that either themselves or others around them have the symptoms of the diseases they are studying. For the most part, psychological disorders are simply normal traits and behaviours displayed to such an excessive degree as to cause impairment in functioning – it is perfectly normal to relate to many, if not all of the disorders and syndromes presented in this chapter.

Section 1: Classifying Disorders: The DSM-IV

We naturally classify and categorize our world to make sense of our surroundings, and to give objects meaning – the same can be said for psychological disorders. A label merely describes a set of *symptoms* or a *syndrome*, wherein a **symptom** is any characteristic of a person's actions, thoughts or feelings that could be a potential indicator of mental illness. By extension, a **syndrome** is a collection of interrelated symptoms manifested by any given individual. Labels describe behaviours, and the accompanying diagnosis helps to explain and distinguish between these labels, hence, the need for an organizational system describing mental illness (Millon, 1975). Furthermore, an organized classification system of psychological disorders facilitates empirical research and enhances communication among scientists and clinicians (Zimmerman & Spitzer, 2005).

The first diagnostic classification system of psychological disorders materialized in 1952 with the first edition of the **Diagnostic and Statistical Manual of Mental Disorders (DSM)** published by the American Psychiatric Association. Since then, enormous efforts have been put forth to improve the DSM with each new edition. The DSM provides official guidelines for the diagnosis of psychological disorders and is used as the standard diagnostic reference guide by clinicians, researchers and psychologists in North America. The most current version is the fourth edition with a text revision (DSM-IV-TR), published in 2000. The DSM-5 (which will no longer utilize roman numerals in the title) is set to be released in May 2013.

The DSM has two main functions, the first is to categorize and describe mental disorders so that clinicians have a common set of criteria for applying a diagnostic label to their patients thereby reducing ambiguity and subjectivity in diagnoses. Secondly, the DSM allows researchers and psychologists to use a common language when discussing their cases and research findings. Thus, a researcher or clinician in Ontario (Canada) reading a journal article conducted by researchers in Florida (United States) on panic disorders can immediately understand the essential features of the patients' syndrome in the study.

DSM Categorization

The DSM-III was the first to introduce a **multiaxial system** of classification, which requires assessment of individuals to be placed on five separate axes describing important mental health factors. Diagnoses of psychological disorders are made on Axes I and II, wherein most disorders are recorded on Axis I, with the exception of personality disorders and mental retardation, which are recorded on Axis II. The distinction between Axis I and II is that diagnoses made on Axis I are *state* dependent (the individual's current condition or state of functioning), whereas Axis II describes disorders that are *trait* dependent (enduring maladaptive problems with the person's functioning).

Axes III through V are used to provide additional information on the individual's overall functioning. Axis III describes current *physical conditions*, such as diabetes or heart disease. This health information is useful because in some cases, medical conditions may cause or contribute to mental illness. Axis IV is used to report *psychosocial* or *environmental stressors* that may affect the diagnosis, treatment, or prognosis of disorders on Axis I or II. Examples of psychosocial or environmental stressors are: a recent death in the family, divorce, or even natural disasters such as devastating earthquakes or floods. Lastly, Axis V provides an estimate of the individual's overall functioning, or *global assessment of functioning*. Estimates are made on the individual's current level of adaptive functioning (i.e., social, occupational and school activities).

Before a diagnosis can be made, two criteria must be met: (1) The disordered behaviour must originate from within the person, and may not be a reaction to external factors, and, (2) The disorder must be involuntary, such that the afflicted person cannot control their symptoms.

Other Features of the DSM-IV

In conjunction with its diagnostic utility, the DSM-IV provides additional information on psychological disorders including epidemiology, prevalence, comorbidity, prognosis, and cultural background information. **Epidemiology** is the study of the distribution of mental or physical disorders in a population. Within epidemiology, **prevalence** is the percentage of a population that exhibits a disorder during a specified time period. Concerning psychological disorders, it is often most interesting to note the *lifetime prevalence* rate of a disorder, which is an estimate of the percentage of people afflicted by a specific disorder at any given point in time. The DSM-IV also details information on the **comorbidity** of psychological disorders, or the coexistence of two or more disorders at the same time. **Prognosis** refers to the forecast about the probable course of an illness. Finally, the DSM-IV also endeavours to include important information about cultural differences, as it acknowledges that we live in a culturally diverse world wherein what may seem abnormal to one culture is regarded as completely normal in another. Furthermore, individuals may present different symptoms based on their cultural backgrounds. In the case of social phobia, individuals from certain cultures (e.g., Japan and Korea) may develop an excessive fear of offending others in social situations, instead of the classic fear of embarrassing oneself, which is evident among North Americans with a social phobia.

Draft

DSM Criticisms

A psychological disorder is not a fixed entity; it is simply the name we give to a set of symptoms that often appear together. However, the DSM-IV employs a system wherein individuals either do or do not meet diagnostic criteria for mental disorders. As such, the main criticisms of the psychiatric classification system center on whether discrete categories are justifiable and if these diagnostic categories are reliable.

Some wonder whether psychological disorders should fall into structured categories, or whether syndromes should fall along a continuum of severity (Lewinsohn, Solomon, Seeley, & Zeiss, 2000; Widiger & Sankis, 2000). The DSM-IV represents a **categorical classification model** in which a psychological disorder differs from normal functioning in kind rather than degree. An example that fits a categorical model is pregnancy – a woman is either pregnant or not, there is no middle ground. The alternative is a **dimensional classification model** in which psychological disorders differ from normal functioning in degree rather than kind. Blood pressure for instance, fits a dimensional model. The use of a categorical model is inherently problematic because discrete categories insinuate that there is a clear boundary between normality and abnormality, and this is simply not true. With the constraints of this system, subclinical cases of disorders that cause severe impairment but do not qualify for the diagnosis of a full-blown psychological disorder may go untreated. It is estimated that subclinical cases are equally common, if not more so, than diagnosable cases of disorders (Zinbarg et al., 1994).

Another problem with the DSM is the high degree of comorbidity among many of its diagnoses. For instance, it is highly common for individuals with mood disorders to also receive a diagnosis of a substance abuse problem and/or an anxiety disorder. On one hand, it may be that these individuals are in fact suffering from more than one distinct disorder. However, on the other hand, it may also be the case that there is too much overlap between psychological disorders, a factor that ultimately undermines the utility of the diagnosis.

We must recognize that changes will inevitably be made to how we categorize mental illness and abnormal behaviour as we pursue higher understanding of human behaviour. These changes represent the self-correcting nature of science, and psychology as a scientific discipline. In conclusion, despite its drawbacks, the DSM-IV constitutes the best current approximation of a comprehensive diagnostic system.

Table 6.2: Lifetime Prevalence Rates of DSM Disorders

Category	Diagnosis	Lifetime Prevalence (%)
Mood Disorders	Major depressive disorder	16.6
	Bipolar I & II disorders	3.9
	Dysthymia	2.5
Anxiety Disorders	Panic disorder	4.7
	Social phobia	12.1
	Specific phobia	12.5
	Generalized anxiety disorder	5.7
	Obsessive-compulsive disorder	1.6
	Post-traumatic stress disorder	6.8
Somatoform Disorders	Somatization disorder	0.2-2.0 (females)
	Conversion disorder	< 1.0
	Hypochrondriasis	1.0-5.0
Schizophrenia	Schizophrenia	1.0
Eating Disorders	Anorexia nervosa	0.5 - 3.7 (females)
	Bulimia nervosa	1.1 - 4.2 (females)

(Source: American Psychiatric Association, DSM-IV-TR, 2000; Government of Canada, The Human Face of Mental Illness, 2006; Kessler et al., 2005)

Section 2: Mood Disorders

Most people can think of a time when they felt extremely down, or exceptionally elated – perhaps in response to failing a test, or in the case of elation, getting into your first choice university for your undergraduate degree. In either of these cases, the emotional response is normal and can be attributed to a specific event. Or maybe, you just wake up one day and feel great – this too is a normal experience.

Mood disorders are a class of disorders marked by intense and prolonged emotional disturbances of varied kinds that may spill over to disrupt physical, perceptual, social, and thought processes. Mood disorders tend to be *episodic* in nature, meaning that they come and go, and are sometimes scattered among periods of normal functioning. Episodes of mood disturbance typically last between 3 and 12 months (Akiskal, 2000).

Types of mood disorders fall into two categories: the depressive disorders and the bipolar disorders. Individuals afflicted by depressive disorders experience intense sadness. Conversely, those with bipolar disorders experience moods from both sides of the mood continuum, and are afflicted by feelings of depression and mania (elation and excitement).

Mood disorders can have devastating social, occupational, and educational effects. According to the Canadian Community Health Survey, 90.1% of Canadians who met diagnostic criteria for depression and 86.9% who met criteria for bipolar disorder in the past 12 months reported that the condition had interfered with their lives (Government of Canada, 2006). Between 62% and 76% of short-term disability episodes resulting from psychological disorders are thought to be due to depression alone (Dewa, Goering, & Lin, 2000). Approximately 60% of all completed suicides occur in individuals suffering from a mood disorder (Shaffer et al., 1996). Mood disorders are frequently comorbid with anxiety disorders, personality disorders, and substance abuse (Health Canada, 2006).

Despite these staggering statistics, many individuals diagnosed with mood disorders live average lives and even achieve great accomplishments. Well-known celebrities including Jim Carrey, Sarah McLaughlin, Ben Stiller and Sting have all battled with mood disorders and still made significant achievements in their lives. This is likely due to a combination of the heterogeneity of severity in symptoms from person to person, the episodic nature of these disorders (allowing for periods of normalcy and regular functioning between episodes), and the successful treatment of mood disorders through the use of a variety of sources.

Box 6.1: Major Depressive Disorder

Julie is a clerical worker who has been experiencing sleeping problems that started about a year and a half ago. During the week, Julie has a hard time getting out of bed to get to work. On weekends, she frequently sleeps all day, only leaving her bed for bathroom breaks and meals. For several months Julie has been having crying spells at work that sometimes came on so suddenly that she is unable to run to the restroom to hide from her coworkers. She has trouble concentrating at her job, and feels no pleasure in completing tasks she used to enjoy. Julie constantly feels guilty because she has allowed her weight and diabetes to get out of control. When questioned about her body, she admits that she thinks she is 30% above her ideal weight. Despite having a full-time job, Julie lives at home with her mother and has no friends outside of her family. At times, Julie feels she might be better off dead.

(Adapted from DSM-IV-TR Casebook, 2004, pp. 143-145)

Draft

Major Depressive Disorder

Major depressive disorder (MDD) or unipolar depression is a mood disorder defined by symptoms such as decreased mood, loss of motivation, significant fluctuations in weight, lack of energy, and thoughts of suicide. Those with MDD frequently report feelings of emptiness, worthlessness, and guilt. In addition to the emotional dysfunction in MDD, many also experience difficulties with memory, attention, decision-making, and cognitive speed in general, all of which are generally known as neurocognitive deficits (Miller, 1975; Beats, Sahakian, & Levy, 1996; Moffoot et al., 1994; Rogers et al., 2004; Taylor Tavares et al., 2007). Crucial considerations in the application of a MDD diagnosis are the length of the depressive episode and the impact on daily functioning, wherein one or more depressive episodes would warrant the diagnosis of MDD. Across North America the lifetime prevalence rate for major depressive disorders is over 16% (Kessler et al., 2005). In Canada alone, 10% will experience a major depressive episode at some point in their lifetimes (Health Canada, 2002; Patten & Juby, 2008).

MDD tends to occur twice as frequently in females than males such that the ratio is about 2:1 (Nolen-Hoeksema, 2002). A recent study found that the age of onset in females was 17.86 years and 18.37 years in males. The rationale behind this gender difference is hypothesized to occur for several reasons. Firstly, females are more likely to engage in *ruminative coping* (Nolen-Hoeksema, 2002). Females tend to focus their attention on their depressive symptoms, thinking things like "What does it mean that I feel this way?" and dwell on personal difficulties or failures. Conversely, males are more likely to attempt to distract themselves to escape their depressive feelings. Others suggest that females adopt a relational self-regulatory style, meaning that they are sensitive to discrepancies between beliefs they hold about themselves and the ideals they perceive others hold for them (Moretti, Rein, & Weibe, 1998). Lastly, some have proposed that females face more adversity as they are subject to higher likelihoods of victimization including sexual abuse, poverty, and gender role constraints (Nolen-Hoeksema, 2001). Thus, while there are various theories proposed to explain this gender difference, we can conclude that it can be best understood as the resultant of a number of complex factors.

Julie, who we met at the beginning of this section, would likely be diagnosed with major depressive disorder. For over a year, she has been feeling depressed, has experienced a decrease in energy and motivation, and has gained a significant amount of weight. Like many others with MDD, Julie is experiencing cognitive functioning problems evidenced by her inability to concentrate at work. Finally, she is riddled by feelings of guilt, and sometimes wishes she were dead. Altogether, these symptoms point to a diagnosis of MDD.

Bipolar Disorders

Previously known as manic-depressive disorder, **bipolar disorders (BD)** are a classification of mood disorders that involve cycles between episodes of depression and mania in patients. **Mania or manic episodes** are characterized by a period of excessively elevated mood. Patients may feel "on top of the world," with racing, grandiose thoughts, and may engage in potentially risky behaviour. The individual may talk rapidly, and shift wildly from one topic to another as their mind races ahead of their speech. Mania is sometimes also described as an irritable mood, and individuals may become argumentative or violent, particularly when someone attempts to rationalize with them or point out problems with their grandiose ideas. As with MDD, individuals with BD frequently experience neurocognitive deficits (Martínez-Arán et al., 2004; Quraishi & Frangou, 2002), which appear to be more severe than those evident in MDD (Borkowska & Rybakowski, 2001). North American prevalence rates for BD are estimated to be around 3.9% (Kessler et al., 2005), while a Canadian study found that 2.4% of people identified symptoms that met criteria for bipolar disorder at some point in their lifetime (Government of Canada, 2006). The average age of onset for BD is 20 years of age, and, dissimilar to MDD, there is no evident gender difference in frequency of diagnosis between males and females. .

The DSM differentiates between two types of bipolar disorder: Bipolar I and II. *Bipolar I* is characterized by at least one manic and one depressive episode. Bipolar I entails the typical conception of bipolar disorder as it incorporates the two most extreme mood states. *Bipolar II* is similar to BD I, except that it requires one hypomanic episode and one depressive episode. Hypomanic episodes are differentiated from full-blown manic episodes in that within hypomania the mood disturbance is not severe enough to cause marked impairment in social or occupational functioning or to require hospitalization, and there are no psychotic features (delusions or hallucinations). Furthermore, the change in functioning in a hypomanic episode may take the form of a dramatic increase in efficiency, accomplishments, or even creativity.

Heterogeneity and Variability within Mood Disorders

Within mood disorders there is great heterogeneity, evidenced by the fact that two people diagnosed with the same disorder may experience different symptoms and their courses of illness may vary greatly . Two disorders that serve as less acute forms of MDD and BD are *dysthymic* and *cyclothymic* disorder. **Dysthymic disorder** or **Dysthymia** is a form of mood disorder that presents with a similar but less severe set of MDD symptoms. Individuals with dysthymia feel mildy depressed all the time as their symptoms are constant as opposed to episodic.

Cyclothymic disorder or **cyclothymia** is characterized by chronic but relatively mild symptoms of bipolar disturbance. Those afflicted by cyclothymic disorder experience numerous periods of hypomanic and depressive symptoms (though not enough to warrant a diagnosis of a major depressive episode) for at least 2 years, with periods of normalcy lasting no longer than 2 months.

Furthermore, the DSM allows for specifiers that contribute additional information that may help with understanding and treatment for an individual. Some of these specifiers include: *postpartum, seasonal pattern*, and *rapid-cycling*. **Postpartum depression** is a type of depression that occurs within four weeks of childbirth. In severe cases of postpartum depression with psychotic features, mothers may commit infanticide and kill their own newborns. The seasonal pattern, also known as **seasonal affective disorder (SAD)** is a type of depression that follows a specific season, such as winter or summer. First described by Rosenthal et al. (1984), it was noted that some patients' syndromes seemed to be tied to fluctuations in latitude and climate. As you may have guessed, the most common season associated with SAD is winter (Lewy, 1993). SAD is more common in countries like Canada and the United States where there is less sunlight in the winter months. In fact, one form of treatment for SAD is phototherapy, during which individuals are exposed to therapeutic light (Labbate, Lafer, Thibault, Rosenbaum, & Sachs, 1995; Lee et al., 1997). *Rapid-cycling* may be applied to either BD I or BD II. The main feature of a rapid-cycling bipolar disorder is the occurrence of four or more mood episodes during the span of 12 months. There is no specified order or combination, but there must be at least four distinct mood states within that timeframe.

Despite the variation in symptoms experienced by individuals diagnosed with a mood disorder, it is clear that these afflictions can cause serious problems in everyday functioning and may even lead to death. Now that we understand the symptoms present in mood disorders, let's explore the cause and development – also known as **etiology** – of these disorders.

Etiology of Mood Disorders

In mood disorders, as with most psychological disorders, there are many factors that contribute to the emergence of symptoms. The complex interactions of biological and psychological factors present the most promising arguments for the etiology of mood disorders.

LIFE EVENTS

As you can imagine, negative life events can trigger depression. Think about the last time you were sad. It was probably because you had some kind of negative experience. Perhaps you broke up with your boyfriend or girlfriend, your family dog passed away, or you failed a class– all of these are examples of life stressors. Life stressors are closely tied to depression (Hammen, 1992). But, how can we account for the fact that many people experience stressful events and do not develop depressive symptoms? The most probable explanation is that some people have an underlying vulnerability that renders them more likely to develop a mood disorder in response to negative or traumatic experiences.

GENETIC VULNERABILITY

Evidence from genetic studies using twin, family, and adoption methods suggest that both MDD and BD have a strong genetic component. When we speak of the similarity in psychiatric diagnosis or in other traits within a pair of twins, we use the term **concordance rates.** Concordance rates for all mood disorders among identical twins average around 65%, but only 14% for fraternal twins (Berrettini, 2006; Kelsoe, 2005). For MDD alone, heritability estimates are approximately 35% (Sullivan, Neale, & Kendler, 2000), and tend to be much higher in BD. One study of genetic influence on BD found that concordance rates were estimated at 85% (McGuffin et al., 2003). Heritability likely creates a predisposition for mood disorders, meaning that some individuals are more likely to have mood disorders based on their genes, but that their environment likely plays a role in determining whether they actually develop the disorder.

Various genes have also been implicated in contributing to mood disorder vulnerability (Craddock & Forty, 2006; McClung, 2007; Neves-Pereira, et al., 2002). However, results are frequently highly inconsistent, and we are far from determining which specific genes play a role in the development and maintenance of mood disorders (Merikangas & Risch, 2003).

BIOLOGICAL AND NEUROCHEMICAL FACTORS

Many researchers have sought to understand the underlying neural anatomical structures and neurochemistry implicated in mood disorders.

Concerning structural and functional abnormalities in individuals with mood disorders, various studies have found irregularities in the amygdala, prefrontal cortex, anterior cingulate, and the hippocampus (Davidson, Pizzagall, Nitschke, & Putnam, 2002).

Three of the most studied neurotransmitters as they relate to mood disorders are serotonin, norepinephrine, and dopamine (Sanacora, Zarate, Krystal, & Manji, 2008). Original theories on the mechanisms of neurotransmitters in mood disorders proposed that low levels of dopamine and norepinephrine (regulated by serotonin) in mood disorders lead to depression and mania. However, the actions of drug therapies (e.g., selective serotonin reuptake inhibitors, monoamine oxidase inhibitors) indicate that it is not solely the change in neurotransmitter levels that cause a change in the presentation of depressive and manic symptoms.

The exact mechanisms of these neurotransmitters are still unclear to some extent, but it would seem that there is a definite role of neurochemistry in the emergence and course of mood disorders (Flores et al., 2004).

DISPOSITIONAL FACTORS

Just as underlying neurochemistry may influence the likelihood of developing a mood disorder, a person's personality traits may contribute to the emergence and maintenance of depression. One of the most frequently researched traits associated with depression is perfectionism, wherein individuals set extremely high standards for themselves (Beck, 1976). Research in this area suggests that perfectionism is not only associated with current depressive symptoms, but also with chronic symptoms (Cox & Enns, 2003; Hewitt, Flett, Ediger, Norton, & Flynn, 1999). Paul Hewitt and Gordon Flett are at the forefront of the research on perfectionism as it relates to depression, and have developed a multidimensional perfectionism scale that assesses three types of perfectionism (MPS; Hewitt & Flett, 1991). The MPS covers the following three types of perfectionism: *self-oriented perfectionism*, setting exceedingly high expectations for oneself; *other-oriented perfectionism*, demanding perfection from others; and *socially prescribed perfectionism*, perceiving that others have expectations of one's self. Research demonstrates that socially prescribed perfectionism is most frequently associated with depression (Flett & Hewitt, 2002).

Subsequent research on personality-based models of depression involves models proposed by Sidney Blatt and Aaron Beck. Blatt (1974, 1995) distinguishes between two personality orientations related to depression: *introjective personality orientation* and *anaclitic orientation*. An introjective depression is characterized by feelings of guilt and worthlessness, and a sense that one has failed to live up to the expectations and standards imposed on them. Conversely, an anaclitic depression is characterized by feelings of helplessness and weakness; individuals often experience intense feelings of abandonment and are desperately dependent on others.

According to Beck, there are two personality types that can be readily associated with depression: *sociotrophy* and *autonomy* (1983). Sociotrophy is associated with being inordinately invested in interpersonal relationships; individuals are overly concerned with pleasing others and actively avoid conflict in their relationships. An autonomous individual prefers to preserve independence and freedom of choice. They engage in solitary activities, place high value on hard work and accomplishments, and are often insensitive to the needs of others.

Dispositional personality traits and types are generally thought of as vulnerability factors in the emergence and onset of depression that may or may not contribute to the illness depending on exposure to other stressors.

Interpersonal Model

For the most part, behavioural approaches to understanding depression focus on how depression creates interpersonal problems that in turn deepen feelings of depression, and so forth (Coyne, 1976; Rudolph et al., 2006). Friends, family, jobs, and relationships in general are positive reinforcers. People with depression lack the social skills to elicit normal positive social reinforcement from others, and are therefore incapable of forming normal social relationships, thus, perpetuating their depression (Coyne, 1999; Gotlib & Robinson, 1982).

Furthermore, depressed individuals are often not much fun to be around (Joiner & Katz, 1999). This finding was illustrated in a classic study conducted by Coyne (1976). Coyne recruited undergraduate students to talk on the phone for 20 minutes with depressed patients, non-depressed patients, and non-patient females randomly drawn from the community. Students were unaware that they would be interacting with individuals with depression. Following their phone interactions students who spoke with depressed patients felt more depressed, anxious, and hostile than those who did not interact with depressed patients. Furthermore, participants reported feelings of rejection towards depressed patients, and had less interest in interacting with them again in the future. These findings suggest that people may be averse to befriending individuals with depression.

COGNITIVE FACTORS

Cognitive processes play an important role in emotion regulation. Cognitive theories of depression focus on the idea that certain patterns of thinking may influence or even cause various emotional states (Haeffel et al., 2008). Two of the best-known cognitive theories of depression are Beck's schema theory and the helplessness/hopelessness theory.

Aaron Beck (1976; 1987) has contributed one of the most important etiologically relevant cognitive theories of depression to date. His theory describes the thought processes proposed to be responsible for feelings of depression. In general, those afflicted by depression are believed to have acquired a negative schema or **depressogenetic schemata**, characterized by the tendency to see and experience the world in a negative fashion. The essential component of Beck's theory states that depressed individuals feel depressed because their thinking is biased toward negative interpretations of themselves, the world and their futures, otherwise known as the *negative cognitive triad*. According to Beck, depressed individuals engage in cognitive biases that perpetuate their feelings of inadequacy and dejection. Two of these proposed cognitive biases include: *selective abstraction* and *overgeneralization*. In selective abstraction, individuals draw a conclusion from a situation on the basis of one of many elements, for instance, a student feels worthless when his group fails their assignment, even though he is only one of six group members who contributed to the project. Overgeneralization occurs when someone makes a broad conclusion drawn on the basis of a single, often trivial, event. For example, a waitress working on a busy Friday night forgets one drink order all night and uses this one instance as proof that she is stupid and useless.

The second important cognitive theory we will discuss is Martin Seligman's *learned helplessness model* of depression, and its recent descendant, *hopelessness theory*. The **learned helplessness theory** was largely formulated on animal research wherein animals were exposed to unavoidable aversive situations. Dogs were exposed to inescapable electric shocks, and after initially trying to escape, the dogs eventually stopped trying to get away and passively accepted the painful shocks. When these same dogs were exposed to shocks that *could* be avoided, they did not attempt to escape and most of them lay down in a corner and whined (Seligman, 1974). Later, this concept was reformulated into an attributional version, and applied to humans to explain depression. According to Seligman (1990), individuals with depression engage in a *pessimistic explanatory style* meaning they tend to attribute any setbacks they encounter to personal ("it's my fault"), global ("this changes everything"), and stable ("things can't change, they will always be this way") causes.

The *hopelessness theory* (Abramson, Metalsky, & Alloy, 1989; Abramson, Alloy, & Metalsky, 1985) posits that individuals with depression expect that desirable outcomes will not happen, and that undesirable outcomes will occur, but feel that they cannot change these outcomes. An important distinction between the helplessness and hopelessness models is that the hopelessness model contends that prior to becoming hopeless individuals have a negative attributional style and experience some unfortunate stressful experience. Only those who already have a pessimistic cognitive style *and* have experienced a traumatic event will then become hopeless.

Section 3: Anxiety Disorders

Everyone experiences anxiety from time to time. Perhaps you have your driving test coming up, a big date with your crush, or a deadline for a big project – all of these situations could understandably make you feel anxious. Anxiety and fear in small doses can even be adaptive in the sense that it can promote quick responses to danger, or encourage you to fix a pressing problem to alleviate your discomfort. For some people, however, anxiety can be chronically debilitating and cause persistent problems that interfere with daily activities. **Anxiety disorders** are a class of disorders marked by feelings of excessive apprehension and anxiety. They are among the most commonly occurring psychological disorders (Government of Canada, 2006), with 29% of people meeting diagnostic criteria at some point in their lives (Kessler et al., 2005). In this section we'll cover the five main types of anxiety disorders: *generalized anxiety disorder, phobic disorder, obsessive-compulsive disorder, post-traumatic stress disorder, panic disorder* and *agoraphobia*. Many of these disorders are overlapping to some extent in that many who have one anxiety disorder will be afflicted by another at some point in their lives.

Box 6.2: Generalized Anxiety Disorder

Dave is a married electrician in his mid-forties. He describes himself simply as being "edgy," but based on what Dave has told you, it is clear that his physical and psychological symptoms interfere with most areas of his life. Dave reports being easily fatigued, and complains of sweaty palms, heart palpitations, and difficulty concentrating – all of which have been ongoing for at least 18 months. Furthermore, he notes that he constantly worries about the health of his parents, his role as a "good father," whether his wife may be thinking about leaving him, and if his coworkers like him. Dave knows that his concerns are somewhat irrational but this does not ease his apprehension. Over the past couple years Dave has had few social contacts because of his nervous symptoms, and on occasion has felt the need to leave work when the symptoms become unbearable. Dave's family is largely unaware of his discomfort because he feels the need to appear "perfect."

(Adapted from DSM-IV-TR Casebook, 2004, pp.135-138)

Generalized Anxiety Disorder

Generalized anxiety disorder (GAD) is a psychological disorder defined by constant, severe, and inescapable anxiety and worry. Feelings of anxiety and apprehension are often uncontrollable and cannot be attributed to a specific target –they involve everything from minor everyday problems to life in general (Brown, O'Leary, & Barlow, 2001). These feelings of uneasiness are frequently accompanied by physical symptoms such as restlessness, fatigue, nausea, irritability, sleeping problems and difficulty concentrating. Many individuals with GAD report high levels of anxiety and nervousness over the course of their whole lives; the progression of symptoms is chronic and tends to worsen at times of stress (Barlow, Blanchard, Vermilyea, Vermilyea, & DiNardo, 1986). GAD occurs more frequently in females than males, and has a lifetime prevalence rate of about 5% (Kessler et al., 2005).

In the case of Dave, there is continued worry about various aspects of his life, from concerns about his parenting skills and role as a husband, to a fear of being disliked by his coworkers. Dave meets diagnostic criteria for GAD because he is experiencing uncontrollable excessive worrying that has been ongoing for over 6 months. He also has at least three physiological symptoms associated with his anxiety including: being on "edge", easily fatigued, and difficulties concentrating. Furthermore, because his anxiety is generalized, he does not meet criteria for any other specific anxiety disorder; for example, Dave's anxiety is not specific to being embarrassed in public, as in social phobia. Finally, Dave's symptoms are not the result of a medical condition or substance abuse, and they interfere with his social and occupational functioning as he has few social contacts and has had to leave work on account of his anxiety.

Phobic Disorders

Phobic disorders are a type of anxiety disorder marked by a persistent and irrational fear of an object or situation that presents no realistic danger. Unlike GAD, the anxiety in phobic disorders has a specific focus. Individuals who suffer from phobias recognize that their fear is irrational, but cannot help themselves. In some, their fear may be so intense that even imagining the phobic object or situation can trigger feelings of anxiety (Thorpe & Salkovkis, 1995). In many cases, phobic reactions tend to be accompanied by physical reactions (e.g., trembling, heart palpitations, and muscle tension). Phobic reactions may develop in response to almost any target, but certain types of phobias are more common than others. Typically, phobias are grouped into two categories entitled *social phobias* and *specific phobias*.

Box 6.3: Social Phobia

> Frank is a 45-year-old postal worker who admits feelings of mild depression over the course of his whole life. He has trouble concentrating and feels little pleasure in any activities. As far back as Frank can remember he has felt socially awkward. Through school from kindergarten to high school, he felt overwhelming anxiety at birthday parties and any other occasion where he might have to be social or interact with other people. As a child, Frank met new people with his eyes lowered, fearing their scrutiny. He expected to feel embarrassed and humiliated, and was

convinced that everyone around him thought he was "dumb" or a "jerk." As a teenager, Frank was terrified of talking to girls, and has yet to have his first kiss or even go on a date. Frank has only ever held jobs where he could apply through an application, because he felt unable to answer questions in an interview setting. At present, he works the evening shift in his job, has little contact with others, and consciously avoids any situations where he might have to talk to people. Frank knows that he shouldn't fear these interactions because everyone around him is able to participate in social activities, but he simply cannot force himself to see past his anxiety.

(Adapted from DSM-IV-TR Casebook, 2004, pp. 299-305)

Individuals afflicted by **social phobia** demonstrate a marked fear of public appearances during which humiliation or embarrassment is possible. These individuals actively avoid situations where they may have to interact with others, and are fearful of being scrutinized or evaluated by others. Most people with a social phobia avoid feared situations, but less commonly some may force themselves to endure the social or performance situation with intense anxiety. This may lead to a vicious cycle of anticipatory anxiety leading to anxiety symptoms in the feared situation, which may in turn lead to actual or perceived poor performance, thus intensifying the fear of the situation even more so than before. Common types of social phobias include fears of public speaking, eating in public places, and meeting new people. Social phobias appear equally frequently in males and females, typically have an onset in the mid-teens (DSM-IV-TR, 2000), and lifetime prevalence rates are generally estimated to be around 12.1% (Kessler et al., 2005).

As you can imagine, social phobias can be quite devastating, particularly if your fear prohibits you from having a social life or holding a regular job, as with Frank from our case study. Frank's story exemplifies many of the symptoms common in social phobia including a persistent fear of interacting with others, despite knowing that his concerns are unreasonable.

Box 6.4: Specific Phobia

Cleo is a 32-year-old schoolteacher living a relatively average life. She lives with her fiancée, has two dogs, and recently bought a new car. Cleo was born in Brazil where she lived until she was 8 with her mother, father, and two brothers. At the age of 7, Cleo witnessed her mother being attacked by a vicious snake at her favourite park close to her family home. Cleo was alone with her mother and had to run to a neighbour's home to call an ambulance. Her mother was given an antidote, and released from the hospital within 24 hours. Despite her mother's quick recovery, this experience fostered an intense fear of snakes. She refuses to go near the snakes at the local zoo, look at photos of snakes, or even talk about them. On one particular occasion Cleo's fiancée rented the movie *Anaconda*, thinking he could help her alleviate her fear of snakes if she watched a film featuring a fake snake. Shortly after the film began, Cleo ran out of the room in tears and crawled into bed visibly terrified by the thought of snakes. Cleo rationally accepts that her mother's snake attack was a freak accident, and that it is extremely unlikely that she will ever encounter a snake now that she lives in a downtown apartment in a busy city. However, these rational ideas do not alleviate her fear of a potential snake attack. Moreover, Cleo refuses to go to parks of any kind for fear of encountering a snake, and walks an extra 10 minutes to work to avoid the park near her apartment.

Specific Phobia

Specific phobias are characterized by a persistent, intense, and irrational fear of specific objects, places, or situations (other than social situations). As with social phobias, individuals with specific phobias avoid the phobic objects and any exposure to the feared target results in an immediate anxiety response. The lifetime prevalence for this disorder is around 12.5% (Kessler et al., 2005), and tends to appear more frequently in females than males. The first symptoms usually appear in childhood or early adolescence, and seem to occur at a younger age in females. The diagnosis can only be applied if fear or anxious anticipation of potentially encountering the phobic object interferes with one's daily routine or functioning, or if the person experiences distress about having a phobia. Types of specific phobias are grouped into five main categories: (1) animals (e.g., snakes, dogs, spiders); (2) natural environment (e.g., water, lightning storms, heights); (3) blood-injury-injection (e.g., sight of blood or an injury, or receiving an injection); (4) situational (e.g., tunnels, bridges, enclosed spaces); or (5) other (e.g., vomiting, choking, costumed individuals such as clowns).

Cleo would be diagnosed as having a specific phobia (animal type). She has a marked fear of parks that is associated with her phobia of snakes, and exposure to the phobic stimulus (a snake in the movie *Anaconda*, or at the zoo) causes an immediate anxiety response. Furthermore, while Cleo is aware that her fear is unreasonable, she still walks the longer route to her job to avoid a park where she fears she may encounter a snake. It is important to note that a fear of snakes is not unreasonable, as some snakes can deliver a deadly bite, but when our fears are so excessive that they interfere with our lives, it becomes a form of mental illness.

Box 6.5: Obsessive-Compulsive Disorder

Sarah is a 14-year-old girl who has recently been admitted to an inpatient ward. When Sarah was living at home she was constantly burdened with fears about cleanliness and germs. At times she would wake up 5 hours before she had to leave the house because her morning rituals would take up so much of her time. Sarah would get out of bed and go to the bathroom to shower where she would scrub her skin for at least a half hour. Then, she would wash her face over the sink, but before washing her face she washed her hands. At first Sarah was content with washing her hands with soap and water, but when this no longer rid her of anxiety and fear, she turned to using rubbing alcohol on her hands which frequently made her bleed. When Sarah put her clothes on she would shake the germs off for a whole half hour and then have to go to school without eating breakfast because she had run out of time. Sometimes thinking about special numbers, for instance multiples of three would ease her anxiety about germs. Sarah has friends, and often felt more comfortable around people because she would forget about germs and disease. When she tried to explain her fears to others, they would say things like "Well, that's stupid," and while she knew her fears were irrational, this did not reduce her anxiety, and she continued to perform her usual rituals to curb her uneasiness.

Obsessions are persistent ideas, thoughts or impulses that are unwanted and inappropriate, and cause marked distress. **Compulsions** are repetitive behaviours or mental acts performed to reduce or prevent distress. **Obsessive-compulsive disorder** (OCD) is an anxiety disorder defined by both obsessions and compulsions. Obsessions are pervasive thoughts and their accompanying anxiety, and compulsions are the ritualized behaviours that temporarily relieve the anxiety. The onset of OCD generally occurs in late adolescence or young adulthood, although there are documented cases of childhood onset. Emergence of OCD occurs earlier in males, but the rate of diagnosis is equally common in males and females (DSM-IV-TR, 2000; Eisen & Rasmussen, 2001). The estimated lifetime prevalence rate of OCD is 1.6% (Kessler et al., 2005).

Common obsessions include: *contamination*, including concerns about dirt and germs; *pathological doubt*, such as fear about making the wrong decisions, or preoccupations about not having completed tasks such as turning off the gas or locking doors; *symmetry, exactness,* or *perfectionism*, for instance experiencing discomfort when things are not symmetrical, lined up or in their place; or *religious*, characterized by worrying about being sacrilegious. Common compulsions include: *washing and cleaning*, engaging in excessive hand washing, grooming, showering, or avoiding touching objects considered to be contaminated; *checking*, such as multiple checking of stoves, faucets, lights, locks; *arranging*, moving various objects around to achieve symmetry; *hoarding*, keeping useless items, and the inability to throw them out; *counting*, counting actions or needing to do things a certain number of times; *repeating*, redoing actions until they feel right (Dell'Osso, Altamura, Mundo, Marazziti, & Hollander, 2007). You may have noticed that specific types of compulsions seem to be directly related to specific obsessions, for instance the *contamination* obsession would likely be paired with the *washing and cleaning* compulsion. Indeed, some obsessions and compulsions are frequently paired together (Leckman, 1997), while others seem to be completely unrelated, for example a woman who dressed and undressed 20 times to prevent her husband getting into a car accident (Marks, 1987).

As with many psychological disorders, OCD can be particularly debilitating, but many people with OCD lead regular lives. Recently, TV personality and comedian, Howie Mandel has spoken about his battle with the disorder. Host of the TV show, *Deal or No Deal*, Mandel never shakes hands with contestants – he simply uses a "knuckle bump" in which he merely touches knuckles with them. Mandel suffers from OCD wherein one of his obsessions is contamination and germs (mysophobia). Mandel avoids shaking hands, but at times it is unavoidable to which Mandel says "I have shaken hands and had a good evening, but I just don't want to trigger whatever I trigger. I would be in the bathroom for hours, and I'll scald [my hands] and I'll come out and then I can't think of anything else. I'll keep thinking I've got something to get off my hands" (Hampson, 2007, R3).

Sarah would be diagnosed with OCD as she demonstrates both obsessions and compulsions (though only one of the two is required to meet clinical diagnosis). Sarah's obsessions are recurrent thoughts that are not simply excessive worries about real-life problems, and fall into the *contamination* category. She is unable to control her obsessional thoughts surrounding contamination and recognizes that they are the product of her own mind. Furthermore, her compulsions meet diagnostic criteria because she engages in repetitive behaviours or mental acts that she feels driven to complete in response to her obsessions that are aimed at reducing distress and anxiety.

Box 6.6: Post-Traumatic Stress Disorder

John is a 23-year-old war veteran. He returned from the Vietnam War one year ago, after being honourably discharged. By all standards, John seemed to return to his regular life – he continued to attend college, married his fiancée, and fell back into his previous favourite pastimes. His wife noticed that he was averse to talking about his experiences in Vietnam but assumed that this was a normal response to unpleasant memories. John began to experience severe symptoms around the time of the fall of Saigon. He became obsessed with watching TV and following the news surrounding this event. His wife noticed that he had problems sleeping, and would wake up in the middle of the night in the midst of a nightmare of reliving his experiences in Vietnam. On one particular occasion, John was in the garden when a plane flew overhead and he found himself in the grips of a full-fledged flashback. John threw himself on the ground and sought cover thinking that the plane was an attacking helicopter. From here his symptoms became progressively worse to the point that he distanced himself from his wife and became seemingly unable to plan for the future because he was living almost exclusively in the past.

(Adapted from DSM-IV-TR Casebook, 2004, pp. 189-194)

Harvard psychiatrist, Dr. Roger Pittman, who studies post-traumatic stress disorder, described the phenomenon as "a memory that has its volume set too loud" (Bean, 2006). Indeed, **post-traumatic stress disorder (PTSD)** is an anxiety disorder triggered by a severely traumatic event, wherein sufferers feel intense anxiety associated with particular stimuli related to the incident, causing them to relive the traumatic event. Sometimes, the anxiety and terror associated with PTSD may not surface until months or even years after exposure. To qualify as an extreme stressor (traumatic event), the victim's response to the experience must have involved intense fear, horror or helplessness. PTSD is often elicited following exposure to a traumatic event such as being raped, watching a murder, experiencing a natural disaster, or involvement in a war. Prevalence rates of PTSD are around 6.8% (Kessler et al., 2005), and the disorder appears to occur with higher frequency and intensity in women than men (Breslau et al., 1998; Tolin & Foa, 2006). Symptoms of PTSD include recurrent and intrusive distressing recollections or dreams of the event, acting or feeling that the event is recurring (including hallucinations and illusions), difficulty sleeping, feeling detached or estranged from others, and attempting to avoid conversations related to the trauma.

It is important to note that experiencing a traumatic event does not dictate that PTSD will certainly follow. One study found that only about 10% of people develop PTSD following a traumatic event, where violent assaults were more likely to trigger the disorder (Breslau, 1999). Other predictors of PTSD include the intensity of the emotions and level of dissociation felt during and immediately following the event, and perceived life threat during the traumatic experience (Ozer, Best, Lipsey, & Weiss, 2003).

John would almost certainly meet criteria for the diagnosis of PTSD. He presumably experienced a series of traumatic events while in the Vietnam War, and it seems that the recent fall of Saigon has triggered post-traumatic stress symptoms. John is experiencing flashbacks and nightmares, and appears to be drifting further from reality as his syndrome intensifies.

Panic Disorder

Panic disorder is type of anxiety disorder characterized by recurrent attacks of overwhelming anxiety that usually occur suddenly and unexpectedly. Panic attacks involve intense feelings of anxiety coupled with physiological symptoms such as dizziness, shortness of breath, heart palpitations, trembling, chest pains, and even a fear of dying (Barlow, 2002). Prevalence rates for panic disorders are around 4.7% (Kessler et al., 2005), and while the age of onset can be considerably variable, it is typically between late adolescence and early adulthood (Pine, 2000).

After victims have experienced a number of panic attacks, they often become terrified about when they might experience their next attack. This fear may become so overpowering that they become afraid to leave their own homes – a condition known as agoraphobia. Agoraphobia is commonly misunderstood as to mean a fear of public places or crowds. In fact, **agoraphobia** pertains to one's fear of being in a situation or place where escape might be difficult or embarrassing (e.g., elevator), or where help would be unavailable should a panic attack occur. Individuals are often able to confront their feared situation when accompanied by a companion. For instance a housebound woman with agoraphobia would likely be better able to endure facing her fears outside the home if her husband accompanied her.

Etiology of Anxiety Disorders

Like mood disorders and many of the remaining psychological disorders we will discuss, the etiology of anxiety disorders appears to be related to an interaction between biological and psychological factors.

BIOLOGICAL FACTORS:

Twin and family studies examining the genetic impact on anxiety disorders have found that there is a moderate genetic predisposition to anxiety disorders (Hettema, Neale, & Kendler, 2001; McMahon & Kassem, 2005). 30-50% of individual variability in risk to develop any given anxiety disorder derives from genetic variability (Gordon & Hen, 2004). Some studies suggest that genetic inheritance of neuroticism, which is the tendency to be high strung, moody, and tense, may be related to the development of anxiety disorders (Zinbarg & Barlow, 1996).

Subsequent research on *anxiety sensitivity* (AS) suggests that some individuals are predisposed to a fear of anxiety-related sensations (Reiss & McNally, 1985) that may make them more vulnerable to anxiety disorders (Schmidt, Zvolensky, & Maner, 2006). Individuals with high AS tend to interpret internal physiological symptoms of anxiety with fear. For instance, one of the items on the questionnaire measuring AS reads, "When I notice that my heart is beating rapidly, I worry that I might have a heart attack" (Peterson & Reiss, 1992). Constant fear of anxiety creates more anxiety, and may subsequently become a vicious circle that develops into a diagnosable anxiety disorder.

Finally, recent evidence suggests that there may be a neurochemical basis to anxiety disorders. Both the neurotransmitters GABA and serotonin have been implicated in the development and maintenance of these disorders (Akimova, Lanzenberger, & Kasper, 2009; Kalueff & Nutt, 2006).

BEHAVIOURAL FACTORS: CONDITIONING & LEARNING

Behavioural theories play a large role in the emergence and maintenance of anxiety disorders, most specifically through *classical conditioning*, *instrumental conditioning*, and *observational learning*.

In general, behavioural explanations of anxiety disorders suggest that anxiety and fear responses may be acquired through classical conditioning and then maintained through instrumental conditioning (see Chapter 3 on Learning for a refresher on these terms). Many individuals with phobias can recall an initial incident that marked the beginning of their fear toward a phobic stimulus (Mineka & Zinbarg, 2006). Consider Cleo's fear of snakes that originated from an initial traumatic incident (mother bitten by a snake). In this example, the snakebite is the unconditional stimulus (US), which elicits fear or the unconditional response (UR). As a result, a contingency was formed between the initial snakebite episode (US) and predictive cues such as parks or snakes in general (the conditional stimulus, CS). Now, Cleo experiences a conditional response (CR) of fear and anxiety whenever she is in the presence of snakes or encounters stimuli that remind her of that original experience (CS).

Instrumental conditioning helps to maintain this fear because the person avoids the feared stimulus (parks and snakes) and this behaviour is reinforced by a reduction in fear and anxiety. This negative reinforcement occurs each time Cleo actively avoids the park on the way to work. Phobias may even arise in the absence of a traumatic experience through the process of observational learning (Rachman, 1990). Parents may pass on their own anxieties to their children. For instance, if Cleo had witnessed her father scream and cry every time he encountered a snake, it is probable that she may too have developed an intense fear of them despite never having experienced a traumatic event with snakes.

Finally, the concept of *preparedness* proposed by Martin Seligman (1971) suggests that we may be evolutionarily predisposed to develop fears and phobias toward certain types of objects and situations. This principle helps to explain why we are more likely to develop a fear in response to ancient sources of threats (e.g., spiders) rather than modern sources of threat (e.g., cars).

COGNITIVE FACTORS

Similar to mood disorders, some types or patterns of thinking may predispose certain individuals to the development of anxiety disorders (Zhang, 2009). Anxious people often interpret ambiguous situations in a negative light (Matthews & MacLeod, 2005). In support of this notion, an interesting study by Eyseneck et al. (1991) demonstrated that anxious people are more likely than non-anxious people to interpret ambiguous sentences as threatening. For example, one of the sentences participants were asked to read was "The doctor examined little Emma's growth." This could be interpreted to mean that the doctor examined the change in Emma's height *or* the growth of a tumour. Anxious people were more likely than non-anxious people to perceive the sentence in a threatening manner to mean that Emma has a tumour.

Draft

Section 4: Somatoform Disorders

Somatoform disorders are a category of disorders in which psychological problems manifest in physical symptoms that cannot be explained. Somatoform literally means "bodily form." The physical characteristics that accompany somatoform disorders do not appear to be the result of a biological cause, however, individuals who are afflicted by somatoform disorders are not faking for personal gain. Individuals who intentionally fake a physical illness may be diagnosed with *malingering* (if the purpose is to avoid some responsibility such as jury detail or conscription into the military) or *factitious disorder* (the psychological motivation is to assume the role of a sick person) and these are quite different from any of the somatoform disorders. Somatoform disorders are frequently comorbid with anxiety or mood disorders (Lieb, Meinlschmidt, & Araya, 2007; Mergl, et al., 2007). Patients with a somatoform disorder tend to spend an average of 2.2 days per year in the hospital, compared to the national average of 0.9 days (Stern & Fernandez, 1991). In general, it is challenging to get reliable prevalence rates for these disorders because the individuals go through the medical system seeing various doctors, and may never receive a psychological disorder diagnosis.

Box 6.7: Somatization Disorder

Marie is a 38-year-old married woman suffering from depression. Over the course of her life, she has drunk heavily and has been hospitalized on two separate occasions for treatment of her alcoholism. After her second hospitalization, at age 29, she remained abstinent. When asked, Marie recalls being a sickly child and experiencing various bouts of illness her whole life with no apparent medical cause. She has seen a number of health professionals to address her complaints of pain in her chest, abdominal cavity, back, and legs. She also suffers from recurrent anesthesia of her fingertips, nausea, bloating, and irregular menses. Aside from being told by medical consultants that she has a "nervous heart" and a "spastic colon," Marie is still searching for an adequate explanation for her physical and psychological problems.

(Adapted from DSM-IV-TR Casebook, 2004, pp. 306-308)

Somatization disorder is a type of somatoform disorder marked by a history of diverse physical complaints that appear to be psychological in origin. For a diagnosis of somatization to be made the individual must present least four bodily pains, two gastrointestinal complaints, one pseudo neurological symptom, and one sexual or reproductive symptom. If any one of these requirements is not met, the diagnosis cannot be applied. Lifetime prevalence rates are estimated to be between 0.2-2% in females, and less than 0.2% among males. Diagnostic criteria are typically met before age 25, but onset of initial symptoms is often present in adolescence. Marie would almost certainly be diagnosed with somatization disorder as she has a history of various physical ailments, and exhibits the required number of somatic symptoms that cannot be explained by a known medical problem. Furthermore, as with many individuals with this disorder, Marie exhibits depressive symptoms not directly related to the diagnosis.

Conversion disorder

Conversion disorder is arguably the most debilitating of the somatoform disorders. **Conversion disorder** is a category of somatoform disorders defined by a specific sensory or motor deficit, such as temporary blindness, deafness, or paralysis. Original research on conversion disorders lead Freud to many of his theories on psychoanalysis, as he concluded that physical complaints with no medial explanation were the product of his patients' unconscious minds attempting to protect themselves from anxiety (Sharp & Mayou, 2004). Current research suggests that severe psychosocial stress (such as life threatening situations) typically occur prior to the onset of conversion disorder (Cloninger & Dokucu, 2008). Symptoms may include impaired coordination or balance, paralysis or localized weakness, blindness, deafness, and hallucinations. Prevalence rates are variable and estimates range from 11 to 500 cases per 100,000 people, and females tend to be afflicted more frequently than males (Singh & Lee, 1997). Diagnoses are more common in rural populations, individuals of lower socioeconomic status, and those who are less knowledgeable about medical and psychological concepts.

Unlike somatization disorder, conversion disorder has betraying clues that reveal the psychological basis of the somatic complaint: patient syndromes tend to be inconsistent with medical knowledge about their apparent disease. For instance, individuals who experience glove anesthesia report no sensation in their hands, but not in any other part of their arm. Medical knowledge on the nervous system indicates that there are no known nerves that innervate the hand without also innervating at least a portion of the arm too. However, part of the criteria for diagnosis is that the symptoms are not intentionally produced or feigned, as would be the case in malingering or factitious disorders.

Box 6.8: Hypochondriasis

> Louis is a 34-year-old unmarried man who works as a programmer at a local computer store. His hours are fairly flexible, and as long as he completes the tasks given to him by his manager in a timely fashion, he can work when he pleases. In his spare time Louis is frequently preoccupied with traveling the country to see various medical experts about his physical condition, which he thinks is of great concern. Over the course of his life, Louis has had an occasional recurring cough, which waxes and wanes relative to the level of stress in his life. He is convinced that his cough and feeling of "tired lungs" are indicative of serious lung disease. His most recent relationship ended because his girlfriend became frustrated and upset when Louis spent their savings on a series of physical examinations and diagnostic tests. Louis went through with these tests despite reassurance from various medical experts that his cough and "tired lungs" were unrelated to any detectable bodily diseases or malfunctions. Due to the flexible nature of his working hours, Louis' obsession with his cough has not impacted his job, but he has lost his longtime girlfriend and has trouble keeping friends because he constantly talks about his "undiagnosed" illness.

Hypochondriasis is a somatoform disorder in which one feels persistent fear of a physical illness, and may feel symptoms when none are present. Individuals with this disorder are constantly preoccupied with fears of having a serious disease based on over-interpretation of one or more bodily signs or symptoms. They constantly monitor their physical condition searching for any possible signs of illness.

Thorough medical examinations, tests, and assurance from medical professionals do not curb their unwarranted fears of disease and illness. The preoccupation may be focused on bodily functions (e.g., sweating); minor physical abnormalities (e.g., occasional cough or small sores); or ambiguous physical symptoms (e.g., "aching veins"). The diagnosis may be applied *with poor insight*, if the individual is unable to recognize that their concern is excessive or unreasonable. Prevalence rates in the general population are thought to be between 1-5%, and the typical age of onset is in early adulthood (DSM-IV-TR, 2000).

Louis would meet diagnostic criteria for hypochondriasis as he demonstrates all of the necessary symptoms including a preoccupation with a fear that has endured for over 6 months, of having a serious physical disease despite reassurance from medical professionals. He has also experienced impairment in his social life (loss of his girlfriend and a lack of friends) as a direct result of his obsession. Furthermore, Louis does not appear to recognize that his pervasive fears are unreasonable; consequently, his diagnosis would likely be noted as *with poor insight.*

As you can probably imagine, people are often resistant to the idea that their pain and suffering might be psychologically related (Hollifield, 2005). Some researchers argue that the concept of 'unexplained by a medical condition' as the core feature of a psychological disorder is highly problematic (Sharp & Mayou, 2004) and it may be best to abolish the existence of somatoform disorders as a whole. Somatization disorder may be better considered as a combination of a personality disorder and anxiety and depressive syndromes (Bass & Murphy, 1995). Further still, some contend that eradication of somatoform disorders would force medical practitioners to pay closer attention to their patients' symptoms rather than attempting to label their disease, and psychiatry would have to place more weight on patients' assertions that their symptoms are genuine (Sharp & Mayou, 2004).

Etiology of Somatoform disorders

Somatoform disorders are largely considered to be related to personality and cognitive factors, but there is some evidence pointing toward physical abnormalities. Some researchers suggest that there may be inherited aspects of physiological functioning, such as a highly reactive autonomic nervous system, which may predispose some people to somatoform disorders (Kirmayer & Looper, 2007). Twin studies have found that some unexplained physical symptoms are heritable (Kendler et al, 1995; Farmer et al. 1999). Furthermore, a recent study presented evidence suggesting that somatoform symptoms are not strictly mental events, but are associated with a diversity of biological processes (Rief & Barsky, 2005). Regardless of these suggestions, the debate on the potential physiological basis of somatoform disorders will continue.

PERSONALITY FACTORS

Individuals with certain types of personalities or specific traits seem to be more prone to the development of somatoform disorders, and there is increasing evidence that somatoform disorders are linked to dysfunction in personality (Bass & Murphy, 1995; Noyes et al., 2001). *Histrionic* and *obsessive-compulsive* are two particular personality types that appear to be the most frequently associated with somatoform disorders. Individuals with histrionic personality types tend to be self-centered, overly dramatic, and are known to go to extreme lengths to get attention (Slavney, 1990). Recent research on the comorbidity of personality disorders and somatoform disorders found a high prevalence (56%) of obsessive-compulsive personality disorder in hypochondriasis (Sakal, Nestoriuc, Nolido, & Barsky, 2010). The personality trait of neuroticism also seems to be elevated in individuals with somatoform disorders (Noyes et al., 2005).

COGNITIVE FACTORS

As one of the main etiologies for somatoform disorders, cognitive patterns have received much attention in the hopes of explaining the sometimes-devastating effects of these disorders. Research by Barsky (1993; 2001) maintains that individuals with somatoform disorders focus an excessive amount of attention on internal physiological processes, and tend to draw catastrophic conclusions about normal bodily sensations. Furthermore, they also adopt what Barsky refers to as a *faulty standard of good health*, meaning that they expect good health to mean a complete lack of discomfort and symptoms of any kind, which is completely unrealistic as even the healthiest people don't feel 100% well every single second of every day.

Subsequent recent research on the cognitive processes involved in somatoform disorders has found that individuals with these disorders have a memory bias for physical threat words (Lim & Kim, 2005). Heightened memory for physical threat words (e.g., peril, dangerous, or hazard) could facilitate recollection of somatic complaints and symptom reporting, and could play an important role in the maintenance of a somatoform disorder.

Section 5: Schizophrenia

Box 6.9: Schizophrenia

George is a 40-year-old man who has arrived at the hospital with his mother, who claims she is afraid of him. This hospitalization marks his twentieth hospitalization since he was 15 years old. George is dressed in ragged clothing including a large overcoat, bedroom slippers, a baseball cap, and several scarves around his neck. Upon questioning, George reveals that he is convinced his mother is feeding him broken glass (even when he has watched her prepare the meal), and frequently shows intense anger toward her as a result. His speech and manner are childlike in that he frequently giggles and walks with exaggerated hip movements. His mother reports that he stopped taking his medication over a month ago and since then has resumed his bizarre behaviour including hearing voices and talking to himself. After each hospitalization he was put on a regimen of antipsychotics, which stabilized him, but after his release George would always refuse to continue taking his medication. George is prone to wandering the apartment all night, refusing to bath, eating very little, and throwing things out of the window. When asked what he has been doing recently, George says "eating wire and lighting fires." George has never been able to hold a job for more than a few weeks, and seems to have no friends outside of his mother and sister with whom he lives.

(Adapted from DSM-IV-TR Casebook, 2004, pp. 232-233)

Schizophrenia is perhaps one of the most interesting and mysterious psychological disorders we will cover in this chapter. This disorder frequently receives media attention, and, as with most media stories, many facts are taken out of context and sensationalized for entertainment. One of the factors that makes schizophrenia so interesting is that is it idiosyncratic in nature, meaning that the disorder generally presents with a somewhat different set of symptoms from person to person. Thus, each person who has schizophrenia is, to some extent, unique from others who have the same diagnosis. No single symptom must be present for the diagnosis to be applied (Walker, Kestler, Bollini, & Hochman, 2004), though it is arguable that the core symptom in schizophrenic disorders is cognitive disturbances.

In 1911, Swiss psychiatrist Eugen Bleuler coined the term schizophrenia, which literally means *split mind*. Bleuler was referring to split mental processes (such as attention, perception, emotion, motivation, and thought), not split personality. Though, even today many people still confuse schizophrenia with dissociative identity disorder (previously know as multiple personality disorder), which, as we will discuss in the next few pages, is an entirely different disorder unto itself. Bleuler argued that schizophrenia was a fitting term because mental processes appear to be operating independently of one another leading to bizarre and disorganized thoughts and behaviour. Thus, schizophrenia is characterized by a single personality that is shattered rather than distinct multiple personalities (the central feature of dissociative identity disorder).

Prevalence & Emergence of Schizophrenia

Schizophrenia is one the most severe psychopathologies. Estimates of prevalence rates range from 0.2% to 2% depending on the specific measurement instrument; however, its lifetime prevalence is generally accepted to be about 1% (Government of Canada, 2006; Walker et al., 2004). Due in part to the debilitating effects of schizophrenia prevalence rates are thought to be around 11% on average in the homeless population (Folsom & Jeste, 2002). Schizophrenia places a substantial financial burden on the patient, their family, and the healthcare system. In 1996, the total cost of care related to schizophrenia in Canada was estimated to be $2.35 billion (annually) in direct costs, and an additional $2 billion for indirect costs (Government of Canada, 2006).

While there are rare cases of schizophrenia beginning in childhood (occurrence is thought to be 1 in 10,000; Remschmidt & Theisen, 2005), it usually emerges in late adolescence or early adulthood. On average, it typically appears 4 years earlier and is more severe in males than females (Riecher-Rossler & Hafner, 2000; Salyers & Meuser, 2001). Incidence rates are significantly higher in males compared to females; in fact, the ratio of men to women diagnosed with schizophrenia is 4:1 (McGrath, 2006). In some cases there may be a sudden presentation of psychosis, but onset of schizophrenia-type symptoms is typically gradual. Many researchers find signs of schizophrenia long before the illness is diagnosed. Children who later develop full-blown schizophrenia often demonstrate deficits in various areas of normal functioning, including cognitive functioning, socializing, and motor function. In measurements of cognitive functioning, these children perform below their healthy peers on intelligence tests, measures of achievement, and tend to have lower grades (Aylward et al., 1984; Jones et al., 1994). Socially, these children are less responsive than children with healthy outcomes, and show more negative facial expressions than their siblings who do not develop schizophrenia (Walker & Lewine, 1990; Walker, Grimes, Davis, & Smith, 1993). Concerning motor function, compared to their siblings, children who develop schizophrenia tend to show more delays and abnormalities in motor development, including walking at a much later age (Walker, Savoie, & Davis, 1994).

The onset of behavioural dysfunction and subclinical symptoms usually escalate over time, a period referred to as the prodomal phase (Lieberman, et al., 2001). Following the diagnosable clinical emergence of schizophrenia, more than half of those afflicted by this disorder suffer from serious disabilities including the inability to maintain close relationships or hold a regular job (Harvey, Reichenberg, & Bowie, 2006). As we move forward to better treatments for schizophrenia, individuals suffering from this disorder are more than ever before able to function in society, though they may need to be hospitalized from time to time when they experience acute episodes of symptoms (Lamb & Buchruch, 2001; McGurk & Mueser, 2004).

Clinical Symptoms of Schizophrenia

As we have already discussed, schizophrenia is a highly heterogeneous disorder. Here we will discuss the two main categories of symptoms – *positive* and *negative* symptoms.

POSITIVE SYMPTOMS

Positive symptoms include behavioural excesses or peculiarities, such as hallucinations, delusions, bizarre behaviour, and wild flights of ideas. In an acute episode of schizophrenia, these are the symptoms that are typically the most prominent. Positive symptoms are the presence of behaviours that are not apparent in most people. Alternatively, negative symptoms, which we will discuss later, are the absence of behaviours that are typically present in most people.

DISORGANIZED THOUGHT AND SPEECH

Disorganized speech, also known as *formal thought disorder*, refers to problems in organizing ideas and communicating in a way that can be understood by a listener. A classic example is this greeting to Bleuler from one of his patients: "I wish you a happy, joyful, healthy, blessed and fruitful year, and many good wine-years to come as well as a healthy and good apple-year, and sauerkraut and cabbage and squash and seed year." This excerpt demonstrates how the patient was completely sidetracked by listing fruits and vegetables, guided by what is known as *loose word associations*. There is a clear chain of associations that had little to do with the original intent of the statement. Communication abnormalities in individuals with schizophrenia are presumed to reflect an underlying inability to think in a logical manner, and as we cannot directly measure thoughts we measure communication, which is a manifestation of these thought patterns. In severe forms, speech may become so jumbled and incoherent that it becomes almost impossible to comprehend and is appropriately labelled as *word salad*.

DELUSIONS

A **delusion** is a false belief that is irrational or maintained despite being unsupported by external evidence. Delusions are considered *psychotic symptoms* because they mark a serious distortion of reality. George, who was presented at the beginning of this section, was deluded in thinking that his mother was feeding him glass. He held this belief despite evidence to the contrary, uch as watching his mother preparing his meal – he certainly would have noticed if she had soiled his food in any way! Delusions are often about thinking or thoughts, including *thought broadcast*, wherein the individual thinks everyone can hear their thoughts; *thought withdrawal*, when the individual is convinced that thoughts are being removed from their head; or *thought insertion*, during which the person is certain that thoughts are being placed in their heads (Maher, 2001). Common types of delusions in schizophrenia are *delusions of grandeur*, commonly regarded as beliefs of one's own self-importance, for instance thinking that you are the president of the United States or Jesus Christ; *delusions of persecution*, beliefs that people are plotting against you; and *delusions of being controlled*, such as believing that one's thoughts are being controlled by radio waves.

HALLUCINATIONS

Hallucinations are sensory perceptions that occur in the absence of a real, external stimulus, or gross distortions of perceptual input. Hallucinations can exist in most sensory modalities: visual, tactile, and olfactory. The most common type of hallucinations in schizophrenia are auditory hallucinations, usually involving hearing voices of people who are either absent or do not exist (Stephan, Barton, & Boutros, 2001). Auditory hallucinations frequently include insults directed at the afflicted individual in the form of a running commentary on their behaviour ("You're a fool for thinking you could trust him"). They may convey demands ("You must hide from the eagle"), or they may be argumentative ("You don't need to leave the house"). Typically hallucinations and delusions work together to form a central theme, for instance, in the movie, *A Beautiful Mind*, John Nash (played by Russell Crowe) suffers from schizophrenia wherein he experiences both delusions and hallucinations.

Some research suggests that auditory hallucinations are rooted in the person's inability to recognize intrusive thoughts as being self-generated and mistakenly identify the source as outside of them (Bentall, 2000; Frith, 1992; Nayani & David, 1996). Neuroimaging research reveals that both speech generation and perception areas are activated during auditory verbal hallucinations (Lennox, Parks, Jones, & Morris, 1999; Shergill, et al., 2004).

Negative Symptoms

Negative symptoms are symptoms of schizophrenia that involve a lack or reduction in expected behaviours, thoughts, feelings, and drives. They include behavioural deficits, such as flattened emotions, social withdrawal, apathy, and poverty of speech. There is a general slowing down of bodily movements, and loss of basic drives such as hunger and loss of pleasure, for instance the pleasure associated with eating your favourite meal, or the content feeling of being full after a good meal. In one aspect, negative symptoms are the opposite of positive symptoms, in that negative symptoms are the presence of a decreased level of behaviours that are apparent in most people.

AFFECT

Individuals with schizophrenia often demonstrate problems with affect, that is, they have disturbed emotions and display deviant emotional responses. Problems with the range of emotions are frequently evident in what is known as *flat affect*. Flat affect or affective flattening is especially common and is usually characterized by the person's face appearing immobile and unresponsive, with exceptionally poor eye contact and reduced body language. Alternatively, disturbance in emotions may appear in the form of *inappropriate affect*. People with inappropriate affect tend to have emotional responses that are out of context; for example, they may laugh upon hearing that their mother has died or remain stone-faced while viewing a hilarious movie. Inappropriate affect is relatively rare, but it appears to be specific to schizophrenia, and therefore has considerable diagnostic importance.

ALOGIA

Alogia is the diagnostic term for poverty of speech. Alogia is manifested by brief, empty replies to questions. Individuals with alogia appear to have a reduction of thoughts that is subsequently reflected in a decreased production of speech.

AVOLITION AND ANHEDEONIA

Apathy or *avolition* is characterized by a lack of energy and a seeming disinterest in continuing to engage in regular activities. People who demonstrate avolition may appear to have an inability to initiate and persist in goal-directed behaviours. They may sit for an inordinately long period of time or show little interest in participating in social activities. Patients tend to become inattentive to their personal hygiene and simply cannot function in a school or work setting. Even when engaging in a normal task such as making a meal, they cannot follow through because they are unable to follow a coherent set of ideas or a plan. *Anhedonia* is the psychiatric term for the inability to experience pleasurable emotions from normally pleasurable life events such as eating, social interaction, or sexual activity. Many people with schizophrenia experience anhedonia in addition to their other symptoms.

Taken together, the negative symptoms have the most detrimental effect on quality of life and deterioration of adaptive behaviours. Research demonstrates that people with schizophrenia are less impaired when their symptoms are predominantly positive rather than negative (Keefe et al., 1987; Harvey, Reichenberg, & Bowie, 2006). This may be partially due to the fact that functional disability is stable, whereas positive symptoms tend to wax and wane over the course of the illness. Another likely cause might be that negative symptoms tend to co-occur with cognitive deficits (Bilder et al., 1985), which are arguably the primary feature of schizophrenia (Heinrichs, 2005).

COGNITIVE DEFICITS IN SCHIZOPHRENIA

Schizophrenia is typically characterized as a cognitive disorder, wherein the course of cognitive disturbances is due to changes in the brain, and the primary deficits are related to problems with processing information (Broome et al., 2005; Heinrichs, 2005).

Primary cognitive impairments in schizophrenia have been found across a wide assortment of tasks including: attention, memory, and *executive functioning* (Green, 1996; Heinrichs & Zakzanis, 1998). Executive functions are high-level processes such as the ability to problem solve, employ abstract thinking skills, and plan ahead. These deficits appear to be a pervasive symptom of schizophrenia and are present from before the initial psychotic break, at the time of diagnosis, over the course of full-blown schizophrenia, and even after remission (when most other symptoms have disappeared or are minimal; Harvey, Reichenberg, & Bowie, 2006). Research suggests that these cognitive impairments are closely related to functional disability, such as social and occupational functioning (Green, 1996; 2006).

An example of a cognitive disturbance that might be evident in individuals with schizophrenia is the inability to regulate attention. For instance, as you learned in the Attention & Memory chapter, most people are able to automatically ignore information in our environment that is not relevant such as the texture or your seat, how your clothes feel on your skin every time you move, or the typing of laptop keyboards around you during your psychology lecture. Using our information processing skills we are able to selectively attend to important stimuli in our environment. Consider that some people with schizophrenia process an excess of information in their environment that would easily drive anyone crazy (e.g., paying attention to the humming of a fan, the feeling of their chair, the flickering of a light bulb, etc.). Given this much sensory input it is not surprising that they have difficulty paying attention to what someone is saying to them or following a recipe to make a meal. This is just one example of a cognitive process that might underlie the disorganized behaviour often observed in this disorder; hence, the argument that the core symptom in schizophrenic disorders is cognitive disturbances.

Subtypes of Schizophrenia

Within schizophrenia there appear to be three general subtypes, including a fourth category for individuals who meet diagnostic criteria for the diagnosis but do not fall into one of the subtypes.

Paranoid schizophrenia is characterized by delusions and hallucinations that center on a theme. A well-known example of a person with paranoid schizophrenia is the character of John Nash from *A Beautiful Mind* (2001). As in the case with Nash, individuals with this subtype may believe that they have many enemies, and develop delusions of grandeur. **Catatonic schizophrenia** is predominantly defined by psychomotor symptoms such as catatonic rigidity, catatonic excitement, or waxy flexibility. These odd movements are not in response to anything in their environment. This subtype is diagnosed fairly infrequently and its prevalence seems to be declining (Mahendra, 1981; Caroff, 2007). **Disorganized schizophrenia** is predominantly defined by incoherent speech, disorganized behaviour, inappropriate affect, and symptoms of both paranoid and catatonic schizophrenia. This subtype causes the most severe and disruptive effects. The delusions are incoherent and fragmentary, though they frequently revolve around bodily functions. Lastly, **undifferentiated schizophrenia** is a subtype of schizophrenia marked by idiosyncratic mixtures of schizophrenic symptoms, and is fairly common. See Table 6.3 for more details on each subtype.

Draft

Table 6.3. Main Subtypes of Schizophrenia

Subtype	Description
Paranoid	Characterized by prominent auditory hallucinations or delusions. In many cases, the delusions are grandiose or persecutory in nature, or both, but can include other themes (e.g., religiosity or jealousy). These delusions and hallucinations typically revolve around a consistent theme. Aside from these specific delusions, the person's ability to reason, expression emotion, and think may not be impaired. Based on this information it is not surprising that individuals with paranoid schizophrenia tend to have higher overall functioning compared with individuals afflicted by other subtypes of schizophrenia.
Catatonic	Includes at least two or more catatonic symptoms (e.g., excessive motor activity, mutism, or peculiar voluntary movement). Individuals with this type of schizophrenia may need supervision to avoid self-harm or harming others during severe motor excitement or immobility.
Disorganized	The main features of this subtype include disorganized speech, disorganized behaviour, and flat or inappropriate affect (e.g., unpredictable giggling). Disorganized behaviour in this diagnosis frequently disrupts the individual's ability to perform daily activities such as showering, preparing meals, or dressing. Any delusions or hallucinations, if present, are not organized around a theme, as is the case with the paranoid subtype.
Undifferentiated	This subtype is typically applied when behaviour does not meet criteria for the paranoid, catatonic, or disorganized subtypes. These people must display two or more features including delusions, hallucinations, disorganized speech, disorganized or catatonic movement, or negative symptoms (e.g., flat affect).

(Source: American Psychiatric Association, DSM-IV, 2000)

Etiology of Schizophrenia

Thus far in the chapter you have probably been able to sympathize and even empathize with many of the disorders we have discussed. It's not hard to envision yourself in a situation where you might develop depression following a traumatic event, or imagine the debilitating effects of anxiety. Many of these disorders feature symptoms that are excessive versions of feelings we encounter in our lives on a daily

Draft

basis. But can you really picture yourself accusing your mother of feeding you glass, or hearing voices that argue with you or tell you what to do? Despite the enigmatic features of schizophrenia, you might be surprised at the similarity of its etiology to some of the disorders previously discussed. Let's explore the biological and neural factors in schizophrenia first.

GENETIC VULNERABILITY

Heredity appears to play a large role in schizophrenia (Kendler, 2000), though it is important to understand that an underlying genetic predisposition to a disorder does not necessarily predict whether or not there will ultimately be an observable pathology. Some form of stressor is usually required for the onset of schizophrenia.

Twin studies demonstrate that concordance rates are around 48% for identical twins, and 17% for fraternal twins (Gottesman, 1991, 2001). Additional research on individuals who were adopted at an early age demonstrates that rates of schizophrenia appear to be higher among biological relatives than adoptive relatives, suggesting that genetic similarity, rather than environment similarity, produces higher rates of schizophrenia (Owen & O'Donovan, 2003).

NEUROCHEMISTRY

Two main neurostransmitters have been implicated in schizophrenia: dopamine and glutamate. The *dopamine hypothesis* advocates that there is excess dopamine in the brains of individuals with schizophrenia. Support for this theory comes from a variety of research avenues, one of which is the effectiveness of antipsychotics used in the treatment of schizophrenia. Antipsychotics are designed to lower the levels of dopamine in the brain by blocking dopamine from binding with postsynaptic receptors, thereby decreasing the amount of dopamine in the brain, and, by proxy, the degree to which positive symptoms are displayed (Kapur, Zipursky, Jones, Remington, & Houle, 2000; Stahl, 2003). Secondly, drugs such as cocaine and amphetamine, known to increase dopamine levels in the brain, can exacerbate the symptoms of schizophrenia in individuals already diagnosed with the disorder (Davis, 1974). In fact, at higher doses cocaine and amphetamine can induce schizophrenia-like (positive) symptoms in people without schizophrenia (Kleven & Seiden, 1991; Shaner, Khalsa, Roberts, Wilkins, Anglin, & Hsieh, 1993). However, the dopamine hypothesis does not account for the negative symptoms in schizophrenia, and not all patients respond to treatments that block dopamine receptors. Therefore, we can conclude that dopamine is not the only neurotransmitter implicated in schizophrenia.

A second important neurotransmitter in schizophrenia may be glutamate (Li, Kim, Ichikawa & Meltzer, 2003). Glutamate is the major excitatory neurotransmitter at fast synapses in the brain (Fonnum, 1984), and recent research suggests that one of the major molecules in glutamate is defective in people with schizophrenia, resulting in a decline in glutamate in the brain (Javitt & Coyle, 2004; Phillips & Silverstein, 2003). A drop in glutamate levels could explain some of the general cognitive deficits evident in schizophrenia. Support for this theory comes from research on the effects of the frequently abused drug, phencyclidine (PCP). PCP is known to interfere with glutamate in the brain, and is capable of producing the full range of schizophrenia symptoms, both positive and negative in nature (Javitt & Coyle, 2004).

Draft

STRUCTURAL ABNORMALITIES

Various studies using brain-imaging techniques have found neuroanatomical and structural differences between schizophrenia and healthy populations. While these differences and deficits are readily apparent in the majority of studies, brain abnormalities are not reliable enough to be useful for diagnosis purposes (Heinrichs, 2005). Researchers have found abnormalities in numerous areas of the brain including: enlargement of the cerebral ventricles (fluid filled spaces in the brain; Suddath, 1990); decreased volume in the temporal (Barta et al., 1990) and frontal lobes (Kim et al., 2000); and, of particular importance, abnormalities found within the prefrontal cortex. Some have hypothesized that frontal lobe dysfunction contributes to positive symptoms, whereas temporal lobe dysfunction underlies negative symptoms (Conklin & Iacono, 2002). The prefrontal cortex garners frequent attention in schizophrenia research because it is this area of the brain that is known to play a role in behaviours such as speech, decision-making, planning, memory, and attention, all of which are disrupted in schizophrenia (Everitt, Lavoie, Gagnon, & Gosselin, 2001; Fuster, 2008; Martínez-Arán, et al., 2002; Zakzanis, Troyer, Rich, & Heinrichs, 2000). Furthermore, brain-imaging research has found that individuals with schizophrenia consistently show decreased activation in the prefrontal cortex (MacDonald & Carter, 2003; O'Donnell & Grace, 1998).

NEURODEVELOPMENTAL HYPOTHESIS

The neurodevelopmental hypothesis of schizophrenia posits that a disruption in the normal maturational processes of the brain before or at birth may be a factor in the development of schizophrenia (Brown, 1999). Two specific prenatal variables that may contribute to the liability of schizophrenia are malnutrition and illness during pregnancy. People born in the western Netherlands between October 15 and December 31, 1945, were prenatally exposed to a severe famine due to a Nazi blockade of food services, and were twice as likely as others born in the Netherlands to develop schizophrenia (Susser et al., 1996). A more recent study detailed a similar effect in people who were born in China immediately following the Chinese famine of 1960-1961 (St. Clair et al., 2005).

Prenatal exposure to viral infection may also be a factor in the predisposition of schizophrenia. For example, people whose mothers had rubella (German measles) during an epidemic in 1964 were more likely to develop psychotic disorders than those not exposed to the virus in utero (Brown, Cohen, Greenwald, & Susser, 2000; Brown et al., 2001). Furthermore, even seemingly negligent factors, such as short periods of oxygen deprivation during birth, may be related to increased rates of schizophrenia (Rosso et al., 2000).

FAMILY ENVIRONMENT AND EXPRESSED EMOTION

While there are many studies on the influence of one's family environment on the emergence of prognosis of schizophrenia, we will briefly review one of the most comprehensive investigations following the effect of family environment on schizophrenia. In a 21-year longitudinal study conducted in Finland, Tienari and colleagues followed two groups of adopted children (2004). One group was genetically at risk for developing schizophrenia because their biological mothers had been diagnosed with either schizophrenia or a milder schizophrenic disorder, whereas the second group was not deemed to be genetically at risk because neither of their parents had been diagnosed with schizophrenia or any related disorder. The main finding was that children in the high-risk group who went on to develop full-blown schizophrenia were more likely to have adoptive parents who communicated in a relatively disorganized, hard-to-follow, or highly emotional manner. By comparison, children in the high-risk group that did not develop schizophrenia or a related disorder were more likely to have adoptive parents who engaged in a more calm and organized pattern of communication. This relationship was not found among the low-risk children. This research demonstrates that when there is an underlying genetic vulnerability, the family environment, particularly the communication, at home may be related to the likelihood of developing schizophrenia.

Expressed emotion (EE) is a measure of the degree to which criticism and negative attitudes are expressed about or toward a person with a mental disorder by the family members with whom the afflicted individual lives. Studies on EE in families have focused more on how EE relates to the course or prognosis of schizophrenia, specifically the likelihood of relapse. One method of examining EE in families is to record and evaluate interviews with family members and the patient to examine the frequency of critical comments, resentment, and over-protectiveness (Hooley, 2004).

Families high in EE tend to blame the diagnosed person for their disorder rather than seeing the disruptive effects of their diagnosis as being out of their control. Various studies demonstrate that a family's expressed emotion is a good predictor of likelihood of relapse once an individual has been released from the hospital (Butzlaff & Hooley, 1998; Hooley, 2004). In fact, patients who return to homes of a family high in EE are three times more likely to relapse as compared to those who return to families low in EE (Hooley & Hiller, 1998). Furthermore, in North American families, the most salient factor predictive of relapse is criticism (McCarty, Lau, Valeri, & Weisz, 2004).

DIATHESIS-STRESS MODEL

The diathesis-stress model encompasses much of what we know about factors related to the etiology of schizophrenia (and various other psychological disorders). The **diathesis-stress hypothesis** suggests a genetic predisposition may be present that is triggered by an environmental stressor. The *diathesis* refers to the underlying predisposition or genetic vulnerability, and *stress* refers to the environmental stressors that may trigger the onset of the illness. Stressors may be in the form of any one of the various events or environmental factors previously discussed (e.g., family environment).

Imagine the diathesis-stress model as having a threshold, and once an individual has surpassed this threshold they will develop schizophrenia. Some individuals will develop full-blown schizophrenia irrespective of environmental factors because of their genetic composition, while others may be less at risk genetically, but could cross the threshold and develop schizophrenia because of the stressors encountered over their lifetimes. Others who are at a lower risk genetically will likely not develop the disorder unless exposed to extreme environmental stressors – these people are extremely unlikely to ever reach the threshold (Fowles, 1992).

Section 6: Dissociative Disorders

Dissociative disorders are among the most controversial of the disorders we will cover in this chapter – they are both strange and the source of fierce controversy (Loewenstein & Putnam, 2005). **Dissociative disorders** are a class of disorders in which people lose contact with portions of their consciousness or memory, resulting in disruptions in their sense of identity. Historically, these disorders have frequently been confused with schizophrenia, likely due to the Greek derived root *schizo*, which means, "splitting away from". Furthermore, both diagnoses share a bizarre break from reality. In this chapter we cover dissociative fugue, dissociative amnesia, depersonalization disorder, and finish with dissociative identity disorder and the controversial feud that surrounds it.

Dissociative Amnesia

Dissociative amnesia is characterized by a sudden loss of memory of important personal information that is too extensive to be due to normal forgetting. Memory losses tend to occur for a single traumatic or extremely stressful event, or for an extended period of time surrounding the event. Cases of dissociative amnesia have been known to occur following episodes of self-mutilation, suicide attempts, physical abuse, or viewing the death of a family member (DSM-IV-TR, 2000; Cardeña & Gleaves, 2007). As with many other diagnoses, this label can only be applied if the symptoms cause clinically significant distress or impairment in social, occupational, or other important areas of functioning.

Dissociative Fugue

Both dissociative amnesia and dissociative fugue entail memory loss in some form; however, dissociative fugue entails a complete loss of one's memory. **Dissociative fugue** is a disorder in which people lose the memory of their entire lives along with their sense of personal identity. Perhaps, you can identify with someone who might wish to leave their lives behind them and start anew in a different city or country – this might seem like an easy way to escape your life circumstances. Individuals with dissociative fugue assert that they have no memory of their prior selves, though motor skills such as being a math whiz or how to drive a car remain intact. Fugues tend to last for a few hours, or in very rare cases, can persist for years. The essential feature of fugue is a sudden, unexpected travel away from home or one's customary places of daily activities. Prevalence rates for all dissociative disorders are relatively hard to come by, but it is generally thought that it occurs in about 2 in every 1000 people (DSM-IV-TR, 2000). It is possible that this sudden break from one's past may be due to neurological causes, such as brain damage or related to a stroke. Ultimately, researchers have not yet been able to uncover the detailed role of psychological factors, trauma, and neurological functioning in dissociative fugue (Kihlstrom, 2005).

Depersonalization Disorder

Have you ever felt that you're detached from your body, almost as if you are living in a dream or movie, watching yourself as an outsider? This sensation is known as depersonalization. In fact, brief depersonalization episodes are fairly common occurrences among adults. **Depersonalization disorder** is a dissociative disorder in which the individual feels estranged from the self and surroundings enough to disrupt functioning. **Derealization** is the sense that the external world is strange or unreal, and often accompanies both depersonalization and panic attacks.

Dissociative Identity Disorder

Dissociative identity disorder (DID) is a type of dissociative disorder characterized by the coexistence in one person of two or more largely complete, and usually very different, personalities. DID was previously known as *multiple-personality disorder*. This disorder frequently captures the attention of the public in films and television shows such as *Identity* (2003), *Sybil* (1976), and *United States of Tara* (2009). The primary symptom of DID is a single individual manifesting multiple personalities that recurrently take control of behaviour (DSM-IV-TR, 2000; Eich, Macaulay, Loewenstein, & Dihle, 1997). Each personality has its own name, mannerisms, self-image, and even distinct memories. Generally, there is a primary identity that carries the individual's given name, and the alternate identities (often termed "alters") are very different from the host personality. In fact, there are documented incidents wherein alters reportedly had varied ages, gender, race, sexual orientation (Kluft, 1996), ethnic background, vocabulary, intelligence scores (Putnam, 1991), handedness (Henniger, 1992), voice patterns and writing style (Lilienfeld & Lynn, 2003). Transitions between identities can occur very suddenly, and it is typically the primary alter who seeks treatment from a health professional. There are usually two to four alters at the time of diagnosis, but more often emerge over the course of treatment. All cases of DID present with gaps in memory, as there is always at least one alter who has no knowledge of the others. Despite the astounding differences among various personalities, we do not have conclusive evidence of the existence of alter personalities. Some hypothesize that these differences could be due to changes in mood, thoughts, or bodily changes such as muscle tension that people may produce on a voluntary basis (Allen & Movius, 2000; Merckelbach, Devilly, & Rassin, 2002). Individuals who meet criteria for DID also frequently meet criteria for mood, sexual, eating, sleep, or substance-related disorders.

As you may have guessed, the controversy surrounding this diagnosis comes down to clinicians and researchers who believe in the presentation of separate personalities or identities within one person, and those who contest that while there may be individuals who are afflicted by dissociation, there can be no distinct identities within a person. DID was first documented in scientific literature in 1962 (Sutcliffe & Jones, 1962) when a total of 77 cases were reported (many of which were between the years 1890-1920). Beginning in the 1970s there was an enormous jump in the number of DID diagnoses (Kihlstrom, 2001), such that by the late 1990s there were allegedly 40,000 diagnosed cases (Lilienfeld & Lynn, 2003). There are various hypotheses that seek to explain this immense change in the diagnosis of DID over such a short period of time. One of these possible hypotheses is that the DSM-III (published in 1980) was the first version of the DSM to clearly spell out the criteria for DID (*DSM-III*, 1980). Furthermore, in this version of the DSM, there was no requirement for amnesia across alters. Thus, the diagnosis may have been applied to individuals who showed great variation in their mood states and behaviour over a short period of time, as is the case with some personality disorders (Kihlstrom & Tataryn, 1991). More recently, a study of 550 Canadian psychiatrists found that more than two thirds had reservations about including DID in the DSM-IV-TR as a formal diagnosis (Lalonde, Hudson, Gigante, & Pope, 2001).

Etiology of Dissociative Disorders

Dissociative amnesia and fugue are usually attributed to extreme stress. It is unclear, though, why a minute portion of the population is prone to these clinically diagnosable responses to stress. Some theorize that certain personality traits, such as being prone to engage in fantasy and becoming abnormally involved in personal experiences, may be related to the emergence of dissociative disorder-like symptoms (Kihlstrom, Glisky, & Anguiulo, 1994).

The etiology of DID has a marred past. There are two primary explanations of the possible emergence of this disorder: DID as a response to early trauma, or a result of cultural and societal pressures. Those who support the early trauma explanation would argue that DID is a defense or coping mechanism as a result of early childhood trauma – usually prolonged sexual abuse. The main personality has no memory of this abuse, but it can resurface by undergoing therapy and hypnosis (Ganaway, 1995). Those who support this model purport that most cases of DID occur in individuals who were severely abused in childhood (Gleaves, 1996; Draijer & Langeland, 1999) but these claims are frequently not supported by objective evidence (Lilienfeld & Lynn, 2003). Conversely, other researchers believe that separate personalities are not genuine and can be explained by intentional role-playing, which is further subtly encouraged by a minority of psychologists who may intentionally, or unintentionally, create alternative personalities (Spanos, 1994; 1996). Furthermore, popular media seems to influence patients' symptoms, for instance before the release of the movie *Sybil* (Schreiber, 1973) the average number of personalities reported in DID was two or three, however, following the movie debut, the average number rose to 15. In conclusion it is fair to say that the controversy surrounding DID is far from over, and that it would seem that there may be more evidence for one explanation over the other, but there are no formal conclusions to be drawn about the etiology of any of the dissociative disorders as of yet.

Section 7: Personality Disorders

Personality disorders are a class of psychological disorders marked by extreme, inflexible personality traits that cause subjective distress or impaired social and occupational functioning. Individuals afflicted by personality disorders tend to have something about their basic personality that leads to maladaptive or rigid behaviours that consequently make it difficult for them to function effectively with others. Features of personality disorders usually become recognizable during adolescence or early adulthood. With the exception of antisocial personality disorder, diagnosis of personality disorders may be applied in childhood or early adolescence under special circumstances.

Unlike the disorders we have discussed thus far in the chapter, personality disorders are placed on Axis II alongside mental retardation, whereas the other disorders presented were Axis I disorders. The DSM-IV-TR includes ten types of personality disorders, which are grouped into three categories, more aptly known as *clusters*. The three clusters include: anxious and fearful; dramatic and erratic; and, odd and eccentric. See Table 6.4 for quick summary of each of the personality disorders.

As we progress through the personality disorders, you may find yourself thinking that many of the *symptoms* are in fact basic personality traits that you encounter in many people, and you would be right in this assessment. The essential feature of personality disorders is the presentation of basic traits to an excessive degree such that they are in opposition to cultural expectations, or create subjective distress.

Anxious & Fearful

Individuals diagnosed with personality disorders in the anxious and fearful cluster tend to be overly fearful of rejection and social disapproval. To control these anxious feelings they engage in maladaptive efforts including being evasive, submissive, or extremely self-controlled. This cluster is comprised of the *avoidant, dependent* and *obsessive-compulsive* personality disorders.

Individuals with **avoidant personality disorder** engage in a pervasive pattern of social inhibition and feelings of inadequacy. They are extremely sensitive to rejection, and have very poor self-esteem. **Dependent personality disorder** is characterized by an excessive and persistent need to be taken care by others. These people are submissive and clingy, lack self-confidence, and frequently allow others (e.g., spouse or parent) to make decisions for them in their everyday lives. **Obsessive-compulsive personality disorder** is a personality disorder in which people tend to be extremely organized and, overly concerned with details and efficiency. They are highly conventional, perfectionistic, serious, and have difficulty relating to others because they need things to be done in their own way.

Odd & Eccentric

Individuals diagnosed with personality disorders in the odd and eccentric cluster are generally described as being distrustful, socially aloof, and unable to connect with others emotionally. The *schizoid, schizotypal,* and *paranoid* personality disorders fall into this category. **Schizoid personality disorder** is characterized as a disorder in which the person is emotionally detached and exhibits a restricted range of expressions of emotion. They are indifferent to the criticism, praise, and feelings of others, and are usually loners with few close friends, and with solitary interests. Individuals with schizoid personality disorder report a decreased experience of pleasure in experiences that most would deem pleasurable, such as walking on the beach or having sex. **Schizotypal personality disorder** is a disorder in which the afflicted individual is overly eccentric, unable to engage in normal social relationships, and has a distorted perception of the world. They are often extremely uncomfortable in social situations, and hold odd beliefs such as beliefs in clairvoyance or telepathy. **Paranoid personality disorder** is characterized by a pervasive pattern of suspiciousness and distrust of others. They interpret others' behaviour as malicious and believe that other people are out to get them and may attack at any time.

Dramatic & Erratic/Impulsive

This cluster of personality disorders includes symptoms such as inflated confidence, anti-social behaviour and wild mood swings. Within the dramatic and erratic cluster are two of the personality disorders that have received the most attention both in research and in the media – *antisocial* personality disorder and *borderline* personality disorder, which we'll discuss separately. **Histrionic personality disorder** is a disorder in which patients show overly dramatic and attention seeking behaviour. These people immediately take on the role of "the life of the party," may go to dramatic extremes to be the focus of attention, and are often dressed in a sexually provocative way. **Narcissistic personality disorder** is a disorder in which patients show a preoccupation with themselves, and a negative attitude toward others. As a means of perpetuating their inflated self-esteem, they frequently overestimate their own abilities and inflate their accomplishments, and expect to be admired.

Borderline personality disorder (BPD) is a personality disorder in which patients display erratic and highly unstable emotions and behaviour. A classic example of an individual portrayed as having BPD is Alex Forrest, played by Glenn Close, in *Fatal Attraction* (1987). Alex is unstable and has highly changeable emotions and behaviours. At one point she is in love with Dan Gallagher (Michael Douglas), and later attempts to murder his wife and child in the hopes that Dan will start a new family with her. The essential feature of BPD is the instability of interpersonal relationships, as they fluctuate between extreme feelings of happiness and despair towards the other party in the relationship. Individuals with BPD experience frequent mood changes; they tend to be irritable, impulsive, sarcastic, easily angered and unpredictable. They often engage in self-mutilating behaviour such as wrist slashing, burning their skin with cigarettes, and carving words on their arms. Furthermore, it is estimated that 1 in 10 patients with BPD commit suicide (Paris, 2002).

Antisocial personality disorder (APD) is a personality disorder also known as psychopathy. Patients show a history of erratic behaviour and are often irresponsible, selfish, and manipulative. While some have argued that APD is distinct from psychopathy (Hare, Hart, & Hapur, 1991; Lilienfeld, 1994), for our purposes we will use the words interchangeably. Psychopathy is frequently shortened to psychopath in movies, which often denotes a murderer. In reality, although individuals with APD are over-represented in the prison population (Hare, 2003), most individuals with this APD are not murderers. Fundamentally, those with APD are essentially selfish and self-centered in the extreme, and have trouble postponing gratification and planning ahead. From this description it may seem as though individuals with APD have no desire to interact with others, yet this is not the case; they interact with others not for the pleasure of company, but rather to use them or get something from them. These people do not shy away from social interactions and place high importance on making good first impressions (Lilienfeld & Arkovitz, 2007); they are antisocial in that they reject widely held social norms. They are skilled at faking affection, and interpersonally they disregard the wishes of others by manipulating and lying, and often use them for profit or pleasure (Fowler & Lilienfeld, 2006). APD is more frequent in males than females (Vitale & Newman, 2001).

Some of the best-known research on psychopathy comes from work by Hervey Cleckley and Robert Hare. Cleckley's original contributions on the description of psychopathy were detailed in *The Mask of Evil*. Later, building off of Cleckley's work, Hare developed the Psychopathology Checklist-Revised (PCL-R; Hare, 1991). The PCL-R is a 20-item checklist that assesses traits such as callousness, lack of guilt, superficial charm, impulsivity, and irresponsibility. The PCL-R remains the most widely used measurement instruments for psychopathy (Hare, 2003).

Despite considerable research on APD, there is no clear explanation of its etiology. Several theories have been proposed to explain the roots of this personality disorder including the influence of family environment, genetics, and deficits in emotion. Individuals with APD frequently come from homes wherein they experienced inconsistent discipline and physical abuse (Johnson, Hunsley, Greenburg, Schlinder, 1999). Furthermore, antisocial behaviours appear to run in families, thus children may learn these behaviours by observing parents (Hutchings & Mednick, 1977; Black, 2001). Most genetic research has focused on the heritability of antisocial personality traits. These studies have found higher levels of antisocial behaviour in adopted children of biological parents with APD (Cadoret, Yates, Troughton, Woodworth, & Stewart, 1995), and higher concordance rates among monozygotic twins relative to dizygotic twins (Lyons et al., 1995). Concerning emotion and arousal, psychopaths tend to show a decreased arousal compared to the average individual in response to imminent electric shock and other forms of stress (Raine, 1996; Lorber, 2004), which may be due to an overall deficit in fear responses (Patrick, 2006). It may be the case that psychopaths are frequently underaroused and in an attempt to increase their arousal to normal levels, seek out excitement and engage in risky behaviours (Raine, 1997). This is known as the *underarousal hypothesis* (Zuckerman, 1989). In conclusion, it is hard to pinpoint the exact cause of APD, but it is likely, as with other disorders, that there are various factors that play into its development.

CLASSIFICATION PROBLEMS WITH PERSONALITY DISORDERS

As we noted earlier, personality disorders are simply normal personality traits that are abnormally extreme and become the prominent feature about a person. But, the diagnostic criteria for each type of personality disorder can be difficult to distinguish from other diagnoses, as there is much overlap between the personality disorder types (Clark, 2007). This may be one of the reasons that the personality disorders are historically the least reliably diagnosed of the DSM disorders (Fowler, O'Donohue, & Lilienfeld, 2007; Zimmerman, 1994). Moreover, there does not appear to be a clear distinction between Axis I and II disorders (Livesely, 2001). As a result, it is not hard to see why some argued that there are fundamental problems with personality disorders, and that there is a need for a reformulation of how we conceptualize these disorders (Widiger, 2007; Widiger & Trull, 2007).

Table 6.4 DSM-IV Classification of Major Personality Disorders

Anxious, Fearful Cluster	
Avoidant personality disorder	Inhibition, feelings of inadequacy, and hypersensitivity to negative evaluation.
Dependent personality disorder	Submissive and clinging behavior related to an excessive need to be taken care of.
Obsessive-compulsive disorder	Orderliness, perfectionism, and control.
Dramatic, Emotional, Erratic Cluster	
Antisocial personality disorder	Disregard for, and violation of, the rights of others.
Borderline personality disorder	Instability in interpersonal relationships, self-image, and affects, and marked impulsivity.
Histrionic personality disorder	Excessive emotionality and attention seeking.
Narcissistic personality disorder	Constant need for grandiosity, admiration, and lack of empathy.

Draft

Odd, Eccentric Cluster

Paranoid personality disorder	Distrustful and suspiciousness, wherein others' motives are interpreted as malevolent.
Schizotypal personality disorder	Acute discomfort in close relationships, cognitive or perceptual distortions, and eccentricities of behavior.
Schizoid personality disorder	Detachment from social relationships and restricted range of emotional expression.

(Source: American Psychiatric Association, DSM-IV-TR, 2000)

Box 6.10: Application / Insanity in the Eyes of the Law

Do you think it is fair that individuals with severe mental illness be subject to the same laws and consequences as those who do not suffer from mental illness? This question has reared its head time and time again over the course of history.

First and foremost, let's define the terms that are used in a court of law concerning psychological illness. In Canada, we do not use the term insane or insanity; we can say that an individual may be judged as 'not criminally responsible on account of mental disorder', though this is not a disorder in and of itself. This is an important distinction because it relates to one of the most basic rules of the law, *mens rea*. Mens rea is the Latin term for "guilty mind" and it infers that there must be criminal intent in a crime. If a person, such as George, who we met at the beginning of the section on schizophrenia, were to kill his mother because he was convinced she was trying to kill him by feeding him glass, can we really conclude that he should be sentenced in the same way as any other criminal? If George's mother really was feeding him glass and he could not escape his environment, would we not conclude that his act was some form of self-defense? To George, the glass is really there and the danger is not imagined, his reality is that his mother is trying to hurt him by feeding him glass. Going back to our point on 'criminal intent', individuals may be deemed 'not criminally responsible on account of mental disorder' when they cannot truly appreciate the significance of their actions.

In Canadian law the old term for this defense was *not guilty by reason of insanity (NGRI)*, but is now known as *not criminally responsible on account of mental disorder (NCRMD)*. This distinction should not be confused to mean that anyone with a diagnosed psychological disorder could escape conviction in a court of law; rather, under specific circumstances it may be the case that individuals with severe mental disturbances frequently related to delusional behaviour may qualify for this defense. One widely held rule entitled the *M'Naughten Rule* was formulated in England following an instance when a delusional man attempted to assassinate the British Prime Minister,

Sir Robert Peel, but mistakenly murdered his secretary, Sir Edward Drummond, instead. According to this rule, the insanity defense can be applied when the individual committed the crime in a mental state wherein they were unable to discern right from wrong. Accordingly, this rule was not in effect for the sentencing of Jeffrey Dahmer, who was charged with (and admitted to) butchering, cannibalizing, and having sex with 15 boys and young men. While it was clear that Dahmer was mentally ill, as he certainly had some form of a paraphilia, the court determined that he was sane and legally responsible, as he had known right from wrong at the time he performed the unspeakable acts and proceeded anyway.

Another interesting addition to criminal proceedings as they relate to psychological disorders is that of *fitness to stand trial*. If at any point during a trial the accused is unable to defend themselves due to their mental illness, the trial will be halted until such a time when (if ever) the defendant is able to stand trial. Individuals may be deemed unfit to stand trial if they are unable to comprehend the proceedings or possible consequences of the outcome of the trial.

Given your newly acquired knowledge about the use of a NCRMD defense, how frequently do you think this actually occurs? Many people overestimate the occurrence of an 'insanity' defense, when in reality less than 1% of all trials make use of the insanity defense and less than 1% of the defendants who plead NCRMD are successful in their claims (Melton et al., 1987).

Final Thoughts

Since its inception, the DSM has seen many more additions than subtractions of disorders. New diagnoses come partly from an increase in understanding of the complexity and scope of mental illness, and partly from a general cultural shift toward seeing mental disorders where people previously saw normal human variation. As informed scientists, we must be wary of the potential consequences of labeling psychological disorders, both in terms of falling victim to perpetuating stereotypes, and the risks of attributing pathological bases to behaviours just because they are different than the norm.

Draft

7

Chapter 7: Psychological Treatment

Introduction

Navigating the options

Remember Julie? We met her in the previous chapter. Julie's worsening history of excessive sleepiness, crying spells, difficulty concentrating, **ahedonia** (absence of pleasure in previously enjoyed activities), guilt, social withdrawal and weight gain were consistent with a DSM-IV diagnosis of Major Depressive Disorder. Since we last caught up with her, Julie's mother has urged her to seek help for her condition, a suggestion that Julie has agreed to in principle. But in practice, Julie has had difficulty sorting out where to turn for help.

Julie has been finding it hard to muster the energy to search for mental health providers given her chronic sleepiness and difficulty concentrating. Neither she, nor her mother has a lot of money to pay for treatment. She knows her workplace has some sort of mental health plan, but isn't sure how to access it, and doesn't want anyone at work to think that she's crazy. As she considers her options, she feels increasingly guilty and embarrassed about her current state and fearful at the prospect of opening up to a stranger about her problems. She thinks to herself that, even if she could find someone suitable, she couldn't possibly pull together a long enough break from her crying spells to get her story out anyway. She thinks, "Really, what would it help to whine about my problems to a stranger? People who do that on TV just look silly and self-indulgent." At home, Julie's mother continues to encourage her to seek treatment, but Julie feels guilty and pessimistic and eventually comes to perceive her mother's words only as a reminder that she has failed at yet another task in life.

One day, Julie awakens with a renewed commitment to get help. She opens the Yellow Pages website and searches for "therapist." She gets over a thousand results, from chiropractors to massage therapists. A suggestion box appears on the side of the screen: Did you mean "Stress Management & Counsellors (100+ hits)," "Marriage, Family, and Individual Counsellors (100+ hits)," "Psychologists and Psychological Associates (10-100 hits)," "Psychiatrists (10-100 hits)," "Psychoanalysts (10-100 hits)…" Overwhelmed, Julie closes the lid of her laptop and crawls back into bed.   The next time her mother prompts her to seek help, Julie angrily snaps back that she is happy the way she is and she doesn't need anybody's so called help.

Julie's situation is in many ways typical for individuals suffering from a range of common psychological conditions. Julie's case illustrates just some of the potential barriers to seeking psychological treatment. These barriers can be both **internal** (e.g., Julie's self-defeating thoughts about her prospects for staving off crying spells in treatment), and **external** (e.g., her lack of funds to pay for treatment). Julie's symptoms, including her low energy and guilty feelings and thoughts, exacerbate the challenges she faces in seeking treatment. When she does muster the energy to begin a search for a provider, she is quickly overwhelmed by the available options.

The treatment of psychological disorders has been a prominent focus throughout the history of psychology, and the diversity of treatment options available today reflects this rich evolution. To navigate these options, you'll need the same critical thinking skills you've been using as you discover and evaluate the science of psychology. To set the stage for the content of this chapter, we'll first review some key issues of diversity in psychological treatment. We'll discuss the **diversity of individuals** who seek out or could benefit from psychological treatment, the **diversity of providers** in the mental health field, and the **diversity of treatment options** available for various psychological conditions. This diversity presents significant challenges that consumers, researchers, and clinicians face when evaluating the **utility** of this wide range of treatment options available for a wide range of individuals delivered by a wide range of providers. These issues provide a backdrop for the content of the bulk of this chapter – a review of psychological, biomedical, and combination treatments for psychological conditions.

Section 1: Diversity of Treatment Consumers

Odds are that either you or someone you know has, at some point, sought out professional treatment for a mental health problem. According to data from the Canadian Mental Health and Well-Being Survey (Health Canada, 2002; Government of Canada, 2006)**,** 8% of adult respondents reported consulting a professional about their mental or emotional health in the past year. However, as Julie's case highlights, it isn't always the case that a person suffering from a psychological disorder successfully finds and completes appropriate treatment. According to the Canadian survey data, of the 10% of the population aged 15 or older who reported symptoms consistent with an anxiety, mood, or substance-related disorder in the past year, 22% reported that they wanted help but could not get it.   It is important to note that potential consumers of mental health services are not limited to those with diagnosed psychological disorders. Of the population aged 15 or older who did not meet criteria for the disorders above, 5% reported that they either sought help for mental health problems, or felt they needed help but did not receive it.

Tailoring treatment to the disorder

Psychological treatment is not a one-size-fits-all operation. Consider the **diversity of disorders** reviewed in the previous chapter. It isn't difficult to imagine that a treatment shown to be useful for Major Depressive Disorder may not be as useful for the treatment of Antisocial Personality Disorder. Now consider that psychological disorders and treatments span an even broader range than that reviewed in the previous chapter. Psychological treatments have been developed for disorders ranging from Autism to Alzheimer's disease, and for behaviours ranging from bedwetting to compulsive shoplifting. Accurate and comprehensive clinical diagnosis of a psychological disorder, or **conceptualization of a psychological condition**, is an important precursor then, to choosing appropriate treatment.

Accurate diagnosis informs more than just treatment selection. It also has implications for the likelihood that an individual will seek out treatment in the first place. Just as a clinician can use the **four D's (deviance, distress, dysfunction, and danger)**, to decide whether an individual's thoughts, emotions, and behaviours are abnormal, we ask ourselves similar questions when trying to sort out whether or not to seek help. Am I functioning outside the realm of societal norms? Am I experiencing distress? Are my symptoms getting in the way of healthy functioning? Am I at risk of hurting myself or someone else? **Ego syntonic disorders** are those in which the symptoms of the disorder are perceived by the individual with the disorder as valued or advantageous. **Ego dystonic disorders**, in contrast, are those in which the symptoms are perceived by the individual as undesirable. For example, Obsessive-Compulsive Disorder tends to be ego dystonic, and the individual with the disorder tends to view their own obsessive thoughts and compulsive behaviours as irrational and a source of psychological distress. Obsessive-Compulsive *Personality* Disorder, in contrast, tends to be ego syntonic, and the individual with the disorder tends to view their rigid and perfectionistic tendencies as positive character traits. Which of these two individuals is more likely to be receptive to psychological treatment?

Tailoring treatment to the individual

Accurate diagnosis provides important information to guide treatment, but does not necessarily provide a complete picture of an individual's treatment needs. Returning again to Julie, suffering from Major Depressive Disorder, do you think a psychological treatment that eventually proves helpful to her in recovering from her depressive episode would be as effective for the 67 year old homeless man in Julie's neighbourhood, who has a physical disability and also suffers from Major Depressive Disorder? What about a woman, close in age to Julie, living in a small community in rural China, who also suffers from Major Depressive Disorder? How about an 11 year old child, a post-partum new mother, an adult with a brain injury and comorbid substance use disorder? Select risk and protective factors can influence the development and expression of mental health problems. Effective psychological treatment should account for these **individual**, **family**, **social**, **circumstantial**, and **cultural contexts** within which the client presents for treatment.

One critical facet of an individual's context is his or her place in what Prochaska and DiClemente (Prochaska & DiClemente, 1983), called **stages of change**. Originally developed based on the study of individuals who successfully quit smoking, these stages identify a stepwise progression of thoughts and actions that characterize effective change of problematic thoughts or behaviours. The first stage, **precontemplation**, is identified by an inability or unwillingness to acknowledge the existence of a problem. In the second stage, **contemplation**, the individual acknowledges the existence of the problem, but may be unsure or unwilling to change the problem. The third stage, **preparation**, is associated with recognition of the problem and preparation for change. **Action**, the fourth stage, involves taking active steps to change the behaviour. The final stage, **maintenance**, represents the continuation of healthy habits formed at the action stage, watching out for potential stressors that may trigger re-emergence of unhealthy behaviours. It is possible for an individual to move both forward and backwards through the stages of this model. **Relapse**, not one of the stages of change per se, is a term often applied in the treatment of substance related disorders to describe the full re-emergence of old unhealthy patterns of behaviour, often returning the afflicted individual all the way back to the precontemplation stage of change. In the therapeutic setting, the application of the stages of change model leads to the use of different interventions at different stages of change.

Section 2: Diversity of Treatment Providers

Range of Provider Backgrounds and Licensure

As Julie's case illustrates, the search for a "therapist" can yield an overwhelming array of options. Providers of mental health services come from a wide range of professional backgrounds and experiences. Although laws and regulations exist at the provincial and national level to provide some degree of consumer protection and clarity in advertising, practitioners of non-traditional methods have ample room for creative practice. For example, the title "psychologist" is restricted in most, but not all, provinces and states to individuals who hold a doctoral degree in psychology. However, the term "therapist" is often freely available to be used by any would-be provider of mental health services.

Licensed psychologists (psychologists with specific training and certification in clinical or counselling psychology) and **psychiatrists** (medical doctors who have advanced training and certification in the practice of psychiatry) may be the most commonly thought of professionals who engage in the practice of psychological treatment. However, not all psychologists or psychiatrists offer all forms of treatment, and some may not offer any treatment at all. There are a wide range of other professionals who provide psychological treatments. Some of these, including social workers, counsellors, mental health workers, and marriage and family counsellors, pursue specific training and offer the types of psychological treatments described below. Many of these professionals (including psychologists and psychiatrists) are subject to **licensure** requirements. Just as obtaining a driver's license demonstrates that you have the basic **competencies**, or skills, to safely operate a motor vehicle, obtaining a professional license demonstrates that the provider has the basic competencies to practice according to the ethical and professional standards of their chosen field. When seeking out a mental health professional, it is generally advisable both to choose a licensed professional, and to research the specific requirements for licensure in that individual's field.

The Art and Science of Psychological Treatment

Of course, the simple fact that you possess a driver's license does not guarantee that you are a *good* driver. Similarly, just because a mental health professional holds a license to practice, does not mean that that practitioner will be able to help every client with every problem. Researchers have studied the characteristics that predict good outcomes in therapy, regardless of the specific techniques employed or psychological problems under consideration. One key factor that has been shown to have an important effect on treatment outcome is the **therapeutic relationship** between therapist and patient.

The American Psychological Association has convened a series of task forces to study the qualities of a good therapeutic relationship (Norcross, 2001; Norcross & Wampold, 2011). They found strong evidence that the quality of the therapeutic relationship between patient and therapist accounts for as much of the treatment outcome as does the treatment methods. Their most recent report categorizes features of therapeutic relationships based on the quality of available evidence. Relationship qualities

Draft

shown to be "demonstrably effective" include, the degree to which the patient and therapist are able to form a working **alliance** (in individual therapy) or show group **cohesion** (in group therapy), the degree to which the therapist is able to demonstrate **empathy** (understanding of the patient's emotions and thoughts), and the degree to which the therapist collects and responds to feedback from the patient. Qualities shown to be "probably effective," include **positive regard** (therapist views the patient as a fundamentally good person), goal consensus, and collaboration.

Section 3: Diversity of Treatment Options

We've reviewed the broad diversity of individuals presenting for, and providing, help for psychological conditions, and considered the implications of this for treatment. The final major source of diversity in the treatment of psychological disorders is the diversity in treatment options. Broadly speaking, treatment for psychological disorders can be broken up into two categories: **psychological** and **biomedical treatments**. In practice, it is not uncommon for these two types of treatments to be offered to a given individual in the form of **combination treatment**, sometimes at the same time, and sometimes one after the other, depending on presenting symptoms, consumer preferences, and provider offerings. We will review important examples of each of these categories of treatment in detail later in the chapter. First, it is important to explore strategies for critically evaluating different forms of treatment.

In the last 20-30 years, there has been a major emphasis on understanding the utility of treatments for psychological disorders. Influenced heavily by the **evidence-based practice** movement in medicine, researchers and providers of psychological treatments responded to the core ideas put forward in this movement (Chambless & Ollendick, 2001; Kazdin, 2008). Specifically, the evidence-based practice movement proposes that (1) patient care is enhanced by the use of up-to-date knowledge, (2) there is a gap between advances in knowledge and individual clinicians' abilities to keep up with these advances, and (3) summaries of evidence presented by experts will bridge this gap and enable clinicians keep up with important advances. Moreover, trainees should learn the most up to date treatments, and clinicians should be held accountable for keeping the practices up to date. This movement led to the creation of expert panels within major professional bodies of psychology (e.g., the Task Force on Promotion and Dissemination of Psychological Procedures of Division 12 [Clinical Psychology] of the American Psychological Association), that set up decision rules for evaluating evidence for specific treatments, and applied these rules to create lists of **empirically supported therapies** for specific psychological disorders (Task Force 1995; Chambless et al., 1996, 1998).

The movement towards empirically supported therapies was not without controversy. Immediate concerns included the extent to which clinicians would be forced to restrict their practices to treatments on the list, either by managed care companies, or by the threat of potential malpractice lawsuit. There were concerns that the existence of the list would prevent clinicians from using treatments they had previously found useful, but lacked formal research support, and prevent them from trying new and potentially innovative strategies. Larger concerns included questions about the validity of the process by which treatments were deemed to be empirically supported. These concerns addressed issues of treatment **efficacy** and **effectiveness.**

EFFICACY

Efficacy is the ability of a treatment to produce a desired effect in highly controlled settings. **Efficacy studies** are the cornerstone of pharmacological treatment research. These studies are designed to demonstrate, in a highly controlled setting, that a medication has a desirable effect on a medical condition of interest. To achieve this, a **randomized controlled trial** design is used wherein participants with the condition (and no other conditions), are randomly assigned to either a **treatment group** that gets the new medication, or a **control group** that gets a **placebo**. In a **single-blind** trial, study participants are not aware which group they are in. In a **double-blind** trial, neither the participant, nor the researcher, is aware which group the participant is in. Because the only thing that differs between the two groups of participants is whether or not they took the active medication, results of these trials can be used to conclusively determine whether the medication is effective.

Efficacy studies of psychological treatments, while desirable, are complicated to implement. Issues faced by researchers designing such studies include: identifying patients with a single, specific condition of interest (e.g., patients with just depression, but no anxiety or substance use), operationalizing the new treatment (e.g., writing detailed treatment manuals for psychological treatments), selecting appropriate "placebos" (e.g., wait-list groups, education-only groups), "blinding" both the participants and the researchers (virtually impossible), and evaluating treatment outcomes (e.g., how is "improvement" operationalized? Does the researcher judge this or the patient? How are potential biases in making this judgement dealt with?). The latter issue, the evaluation of treatment outcomes, is of particular importance. Efficacy studies are often criticized for failing to differentiate between **statistical significance** (e.g., the treatment group showed lower scores on a depression symptom checklist, and the difference was statistically significant) and **clinical significance** (e.g., the patients felt noticeably better, were better able to function in their day-to-day lives, etc.). Despite these issues, efficacy studies are the cornerstone on which a treatment is deemed to be "empirically supported."

EFFECTIVENESS

Effectiveness is the ability of a treatment to produce a desired effect in real-world settings. In contrast with efficacy studies that evaluate the utility of a treatment for an "ideal" patient within a highly controlled treatment setting, effectiveness studies attempt to gauge the utility of a treatment for a real patient in an ordinary treatment setting. Studies have estimated that the prevalence of **comorbidity** of psychological disorders is high. Anxiety and mood disorders, especially depressive mood disorders, tend to co-occur. Suppose you are a clinician, meeting a new patient diagnosed with both Generalized Anxiety Disorder and Major Depressive Disorder. When searching for an empirically supported treatment, do you refer to the list for the anxiety disorder, the mood disorder, or both? Suppose now that this client reports that his primary concern is decreasing his social anxiety so that he can deliver a speech at his best friend's wedding. How do you think he would respond if you reached for the treatment manual for the 12-session Major Depressive Disorder intervention program, choosing his low mood and guilty feelings as a treatment target?

Effectiveness studies of psychological treatments relax many of the methodological controls of efficacy studies, in order to study treatment in a more naturalistic setting. For example, a highly influential effectiveness study of psychotherapy was conducted in the 1990s by the popular press magazine, Consumer Reports (Seligman, 1995). Collecting survey data from over 4000 respondents, the Consumer

Reports study asked individuals who had received treatment for a mental health problem about their experience. Of the respondents, 9 out of 10 reported symptom improvement after treatment. Longer therapy was associated with greater reported treatment. Interestingly, the degree of symptom improvement was not different depending on the profession of the therapist (e.g., psychologist, psychiatrist, social worker, etc.). Similarly, the degree of symptom improvement was not different depending on whether individuals reported receiving psychotherapy alone, or psychotherapy plus medication.

There are, of course, many notable weaknesses to effectiveness studies such as the Consumer Reports project. First, the respondents may be a representative sample of the population of individuals who seek out and persist with treatment for psychological disorders, but they may not be a representative sample of the entire population. Other issues include the absence of a control group of similar individuals who did not receive treatment. Without such a control group (preferably one to which participants were randomly assigned across the entire study), we are unable to differentiate the effects of psychotherapy from "placebo" effects such as expectations of improvement associated with any therapy, and related effects such as social contact and the simple passage of time. Further issues include potential bias in the self-report data, and limitations of the scale by which improvement was measured.

EVALUATING THE EVIDENCE

We've reviewed the diversity of individuals, providers, and treatment options within the mental health field. This diversity presents significant challenges for consumers (consider Julie evaluating the thousands of options in the yellow pages), clinicians (consider Julie's eventual therapist devising an appropriate intervention to treat her symptoms), and researchers. Researchers who work to address these questions from the perspective of each of these parties have a substantial task to complete.

Alan Kazdin, a psychologist who does research on treatment for childhood disorders, generated a comprehensive list of questions that can be used to guide research on psychological treatment (Kazdin, 2003). These include: What is the effect of treatment compared to no treatment? What specific treatment components contribute to positive change? What treatment components can be added to optimize change? What characteristics of the treatment can be changed to improve outcome? How effective is this treatment compared to other treatments for this problem? What contextual features **mediate** (cause) and **moderate** (influence) therapeutic change? To what extent are treatment effects generalizable to other psychological problems and other treatment settings?

These important questions represent a movement in the field beyond the generation of simple lists of empirically supported treatments, or lists of specific patient and therapist qualities that predict good outcomes. The American Psychological Association defines evidence-based practice as "the integration of the best available research with clinical expertise in the context of patient characteristics, culture and preferences" (APA Task Force on Evidence-Based Practice, 2006). Although the treatments reviewed in this chapter are some of the most well-established and well-researched in the field, very few have been studied thoroughly enough to be associated with answers to each and every one of the questions above.

Section 4: Historical Psychological Treatments

Psychotherapy, also known as "talk" therapy, is the process of treating mental and emotional problems through verbal communication between a patient and therapist. As reviewed above, there is a great diversity of options available to an individual seeking psychotherapy. In the following section, we will review some of the major schools of psychotherapy practiced in North America both historically and in present day.

PSYCHOANALYTIC AND PSYCHODYNAMIC THERAPY

For many of you, an image of a **patient** lying back on a couch, with a stoic, bearded doctor taking notes just out of the patient's line of sight, is the first thing that may come to mind when you think of psychotherapy. This is the iconic image of a patient undergoing Freudian **psychoanalysis**. **Sigmund Freud**'s (1856-1939) psychoanalysis is generally thought of as the first of the **"talk" therapies**. Working primarily with female patients suffering from **hysteria**, a common condition of the time, Freud developed rich theories on the origins and treatment of psychological disorders. Though some of his ideas have been heavily criticized over time, and are discordant with our current cultural context (especially ideas around the fragility of women and the importance of infantile sexual development), the traditions of this school of therapy still very much inform our popular culture representations of therapy (e.g., HBO's television show *In Treatment*), and are well-represented in the treatment options available to us today.

Conceptualization of psychological maladjustment In classic psychoanalysis, psychological distress is thought to arise from the presence of internal, unconscious conflicts, usually rooted in psychological trauma associated with childhood development (Freud, 1940). In Freud's view, the mind, or **psyche**, contained three levels of awareness – the **conscious**, containing the thoughts and feelings that you have access to at any given moment, the **preconscious**, the contents of which can be actively brought to mind as needed, and the **unconscious**, where a vast repository of inaccessible thoughts, repressed traumatic memories, and primitive urges resides.

Freud believed that an individual's personality was composed of three segments that reside at different levels of consciousness. The **id**, operating at the unconscious level, is motivated to fulfill our innate, primitive instincts. The **ego**, bridging the unconscious, preconscious, and conscious levels of awareness, is responsible for executing the urges of the id in a way that is acceptable to the external environment. The **superego** bridges all three levels of consciousness and seeks to govern your behaviour in such a way that is congruent with internalized parental and societal standards of morality.

Unsuccessful management of the conflicting urges of the id, ego, and superego, taking place at the unconscious level, is thought to drive unhealthy behaviours and cause anxiety and distress. The goal of psychoanalytic therapy, then, is to resolve suffering by bringing unconscious conflicts into conscious awareness, providing the patient with insight, and enabling them to delve deeper in search of further unconscious conflicts. The process of resolving of conflicts brought into conscious awareness is thought to relieve psychological distress through **catharsis** and free the patient to develop more adaptive patterns of behaviour.

Therapeutic techniques In order to successfully complete psychoanalytic therapy, the patient must bring thoughts, emotions, memories, and actions of the unconscious into conscious awareness. According to Freud, this task is made especially difficult by the development of sophisticated **ego defense mechanisms** that prevent unconscious material from coming to light. The analyst's task then, is to circumvent the defenses of the ego, allowing the patient to reveal material that may provide insight into the unconscious. Freud developed a number of techniques to diminish the influence of the ego and facilitate access to the unconscious. The iconic couch and distant therapist are examples of this – this arrangement of the patient lying comfortably and the therapist out of view was designed to place patients at ease and minimize the feeling of being observed.

Major techniques of psychoanalytic therapy include **free association**. In free association, the patient is encouraged to let his or her mind wander, reporting the content to the therapist without self-censorship. The analyst attends to the content with minimal verbal feedback, thereby facilitating the patient's sense of being alone with their thoughts, and fostering an environment where truly uncensored associations can be reported, providing the analyst with clues as to the secrets of the unconscious. A second technique, **dream analysis**, is based on similar principles. Similar to uncensored mind-wandering, the state of dreaming was believed to be one in which the defenses of the ego relaxed. Because the ego's defenses were thought to be lowered, but not completely eliminated during sleep, dreams were understood to involve two levels of content. The first level, the **manifest content**, includes the described elements of the dream itself (e.g., the patient unlocking the door to his house). The second level, the **latent content**, is where the true underlying meaning of the dream resides. A third technique employed in psychoanalysis is the **analysis of resistance**. In this case, the analyst is cued to the emergence of painful, or potentially embarrassing thoughts and feelings by the patient's resistance (either unwillingness or inability) to discuss certain topics. Freud believed that the more potentially damaging the emergence of an unconscious thought or memory could be, the more patients would be motivated to steer clear of it.

As Freud's theories and practice evolved, he began to place increasing emphasis on the analyst-patient relationship in therapy. The concept of **transference** describes the process by which a patient's thoughts, feelings, and drives developed in early childhood and experienced in significant relationships, are re-expressed, or "transferred" onto the relationship with the analyst. Analysis of the patient's thoughts, feelings, and behaviours towards the analyst then, can provide insight into unconscious conflicts causing distress in the patient's relationships with others. Acknowledging the humanity of the analyst, the concept of **counter-transference** describes the analyst's reactions to the patient's transference. In classic psychoanalysis, a therapist undertakes significant personal psychoanalysis to gain insight into his or her counter-transference reactions, with the aim of minimizing counter-transference reactions, and presenting a blank slate for the patient to re-enact their own relationship style, free from the potentially modifying influence of any reactions from the analyst.

As noted above, Freud believed the mechanism by which psychoanalysis brought about the relief of psychological distress was twofold. One the one hand, the techniques outlined above can provide catharsis associated with bringing unconscious material into conscious awareness. On the other hand, the material generated using the techniques above serve as the raw material for the analyst's most critical task, **interpretation**. To form interpretations, the analyst sifts through the content generated through free association, dream analysis, analysis of resistance and transference, identifying patterns, illuminating hidden conflicts, and, when the time is right, explaining the true meaning of the patient's thoughts, feelings, drives, and conflicts. The goal is to provide the patient with **insight**, enabling the patient to work through identified conflicts and delve deeper into the unconscious to discover further truths.

Critique　　　Freud's theories and practices were foundational to the modern practice of psychotherapy and have continuing influence to this day. However, some important limitations to the practice of classic psychoanalysis have been described. Freud's conceptualization of psychological maladjustment relies heavily on constructs that cannot be directly observed (i.e., unconscious conflicts) and are therefore difficult to validate scientifically. Consequently, the mechanism by which Freudian therapy "works" (by bringing unconscious conflicts into conscious awareness, thereby providing the patient with insight) is not possible to test scientifically. If a patient improves clinically, it is assumed to be because they have gained insight, but if they gain insight but do not improve clinically, it is assumed to be the case that the insight was not fully accepted. Finally, classic psychoanalysis has been criticized for its limited generalizability. To participate, a patient must be intelligent, motivated, articulate, and rational. This is not the case for all individuals with psychological disorders.

Modern iterations of psychoanalytic therapy are known as **psychodynamic** approaches. These techniques differ from historical approaches in that the therapist takes a more active stance, engaging with the patient to discover areas of present-day (rather than childhood) conflict. **Interpersonal therapy** is a specific psychodynamic approach that is time-limited, present-focused, empirically supported for the treatment of depression, and applicable to a broader range of psychological problems (Klerman, Weissman, Rounsaville, & Chevron, 1984). In interpersonal therapy, therapy focuses on current relationships and issues within those relationships. By helping the patient learn to solve present relationship problems, the goal is to provide them with skills to develop more healthy relationships, reducing the psychological symptoms that invariably come with unhealthy relationships with others.

BEHAVIOURAL THERAPY

Behaviour therapies stand in stark contrast to psychoanalytic techniques. Although the psychoanalyst and the behaviourist may both agree that psychological distress is, to some degree, based on historical personal experiences, the similarities end there. Where the psychoanalyst constructs arguably subjective interpretations of a patient's underlying drives, motives, and conflicts based on elaborate (and largely untestable) theories of development and personality and bestows these enlightened interpretations on the patient to effect change, the behaviourist ignores the patient's unobservable internal state, and focuses instead on observable behaviours, seeking to allow for positive change in a measurable way (Wolpe, 1969). Behaviour therapies are built on the principles of **classical and operant conditioning** articulated by the likes of **Pavlov**, **Thorndike**, and **Skinner**. The behaviour therapist considers him or herself as an applied scientist, identifying a patient's problematic behaviours, uncovering the **reinforcement contingencies** that perpetuate them, and implementing strategies to eliminate them.

Conceptualization of psychological maladjustment　　To a behaviourist, psychological symptoms and disorders arise as a result of **maladaptive learning histories** that give rise to problematic behaviours. The consequences of such **maladaptive behaviours** are often negative, leading to psychological distress. The behavioural therapist operates under the theory that modifying a patient's present-day maladaptive behaviour patterns and replacing these patterns with more adaptive alternatives will lead to positive consequences for the patient, including a reduction in psychological distress. These consequences will serve to positively reinforce the adaptive behaviours, increasing the likelihood that the positively changed behaviours will persist over time.

To a pure behaviourist, positive therapeutic change can occur without attention to the patient's internal thoughts and feelings. That is, although the behaviourist would not deny the existence of the patient's internal world, she would regard it as unobservable, immeasurable, and unessential for effecting behavioural change. Similarly, the patient's early life learning history, information that could provide insight as to how specific problematic behaviours evolved, is not typically a focus of attention in behavioural therapy. The way to reduce psychological distress is to change the present-day maladaptive behaviours; seeking insight into how the behaviours evolved is simply not required.

Therapeutic techniques　Behavioural therapists draw on a wide range of tools based on the principles of classical and operant conditioning. One sphere of psychological distress that the behaviour therapies devoted much attention is that of reducing symptoms of fear and anxiety. Remember Cleo from the previous chapter whose powerful specific phobia for snakes prevents her from going to parks of any kind? Since we last met her, she and her fiancée have had endless arguments about her strong desire to have their wedding in Central Park.

The technique of **systematic desensitization**, initially developed by **Joseph Wolpe** [1915-1997] is a powerful tool in the behavioural therapist's arsenal that may be helpful to Cleo. In this technique, principles of **classical conditioning** are used to decouple the snake-fear stimulus-response association. This goal is achieved by taking gradual steps to **counter-condition** the feared stimulus (snake) with an adaptive response that is incompatible with fear. Systematic desensitization, then, is a multi-stage process that typically begins with practice in a response incompatible with fear. In the first stage, **relaxation training**, the therapist instructs the client in skills such as **progressive muscle relaxation**, and **abdominal breathing**. The patient and therapist work at these skills, often including homework assignments for the patient, until the patient is able to efficiently and effectively put themselves in a relaxed state on demand.

The next stage in systematic desensitization is for the therapist and patient to collaboratively generate an **anxiety hierarchy** where feared situations are listed out in order of least to most anxiety provoking. The anxiety hierarchy may include both imagined events and real-world events. For Cleo, the hierarchy may include, ordered from least to most fearful: encountering a worm on the sidewalk, imagining a toy snake, seeing a snake on tv, entering a park, getting married in a park…staring down a python. The therapist and patient work up the hierarchy, from least threatening situation to most. At each stage of the hierarchy, the conditioned fear responses are slowly extinguished through a technique called **exposure**. In this technique, the therapist guides the patient in putting herself into a state of deep relaxation using her practiced techniques, then guides the patient to imagine or actually put herself in a given feared situation. The ultimate goal is, over repeated trials, to slowly and progressively re-condition the previously feared stimuli in the hierarchy with an adaptive relaxation response. Once a stimulus at the bottom of the hierarchy can be reliably encountered without fear, the patient and therapist move up the ladder to the next most feared item, until even the most feared stimuli can be encountered without anxiety.

Other behaviour therapy techniques have been developed based on principles of **operant conditioning**. Collectively, such techniques have been labelled **behaviour modification**. In behaviour modification techniques, analysis of the consequences of specific behaviours is undertaken to understand how certain contingencies either increase or decrease the likelihood of recurrence of the behaviours. Think back to Steve from Chapter 1. What were the consequences of his behaviour when he first started taking his prescribed painkillers? How do you think these consequences (e.g., reduced pain, return to work), affected his later drug-related behaviour when he was faced with other minor injuries? What consequences were in play when Steve began to experience withdrawal symptoms? By analyzing his behaviour and the resulting consequences, you should be able to see how Steve's escalating pattern of maladaptive drug-seeking behaviour is closely tied to a pattern of initial positive reinforcement (i.e., he felt good when he took the pills), and later negative reinforcement (i.e., he felt relief from withdrawal symptoms when he took the pills). As you may reason, one component of many substance-related disorders treatment programs involves adjusting the real and perceived consequences of alcohol or drug-seeking behaviour to shift the balance of reinforcement and punishment such that the problematic behaviours are more likely to decrease in frequency. In Steve's case, even without treatment, the negative consequences of his behaviour that emerged over time (i.e., ultimatum from his wife, legal risks, suicide attempt) are now strong competitors to the reinforcing properties of the drug. If his future treatment were to include a behavioural component, his therapist would be likely to work with Steve to emphasize these negative consequences, and identify the reinforcing positive consequences of an emerging sober lifestyle.

Critique   Behavioural techniques are widely used in present-day practice and lend themselves well to scientific study. Research shows that behavioural techniques are effective for reducing symptoms of mood disorders (especially major depressive disorder and dysthymia), anxiety disorders (especially phobias and OCD), and substance-related disorders. These approaches can be applied to a much broader range of patients than psychoanalysis. Effective behavioural treatments have been developed for individuals with autism, mental retardation, brain injury, and Alzheimer's disease. Although these treatments are widely accepted today, they are not free from criticism. A primary critique relates to the generalizability of these techniques. Skills learned in the therapy relationship may not easily translate into the real world setting. A second critique relates to the ethics of behaviour modification. Although in present-day practice patients who undergo behavioural therapy first provide informed consent, some critics argue that it is unethical for one person to endeavour to change the behaviour of another. The same argument can be applied to most forms of psychotherapy.

HUMANISTIC/CLIENT-CENTERED THERAPY

At the same time the behaviourists were challenging the validity and relevance of psychoanalytic theories of personality development, another group of psychologists critiqued both the psychoanalytic and the behaviourist approaches for being too manipulative and mechanistic. Influenced most heavily by the work of **Carl Rogers** [1902-1987], **humanist** or **client-centered therapy** emphasizes and celebrates the autonomy of the individual patient. For Carl Rogers, the patient is neither to be perceived as a collection of unconscious drives and conflicts, nor a set of adaptive and maladaptive behaviours. Rather, the patient is to be treated as a whole person, expert in their own feelings, thoughts, and desires. The goal of humanist therapy is to work *with* the patient, *joining* her in her current thoughts, feelings, and struggles, and working *together* to enable her to follow her own innate tendencies towards **self-actualization**, the realization of her full human potential (Rogers, 1951).

Draft

Conceptualization of psychological maladjustment
To a humanist, psychological distress develops when a person's sense of **self-concept,** their internal representation of themselves as worthwhile human beings, becomes incongruent with their **experience**, their moment-to-moment interactions with the external world. One of the main precursors to the development of **incongruence** is the formation of **conditions of worth** within the self-concept. For example, a university student may possess, as a condition of worth, an internal belief that he is only worthwhile as a person if he earns straight A's on his report card. When he earns a B in his Introduction to Psychology course, his experience fails to match his self-perceived conditions of worth, he experiences incongruence and consequent psychological distress.

Rogers believed that a person's self-concept was heavily influenced by their relationships with significant others. To Rogers, a healthy self-concept contained few conditions of worth, and developed through the experience of **unconditional positive regard** in relationships, especially formative relationships with caregivers in early life. To show an individual unconditional positive regard is to demonstrate, through words and actions, an unwavering empathy for their feelings, understanding of their thoughts, and prizing of their inner experience as a human being. In such a relationship, individuals develop a self-concept that is free from restrictive conditions of worth.

Consider the mother who praises her son for earning an 'A' in his kindergarten class. His mother's statement, "Johnny, I am proud of you always and happy you earned an 'A' in class," communicates unconditional positive regard in that her pride in Johnny is not dependent on his earning an A. In contrast, **conditional positive regard** is shown in the statement, "Johnny, I am proud of you when you earn 'A's." It is important to note that unconditional positive regard does not dictate universal acceptance of behaviour. Consider the reprimands, "Johnny, I can see that you are upset, and I understand your feelings, but throwing food at the table is not an acceptable action," versus "Johnny, you are a bad boy for throwing food." Which is more consistent with a parenting approach of unconditional positive regard?

Therapeutic techniques
At first glance, it may appear as though the humanist therapist would have few options available to her when it comes to choosing therapeutic techniques. If you truly believe, as the humanist therapist would, that each patient is the expert in his own experience, and each patient has, within himself, an innate tendency to realize his full human potential, then what exactly is your role in the therapeutic relationship? Certainly, the authoritative stance employed by both the psychoanalyst and behavioural therapist serve as opposing examples to the application of the humanist philosophy. In fact, the earliest versions of humanist approach went by the name **nondirective therapy**, because the therapist's techniques were restricted only to reflection and response to the **client's** (note that the humanists' prefer the term "client" to "patient") stated thoughts and feelings. The therapist was explicitly instructed never to direct the conversation. With time, the label 'nondirective therapy' was abandoned in favour of the term **client-centered therapy**, placing emphasis on the client, rather than the therapist, and keeping with the humanist ideals.

The goal of client-centered therapy is to enhance healthy functioning by enhancing a person's congruence between self-concept and their experience. Rogers theorized that this goal could be achieved in the context of a safe, social relationship in which the client is free to discover and explore their areas of incongruence. The therapist's task is to foster this social environment by demonstrating three **core conditions** in the therapeutic relationship. The first, **unconditional positive regard,** is the application of the concepts discussed above. That is, the therapist shows, through words and actions, that the client is a person of worth and goodness, and that no revelation, however embarrassing or anxiety-provoking for the client, will be met with a judgmental attitude by the therapist. The second, **empathy**, means that the therapist makes every effort to understand the client's feelings in the moment, and validates those feelings back to the client by communicating this understanding. The third, **genuineness**, means that the therapist is present as a congruent human being in the social relationship. The therapist is neither a distant expert, nor a paid consultant; rather the client-centered therapist is a fellow human, joining with the client on his journey of self-actualization.

Critique Like psychoanalytic approaches, the humanist conceptualization of psychological maladjustment relies on constructs that are difficult to validate scientifically (i.e., self-actualization). However, because client-centered approaches to therapy take an optimistic view of the human condition and endorse practices that few would argue could be in any way harmful, criticisms of humanist therapies do not generally criticize the therapeutic approach as incorrect. Rather, criticisms tend to center on whether such a mild form of therapy can be effective at all.

Over time, even Rogers himself came to see that non-directive ideals of the humanist practice were not as "non-directive" in practice. Based on careful study of therapy transcripts, researchers found evidence that Rogers tended to respond more positively to his clients' statements of well-being and therapeutic improvement (Traux, 1966). In this way, client-centered therapy could be considered behaviourism in action, where statements of therapeutic improvement are reinforced and shaped via the therapist response.

These criticisms aside, client-centered therapy is a widely-used approach today. Because of its universal applicability and its emphasis on forming positive therapist-client relationships, it is often one of the first types of therapy taught in training programs, and is often used as a starting point among eclectic therapists (therapists who employ more than one approach based on each client's individual needs).

Section 5: Modern Psychological Treatments

Cognitive Therapy

So far, we've reviewed three very different foundational approaches to psychological treatment. We turn our attention now to some more recently evolved schools of therapy. The first of these, **cognitive therapy**, is most closely associated with the work of **Aaron Beck** [1921-present] in the 1960's and onward. Originally trained as a psychoanalyst, through his work as a researcher and therapist Beck became dissatisfied with the limitations in psychoanalytic notions and techniques, and developed his own ideas about the organization of personality and the development of psychological distress. Preserving the psychoanalytic emphasis on the patient's inner experience and integrating the behaviourist emphasis on a scientific approach, Beck's cognitive therapy focused on changing the **maladaptive cognitions** (thoughts) that characterize the inner world of an individual suffering from psychological distress.

CONCEPTUALIZATION OF PSYCHOLOGICAL MALADJUSTMENT

To a cognitivist, psychological distress arises from the cyclical interaction between our **thoughts**, **feelings**, and **behaviours** (Beck, Rush, Shaw, & Emery, 1979). Beck believed that *thoughts* were the

Draft

critical target of intervention in breaking a maladaptive cycle of thoughts, feelings and behaviours. To a cognitivist, maladaptive thoughts are expressed, and can be targeted for intervention at multiple levels. Key targets for intervention may include automatic thoughts, cognitive distortions, and core schemas.

In the day-to-day expression of psychopathology, an individual has frequent, negative **automatic thoughts**; habitual, instantaneous thoughts that are generated internally and affect our mood and behaviour. Consider an example from the story of Julie. We can see how her **automatic thought**, "*Really, what would it help to whine about my problems to a stranger?*" is associated with *feelings* of guilt and embarrassment and her eventual *behaviour* of closing down her computer and giving up her search for help. Automatic thoughts are often fleeting, and an individual is often unaware of the frequency or severity with which they occur.

Cognitive distortions are a related phenomenon. These are self-generated misrepresentations of reality, often representing the underlying assumptions for automatic thoughts, which reinforce maladaptive perceptions about the self. Julie's perception that her mother's reminder's to seek treatment are actually reminders that she has failed in life are an example of the cognitive distortion of overgeneralization (a single instance taken as evidence applying to a wide range of situations). Other distortions described by Beck include dichotomous thinking (considering only extreme points of view), selective abstraction (paying attention only to negative features of a situation), personalising (blaming oneself for negative events, even when there is no evidence that one is to blame), catastrophizing (overemphasizing negative outcomes) and minimizing (downplaying positive outcomes). Beck believed that content of these automatic thoughts and cognitive distortions were rooted in early life histories, where core beliefs or **schemas** about the self, other people, and the world were learned. Julie's automatic thought and cognitive distortions above might be rooted in a core belief that she is a failure in life and not worth helping.

Note here that the cognitivist and the behaviourist share similar views about the role of early life learning histories and about the role of behaviour and its contingencies in the development and maintenance of psychological distress. The difference, however, is that where the behaviourist views the patient's internal thoughts as unobservable and unavailable for therapeutic action, the cognitivist argues that thoughts can be observed and are *critical* for therapeutic action. Modern versions of cognitive therapy preserve the focus on internal cognitions, but incorporate many techniques from the behavioural approaches, and are often labelled **cognitive-behavioural therapy**. Like behavioural approaches, cognitive approaches tend to be present-focused, working to examine and change automatic thoughts, thereby causing reduction in psychological distress and possibly leading to revision of core schemas through new learning. Understanding the historical evolution of maladaptive core schemas is not typically a focus of cognitive therapy, though cognitive-based approaches targeting schemas have been developed and implemented (Young, 1999).

Therapeutic techniques　　The techniques of a cognitive therapist are designed to first increase the patient's awareness of his or her automatic thoughts and the consequences of these thoughts for their feelings and behaviours, and second, to teach them to challenge those thoughts and replace them with more adaptive and rational alternatives. Beck believed that these goals were best achieved by fostering a therapeutic atmosphere of "**collaborative empiricism.**" In this way, the patient and therapist embark together on a task-oriented, scientific exploration of the patient's problematic thoughts, feelings, and behaviours, working specifically at identifying and challenging maladaptive thoughts. Cognitive therapy is often highly structured, with each therapy session following a specific agenda, and the overall number of sessions typically agreed upon at the outset. Empirically supported cognitive therapy protocols for major mood and anxiety disorders often last in the range of 12-16 weekly sessions.

Psychoeducation is a critical first step in cognitive therapy, with the therapist educating the patient about the cognitive conceptualization of psychological distress and teaching them how to identify their own automatic thoughts. Once patients have a working understanding of the concepts involved, they are often given **homework** designed to help them identify maladaptive thoughts, which can then be examined in the therapy session. One commonly used homework tool in the cognitive therapist's arsenal is the **daily thought record**. In the simplest form, this tool is a written log of problematic events and the client's reactions (thoughts, and sometimes also emotions and behaviours) to these events. Initially, this tool is used to help the client identify and articulate negative automatic thoughts that may typically pass by unnoticed. Later, this tool can be expanded to help the client (1) identify relationships between these thoughts and associated emotions and behaviours, (2) identify cognitive distortions that underlie maladaptive automatic thoughts, and (3) to develop rational, healthier alternatives to their maladaptive responses.

Within the therapeutic session, the daily thought record is often used as a focal point. The therapist and patient may select a single event from the thought record, and embark together on a scientific exploration of the chain of events. The therapist works to demonstrate techniques designed to challenge maladaptive thinking patterns and replace these with more rational alternatives. These techniques may include **Socratic questioning**, in which the therapist probes the patient with questions designed to illicit logical flaws in the patient's thoughts and assumptions. The patient is encouraged to apply this technique to him or herself, developing a curious and sceptical attitude towards their own automatic ways of thinking. Other techniques may include **examining the evidence** (listing all the facts that support or refute a belief), **generating alternatives** (brainstorming alternative explanations for negative events, such as "She didn't call because she hates me" versus "She didn't call because she was busy."), **reframing** (identifying the positive features of a negative situation), **cost-benefit analysis** (evaluating what could be gained or lost by changing a belief), and **testing the thoughts** (designing a behavioural experiment to test the validity of a belief). The ultimate goal of cognitive therapy is to empower the patient to challenge their own maladaptive thoughts and react to events in more rational and healthy ways.

Critique   Cognitive-behavioural therapies are strongly rooted in an empirical tradition and lend themselves well to scientific study. Detailed treatment manuals are produced for most CBT approaches, and therapists are trained to administer therapy in a highly structured way. Efficacy evidence for CBT approaches has been found for a wide range of disorders including mood, anxiety, substance-related, and eating disorders. In some cases, these approaches have been studied in combination with pharmacological interventions, and have shown evidence for improved outcomes for patients compared to the administration of medication alone (e.g., reduced risk of relapse in depression).

Criticisms of CBT approaches center on the very qualities that make them amenable to research. The use of manualized treatments may be appropriate for efficacy studies, in which the patients are carefully selected to have a very similar set of symptoms and no comorbid conditions. However, the effectiveness of such treatments for patients with more complex symptoms in the real-world setting is more challenging to determine. It may not be appropriate to pursue a structured, manualized CBT treatment for anorexia in a patient who has anorexia, has recently lost a parent to suicide, and has an addiction to methamphetamine. Some argue that CBT treatments, by focusing on present symptoms and behaviour, ignore root causes of psychopathology. Schema-focused cognitive treatments evolved, in part, to address such criticisms.

MINDFULNESS-BASED APPROACHES TO THERAPY

Mindfulness-based approaches to psychotherapy are the most recently evolved (from a Western perspective) of the psychological treatments considered in this chapter, first emerging in various forms in the 1970s and gaining prominence even today. The collection of approaches reviewed in this section share common historical features with behavioural and cognitive approaches, but integrate ideas and practices rooted in Buddhist philosophy and meditation techniques. The overarching goal of these approaches is to alleviate psychological distress and achieve a sense of well-being and purposeful living by developing a present-focused mindset characterized by nonjudgmental acceptance. A key tenet of mindfulness-based approaches is that pain and suffering is an important part of the human experience. A major thrust of therapy then is to develop the ability to differentiate the negative thoughts, feelings, and behaviours that can be reduced without further negative consequences, from the negative experiences in which attempts to avoid, escape, or change the outcomes would lead to further pain and suffering. Mindfulness techniques are designed to facilitate the acceptance of the latter type of negative experience, believed to be important for mental health and personal growth. Examples of mindfulness-based approaches that have been subject to empirical study include Acceptance and Commitment Therapy (Hayes, Strosahl, & Wilson, 1999), Dialectical Behavior Therapy (Linehan 1993a, 1993b), and Mindfulness-Based Cognitive Therapy (Segal et al., 2002).

Conceptualization of psychological maladjustment While the collection of therapies grouped together here as mindfulness-based approaches to psychotherapy differ in terms of their historical evolution and theoretical underpinnings, they share a core conceptualization of psychological maladjustment. Much like the cognitive approaches, the mindfulness-based approaches posit that our thoughts, emotions, and behaviours are closely associated. Unlike the cognitive approaches, however, the mindfulness-based approaches do not believe that changing negative thoughts is the mechanism by which psychological suffering can be alleviated. Some research on cognitive therapy has shown that much of the benefits of the cognitive approach are achieved early in the therapeutic process. Mindfulness theorists point to these findings as evidence that the mechanism of change in cognitive therapy lies in the development of a person's *awareness* of their negative thoughts, rather than in the development of skills in *challenging and changing* those thoughts, which occurs later in therapy.

In the mindfulness approaches, psychological distress is thought to be alleviated when we are able to distance ourselves from our negative thoughts and emotional reactions (factors we cannot control or change). By distancing ourselves from our internal reactions through mindfulness practice, we can change our behavioural reactions to our negative internal states. The alleviation of psychological distress occurs when we are able to be fully aware of our negative thoughts and feelings, accept them without judgment, and choose healthy behavioural actions in spite of these negative internal experiences. Importantly, the mindfulness approaches share the idea that negative thoughts, emotions, and experiences are not to be unnecessarily avoided, as this avoidance may lead to maladaptive consequences such as missed opportunities, failure to meet responsibilities, and increases in future anxieties. Psychological health then is achieved through practice in attending to our thoughts as they occur in the present, accepting these thoughts as they are without judgment and choosing adaptive behavioural actions congruent with our goals and values.

Therapeutic Techniques   A fundamental goal of mindfulness-based approaches to psychotherapy is to increase the patient's awareness of his or her present experience, including internal thoughts, emotions, and bodily sensations, as well as items in the external environment. Critically, this awareness must be accompanied by a nonjudgmental, nonreactive stance of open acceptance to all experiences, both positive and negative. Mindfulness-based therapeutic approaches include explicit teaching of strategies to develop this present-focused nonjudgmental mindset. Patients are provided with coaching in these strategies and encouraged to engage in regular and sustained practice.

The rationale for cultivating mindfulness skills differs in specific versions of mindfulness-based therapies. In **Acceptance and Commitment Therapy** (ACT), which has been applied to a broad range of psychological conditions, clients engage in a process of values clarification in which they articulate the life directions to which they aspire (e.g., being a loving partner), and set specific goals to be met that are representative of their values (e.g., accompanying your partner to a stressful event). In ACT then, mindfulness skills are deployed in order to help the patient engage in behaviours that serve their goals, regardless of any fears, anxieties, or pessimistic thoughts that might push them away from achieving these goals.

The specific techniques employed in ACT are wide ranging. Mindfulness exercises are practiced in conjunction with many of the behavioural and cognitive techniques reviewed previously in this chapter. A central concept in ACT is that of **defusion**, the process of learning to see internal experiences as harmless, passing sensations that do not have to control our behaviour. One exercise used in ACT to facilitate defusion is the **leaves on the stream exercise**. In this task, clients imagine themselves sitting beside a stream with leaves floating on top. As thoughts and emotions enter their awareness, they imagine placing each one on top of a single leaf and watching it gently float away. In another exercise, they learn to describe internal events starting with, "I'm having the thought that..." such that powerful negative self-statements such as "I'm worthless," are recognized as fleeting thoughts, "I'm having the thought that I'm useless," rather than absolute truths. Metaphors are used heavily in ACT. The metaphor of the **passengers on the bus** illustrates the concept of defusion by likening negative internal experiences to unruly passengers on a bus. They may exist and be unpleasant, but regardless of their actions, the driver maintains control and chooses which direction to take the bus.

The application of mindfulness skills in **Dialectical Behaviour Therapy** (DBT), initially developed by clinicians working with severely distressed individuals, follows a hierarchy of treatment targets. First, patients practice mindfulness skills in the service of reducing self-harming (e.g., suicidal gestures) and treatment-interfering (e.g., missed sessions) behaviours. As therapy continues, mindfulness skills are deployed in the service of reducing negative behaviours that interfere with quality of life (e.g., maintaining employment, relationships). It is only after considerable progress and practice that the focus of therapy may turn to issues of personal and spiritual growth.

Dialectical behaviour therapy is a multi-faceted treatment approach that typically includes group and individual therapy sessions, as well as telephone consultations with the therapist as needed. Like ACT, DBT employs behavioural and cognitive techniques alongside a set of mindfulness-based interventions. Mindfulness skills are typically taught in group sessions, with individualized application of these skills reviewed during one-on-one sessions. A core concept in DBT is that of the three **states of mind**. First, the **reasonable mind** is the logical part of the mind that knows facts, solves problems, and thinks rationally. Second, the **emotion mind** perceives the world through the lens of feelings and compels us to act according to our emotions. Through mindfulness skill practice, the goal is to achieve the **wise mind**, where the reasonable and emotion mind are synthesized and balanced. Specific skills trained in DBT include the **"what" skills** of **observing** (attending to the experience of the present moment), **describing** (labelling observations with words), and **participating** (fully engaging in the present activity without self-consciousness). The **"how" skills** trained in DBT include being nonjudgmental, being one-mindful (focusing attention on one thing at a time), and behaving effectively.

Critique   Despite notable differences in the two approaches, criticisms of mindfulness-based therapies echo the CBT critique that such approaches do not address root causes of psychopathology. The research on mindfulness-based approaches is in a relative state of infancy, but the body of evidence to support its use in certain situations is growing. The efficacy of DBT for borderline personality disorder is well-established, and studies are underway to use DBT for a broader range of psychological disorders.

Systems Approaches to Therapy

Systems approaches to psychotherapy have been employed at least as long as behavioural approaches, but are reviewed here as our final psychological treatment as they employ a radically different approach to the conceptualization and treatment of psychological problems. In contrast to all the treatments reviewed above, systems approaches to therapy place a primary focus on the relationships between two or more co-participants, rather than the single individual. The co-participants comprise a single **system**, characterized by emotional interconnectedness, repetitive patterns of interactions, emotional and structural boundaries, alliances and coalitions, subsystems (e.g., siblings or spouses within a family), and rules that reflect interaction patterns and maintain equilibrium. While each participant is considered to be a fully independent part of the system, all parts of the system must be taken into account when devising strategies for creating positive change.

Conceptualization   One of the most influential historic research hypotheses that supported the systems
of psychological   approach was that of the **double-bind hypothesis** of schizophrenia development
maladjustment   (Bateson, Jackson, Haley, & Weakland, 1956). Based on extensive study of individuals with schizophrenia and their families, these authors hypothesized that the cause of schizophrenia was a consistent and contradictory pattern of relating from parent to child. Specifically, the parent would habitually place the child in a double-bind by giving them a choice of two actions, each of which would be followed by a negative response. Over time, the child in this no-win situation, subject to repeated invalidating messages, would develop the severe psychopathology of schizophrenia. Later research failed to support this specific hypothesis with respect to schizophrenia, but the principle underlying it – that psychopathology can be related to maladaptive patterns of relating within a system – has received empirical support and is a core principle of systems therapy.

Contemporary approaches to systems therapy hold that psychological maladjustment can be caused and perpetuated by maladaptive patterns of communication and behaviour within a system, such as a family (Minuchin &Fishman, 1981). The systems therapist does not view psychological maladjustment as rooted in the individual. Note that many forms of systems therapy avoid applying psychiatric diagnoses to individuals, as it would be inappropriate to label one individual within a system as pathological. In the language of systems therapy, the terms "psychological maladjustment," "distress," and "problems" are more commonly used than the term "psychopathology." The mechanism by which psychological maladjustment can be reduced or eliminated then is by identifying and positively changing the patterns of communication and behaviour within the family.

Therapeutic techniques

The goals of systems therapy are to establish, or re-establish, a healthful state of interrelatedness within the system, as characterized by healthy patterns of communication, behaviour, boundaries and problem-solving strategies. As systems are complex entities, the therapist's first task is to establish a productive working relationship with the family, joining their system and mapping out the hierarchies, subsystems, alliances, etc. As the therapist develops a working understanding of the system, he or she employs interventions designed to destabilize unhealthy patterns of relating and provide opportunities to develop healthy patterns. This process, like the family system itself, is often cyclical. That is, changes in patterns of behaviour and communication, even between members of a subsystem, will have a ripple effect through the entire system. The therapist and family must work to constantly realign their understanding of the system's working as each intervention shifts the patterns within the system.

Specific examples of interventions employed in systems therapy include **reframing** in which the therapist provides an alternate viewpoint on a problematic situation with the goal of shifting the interpretation of the situation from negative to positive. For example, a mother may complain that her teenage daughter refuses to accept help, even when she's struggling with her homework. The therapist could reframe this behaviour as her daughter showing a sense of herself as independent and capable. This may help the mother set aside her frustration with a daughter who won't accept help, and instead foster a sense of pride in a daughter who believes in herself as capable.

Another commonly used technique in systems therapy is that of **prescriptions** or instructions given to the family by the therapist to engage in certain patterns of behaviour. These prescriptions are designed to increase the family's awareness of dysfunctional patterns of behaviour and provide opportunities for change. Consider the case of a father, frustrated because his children never clean up after themselves, leaving him perpetually tidying up in their wake. A **counter systemic** prescription in this case could be a directive in which the father is forbidden to clean up after the children for a week. After a week, the therapist follows up with the family to assess the impact of this prescription on the father (was it hard to refrain from cleaning?), the children (did they respond to the lack of cleaning?), and other members of the family member (did they respond to the now-open job of cleaner?). A **restructuring** prescription in this case would be an explicit directive to elicit cooperation among disengaged family members, such as a prescription for the children to clean up after themselves.

Critique

Evaluation of outcomes in systems therapy is difficult, given the complexity of the systems and the number of individuals involved. Criticisms of systems therapy magnify the complexity of the approach. For example, some have pointed out that systems therapy, by focusing on each participant's role in relational conflicts, may ignore unhealthy power distributions in family systems (e.g., cases of spousal abuse) or unjust societal norms (e.g., disparaging attitudes towards women or individuals of certain social classes). As with the behavioural, cognitive, and mindfulness approaches, the present-focuses systems therapies have been criticized for ignoring the historical development of unhealthy patterns of relating. Despite these considerable challenges, there is efficacy evidence for systems approaches applied with families of individuals with schizophrenia, depression and substance related disorders.

Common Factors

At this stage, we have reviewed six different major schools of psychotherapy, each holding very different views about the nature of psychological maladjustment and the therapeutic techniques which facilitate psychological change. Further, each has accumulated at least some empirical support for its efficacy. What accounts for these very different approaches each holding the potential for effecting positive psychological outcomes? Some researchers have proposed that, despite the striking differences in theoretical foundations of each school of psychotherapy, **common factors** exist within each and account for much of the therapeutic benefit. As early as 1936, psychologist Saul Rosenzweig, a classmate of B.F. Skinner's, speculated that shared elements of different schools of therapy likely accounted for the bulk of therapeutic change.

More recently, Michael Lambert's reviews of a broad range of psychotherapy outcome studies has identified four categories of common factors that together account for the bulk of therapeutic change. These factors include (1) client resources, (2) therapeutic relationship, (3) intervention strategies, and (4) expectancy (Lambert, 1992). **Client resources**, also known as **extratherapeutic factors** (factors that operate outside of the therapy itself) are the internal and external resources that a client brings into the therapeutic relationship, such as readiness for change, social skills, support networks, resilience, positive life events, etc. Lambert's research suggests, across studies, client resources account for 40% of the variance in predicting therapeutic outcome. The **therapeutic relationship**, or the degree to which the patient and therapist establish a relationship in which the client feels safe, understood, and hopeful, accounts for another 30% of the therapeutic outcome. **Intervention strategies** include interpretation, free association, reframing, counter-conditioning, exposure, etc. While these may differ across schools of psychotherapy, taken together they account for only 15% of variance in therapeutic outcome. Finally, **expectancy**, or the patient's belief that therapy and the therapist are likely to be helpful, accounts for the final 15% of the variance in outcome.

Section 6: Biological Treatments

The treatment of psychological disorders through biological means, especially pharmacological means, is common practice today. The first **psychotropic medications** (chemical agents used to treat psychological problems), introduced in the 1950's, had a profound impact on the medical field of psychiatry and the treatment of individuals with severe psychological disorders. Prior to this period, biological interventions, including relatively crude versions of **electroconvulsive therapy** and **psychosurgery**, were used on only those individuals with the most severe disorders. Institutionalization of patients in overcrowded mental hospitals was common practice. In the following section, we will briefly review some of the major biological treatments for psychological disorders presently practiced in North America.

Pharmacotherapy

Pharmacotherapy is the treatment of psychological conditions using medications. The first psychotropic medication employed in modern psychiatric practice was chlorpromazine, discovered in 1952 by French psychiatrists Jean Delay and Pierre Deniker. Initially used for its powerful calming effects on severely agitated patients, the drug was soon found to also reduce patients' hallucinations and delusions. This, and similar medications developed shortly thereafter and collectively known as typical **antipsychotics**, are still used in practice today. These medications are not curative; rather they simply reduce the potency of the positive symptoms (hallucinations and delusions) of schizophrenia. In the brain, the action of typical antipsychotics is to block dopamine receptors. Over-activity of dopamine-secreting neurons in specific regions of the brain, especially the cerebral cortex and frontal limbic areas, is hypothesized to underlie positive symptoms of schizophrenia. By blocking the receptors in these neurons, antipsychotic medications are thought to block the positive symptoms. Unfortunately, a different system of dopamine-secreting neurons involved in the control of movement can also be affected by antipsychotic medications. Long-term use of antipsychotics increases the risk of developing a serious movement disorder known as **tardive dyskinesia**, characterized by involuntary movements of the face, trunk and limbs.

Modern **antidepressant medications** were discovered shortly after the first antipsychotics. In the late 1950s, the drug imipramine was synthesized in an attempt to create another antipsychotic medication. It was found to have no effect on symptoms of schizophrenia, but did appear to alleviate symptoms of depression in patients who were both psychotic and depressed. Imipramine, still used today, belongs to a class of antidepressants known as the **tricyclics** that block the reuptake of the neurotransmitters norepinephrine and serotonin at presynaptic nerve endings, thereby elevating the levels of these neurotransmitters in the synapse. A second class of antidepressants, the **monoamine oxidase inhibitors**, block the function of the enzyme responsible for the degradation of neurotransmitters tyramine, serotonin, dopamine, and norepinephrine, thereby elevating the levels of these neurotransmitters in the central nervous system. A third class, the **selective serotonin reuptake inhibitors** (SSRIs), block the reuptake of serotonin, thereby elevating serotonin levels at the synapse. SSRIs, the most recently-developed of the three classes, are most commonly used today because they are generally effective, well-tolerated, and importantly, cannot be used as an effective means of suicide. A fourth group of antidepressant medications is presently emerging, consisting of drugs that block reuptake of specific neurotransmitters, either alone, or in combination with serotonin. Collectively, these medications are thought to improve depressive symptoms by increasing the availability of specific neurotransmitters in the central nervous system.

Antianxiety medications, also known as **anxiolytics**, are among the most prescribed, and most abused, form of psychotropic medications. Collectively known as the **benzodiazepines**, these medications work by activating the benzodiazepine receptor, leading to an enhancement in the attachment of the neurotransmitter gamma-aminobutyric acid (GABA) at the postsynaptic neuron. Because benzodiazpines are relatively fast-acting, yield a marked reduction in the experience of anxiety in a very short time, and have relatively few side effects they have high potential for abuse or dependence and are generally prescribed today for only short-term use. Antidepressants, specifically SSRIs, have been shown to be effective for longer-term treatment of some anxiety disorders.

Draft

Electroconvulsive Therapy

Electroconvulsive therapy (ECT) is a procedure involving the brief passage of an electrical current through electrodes applied to the scalp, stimulating a **generalized seizure** (a sudden, widespread alteration in electrical signalling across both hemispheres in the brain). These seizures, lasting about 15-30 seconds, are associated with a loss of consciousness and full-body convulsions (a dramatic stiffening of the limbs followed by rhythmic contractions of the head and limb). Historically, ECT was delivered with high doses of electricity. Memory loss, fractured bones, and other serious side effects were common. In present-day ECT, lower doses of electricity are used, a fast-acting anaesthetic is given to the patient to ensure that the patient is asleep when the electrical current is applied, and a muscle relaxant is given to prevent the convulsions. Some memory loss for the period of time close to the treatment may still occur.

Historically, ECT was used to treat a wide range of psychiatric disorders, sometimes with no benefit. In present-day practice, ECT is used only in cases where there is strong evidence for efficacy. Disorders for which ECT can be used today include severe depression and severe mania. In some cases it is used to treat certain symptoms of schizophrenia and catatonia. The mechanism by which ECT exerts a therapeutic effect is unknown, but the efficacy of ECT has been found to be similar to pharmacological interventions. Although many individuals do not elect to pursue ECT as a first-line treatment, there are some advantages of ECT compared to pharmacological interventions. For example, ECT may be more appropriate in pregnancy where pharmacologic treatments may harm the fetus, and in older adults, who may be more susceptible to side effects of medications. Notably, ECT can yield a faster clinical response to treatment. For example, in severe depression, symptoms may begin to improve immediately following ECT treatment, whereas therapeutic effects of SSRIs generally take ten days to two weeks to emerge.

Psychosurgery

Psychosurgery is the treatment of psychological disorders through brain surgery. Psychosurgery is controversial because, unlike cases where there is obvious brain pathology causing symptoms (e.g., a brain tumor or aneurysm), in psychosurgery there is no obvious brain damage that can be "repaired" through surgical intervention. A gruesome chapter in the history of psychological treatment occurred in the 1930s to 1950s where a simple form of psychosurgery, the frontal or "icepick" lobotomy was used to treat a wide variety of symptoms. This procedure, in which a long metal implement was inserted into the frontal lobe via the eye socket, caused severe intellectual impairment, blunting of emotions, and deficits in judgment.

Present-day application of psychosurgery takes a more cautious approach. Surgery is only considered in cases where symptoms are severe and **refractory** (unresponsive to treatment) to medication, psychotherapy, or electroconvulsive therapy. In one exemplary psychosurgery program at the Massachusetts General Hospital, a team of psychiatrists, neurosurgeons and neurologists must thoroughly evaluate the patient and come to a consensus agreement that surgery is a clinically appropriate option. Then the patient and all involved family members must give their informed consent before the surgery can proceed (Mashour, Walker, & Martuza, 2005). The most common surgical intervention used in North America today includes targeted lesions in the limbic system, most often in the anterior cingulate, where elevated activity has been associated with Obsessive-Compulsive disorder symptoms. This intervention is primarily used for individuals with severe and refractory OCD, but is also occasionally used for other anxiety and affective disorders.